W9-CSX-230

When should I travel to get the best airfare?
Where do I go for answers to my travel questions?
What's the best and easiest way to plan and book my trip?

frommers.travelocity.com

Frommer's, the travel guide leader, has teamed up with **Travelocity.com**, the leader in online travel, to bring you an in-depth, easy-to-use resource designed to help you plan and book your trip online.

At **frommers.travelocity.com**, you'll find free online updates about your destination from the experts at Frommer's plus the outstanding travel planning and purchasing features of Travelocity.com. Travelocity.com provides reservations capabilities for 95 percent of all airline seats sold, more than 47,000 hotels, and over 50 car rental companies. In addition, Travelocity.com offers more than 2,000 exciting vacation and cruise packages. Travelocity.com puts you in complete control of your travel planning with these and other great features:

> **Expert travel guidance from Frommer's** - over 150 writers reporting from around the world!

> **Best Fare Finder** - an interactive calendar tells you when to travel to get the best airfare

> **Fare Watcher** - we'll track airfare changes to your favorite destinations

> **Dream Maps** - a mapping feature that suggests travel opportunities based on your budget

> **Shop Safe Guarantee** - 24 hours a day / 7 days a week live customer service, and more!

Whether traveling on a tight budget, looking for a quick weekend getaway, or planning the trip of a lifetime, Frommer's guides and Travelocity.com will make your travel dreams a reality. You've bought the book, now book the trip!

Travelocity.com
A Sabre Company

Frommer's®

Other Great Guides for Your Trip:

Frommer's Austria

Frommer's Europe

Europe For Dummies

Frommer's Europe from $70 a Day

Frommer's Road Atlas Europe

Frommer's Europe's Greatest Driving Tours

Frommer's Gay & Lesbian Europe

Hanging Out in Europe

Here's what the critics say about Frommer's:

"Amazingly easy to use. Very portable, very complete."
—*Booklist*

♦

"The only mainstream guide to list specific prices. The Walter Cronkite of guidebooks—with all that implies."
—*Travel & Leisure*

♦

"Complete, concise, and filled with useful information."
—*New York Daily News*

♦

"Hotel information is close to encyclopedic."
—*Des Moines Sunday Register*

♦

"I use a lot of travel guides when preparing my trips, but I have learned to especially trust Frommer's when it comes to picking lodgings."
—*The Orange County Register*

Vienna & the
Danube Valley
3rd Edition

by Darwin Porter & Danforth Prince

HUNGRY MINDS, INC.

New York, NY • Cleveland, OH • Indianapolis, IN

ABOUT THE AUTHORS

Co-authors **Darwin Porter,** a native of North Carolina, and Ohio-born **Danforth Prince** wrote and researched the first-ever Frommer's guide to Austria. These veteran travel writers are also authors of several best-selling Frommer's guides, notably to Germany, the Caribbean, Spain, England, and France. As frequent travelers to this alpine country's illustrious capital, Vienna, they know their destination well.

Published by:

HUNGRY MINDS, INC.

909 Third Ave.
New York, NY 10022
www.frommers.com

ISBN 0-7645-6353-X
ISSN 1090-3178

Editor: Justin Lapatine
Production Editor: Jennifer Connolly
Photo Editor: Richard Fox
Design by Michele Laseau
Cartographer: Elizabeth Puhl
Production by Hungry Minds Indianapolis Production Services
Front cover photo: Strauss Statue in Stadt Park

SPECIAL SALES

For general information on Hungry Minds' products and services please contact our Customer Care department; within the U.S. at 800-762-2974, outside the U.S. at 317-572-3993 or fax 317-572-4002. For sales inquiries and reseller information, including discounts, bulk sales, customized editions, and premium sales, please contact our Customer Care department at 800-434-3422.

Manufactured in the United States of America

5 4 3 2 1

Contents

List of Maps

An Invitation to the Reader

In researching this book, we discovered many wonderful places—hotels, inns, restaurants, shops, and more. We're sure you'll find others. Please tell us about them, so we can share the information with your fellow travelers in upcoming editions. If you were disappointed with a recommendation, we'd love to know that, too. Please write to:

Frommer's Vienna & the Danube Valley, 3rd Edition
Hungry Minds, Inc.
909 Third Ave.
New York, NY 10022

An Additional Note

Please be advised that travel information is subject to change at any time—and this is especially true of prices. We therefore suggest that you write or call ahead for confirmation when making your travel plans. The authors, editors, and publisher cannot be held responsible for the experiences of readers while traveling. Your safety is important to us, however, so we encourage you to stay alert and be aware of your surroundings. Keep a close eye on cameras, purses, and wallets, all favorite targets of thieves and pickpockets.

What the Symbols Mean

✪ **Frommer's Favorites**

Our favorite places and experiences—outstanding for quality, value, or both.

The following abbreviations are used for credit cards:

AE	American Express	ER	EnRoute
CB	Carte Blanche	JCB	Japan Credit Bank
DC	Diners Club	MC	MasterCard
DISC	Discover	V	Visa
EC	Eurocard		

Find Frommer's Online

www.frommers.com offers up-to-the-minute listings on almost 200 cities around the globe — including the latest bargains and candid, personal articles updated daily by Arthur Frommer himself. No other Web site offers such comprehensive and timely coverage of the world of travel.

Introducing Vienna

City of music, cafes, waltzes, parks, pastries, and wine—that's Vienna. Vienna is a true cosmopolitan center, where different tribes and nationalities have for centuries fused their cultural identities to produce the intriguing and often cynical Viennese.

From the time the Romans selected a Celtic settlement on the Danube River as one of its most important central European forts, "Vindobona," the city we now know as Vienna has played a vital role in European history. Austria grew up around the city and developed into a mighty empire. The capital became a showplace city during the tumultuous reign of the Habsburg dynasty, whose court was a dazzling spectacle. Before the fall of the empire, Vienna was described as a "royal palace amidst surrounding suburbs."

The face of the city has been altered time and again by war, siege, victory, defeat, the death of an empire, the birth of a republic, foreign occupation, and the passage of time. Fortunately, the Viennese character—a strict devotion to the good life—has remained solid.

Music, art, literature, theater, architecture, education, food, and drink are all part of Vienna's allure.

The Viennese have always been hospitable to foreigners, but there was a time at the end of the 18th century when the emperor felt that tourists might spread pernicious ideas, and all non-Austrians were limited to a 1-week stay in the capital. This, of course, is no longer the case. In the pages that follow, we'll show you all the brilliance this city has to offer.

1 Frommer's Best of Vienna

- **Listening to Mozart:** It is said that at any time of the day or night in Vienna, someone somewhere is playing the music of Wolfgang Amadeus Mozart. You might hear it at an opera house, a church, a festival, an open-air concert, or, more romantically, in a *belle époque* cafe performed by a Hungarian orchestra. Regardless, "the sound of music" drifting through Vienna is likely to be the creation of this prodigious genius. (See chapter 9.)
- **Cruising the Danube (Donau):** Johann Strauss used a bit of poetic license when he called the Donau "The Blue Danube"— it's actually a muddy-green color. But cruising the river by boat is nevertheless a highlight of any Viennese vacation. The legendary **DDSG** (Blue Danube Shipping Co.; ☎ **01/727-500**), offers 1-day trips with cruises priced for every budget. While on board,

you'll pass some of the most famous sights in eastern Austria, including quintessential towns like Krems and Melk. (See chapter 6.)

- **Watching the Lippizaner Stallions:** Nothing evokes the heyday of imperial Vienna more than the **Spanish Riding School** (☎ 01/533-9032). Here, the sleek, white stallions and their expert riders demonstrate the classic art of "dressage" in choreographed leaps and bounds. The stallions, a crossbreed of Spanish thoroughbreds and Karst horses, are the finest equestrian performers on earth. Riders wear black bicorn hats with doeskin breeches and brass buttons. The public is admitted to watch, but reservations should be made 6 to 8 weeks in advance. (See chapter 6.)

- **Heurigen Hopping in the Vienna Woods:** *Heurigen* are rustic wine taverns that celebrate the arrival of each year's new wine (*Heuriger*) by placing a pine branch over the door. The Viennese rush to these taverns to drink the new local wines and feast on a country buffet. Some Heurigen have garden tables with panoramic views of the Danube Valley, and others provide shaded, centuries-old courtyards where revelers can enjoy live folk music. Try the red wines from Vöslau, the Sylvaner of Grinzing, or the Riesling of Nussberg. (See chapter 9.)

- **Feasting on *Tafelspitz*, "The Emperor's Dish":** No Austrian dish is more typical than the fabled *tafelspitz* (boiled beef dinner) favored by Emperor Franz Joseph. Boiled beef sounds dull, but *tafelspitz* is far from bland. A tender delicacy, the "table end" cut is flavored with a variety of spices, including juniper berries, celery root, and onions. An apple-and-horseradish sauce further enlivens the dish, which is usually served with fried grated potatoes. For Vienna's best *tafelspitz*, try the **Hotel Sacher** (☎ 01/514560). (See chapter 5.)

- **Revisiting the Habsburgs:** One of the great dynastic ruling families of Europe, the Habsburgs ruled the Austro-Hungarian Empire from their imperial court in Vienna. You can still witness their grandeur as you stroll through the Inner City. The Hofburg, the family's winter palace, is a living architectural textbook, dating from 1279. Also, be sure to visit Schönbrunn, the sprawling summer palace, which lies on the outskirts of the city and boasts magnificent gardens. (See chapter 6.)

- **Biking Along the Danube:** The most exciting villages and stopovers along the Danube, including Melk and Dürnstein, are linked by a riverside bike trail between Vienna and Naarn. As you pedal along, you'll pass castles of yesteryear, medieval towns, and latticed vineyards. Route maps are available at the Vienna Tourist Office, and you can rent bikes from the ferry or train stations. (See chapter 6.)

- **Attending an Auction at Dorotheum:** Vienna is a treasure trove of art and antiques, and as many estates break up, much of it goes on sale. The main venue for buying art and antiques is **Dorotheum,** Dorotheergasse 17 (☎ 01/5156-0449), the state-owned auction house. Founded in 1707, it remains one of the great European depositories of *objets d'art*. Items here are likely to be expensive; if you're looking for something more affordable, try the summer Saturday and Sunday outdoor art and antiques market along the Danube Canal (between Schwedenbrücke and Salztorbrücke). (See chapter 8.)

- **Savoring the Legendary Sachertorte:** Café Demel (☎ 01/533-5516), the most famous cafe in Vienna, has a long-standing feud with the **Hotel Sacher** (☎ 01/514560) over who has the right to sell the legendary and original Sachertorte, a rich chocolate cake with a layer of apricot jam. Actually, the court settled that matter in 1965, ruling in favor of Hotel Sacher. But Demel still claims that the chef who invented the torte brought "the original recipe" with him when he left the Sacher to work for Demel. Settle the dispute yourself by sampling the Sachertorte at both of these venerated establishments. (See chapter 5.)

- **Unwinding in a Viennese Coffeehouse:** The coffeehouse still flourishes here in its most perfect form. You can spend hours reading newspapers (supplied free), writing memoirs, or planning the rest of your stay in Vienna. And, of course there's the coffee, prepared 20 to 30 different ways, from *Weissen Ohne* (with milk) to *Mocca Gespritzt* (black with a shot of rum or brandy). A glass of ice-cold water always accompanies a cup of coffee in Vienna, as well as the world's most delectable pastry or slice of cake. (See chapter 5.)
- **Strolling the Kärntnerstrasse:** Lying at the heart of Viennese life is the bustling, pedestrian-only Kärntnerstrasse. From morning to night, shoppers parade along this merchandise-laden boulevard; street performers, including musicians and magicians, are always out to amuse. For a break, retreat to one of the cafe terraces for some of the best people-watching in Vienna. (See chapter 7.)
- **Playing at the Prater:** Ever since Emperor Joseph II opened the Prater to the public in the 18th century, the Viennese have been flocking to this park for summer fun—and understandably so. The Prater has abundant tree-lined paths in which to jog or stroll (the Viennese, in general, are much fonder of strolling). The amusement park boasts a looming Ferris wheel that was immortalized in Orson Welles's film *The Third Man*. Open-air cafes line the park, which also provides an array of sports facilities, including tennis courts and a golf course. (See chapter 6.)
- **Enjoying a Night at the Opera:** There is nothing more Viennese than dressing up and heading to the Staatsoper, one of the world's greatest opera houses, where ascending the grand marble staircase is almost as exhilarating as the show. Built in the 1860s, the Staatsoper suffered severe damage during World War II but reopened in 1955 with a production of Beethoven's *Fidelio*, marking Austria's independence from occupation. Both Richard Strauss and Gustav Mahler directed here, and the world's most renowned opera stars continue to perform, accompanied, of course, by the Vienna Philharmonic Orchestra. (See chapter 9.)
- **Hearing the Vienna Boys' Choir:** In this city steeped in musical traditions and institutions, one group has distinguished itself among all others: the Vienna Boys' Choir or *Wiener Sängerknaben*. Created by that great patron of the arts, Maximillian I, in 1498, the choir still performs masses by Mozart and Haydn at the Hofburgkapelle on Sundays and holidays, except in July and August. (See chapter 6.)
- **Discovering the Majesty of St. Stephan's Cathedral:** Crowned by a 450-foot steeple, Dompfarre St. Stephan, Vienna's cathedral, is one of Europe's great Gothic structures. Albert Stifter, the acclaimed Austrian writer, wrote that its "sheer beauty lifts the spirit." The cathedral's vast tiled roof is exactly twice the height of its walls. Intricate altarpieces, stone canopies, and masterful Gothic sculptures are just some of the treasures that lie within. Climb the spiral steps to the South Tower for a panoramic view of the city. (See chapter 6.)

2 Best Hotel Bets

For the details on these and other hotels, see chapter 4.

- **Best Historic Hotel:** Built in 1869, the **Hotel Imperial** (☎ **800/325-3589** in the U.S., or 01/501100) is actually the "official guest house of Austria." It has presided over much of the city's history, from the heyday of the Austro-Hungarian Empire to defeat in two world wars. All the famous and infamous of the world have checked in here. Wagner, for example, worked on key sections of both *Tannhäuser* and *Lohengrin* here in 1875, and some of the great cultural icons of this century—from Margot Fonteyn to Herbert von Karajan—have been guests.

- **Best Trendy Hotel:** Created by the famous English architect Sir Terence Conran, **Das Triest** (☎ 01/589-18), attracts the artistic elite to its stylish precincts near St. Stephan's. Originally a stable, it's "come a long way, baby," and now is elegant, luxurious, and stylish. Rooms are decorated with a distinctive flair.

- **Best New Hotel:** A block from the state opera house, **ANA Grand Hotel Wien** (☎ 01/525-800) is now preferred by many discerning and well-heeled guests to the more famous Imperial or Bristol. It is luxury in the grand hotel sense, with a stunning interior and commodious, elegantly decorated bedrooms.

- **Best for Business Travelers:** With state-of-the-art business equipment and an incredibly helpful staff, the **Hotel Bristol** (☎ 800/325-3535 in the U.S., or 01/515-160) is the preferred choice of international business travelers. Some suites are large enough for business meetings, and room service will quickly deliver hors d'oeuvres and champagne (for a price, of course) when the deal is closed. Many guests like to treat their clients to dinner at the Bristol's elegant restaurant, Korso.

- **Best for a Romantic Getaway:** Set on 15 acres of manicured gardens, **Hotel im Palais Schwarzenberg** (☎ 01/798-4515) has an elegant, even noble atmosphere. Although perched in the center of a city, you feel like you've escaped to an old country estate. The palace was built 3 centuries ago by the baroque masters Hildebrandt and Fisher von Erlach and remains a luxurious world of crystal, marble, and gilt.

- **Best for Families:** Only a 4-minute walk from St. Stephan's Cathedral, **Hotel Kärntnerhof** (☎ 01/512-1923) is a small, kid-friendly hotel in the center of Vienna. It offers a superb location, attentive staff, and good prices. Also, bedrooms are roomy enough to accommodate families and come equipped with modern amenities.

- **Best Moderately Priced Hotel:** Also in the heart of Old Vienna, less than a block from the cathedral, **Hotel Royal** (☎ 01/515680) was completely rebuilt in 1982. Within this price bracket, not many hotels can compete with the Royal in terms of class. In the lobby, you'll find the piano Wagner used when he was composing *Die Meistersinger Von Nürnberg*.

- **Best Budget Hotel:** Between the State Opera and the famous Nasch Market, **Hotel Schneider** (☎ 01/588380) is a modern five-story building, traditionally furnished with 19th-century antiques. Comfortable and cozy, it attracts singers, musicians, artists, and actors (not the big stars). This hotel is also popular among families because many of the rooms have kitchenettes.

- **Best Pension (B&B):** Near the busy Mariahilferstrasse, **Pension Altstadt Vienna** (☎ 01/5263-3990) has an elegant atmosphere as exemplified by its colorful, velvet-laden Red Salon lounge. The rooms don't disappoint either, as each was decorated by an individual designer and graced with high ceilings, antiques, and parquet floors. This is hardly a lowly pension but a fair-priced and prestigious address with its own special charms.

- **Best Service:** The **Hotel de France** (☎ 800/223-5652 in the U.S., or 01/313680) near the Votivkirche is hardly the best hotel in Vienna, but what makes a stay here particularly delightful is the attentive and highly professional staff. Room service is efficient, messages are received and delivered promptly, and the housekeepers turn down your bed at night.

- **Best Location:** Although it's no Bristol or Imperial, the **Hotel Ambassador** (☎ 01/961610) is definitely where you want to be. The hotel lies between the State Opera and St. Stephan's, with the Kärntnerstrasse on the other side. The Ambassador has enjoyed its position here since 1866—playing host to both Mark Twain and Theodore Roosevelt.
- **Best Health Club:** The **Vienna Hilton** (☎ 800/445-8667 in the U.S., or 01/717000), under different management, sponsors the Pyrron Health Club on its premises. This is, by far, the most professional health club in town, with state-of-the-art equipment and facilities for both men and women. The price for hotel guests is 180AS ($12.05) and 200AS ($13.40) for nonguests.
- **Best Hotel Pool:** Hotels are not known for the breadth of their pools, but of the three hotels in town that have them, the biggest and best awaits in the Body and Soul health spa in the windowless cellar of the **Vienna Marriott** (☎ 800/228-9290 in the U.S., or 01/515180). It's about 36 feet by 24 feet and ringed with potted plants and tables. There's a pair of saunas, an exercise room, and massage facilities. Residents of the Marriott use the pool for free; nonresidents pay 350AS ($23.45). It's open daily from 7am to 10pm.
- **Best Views:** Overlooking the Danube Canal, the 18-story **Vienna Hilton** (☎ 800/445-8667 in the U.S., or 01/717000) offers the most panoramic views from its top floors. Plush accommodations and elegant public rooms also lure guests. The cityscape views are quite dramatic at both dawn and sunset.

3 Best Dining Bets

For the details on these and other restaurants, see chapter 5.

- **Best Spot for a Romantic Dinner:** The **Sacher Hotel Restaurant** (☎ 01/514560) is a showcase for imperial Vienna. Franz Joseph's favorite dish was *tafelspitz*, a delectable boiled beef dinner that's still served here, along with various Viennese and international dishes. Of course, the fabled Sachertorte was invented here.
- **Best Spot for a Business Lunch:** Most afternoons you'll find the movers and shakers of Vienna at **Korso bei Der Oper** (☎ 01/5151-6546) in the Hotel Bristol. The refined menu features Viennese/International cuisine, and business can be conducted with the assurance of good food and impeccable, unobtrusive service.
- **Best Spot for a Celebration:** When you want to take your significant other or a close group of friends to a special place, **Altwienerhof** (☎ 01/892-6000), serving Austrian/French cuisine, is a discriminating choice. A private home in the 1870s, it was transformed into one of the city's premier restaurants. Of course, if it's a real celebration, you'll order champagne, but if not, you'll find one of Vienna's largest wine cellars here.
- **Best Cafe Dining:** Installed in the old glassed-in palm garden of Kaiser Franz Josef's palace, **Palmenhaus** (☎ 01/533-1033) has been restored to its original splendor. Currently, it is the hottest cafe restaurant in Vienna, featuring well-honed Italian cuisine.
- **Best Decor:** At **Steirereck** (☎ 01/713-3168), which means "corner of Styria," the decor is pristine and pure, with original beams and archways transplanted from an old Styrian castle. Murals also add to the elegant ambience, but it's still the food that brings most guests here.

- **Best Wine List:** There are far more elegant restaurants in Vienna and far better places serving haute cuisine, but the wine list at **Wein-Comptoir** (☎ 01/ 512-1760) is tops. Wines are mostly Austrian and reflect the best vintages from every province. Some discriminating diners come just for the wine.
- **Best Value:** If you're seeking a reliable Austrian/International kitchen, and don't want to go broke sampling its wares, head for the **Hotel Astoria Restaurant** (☎ 01/5157-7172). This time-honored favorite retains the authentic *Jugendstil* (art nouveau) look of its past and is an elegant spot to try moderately priced, Old Viennese cooking.
- **Best for Kids:** When your kids rebel against sauerkraut and sausage, they may find that **A Tavola** (☎ 01/512-7955) offers them something more familiar. It's one of the more reasonably priced restaurants in town, and the many different varieties of pasta will please the palates of young and old alike.
- **Best Viennese Cuisine:** If the empire was ever to be restored in Austria, you'd want to take the new Kaiser or Kaiserin to **Drei Husaren** (☎ 01/512-1092). Expect an impeccably prepared meal containing the finest ingredients. Antiques and abundant flowers add to the elegant setting, but it is the delectable menu itself that wins favor, including a nightly repertoire of some 35 hors d'oeuvres.
- **Best Italian Cuisine:** Homemade pastas in savory sauces are served at **Firenze Enoteca** (☎ 01/513-4374), in the heart of Vienna, near St. Stephan's Cathedral. Most of the food is Tuscany-inspired, but other regions of Italy are represented.
- **Best Hungarian Cuisine:** If you can't visit neighboring Budapest, you can get a good preview of Hungarian fare at **Kardos** (☎ 01/512-6949). Try all the Gypsy *schmaltz* favorites, including Lake Balaton–style fish soup.
- **Best Seafood:** The freshest seafood in Vienna—flown in either from the North Sea or the Bosphorus—is served in the center of town at the **Kervansaray und Hummer Bar** (☎ 01/512-8843). Here, you'll find Vienna's finest lobster catch.
- **Best for Game:** In a land of hunters, wild game is still very popular among the Viennese, who flock to **Sailer** (☎ 01/4792-1210). The chefs here prepare such dishes as wild boar, pheasant, and partridge—all according to time-honored recipes.
- **Best Place for** *Tafelspitz:* Go to **Plachutta** (☎ 01/512-1577) to sample the delectable boiled beef dish that enchanted Emperor Franz Joseph I. It's a Viennese tradition.
- **Best Desserts:** Sweet tooths flock to the legendary **Café Demel** (☎ 01/ 533-5516). Café Demel took the Hotel Sacher to court over the recipe for the original Sachertorte, but you can weigh in on the debate with your taste buds. Demel also boasts Vienna's finest array of pastries and delectable desserts like *Gugelhupfs* (cream-filled horns).
- **Best Outdoor Dining: Restaurant at Palais Schwarzenberg** (☎ 01/798-4515), in one of Vienna's most famous hotels, boasts the most beautiful dining terrace in the entire city. Classic Viennese cuisine and a stellar wine list only enhance this summer delight.
- **Best Afternoon Tea:** Situated across from the Hofburg, the grand **Café Central** (☎ 01/533-3763) is an ideal location for a spot of tea as the decor evokes the rich trappings of late imperial Vienna. You'll not only find a wide selection of tea (and coffee) but a rich variety of pastries and desserts.
- **Best Brunch:** In a style that would have impressed Maria Theresa herself, **Café Imperial** (☎ 01/5011-0389), in the Hotel Imperial, prepares an outstanding breakfast buffet on Sundays, beginning at 7am. After brunch and a little champagne, the day is yours!

- **Best Music Feast:** To a true Viennese, a meal is not a meal without music. At **Wiener Rathauskeller** (☎ **01/4051-2190**), in City Hall, you'll enjoy all the schnitzel and sauerkraut you can eat while listening to musicians ramble through the world of operetta, waltz, and *Schrammerl.*
- **Best Picnic Fare:** Head for the **Naschmarkt,** the open-air food market that's a 5-minute stroll from the Karlsplatz. Here you can gather all the ingredients for a spectacular picnic and then enjoy it at the Stadtpark, the Volksgarten, or even an excursion into the Vienna Woods.

2

Planning a Trip to Vienna

So, you've decided on a trip to Vienna. Now you need to figure out how much it will cost, how to get there, and when to go. This chapter will answer these questions and more, with useful tips on pretrip planning to help you get the most from your stay.

1 Visitor Information

TOURIST OFFICES

Before you go, we recommend you contact the **Austrian National Tourist Office.** Write or call the East Coast branch at P.O. Box 1142, New York, NY 10108-1142 (☎ **212/944-6880;** www.anto.com) or the West Coast branch at P.O. Box 491938, Los Angeles, CA 90049 (☎ **310/477-2038**).

As you travel, throughout Vienna and Austria you'll see signs with a fat "i" symbol. Most often that will stand for "information," and you'll be directed to a local tourist office where, chances are, you can obtain maps of the area and might even be assisted in finding a hotel should you arrive without a reservation.

WEB SITES

Here are a few sites where you can begin your Net search for Vienna information: **Austrian National Tourist Office** (www.anto.com), **Vienna Tourist Board** (www.info.wien.at), **LiveCam Vienna** (http://rhwcam.markant.at/snap.cgi), and **Mozart Concerts** (www.mozart.co.at/concerts).

2 Entry Requirements & Customs

ENTRY REQUIREMENTS

Citizens of the United States, Canada, the United Kingdom, Australia, Ireland, and New Zealand need only a valid passport to enter Austria. No visa is required.

CUSTOMS

Visitors who live outside Austria in general are not liable to pay duty on personal articles brought into the country temporarily for their own use, depending on the purpose and circumstances of each trip. Customs officials have great leeway here. Travelers 17 years of age and older may carry up to 200 cigarettes or 50 cigars or 250 grams of tobacco; 1 liter of distilled liquor; and 2.25 liters of wine or 3 liters of beer duty-free. Gifts not exceeding a value of 2,500AS ($167.50) are also exempt from duty.

U.S. CUSTOMS   Returning U.S. citizens who have been away for 48 hours or more are allowed to bring back, once every 30 days, $400 worth of merchandise duty-free. You'll be charged a flat rate of 10% duty on the next $1,000 worth of purchases. Be sure to have your receipts handy. On gifts, the duty-free limit is $100. For more specific guidance, write to the **U.S. Customs Service,** P.O. Box 7407, Washington, DC 20044 (☎ **202/927-6724;** www.customs.ustreas.gov), and request the free pamphlet "Know Before You Go." You can also download the pamphlet from the Internet at **www.customs.ustreas.gov/travel/kbygo.htm**.

BRITISH CUSTOMS   Citizens of the United Kingdom can buy wine, spirits, or cigarettes in an ordinary shop in Austria and bring home almost as much as they like. (U.K. Customs and Excise does set theoretical limits.) But if goods are bought in a duty-free shop, then the old rules still apply—the allowance is 200 cigarettes and 2 liters of table wine, plus 1 liter of spirits or 2 liters of fortified wine. If you're returning home from a non-European Union country, the same allowances apply, and you must declare any goods in excess of these allowances. British Customs tends to be strict and complicated in its requirements. For details, get in touch with **Her Majesty's Customs and Excise Office,** Dorset House, Stamford Street, London SE1 9PY (☎ **020/ 7202-4510;** fax 020/7202-4131; www.hmce.gov.uk).

CANADIAN CUSTOMS   For a clear summary of Canadian rules, write for the booklet "I Declare," issued by **Revenue Canada,** 1165 St. Laurent Blvd., Ottawa K1G 4KE (☎ **506/636-5064;** www.ccra-adrc.gc.ca). Canada allows its citizens a $750 exemption, and you're allowed to bring back duty-free 200 cigarettes, 200 grams of tobacco, 1.5 liters of liquor, and 50 cigars. In addition, you are allowed to mail gifts to Canada from abroad at the rate of C$60 a day, provided they are unsolicited and aren't alcohol or tobacco (write on the package: "Unsolicited gift, under $60 value"). All valuables should be declared on the Y-38 Form before departure from Canada, including serial numbers of, for example, expensive foreign cameras that you already own. Note: The $750 exemption can be used only once a year and only after an absence of 7 days.

AUSTRALIAN CUSTOMS   The duty-free allowance in Australia is A$400 or, for those under age 18, A$200. Personal property mailed back from Austria should be marked "Australian goods returned" to avoid duties. Australian citizens are allowed to mail gifts to Australia from abroad duty-free up to A$200 per parcel. There are no other restrictions on unsolicited gifts; however, you could be subject to a Customs investigation if you send multiple parcels of the same gift to the same address. Upon returning to Australia, citizens can bring in 250 cigarettes or 250 grams of loose tobacco, and 1,125 milliliters of alcohol. If you're returning with valuable goods you already own, such as foreign-made cameras, you should file Form B263. A helpful brochure, available from Australian consulates or Customs offices, is "Know Before You Go." For more information, contact **Australian Customs Services,** GPO Box 8, Sydney NSW 2001 (☎ **02/9213-2000;** www.customs.gov.au).

NEW ZEALAND CUSTOMS   The duty-free allowance for New Zealand is NZ$700. New Zealanders are allowed to mail gifts to New Zealand from abroad duty-free to a limit of NZ$70 per parcel. Beware sending multiple parcels of the same gift to the same address; a Customs investigation could await your return home. Citizens over 17 years of age can bring in 200 cigarettes, or 50 cigars, or 250 grams of tobacco (or a mixture of all three if their combined weight doesn't exceed 250 grams), plus 4.5 liters of wine and beer or 1.125 liters of liquor. New Zealand currency does not carry import or export restrictions. Fill out a certificate of export, listing the valuables you are taking out of the country; that way, you can bring them back without paying duty. Most questions are answered in a free pamphlet available at New Zealand consulates and Customs offices, "New Zealand Customs Guide for Travellers, Notice no. 4." For more information, contact **New Zealand Customs Services,** 50 Anzac Ave., P.O. Box 29, Auckland (☎ **09/359-6655;** www.customs.govt.nz).

IRELAND CUSTOMS Citizens of Ireland must declare all goods in excess of IR£142 per person obtained tax- or duty-free within a EU country above the following allowances: 50 cigars, 100 cigarillos, or 250 grams of tobacco; 1 liter of liquor or 2 liters of wine, 2 liters of still wine; 50 grams of perfume; and 250 milliliters of toilet water. If goods were duty or tax paid in another EU country up to a value of IR£460, no extra tax is levied at the Irish border. For more information, contact **The Revenue Commissioner,** Dublin Castle (☎ **01/679-2777**); fax 01/679-3261; www. revenue.ie) or write The Collector of Customs and Excise, The Custom House, Dublin 1.

3 Money

Foreign and Austrian money can be brought into Vienna without any restrictions. There is no restriction on taking foreign money out of the country either.

CURRENCY

The basic unit of currency is the **Austrian schilling (AS),** which is made up of 100 **groschen.** There are coins with denominations of 2, 5, 10, and 50 groschen, and 1, 5, 10, and 20 schillings, and banknotes with denominations of 20, 50, 100, 500, 1,000, and 5,000 schillings.

The **Euro** ([eu]) the new European currency, became the official currency of Austria and 10 other participating countries on January 1, 1999, but not in the form of cash. The traveler will see prices displayed in euros as well as schillings, and the euro can be used in noncash transactions, such as credit cards. The euro will be introduced in the form of cash in January 2002. For the following six months or so, Austria will operate under a dual-currency system of both euros and schillings. In July 2002, euros will become the only form of currency, replacing the schilling in Austria and the national currencies of the other participating EU countries.

It's always wise to exchange enough money before departure to get you from the airport to your hotel. This way, you avoid delays and the lousy rates at the airport exchange booths.

Austrian banks generally offer the best rates of exchange; they're open Monday to Wednesday, and Fridays from 8am to 3pm, and Thursdays from 8am to 5:30pm (most banks also close daily from 12:30 to 1:30pm). The most tourist-friendly bank in Vienna is the one run by American Express at Kärntnerstrasse 21–23 (☎ **01/ 515400**), open Monday to Friday, 9am to 5:30pm, and Saturday, 9am to noon. During off-hours you can exchange money at *bureaux de change* throughout the Inner City (there's one at the intersection of Kohlmarkt and the Graben), as well as at travel agencies, train stations, and at the airport. There's also a 24-hour exchange service at the post office (*Hauptpostamt*) at Fleischmarkt 19. Examine the prices and rates carefully before handing over your dollars, and try not to exchange money at your hotel; the rates they offer tend to be horrendous.

If you need to prepay a deposit on hotel reservations by check, it's cheaper and easier to pay with a check drawn on an Austrian bank. This can be arranged by a large commercial bank or **Ruesch International,** 700 11th St. NW, Washington, DC

The Austrian Schilling

For American Readers   At this writing $1 = approximately 15 schillings (or 1 schilling = approximately 6.7¢), and this was the rate of exchange used to calculate the dollar values given throughout this book, rounded to the nearest nickel.

For British Readers   At this writing £1 = approximately 22 schillings (or 1 schilling = approximately 4.3 pence), and that was the rate of exchange used to calculate the pound values in the table below.

The Euro   At this writing, the schilling was fixed to the euro at the constant rate of 13.76 schillings per euro. (Stated differently, 1 schilling was worth [eu].0727.)

Note: Because most international exchange rates fluctuate freely, this table should be used only as an approximate indicator of relative currency values.

AS	U.S.$	U.K.£	Euro€	AS	U.S.$	U.K.£	Euro€
1	0.07	0.04	0.07	75	5.03	3.23	5.45
2	0.13	0.09	0.15	100	6.70	4.30	7.27
3	0.20	0.13	0.22	125	8.38	5.38	9.09
4	0.27	0.17	0.29	150	10.05	6.45	10.91
5	0.34	0.22	0.36	175	11.73	7.53	12.72
6	0.40	0.26	0.44	200	13.40	8.60	14.54
7	0.47	0.30	0.51	225	15.08	9.68	16.36
8	0.54	0.34	0.58	250	16.75	10.75	18.18
9	0.60	0.39	0.65	275	18.43	11.83	19.00
10	0.67	0.43	0.73	300	20.10	12.90	21.81
15	1.01	0.65	1.09	350	23.45	15.05	25.45
20	1.34	0.86	1.45	400	26.80	17.20	29.08
25	1.68	1.08	1.82	500	33.50	21.50	36.35
50	3.35	2.15	3.64	1000	67.00	43.00	72.70

20005 (☎ **800/424-2923** or 202/408-1200; www.ruesch.com), which performs many conversion-related tasks, usually for only $15 per transaction.

CREDIT CARDS

The way to get the best rate of exchange is to use your credit cards whenever possible. They virtually always offer the best exchange rate, and there's no accompanying service charge. Credit cards are widely accepted in Austria; American Express, Visa, and Diners Club are the most commonly recognized. A Eurocard or Access sign displayed at an establishment means that it accepts MasterCard.

ATM NETWORKS

Plus, Cirrus, and other networks connecting automated-teller machines (ATMs) operate in Vienna and throughout Austria. When using an ATM abroad, the money will be in local currency; the rate of exchange tends to be as good, if not better, than the rates at airport money counters or hotels. Note that international withdrawal fees will be higher than domestic—ask your bank for specifics. Always determine the frequency limits for withdrawals and cash advances off your credit card. Also, check to see if your PIN code must be reprogrammed for usage in Austria. Most ATMs outside the United States require a four-digit PIN number.

What Things Cost in Vienna	U.S. $	U.K. £	Euros €
Taxi from the airport to the city Center	30.15	19.35	32.70
U-Bahn (subway) from St. Stephan's to Schönbrunn Palace	1.50	95p	1.60
Local phone call	.17	11p	0.18
Double room at Hotel Astoria (expensive)	194.30	124.70	211
Double room at the Am Parkring (moderate)	133.30	85.60	145
Double room at the Pension Nossek (inexpensive)	87.10	55.90	95
Lunch for one, without wine, at Drei Husaren (expensive)	29.50	18.90	32
Lunch for one, without wine, at Griechenbeisl (moderate)	18	11.60	20
Dinner for one, without wine, at Hauswirth (expensive)	58.65	37.65	64
Dinner for one, without wine, at Plachutta (moderate)	50.25	32.25	55
Dinner for one, without wine, at Zwolf-Apostelkeller (inexpensive)	18.40	11.60	20
Glass of wine (one-eighth liter)	2.80	1.80	3.05
Half-liter of beer	3.20	2.05	3.50
Coca-Cola (in a cafe)	2.50	1.60	2.75
Cup of coffee (in a cafe)	3.0	1.95	3.30
Roll of color film, 36 exposures	8.50	5.50	9.30
Admission to Schönbrunn Palace	8.40	5.40	9.10
Movie ticket	6–8.50	3.90–5.50	6.50–9.25
Theater Ticket	10–168	6.45–108	10.90–182

To receive a directory of **Cirrus** ATMs, call ☎ **800/424-7787**; for **Plus** locations, call ☎ **800/843-7587**. You can also access the Visa/PLUS International ATM Locator Guide through the Internet: www.visa.com.

TRAVELER'S CHECKS

Traveler's checks are the safest way to carry cash while traveling. Most banks will give you a better exchange rate for traveler's checks than cash.

Major issuers of traveler's checks include **American Express** (☎ **800/221-7282**); **Citicorp** (☎ **800/645-6556** in the U.S. and Canada, or 813/623-1709 collect from anywhere else in the world); **Thomas Cook** (☎ **800/223-7373** in the U.S. and Canada, or 609/987-7300 collect from other parts of the world); and **Visa** traveler's checks (☎ **800/221-2426** in the U.S. and Canada, or 212/858-8500 collect from other parts of the world).

MONEYGRAMS

If you find yourself out of money, a new wire service provided by American Express can help you tap willing friends and family for emergency funds. Through **MoneyGram**,

7401 W. Mansfield, Lakewood, CO 80235 (☎ **800/926-9400**; www.moneygram. com) money can be sent around the world in less than 10 minutes. Call AMEX to l earn the address of the closest outlet that handles MoneyGrams. Cash, credit card, or the occasional personal check (with ID) are acceptable forms of payment. AMEX's fee for the service is $19 for the first $300 with a sliding scale for larger sums. The service includes a short telex message and a 3-minute phone call from sender to recipient. The beneficiary must present a photo ID at the outlet where the money is received.

4 When to Go

Vienna experiences its high season from April through October, with July and August and the main festivals being the most crowded times. Bookings around Christmas are also heavy because many Austrians themselves visit the capital city during this festive time. Always arrive with reservations during these peak seasons. During the off-seasons, hotel rooms are generally plentiful and less expensive, and there is less demand for tables in the top restaurants.

CLIMATE

The temperature in Austria varies greatly depending on your location. However, in Vienna—which has a moderate subalpine climate—the January average is 32°F, and in July it's 66°F. A New Yorker who lived in Vienna for 8 years told us that the four seasons were "about the same." Summers in Vienna, which generally last from Easter until mid-October, are not usually as humid as those in coastal New York City, but they can sometimes be uncomfortably sticky. The ideal times for visiting Vienna are spring and fall, when mild weather prevails, but the winter air is usually crisp and clear, with plenty of sunshine.

Average Daytime Temperature (°F) & Monthly Rainfall (inches) in Vienna

	Jan	Feb	Mar	Apr	May	June	July	Aug	Sept	Oct	Nov	Dec
Temp.	30	32	38	50	58	64	68	70	60	50	41	33
Rainfall	1.2	1.9	3.9	1.3	2.9	1.9	.8	1.8	2.8	2.8	2.5	1.6

HOLIDAYS

Bank holidays in Vienna are as follows: January 1, January 6 (Epiphany), Easter Monday, May 1, Ascension Day, Whitmonday, Corpus Christi Day, August 15, October 26 (Nationalfeiertag), November 1 and 26, and December 25 and 26.

Vienna Calendar of Events

January

- **New Year's Eve/New Year's Day.** Vienna's biggest night is launched by the famed concert of the Vienna Philharmonic Orchestra. The New Year also marks the beginning of **Fasching,** the famous Vienna Carnival season, which lasts through Shrove Tuesday (Mardi Gras). For tickets and information, contact the Wiener Philharmoniker, Bösendorferstrasse 12, A-1010 Vienna (☎ **01/505-6525**). The concert is followed by the **Kaiserball** in the Hofburg. For information and tickets, contact the WKV, Hofburg, Heldenplatz, A-1014 Vienna (☎ **01/587-3666**).
- **Eistraum (Dream On Ice).** During the coldest months of Austrian winter, the monumental plaza between the Town Hall and the Burgtheater is flooded and

frozen; lights, loudspeakers, and a stage are hauled in, and the entire civic core is transformed into a gigantic ice-skating rink. Sedate waltz tunes accompany the skaters during the day, and DJs spin rock, funk, and reggae after the sun goes down. Around the rink, dozens of kiosks sell everything from hot chocolate and snacks to wine and beer. For information, contact the Vienna Tourist Board (☎ **01/211-14-222**). January 22 to March 7.

February

- **Opera Ball.** On the last Thursday of the Fasching, Vienna's high society gathers at the Staatsoper for the grandest ball of the Carnival season. The evening opens with a performance by the Opera House Ballet. You don't need an invitation, but you do need to buy a ticket, which, as you might guess, isn't cheap. For information call the Opera House (☎ **01/5144-2606**) directly.

April

- **Osterklang Wien (Sound of Easter in Vienna).** The Vienna Philharmonic usually opens these festivities, first launched in 1997. You might also hear the Vienna Symphony Orchestra perform *Spring in Vienna*. Various venues are used for this festival, including the Vienna State Opera. Ringing out the festival is an Easter oratorio at St. Stephan's Cathedral. Concerts during the festival usually last 2 hours. For information, write Osterklang Wien/Klangbogen, Laudongasse 29, A-1080, Vienna (☎ **01/400-8410**). Book by phone with a credit card by calling ☎ **01/01-42-717.** Palm Sunday to Easter Sunday.

- **Vienna Mozart Week.** In its sixth year, Vienna's musicians will devote an entire week to the works of Wolfgang Amadeus Mozart. The Neues Wiener Barock-ensemble sets the tone with orchestral works by the musical genius, followed by performances by the Vienna Philharmonic. Mozart Week culminates in a performance of the Coronation Mass and church sonatas during Sunday mass at the Church of the Augustinian Friars. Organizers of the festival also conduct guided walks following in "Mozart's Footsteps in Vienna." For bookings, contact Wiener Mozartwoche, Postfach 55, A-1181 Vienna (☎ **01/408-7586**). Festival dates change every year but usually begin the end of the first week in April, lasting for 1 week.

- **Vienna Spring Festival.** The festival has a different central theme every year (still undecided for 2001), but always count on music by the world's greatest composers, including Mozart and Brahms, at the Konzerthaus. The booking address is Wiener Konzerthaus, Lothringerstrasse 20, A-1030 Vienna (☎ **01/712- 1211**). Mid-April through the first week of May.

May

- **International Music Festival.** This traditional highlight of Vienna's concert calendar features top-class international orchestras, distinguished conductors, and classical greats. You can hear Beethoven's *Eroica* as it was meant to be played, Mozart's *Jupiter Symphony,* and perhaps Bruckner's *Romantic.* The list of conductors and orchestras reads like a "Who's Who" of the international world of music. The venue and also the booking address is Wiener Musikverein, Karlsplatz 6 (☎ **01/505-8190**). Early May through the first 3 weeks of June.

- ✪ **Vienna Festival.** An exciting array of operas, operettas, musicals, theater, and dances are performed. New productions of treasured classics are presented alongside avant-garde premieres, all staged by international leading directors. In addition, celebrated productions from renowned European theaters offer guest performances. Anticipate such productions as Mozart's *Così fan tutte*, Monteverdi's *Orfeo*, and Offenbach's *La Vie Parisienne*. For bookings, contact Wiener Festwochen, Lehárgasse 11, A-1060 Vienna (☎ **01/589-220**). The second week of May until mid-June.

June

- **Euro Gay Pride 2001.** The largest gay, lesbian, bisexual, and transgendered Pride Parade in the history of Europe is to be staged in Vienna over a 1-month period beginning June 1, 2001. Major events, from speeches to entertainment at various venues, are planned for this colossal happening, which is expected to draw crowds from all over the world. For more information, contact Verein Christopher Street Day, Wasagasse 12, A-1090 Vienna (☎ **01/319-4472;** e-mail: pr@pride.at).

July

- **Vienna Jazz Festival.** This is one of the world's top jazz events, using the Vienna State Opera as its central event venue. The program calls for appearances by more than 50 international and local stars. For information and bookings, contact the Vienna Jazz Festival, Frankenberggasse 13 (☎ **01/503-561**). July 1 to July 10, 2001.

- **Klangbogen.** A wealth of musical events, ranging from opera, operetta, and chamber music to orchestral concerts. World-renowned orchestras perform in the Golden Hall of the Vienna Musikverein. For bookings and information, contact Klangbogen, Laudongasse 29, A-1080 Vienna (☎ **01/4000-8410**). The second week of July through the first week of September.

- **Music Film Festival.** Opera, operetta, and masterly concert performances captured on celluloid are enjoyed free under a starry sky in front of the neo-Gothic City Hall on the Ringstrasse. Programs focus on works by Franz Schubert, Johannes Brahms, or other composers. You might view Rudolf Nureyev in *Swan Lake* or see Leonard Bernstein wielding the baton for Brahms. For more information, contact Ideenagentur Austria, Opernring 1R, A-1010 Vienna (☎ **01/587-0150**). July and August.

October/November

- **Wien Modern.** Enjoying its 14th year in 2001, the Wien Modern was founded by Claudio Abbado and is devoted to the performance of contemporary works in music. You might catch works from Iceland, Romania, or Portugal, as well as Austria. Some of the composers make live appearances and discuss their compositions. Performances are at Verein Wien Modern, Lothingerstrasse 20 (☎ **01/7124-6800**), but the booking address is Wiener Konzerthaus, Lothringerstrasse 20 (☎ **01/712-468**). End of October until the end of November.

December

- **Christkindlmärte.** Between late November and New Year's, look for pockets of folk charm (and in some cases kitsch) associated with the Christmas holidays. Small outdoor booths known as *Christkindlmarkts*—usually adorned with evergreen boughs, red ribbons, and in some cases religious symbols—sprout up in clusters around the city. They're selling old-fashioned toys, *Tannenbaum* (tree) decorations, and gift items. Food vendors will also be nearby offering sausages, cookies and pastries, roasted chestnuts, and *Kartoffel* (charcoal-roasted potato slices). The greatest concentration of these open-air markets can be found in front of the Rathaus, in the Spittelberg Quarter (7th District), at Freyung, the historic square in the northwest corner of the Inner City.

5 Health & Insurance

STAYING HEALTHY

You'll encounter few health problems while traveling in Vienna. The tap water is generally safe to drink, the milk is pasteurized, and health services are good. Occasionally, the change in diet and water may cause some minor disturbances, so you may want to talk to your doctor.

Bring enough prescription medicines to last throughout your stay. Bring along copies of your prescriptions written in the generic—not brand-name—form. Generally, any prescription can easily be filled. If you need a doctor, your hotel can recommend one, or you can contact your embassy or consulate. You can also obtain a list of English-speaking doctors before you leave from the **International Association for Medical Assistance to Travelers (IAMAT)** in the United States at 417 Center St., Lewiston, NY 14092 (☎ **716/754-4883**); in Canada at 40 Regal Rd., Guelph, ON N1K 1B5 (☎ **519/836-0102**).

INSURANCE

Before going, check your existing policies to see if they'll cover you while you're traveling. For example, your homeowner's or renter's insurance might cover off-premises theft and loss wherever it occurs. And check that your health insurance will cover you when you're away from home. Note that Medicare does not cover you when you are outside the United States.

Some credit and charge cards offer automatic flight insurance when you purchase an airline ticket with that card. These policies insure against death or dismemberment in case of an airplane crash. If you are traveling on a tour or have prepaid a large chunk of your travel expenses, you might want to ask your travel agent about trip-cancellation insurance.

If you are going to rent a car in Austria, check to see whether your automobile insurance, automobile club, or charge card covers personal accident insurance (PAI), collision damage waiver (CDW), or other insurance options. You may be able to avoid additional rental charges if you already covered. See "Car Rentals" for more information.

The following companies sell a variety of travel insurance policies:

- **HealthCare Abroad,** c/o Wallach & Co., 107 W. Federal St., Middleburg, VA 20118 (☎ **800/237-6615;** www.wallach.com), offers $250,000 of comprehensive medical expense protection, plus the multilingual services of a worldwide travelers' assistance network. Any U.S. resident under the age of 85 traveling outside the country is eligible to participate. Provisions for trip cancellation can also be written into the policy for a nominal cost.

- **Travelex,** 11717 Burt St., Suite 202, Omaha NE 68175 (☎ **800/228-9792;** www.travelex-insurance.com), offers insurance packages based on the age of the traveler as well as the cost of the trip per person. Included in the packages are travel-assistance services and financial protection against trip cancellation, trip interruption, flight and baggage delays, accident-related medical costs, accidental death, dismemberment, and medical evacuation.

   Another good company with similar plans is **Travel Guard International,** 1145 Clark Street, Stevens Point, WI 54481 (☎ **800/826-1300** or 715/ 345-0505; www.noelgroup.com).

- **Travelers Insured International, Inc.,** P.O. Box 280568, Hartford, CT 06128-0568 (☎ **800/243-3174,** or 860/528-7663 outside the U.S. between 7:45am and 7pm EST; www.travelinsured.com), provides trip cancellation and emergency evacuation polices costing $5.50 for each $100 of coverage. Travel accident and illness insurance start from $10 for 6 to 10 days; $500 worth of coverage for lost, damaged, or delayed baggage costs $20 for 6 to 10 days; and trip cancellation goes for $5.50 per $100 worth of coverage (written approval is necessary for cancellation coverage above $10,000).

INSURANCE FOR BRITISH TRAVELERS   Most big travel agencies offer their own insurance and will probably try to sell you their package when you book a holiday. Think before you sign. Britain's Consumers' Association recommends that you insist on seeing the policy and reading the fine print before buying travel insurance.

You should also shop around for better deals. You might contact **Columbus Travel Insurance Ltd.** (☎ **020/7375-0011** in London) or, for students, visit **Campus Travel** (☎ **0870/240-1010** in London). Columbus Travel will sell travel insurance only to people who have been official residents of Britain for at least a year.

6 Tips for Travelers with Special Needs

FOR TRAVELERS WITH DISABILITIES

BEFORE YOU GO   For a $35 annual fee, **Mobility International USA,** P.O. Box 10767, Eugene, OR 97440 (☎ **541/343-1284** voice and TDD; www.miusa.org), will answer your questions on various destinations and also give discounts on videos, publications, and programs it sponsors.

You can also obtain a copy of **"Air Transportation of Handicapped Persons,"** published by the U.S. Department of Transportation. It's free if you write to Free Advisory Circular No. AC12032, Distribution Unit, U.S. Department of Transportation, Publications Division, M-4332, Washington, DC 20590.

If you're interested in tours for travelers with disabilities, contact the **Society for the Advancement of Travel for the Handicapped,** 347 Fifth Ave., New York, NY 10016 (☎ **212/447-7284;** www.sath.org). Annual membership dues are $45, $30 for seniors and students. Send a stamped, self-addressed envelope.

For persons who are blind or have visual impairments, the best source is the **American Foundation for the Blind,** 11 Penn Plaza, Suite 300, New York, NY 10001 (☎ **800/232-5463,** or 212/502-7600; www.afb.org). It offers information on travel and various requirements for the transport and border formalities for Seeing Eye dogs.

IN VIENNA   As with most European cities, services for travelers with disabilities in Vienna are limited, but luckily a lot of the sights in the city center are close together and wheelchair-accessible. The **Vienna Tourist Board,** Obere Augartenstrasse 40, A-1025 (☎ **01/211140;** fax 01/216-8492) publishes a helpful booklet for visitors with disabilities, including information on riding public transportation.

FOR BRITISH TRAVELERS   RADAR (the Royal Association for Disability and Rehabilitation), Unit 12, City Forum, 250 City Rd., London ECIV 8AF (☎ **020/7250-3222**), publishes holiday "fact packs"—three in all—which sell for £2 each or £5 for all three. The first provides general information, including planning and booking a holiday, insurance, finances, and useful organizations. The second outlines transport and equipment options for traveling abroad, and the third deals with specialized accommodations.

Another good resource is the **Holiday Care,** 2nd Floor Imperial Building, Victoria Road, Horley, Surrey RH6 7PZ (☎ **01293/774535;** fax 01293/784647; www.holidaycare.org.uk), a national charity that advises on accessible accommodations for the elderly and travelers with disabilities. It also provides a free reservations service offering discount rates. Annual membership costs £30.

FOR GAYS & LESBIANS

Unlike Germany, Austria still has a prevailing anti-homosexual attitude, in spite of the large number of gay people who live there. There is still much discrimination; gay liberation has a long way to go. Vienna, however, has a large gay community with many bars and restaurants. For information about gay-related activities in Vienna, call the **Gay/Lesbian Visitor Center** at Novargasse 40 (☎ **01/216-6604**).

To learn about gay and lesbian travel in Austria, you might want to consult the following publications before you go. Men can order *Spartacus,* the international gay guide ($32.95), or *Odysseus 2001* ($29). Both lesbians and gay men might want to pick up a copy of *Gay Travel A to Z* ($16), which provides general information and lists bars, hotels, restaurants, and places of interest for gay travelers throughout the world. These books and others are available from **Giovanni's Room,** 345 S. 12th St. Philadelphia, PA 19107 (☎ **215/923-2960;** www.giovannisroom.com).

The magazine *Our World,* 1104 North Nova Rd., Suite 251, Daytona Beach, FL 32117 (☎ **904/441-5367;** www.ourworldmag.com), covers options and bargains for gay and lesbian travel worldwide. It costs $35 for 10 issues. *Out and About,* 657 Harrison St., San Francisco, CA 94107 (☎ **800/929-2268;** 415/229-1793; www. outandabout.com), has been hailed for its "straight" reporting about gay travel. It profiles the best gay or gay-friendly hotels, gyms, clubs, and places of interest throughout the world. It costs $49 for 10 information-packed issues.

The **International Gay and Lesbian Travel Association (IGLTA),** 4331 N. Federal, Suite 304, Ft. Lauderdale, FL 33308 (☎ **800/448-8550** for voice mailbox, or 954/776-2626), encourages gay and lesbian travel worldwide. With around 1,200 member agencies, it specializes in networking travelers with the appropriate gay-friendly service organization or tour specialist. It offers quarterly newsletter, marketing mailings, and a membership directory updated four times a year.

In Austria, the minimum age for consensual homosexual activity is 18.

FOR SENIORS

Many senior discounts are available, but note that some may require membership in a particular association.

If you're a member of **AARP (American Association of Retired Persons),** 601 E St. NW, Washington, DC 20049 (☎ **800/424-3410** or 202/434-AARP; www. aarp.org), you may get discounts on car rentals, hotels, and airfares.

SAGA International Holidays, 222 Berkeley St., Boston, MA 02116 (☎ **800/ 343-0273;** www.sagaholidays.com), runs all-inclusive tours for those aged 50 years and older.

You can write for a helpful publication, *101 Tips for the Mature Traveler,* available free from Grand Circle Travel, 347 Congress St., Suite 3A, Boston, MA 02210 (☎ **800/221-2610** in the U.S., or 617/350-7500).

Travel information for seniors is also available from the **National Council of Senior Citizens,** 8403 Colesville Rd., Suite 1200, Silver Spring, MD 20910 (☎ **301/ 578-8800;** www.ncscinc.org). For $13 per person or per couple you receive a monthly newsletter and membership benefits, including discounts on hotel and car rentals.

Sears Mature Outlook, P.O. Box 9390, Des Moines, IA 50306 (☎ **800/ 336-6330**), is a membership program for people over 50 years of age. Members are offered discounts at ITC-member hotels and will receive a bimonthly magazine. The annual membership fee of $39.95 entitles you to discounts on selected car rentals and restaurants, plus free coupons for discounted merchandise from Sears.

Uniworld, 16000 Ventura Blvd., Suite 200, Encino, CA 91436 (☎ **800/ 733-7820** in the U.S. or 818/382-7820; www.uniworldcruisers.com), specializes in singles tours for the mature person. They either arrange for you to share an accommodation with another single person or get you a low-priced single supplement.

Elderhostel, 75 Federal St., Boston, MA 02110-1941 (☎ **617/426-7788;** www.elderhostel.org), offers an array of university-based summer educational programs for seniors worldwide, including in Vienna. Most courses are 3 weeks long and are remarkable values, considering that airfare, accommodations (in student dormitories or modest inns), meals, and tuition are included. Courses include field trips but no homework, and participants must be at least 55 years old.

FOR FAMILIES

Vienna is a great place to take your kids. The pleasures available for children (which most adults enjoy just as much) range from watching the magnificent Lippizaner stallions at the Spanish Riding School to exploring the city's many castles and dungeons.

Another outstanding and kid-friendly Viennese attraction is the Prater amusement park, with its giant Ferris wheel, roller coasters, merry-go-rounds, arcades, and tiny railroad that loops around the park. Even if your kids aren't very interested in touring palace state rooms, take them to Schönbrunn, where the zoo and coach collection will tantalize. In summer, beaches along the Alte Donau (an arm of the Danube) are suitable for swimming. And, don't forget the lure of the *Konditorei,* those little shops where scrumptious Viennese cakes and pastries are sold.

Baby-sitting services are available through most hotel desks or by applying at the Tourist Information Office in the town where you're staying. Many hotels have children's game rooms and playgrounds.

Family Travel Times online newsletter costs $40 (www.familytraveltimes.com), and it's updated every 2 weeks. Subscribers can call in with travel questions on Wednesday from 10am to 1pm EST. Contact Family Travel Times, 40 5th Ave., New York, NY 10011 (☎ **888/822-44322,** or 212/477-5524).

FOR STUDENTS

Council Travel (a subsidiary of the Council on International Educational Exchange) is America's largest student, youth, and budget travel group, with more than 60 offices worldwide. The main office is at 205 E. 42nd St., New York, NY 10017 (☎ **888/COUNCIL;** www.counciltravel.com); call to find the location nearest you. Council Travel sells publications for young people about how to work, study, and travel abroad.

International Student Identity Cards entitle bona fide students to generous travel and other discounts. Discounted international and domestic air tickets are available, as well as Eurotrain rail passes, YHA passes, weekend packages, overland safaris, and hostel/hotel accommodations. The card, which costs only $20, is available at Council Travel offices nationwide (☎ **212/822-2700**), as well as on hundreds of college campuses. Proof of student status and a passport-size (2-by-2-inch) photograph are necessary.

For real budget travelers, it's worth joining **IYHF (International Youth Hostel Federation).** For information, write Hostelling Information/American Youth Hostels (HI-AYH), 733 15th St. NW, Suite 840, Washington, DC 20005 (☎ **202/783-6161;** www.hiayah.org). Membership, which provides discounts at hostels, costs $25 annually; those under age 18 are free and those over age 54 pay $15.

TIPS FOR BRITISH STUDENTS   USIT Campus, 52 Grosvenor Gardens, London SW1W 0AG (☎ **0870/240-1010**) opposite Victoria Station, open 7 days a week, is Britain's leading specialist in student and youth travel worldwide. It provides comprehensive travel service specializing in low-cost rail, sea, and air travel; holiday breaks; and travel insurance; plus student discount cards.

The **International Student Identity Card (ISIC)** is an internationally recognized proof of student status that will entitle you to savings on flights, sightseeing, food, and accommodations. You can purchase the card at Campus Travel (☎ **020/7938-2948**) for £5 and it is well worth the cost. Always show your ISIC when booking a trip—you may not get a discount without it.

Youth hostels are the place to stay if you're a student. You'll need an **International Youth Hostels Association** card, which you can purchase from the youth hostel store at 14 Southampton St., London WC23 7HY (☎ **020/7836-8541**), or Campus Travel, 52 Grosvenor Gardens, London SW1W 0AG (☎ **020/7938-2948**). Take both your passport and some passport-size photos of yourself, plus £9 for your membership.

The Youth Hostel Association puts together *The Hostelling International Budget Guide,* listing every youth hostel in 31 European countries. It costs £7 when purchased at the Southampton Street store in London. Add 61p postage if it's being delivered within the United Kingdom.

If you're traveling in summer, many youth hostels will be full. To avoid disappointment, it's best to book ahead. In London, you can make advance reservations at the membership department at 14 Southampton St. (see above).

7 Getting There

BY PLANE

As a gateway between Western and Eastern Europe, Vienna has seen an increase in air traffic into the city. Although Vienna is serviced by a number of well-respected European airlines, most flights coming from America require a transfer in other European cities, such as London or Frankfurt.

THE MAJOR AIRLINES

From the United States, you can fly directly to Vienna on **Austrian Airlines** (☎ **800/ 843-0002** in the U.S. and Canada; www.aua.com), the national carrier of Austria. There's nonstop service from New York to Vienna (approximately 9 hours) and more recently from Chicago and Washington to Vienna.

In 1994, Austrian Airlines inaugurated a block seat arrangement with **Delta Airlines** (☎ **800/241-4141** in the U.S.; www.delta.com), whereby certain flights from New York's JFK airport would be operated by both carriers. Delta also maintains two independent routings into Vienna from New York and Atlanta. The first departs daily from New York's JFK and stops in Paris with no change of aircraft. Flights from Atlanta to Vienna depart every day, although a change of equipment is required in Paris.

British Airways (☎ **800/AIRWAYS** in the U.S. and Canada; www.british-airways.com) provides excellent service to Vienna. Passengers fly first to London—usually nonstop—from 18 gateways in the United States, 3 in Canada, 2 in Brazil, and 1 in Bermuda, Mexico City, and Buenos Aires. From London, British Airways has two to five daily nonstop flights to Vienna from either Gatwick or Heathrow airports.

Flights on **Lufthansa** (☎ **800/645-3880** in the U.S. and Canada; www.lufthansa-usa.com), the German national carrier, depart from North America frequently for Frankfurt and Düsseldorf, with connections to Vienna.

Affiliated with Lufthansa is **Lauda Air** (☎ **800/588-8399;** www.laudaair.com), which offers direct service five times a week between Miami and Vienna, with a brief touchdown in Munich. Lauda also operates flights to Vienna from European hubs, such as Barcelona, Madrid, London, and Paris.

American Airlines (☎ 800/433-7300 in the U.S. and Canada; www. americanair. com), funnels Vienna-bound passengers through gateways in Zurich, London, or Frankfurt.

If you're traveling from Canada, you can usually connect from your hometown to **British Airways** (☎ 800/AIRWAYS in Canada; www.british-airways.com) gateways in Toronto, Montréal, and Vancouver. Separate nonstop flights from both Toronto's Pearson Airport and Montréal's Mirabelle Airport depart every day for London, and flights from Vancouver depart for London three times a week. In London, you can stay for a few days (arranging discounted hotel accommodations through the British Airways tour desk) or head directly to Vienna on any of the two to five daily nonstop flights from either Heathrow or Gatwick.

There are frequent flights between London and Vienna, the majority of which depart from London's Heathrow Airport. Flight time is 2 hours and 20 minutes.

Austrian Airlines (☎ 020/7434-7373 in London; www.aua.com) has four daily nonstop flights into Vienna from Heathrow.

British Airways (☎ 0345/222-111 in London; www.british-airways.co.uk) surpasses that, offering three daily nonstops from Heathrow and two from Gatwick, with easy connections through London from virtually every other part of Britain.

The lowest fares are offered to travelers who stay a Saturday night abroad and return to London on a predetermined date within 1 month of their initial departure. To qualify for this type of ticket on either of the above-mentioned airlines, no advance purchase is necessary.

FINDING THE BEST AIRFARE

The lowest airfares at **Austrian Airlines** (www.austrianair.com) are called nonrefundable PEX (not to be confused with APEX), and these require a 21-day advance purchase and a European stopover of 7 to 30 days. Once issued, no changes or refunds are permitted unless you're willing to pay more for your fare. A slightly different, slightly more expensive ticket is an Advance Purchase Excursion fare, or APEX, which requires only 14-day advance purchase and a stopover of 7 days to 2 months. For changes in flight dates within 14 days prior to the initial departure, a $150 penalty is imposed.

With a regular excursion fare, no advance purchase is necessary. There are no restrictions about early reservations or minimum time logged abroad. The return half of the ticket is valid for a year after departure.

Austrian Airlines offers a 10% discount off regularly published fares between New York and Vienna and Chicago and Vienna for passengers age 62 and over and for a traveling companion regardless of that companion's age.

The airline also offers breaks to anyone between the ages of 12 and 24. Its round-trip Youth Fare requires only that tickets be reserved and purchased 3 days or less before departure. The return half of the ticket can be used any time within a year of departure.

CHARTER FLIGHTS   A charter flight is a one-time-only transit to some predetermined point, with the aircraft reserved months in advance. Before paying for a charter, check the restrictions on your ticket or contract. You'll pay a stiff penalty (or forfeit the ticket entirely) if you cancel. Charters are sometimes canceled when the plane doesn't fill up.

One reliable charter-flight operator is **Council Charter,** run by the Council on International Educational Exchange, 205 E. 42nd St., New York, NY 10017 (☎ 800/ 2-COUNCIL; www.ciee.org). You could also try **Travac,** 989 Sixth Ave., New York, NY 10018 (☎ 800/TRAV-800 or 212/563-3303; www.thetravelsits.com).

BUCKET SHOPS & CONSOLIDATORS   You might be able to get a great deal on airfare by calling a bucket shop or a consolidator, outfits that act as clearinghouses for blocks of tickets that airlines discount and consign during normally slow periods of air travel. Tickets are usually priced 20% to 35% below the full fare. However, payment terms can vary, and you might be assigned a poor seat on the plane at the last minute.

In the United States, bucket shops abound from coast to coast. You might try **Travac,** 989 Sixth Ave., New York, NY 10018 (☎ **800/TRAV-800** in the U.S., or 212/563-3303) or 2601 E. Jefferson St., Orlando, FL 32803 (☎ **407/896-0014**); **TFI Tours International,** 34 W. 32nd St., 12th Floor, New York, NY 10001 (☎ **800/745-8000** outside of New York State, or 212/736-1140); or **Travel Avenue,** 10 S. Riverside Plaza, Suite 1404, Chicago, IL 60606 (☎ **800/333-3335;** www. travelavenue.com). There's also **1-800-FLY-4-LESS,** RFA Building 5440 Morehouse Dr., San Diego, CA 92121, a nationwide airline reservation and ticketing service that specializes in finding the lowest fares. For information on available consolidator airline tickets for last minute travel, call ☎ **800/359-4537.**

REBATORS   Most rebators offer discounts ranging from 10% to 25% plus a $25 handling charge. They are not the same as travel agents but sometimes offer similar services, including discounted accommodations and car rentals.

Try **Travel Avenue,** 10 S. Riverside Plaza, Suite 1404, Chicago, IL 60606 (☎ **800/333-3335** or 312/876-1116).

TRAVEL CLUBS   Travel clubs supply an unsold inventory of tickets at 20% to 60% discounts. After you pay an annual fee, you're given a "hot line" number to call to find out what's available. You have to be fairly flexible in your travel plans to take advantage of these offers. Some good travel clubs include **Moment's Notice,** 7301 New Utrecht Ave., New York, NY 11228 (☎ **718/234-6295;** www. moments-notice.com), with a members' 24-hour hot line (☎ 718/234-6295) and a $25 annual fee; and the **Sears Discount Travel Club,** 3033 S. Parker Rd., Suite 900, Aurora, CO 80014 (☎ **800/ 433-9383** in the U.S.; www.travelersadvantage.com), with a $49 annual fee and a catalog listing offers. **Encore Travel Club,** 4501 Forbes Blvd., Lanham, MD 20706 (☎ **800/638-8976**), charges $59.95 a year for membership and offers up to a 50% discount at more than 4,000 hotels, usually during off-peak periods; it also offers substantial discounts on airfare, cruises, and car rentals through its volume-purchase plans. Membership includes a travel package outlining the company's many services and use of a toll-free telephone number for advice and information.

TRAVEL BARGAINS ON THE WEB   Savvy travelers are finding excellent deals and great vacation packages through the Internet. Increasingly, travel agencies and companies are using the Web to offer everything from vacations to plane reservations to budget airline tickets on major carriers. We have found the following sites that may be useful to you and your travel endeavors.

- **www.travelocity.com (www.previewtravel.com, www.frommers.travelocity. com)** is now Frommer's online travel planning/booking partner. It can arrange international flights to Austria, hotel and car rental bookings, as well as vacation packages. Its Destination Guide includes updated information on some 260 destinations worldwide—supplied by Frommer's.

- **www.travelcom.es** allows you to search travel destinations to decide on that perfect vacation and offers link sites to travel agencies all over the world and in all 50 states.

- **www.moments-notice.com** promotes itself as a travel service, not an agency, providing a bargain-hunter's dream. Updated each morning, many of the deals are snapped up by the end of the day. A drawback is that many of these offerings require you to drop everything and go almost immediately. Also see "Travel Clubs," above.

- **www.discount-tickets.com** lists discounts on airfares, accommodations, car rentals, and tours.
- **America Online** at **www.aol.com** offers many travel sites that can be customized to a particular region of the world.

A NOTE FOR BRITISH TRAVELERS   A regular fare from the United Kingdom to Vienna is extremely expensive, so call a travel agent about a charter flight or special air-travel promotions. If this is not possible, then an APEX ticket (see above) might be the way to trim costs. You might also ask the airlines about a "Eurobudget ticket," which carries restrictions or length-of-stay requirements.

British newspapers are always full of classified ads touting "slashed" fares from London to other destinations. One good source is *Time Out,* a magazine filled with cultural information about London. The *Evening Standard* maintains a daily travel section, and the Sunday editions of virtually any newspaper in the British Isles will run ads.

Although competition among airline consolidators is fierce, one well-recommended company is **Trailfinders** (☎ 020/7937-5400 in London; www.trailfinder.com). Buying blocks of tickets from such carriers as British Airways, Austrian Airlines, and KLM, they offer cost-conscious fares from London's Heathrow or Gatwick to Vienna.

In London, many bucket shops around Victoria and Earl's Court offer low fares. Make sure that the company you deal with is a member of the IATA, ABTA, or ATOL. These umbrella organizations will help you if anything goes wrong.

CEEFAX, a British television information service, airs on many home and hotel TVs and runs details of package holidays and flights to Vienna and beyond. Just switch to your CEEFAX channel and you'll find a menu of listings that includes travel information.

Make sure that you understand the bottom line on any special deal. Ask if all surcharges, including airport taxes and other hidden costs, are included before committing. Upon investigation, some of these "deals" are not as attractive as advertised. Also, find out about any penalties incurred if you're forced to cancel at the last minute.

BY TRAIN

If you plan to travel a lot on the European and/or British railroads on your way to or from Vienna, you'd do well to secure the latest copy of the Thomas Cook European Timetable of Railroads. It's available exclusively in North America from **Forsyth Travel Library,** 226 Westchester Ave., White Plains, NY 10604 (☎ 800/FORSYTH; www.forsyth.com), at a cost of $27.95 plus $4.95 postage (priority airmail) in the United States and $2 (U.S.) for shipments to Canada.

Vienna has rail links to all the major cities of Europe. From Paris, a train leaves the Gare de l'Est at 7:49am, arriving in Vienna at 9:18pm. From Munich, a train leaves daily at 9:24am, arriving in Vienna at 2:18pm, and then again at 11:19pm, arriving in Vienna at 6:47am. From Zurich you can take a 9:33pm train that arrives in Vienna at 6:45pm.

Rail travel within Austria itself is superb, with fast, clean trains taking you just about anywhere in the country and going through some incredibly scenic regions.

Train passengers using the **Chunnel** under the English Channel can go from London to Paris in just 3 hours and then on to Vienna (see above). Le Shuttle transports passengers along the 31-mile journey in just 35 minutes. The train also accommodates passenger cars, charter buses, taxis, and motorcycles through a tunnel from Folkestone, England, to Calais, France. Service is year-round, 24 hours a day.

EURAIL PASSES

Austria is part of the Eurail system, and a **Eurailpass** (www.raileurope.com) is good for unlimited trips on all routes of the Austrian Federal Railways and on many Danube boats. The Eurailpass permits unlimited first-class rail travel in any country in Western Europe (except the British Isles) and also includes Hungary in Eastern Europe.

Here's how it works: The pass is sold only in North America. A 15-day pass costs approximately $554, a 21-day pass $718, a 1-month pass $890, a 2-month pass $1,260, and a 3-month pass $1,558. Children under age 4 travel free provided they don't occupy a seat (otherwise, they're charged half fare); children under age 12 pay half fare. If you're under age 26, you can obtain unlimited second-class travel wherever Eurailpass is honored, on a Eurail Youthpass, which costs $623 for 1 month or $882 for 2 months.

You can buy a Eurailpass from your travel agent or at a railway agent in major cities. You can also buy the pass at the North American offices of CIT Travel Service, the French National Railroads, the German Federal Railroads, and the Swiss Federal Railways.

Eurail Saverpass offers discounted 15-day travel for a group of three people who travel constantly and continuously together between April and September, or if two people travel constantly and continuously together between October and March. The price of a Saverpass, valid all over Europe, good for first class only, is $470 for 15 days.

Eurail Flexipass allows passengers to visit Europe with more flexibility. It's valid in first class and offers the same privileges as the Eurailpass. However, it provides a number of individual travel days, which can be used over a much longer period of consecutive days. That makes it possible to stay in one city and yet not lose a single day of travel. There are two passes: 10 days of travel within 2 months for $654 and 15 days of travel within 2 months for $862.

With many of the same qualifications and restrictions as the previously described Flexipass is a **Eurail Youth Flexipass.** Sold only to travelers under age 26, it allows 10 days of travel within 2 months for $458 or 15 days of travel within 2 months for $599.

TRAVEL PASSES FROM THE U.K.

Eurotrain "Explorer" tickets are a worthwhile option for travelers under age 26. They allow passengers to move leisurely from London to Vienna with unlimited stopovers. All travel must be completed within 2 months of departure. Such a ticket sells for £204 round-trip.

Persons under age 26 (with proof of age) who want to travel from London to Vienna quickly and directly pay £155 round-trip for a ticket that allows no stopovers and retraces an identical route (exclusively through France) both ways. The cost includes ferryboat transport across the Channel. **USIT Campus,** 52 Grosvenor Gardens, London SW1W OAG (☎ **0870/240-1010**), can give you prices and help you book tickets.

BY CAR

If you're already on the continent, you might want to drive to Vienna. That is especially true if you're in a neighboring country, such as Italy or Germany; however, arrangements should be made in advance with your car-rental company.

Inaugurated in 1994, the Chunnel running under the English Channel cuts driving time between England and France to 35 minutes. Passengers drive their cars aboard the train, *Le Shuttle,* at Folkestone in England, and vehicles are transported to Calais, France.

Vienna can be reached from all directions via major highways called *Autobahnen* or by secondary highways. The main artery from the west is Autobahn A-1, coming in from Munich (291 miles/466km), Salzburg (209 miles/334km), and Linz (116 miles/186km). Autobahn-2 arrives from the south from Graz and Klagenfurt (both in Austria). Autobahn-4 comes in from the east, connecting with route E-58, which runs to Bratslavia and Prague. Autobahn A-22 takes traffic from the northwest, and Route E-10 brings you to the cities and towns of southeastern Austria and Hungary.

Unless otherwise marked, the speed limit on autobahns is 130kmph (80 m.p.h.); however, when estimating driving times, figure on 50 to 60 m.p.h. because of traffic, weather, and road conditions.

As you drive into Vienna, you can get maps, information, and hotel bookings at **Information-Zimmernachweis** at the end of the A-1 (Westautobahn) at Wientalstrasse/Auhof (☎ **01/211140**).

BY BUS

Because of the excellence of rail service funneling from all parts of the Continent into Vienna, bus transit is not especially popular. But there is some limited service. **Eurolines,** 52 Grosvenor Gardens, Victoria, London SW1 England (☎ **0990/143-219** or 020/7730-8235), operates two express buses per week between London's Victoria Coach Station and Vienna. The trip takes about 29 hours and makes 45-minute rest stops en route about every 4 hours. Buses depart from London at 8:30am every Friday and Sunday, traverse the Channel between Dover and Calais, and are equipped with reclining seats, toilets, and reading lights. The one-way London-Vienna fare is £72. If you opt for a round-trip fare, priced at £115, you won't need to declare your intended date of return until you actually use your ticket (although advance reservations are advisable), and the return half of your ticket will be valid for 6 months. The return to London departs from Vienna every Sunday and Friday at 7:45pm, arriving at Victoria Coach Station about 29 hours later. You can reserve tickets in advance through the Eurolines office listed above, through most British travel agencies, or through Eurolines' largest sales agent, National Express (☎ **0990/808-080**).

Eurolines also maintains affiliates in every major city of Western Europe. In Vienna, contact O.B.B./Blaguss Reisen (☎ **01/5018-0147**).

Austria is serviced by a wide network of buses that service towns, cities, and villages far from Vienna. For more bus information, call ☎ **01/71101.**

BY BOAT

To arrive in Vienna with flair befitting the city's historical opulence, take advantage of the many cruise lines that navigate the Danube. One of the most accessible carriers is **DDSG, Blue Danube Shipping Company,** Donaureisen, Handelskai 265, in Vienna (☎ **01/588800;** fax 01/5888-0440), which offers mostly 1-day trips into Vienna from as far away as Passau, Germany. They also travel from Bratislava (in Slovakia), Budapest, and beyond, depending on the season and itinerary. Extended trips can be arranged and cruises are priced to meet every budget. See "Cruising the Danube" in chapter 6.

8 Package Tours & Escorted Tours

Although a sampling of some well-recommended tour operators follows, you should always consult a good travel agent for the latest offerings and advice.

A far-flung and reliable touring experience is offered by **British Airways** (☎ **877/428-2228;** www.britishairways.com). Trips usually combine Vienna and other

Austrian attractions with major sights in Germany and Switzerland. BA can arrange a stopover in London en route for an additional fee and allow extra time in Vienna before or after the beginning of any tour for no additional charge.

Other attractive options are provided by North America's tour-industry giants, **Delta Dream Vacations** (☎ 800/872-7786; www.deltavacations.com), **American Express Vacations** (☎ 800/446-6234; www.americanexpress.com), and an unusual, upscale (and very expensive) tour operator, **Abercrombie and Kent** (☎ 800/ 323-7308; www.abercrombiekent.com), long known for its carriage-trade rail excursions through Eastern Europe and the Swiss and Austrian Alps.

Getting to Know Vienna 3

This chapter will help you get your bearings in Vienna. It will introduce you to Vienna's neighborhoods, explain how the city is laid out, and tell you how to get around. There's also a convenient list of "Fast Facts," covering everything from embassies to electrical outlets.

1 Orientation

ARRIVING

BY PLANE   Vienna's international airport, **Wien Schwechat** (☎ **01/70070** for flight information), is about 12 miles southeast of the Inner City. One of Europe's most modern airports, the Schwechat is quick and easy to navigate. There's even a supermarket here, in addition to several banks, restaurants, and duty-free shops. In the arrival hall, don't miss the official **Vienna Tourist Information Office,** which is open daily June to September from 9am to 10pm, October to May from 8:30am to 9pm.

Getting to the Center   When you come out of Customs, signs for taxis and buses are straight ahead. A one-way **taxi** ride from the airport into the Inner City is likely to cost 450AS ($30.15), maybe more if traffic is bad. Therefore, it's better to take the bus.

There is regular **bus** service between the airport and the **City Air Terminal,** which is adjacent to the Vienna Hilton and directly across from the **Wien Mitte/Landstrasse** rail station, where you can easily connect with subway and tram lines. Buses run every 20 minutes from 5:30am to 11:30pm, and then every hour from midnight until 5am. The trip takes about 25 minutes and costs 70AS ($4.70) per person. Tickets are sold on the bus and must be purchased with Austrian money. There's also bus service between the airport and two railroad stations, the Westbahnhof and the Südbahnhof, leaving every 30 minutes to an hour. Fares are also 70AS ($4.70).

There's also local **train** service, *Schnellbahn,* between the airport and the Wien Nord and Wien Mitte rail stations. Trains run hourly between 4:30am and 9:30pm and leave from the basement of the airport. Trip time varies from 40 to 45 minutes, and the fare is 38AS ($2.55).

BY TRAIN   Vienna has four principal rail stations with frequent connections to all Austrian cities and towns and to all major European centers, from Munich to Milan. Train information for all stations can be obtained by calling ☎ **05/1717.**

The **Westbahnhof,** on Europaplatz, is for trains arriving from western Austria, France, Germany, Switzerland, and some Eastern European countries. It has frequent links to all major Austrian cities, such as Salzburg, which is a 3-hour train ride from Vienna. The Westbahnhof connects with local trains, the U3 and U6 underground lines, and several tram and bus routes.

The **Südbahnhof,** on Südtirolerplatz, has train arrivals from southern and eastern Austria, Italy, Hungary, and the new countries of Slovenia and Croatia. It is linked with local rail service and tram and bus routes.

Both of these stations house useful travel agencies (**Österreichisches Verkehrsbüro**) that provide tourist information and help with hotel reservations. In the Westbahnhof it's in the upper hall and at the Südbahnhof, in the lower hall.

Other stations in Vienna include **Franz-Josef Bahnhof,** on Franz-Josef-Platz, used mainly by local trains, although connections are made here to Prague and Berlin. You can take the D-tram line to the city's Ringstrasse from here. **Wien Mitte,** at Landstrasser Hauptstrasse 1, is also a terminus of local trains, plus a depot for trains to the Czech Republic and to Vienna's Schwechat Airport.

BY BUS The **City Bus Terminal** is at the Wien Mitte rail station, at Landstrasser Hauptstrasse 1. This is the arrival depot for Eurolines, all of Austria's postal and federal buses, and private buses from other European cities. The terminal has lockers, currency-exchange kiosks, and a ticket counter open daily from 6:15am to 6pm.

VISITOR INFORMATION

Once you've arrived safely in Vienna, head for either of two information points that make it their business to have up-to-the-minute data about what to see and do in Vienna. The more centrally located of the two is the **Wien Tourist-Information** office at Kärntnerstrasse 38 (☎ **01/513-8892;** tram 1 or 2). Located in the heart of the Inner City (directly behind the Opera, on the corner of Philharmoniker Strasse), it's open daily from 9am to 7pm. The staff will make free hotel reservations for anyone in need of lodgings. Larger and more administrative but also willing to handle questions from the public is the headquarters of the **Vienna Tourist Board,** at Obere Augartenstrasse (☎ **01/2111-4412;** tram 31). Both branches stock free copies of a tourist magazine, *Wien Monatsprogramm,* which lists what's going on in Vienna's concert halls, theaters, and opera houses. Also worthwhile here is *Vienna A to Z,* a general, pocket-size guide with descriptions and locations for a slew of attractions. This booklet is also free, but don't rely on its cluttered map.

For information on Vienna and Austria, including day trips from the city, visit the **Austrian National Tourist Office** (☎ **01/58866**) at Margaretenstrasse 1, A-1040. The region surrounding the city (lower Austria, or *Niederösterreich*) contains dozens of attractions worth a visit. For a rundown on the Wachau (Danube Valley) and the Weinerwald (Vienna Woods), you might want to contact **Niederösterreich Information,** Fishhoffe 3 (☎ **01/53-610-0**).

CITY LAYOUT

From its origins as a Roman village on the Danubian plain, Vienna has evolved over the years into one of the largest metropolises of central Europe, with a surface area covering 160 square miles. It is divided into 23 districts (*Bezirke*), which are identified with Roman numerals. Each district has its own character or reputation; for example, the 9th District is known as Vienna's academic quarter, whereas the 10th, 11th, and 12th Districts are home to blue-collar workers and are the most densely populated.

The 1st District, known as the **Innere Stadt (Inner City),** is where most foreign visitors spend their time. This compact area is historic Vienna and boasts the city's most astonishing array of monuments, churches, palaces, and museums in addition to its finest hotels and restaurants. Its size and shape roughly correspond to the original borders (then walls) of the medieval city; however, other than **St. Stephan's Cathedral,** very few buildings from the Middle Ages remain.

The Inner City is surrounded by **Ringstrasse,** a circular boulevard about 2½ miles long. Constructed between 1859 and 1888, it's one of the most ambitious examples of urban planning in central European history. The Ringstrasse was imposed over the foundations of Vienna's medieval fortifications, and it opened new urban vistas for the dozens of monumental 19th-century buildings that line it today. The name of this boulevard changes as it moves around the Inner City; this can be confusing. Names that correspond with the boulevard carry the suffix *ring:* Opernring, Schottenring, Burgring, Dr.-Karl-Lueger-Ring, Stubenring, Parkring, Schubertring, and Kärntner Ring.

Ironically, the river for which Vienna is so famous, the Danube, doesn't really pass through the city. This is often disappointing for visitors. Between 1868 and 1877 the river was channeled into its present muddy banks east of town, and was replaced with a small-scale substitute, the **Donaukanal (Danube Canal),** which was dug for shipping. The canal sits against the eastern edge of the Ring and is traversed by five bridges in the 1st District alone.

Surrounding Ringstrasse and the Inner City, in a more or less clockwise direction, are the inner suburban districts (2nd–9th), which contain many hotel and restaurants as well as the villas and palaces of Vienna's 18th-century aristocrats, modern apartment complexes, and the homes of 19th-century middle-class entrepreneurs. There are plenty of quality hotels and restaurants in these districts because of their proximity to the center of town. We'll profile them later in this chapter under "Neighborhoods in Brief."

The outer districts (10th–23rd) form another concentric ring of suburbs, hosting a variety of neighborhoods from industrial parks to rural villages. **Schönbrunn,** the Habsburg's vast summer palace, is located in an outlying area, the 13th District, **Hietzing.** Also noteworthy is the 19th District, **Döbling,** with its famous Heuriger villages like Grinzing and Sievering, and the 22nd District, **Donaustadt,** which is home to the verdant Donau Park and the adjoining UNO-City, an impressive modern complex of United Nations agencies.

FINDING AN ADDRESS   Street addresses are followed by a four-digit postal code, or sometimes a Roman numeral, that identifies the district in which the address is located. Often, the code is preceded by the letter *A.* The district number is coded in the two middle digits, so if an address is in the 1st district ("01"), the postal code would read A-1010; in the 7th District, A-1070; and in the 13th District, A-1130. The layouts of many neighborhoods—especially those around St. Stephan's—are labyrinths of narrow side streets and are often hard to navigate. Fortunately, the most confusing of the Inner City's streets tend to be the shortest, a fact that limits numbers within its boundaries. If you're doubtful about finding a street address, ask a well-meaning passerby to point you in the right direction or make a quick call before heading out to get the name of the nearest *Ecke* (cross street or corner).

A rule of thumb used by hotel concierges and taxi drivers is based on the following guidelines: Odd street numbers are on one side of the street, and even numbers on the other. The lowest numbers are usually closest to the city's geographic and spiritual center, Stephansplatz, and get higher as the street extends outward. Naturally, this system won't work on streets running parallel to the cathedral, so you'll have to test your luck.

What about the broad expanses of Vienna's Ring? Traffic always moves clockwise on the Ring, and any backtracking against the direction of the traffic must be done via side streets that radiate from the general traffic flow. Numeration on the Ring always

Vienna at a Glance

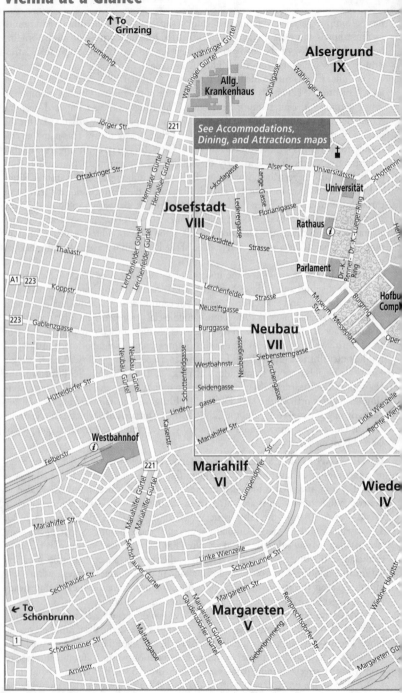

↑ To Grinzing

Schumanng.

Währinger Gürtel

Spitalgasse

Währinger Str.

Alsergrund IX

Allg. Krankenhaus

Jörger Str.

221

Ottakringer Str.

See Accommodations, Dining, and Attractions maps

✝

-Kodagasse

Alser Str.

Universitätsstr.

Schottenr

Lange Gasse

Universität

Josefstadt VIII

Florianigasse

Lederergasse

Josefstädter

Rathaus ℹ

Strasse

Parlament

Dr.-K.-Renner-/Dr.-K.-Lueger-Ring

Herr

Thaliastr.

Hernalser Gürtel

Hernalser Gürtel

A1 223

Koppstr.

Lerchenfelder Gürtel

Lerchenfelder Gürtel

Lerchenfelder

Strasse

Museum Str.

Burgring

Messeplatz

Hofbu Compl

223

Gablenzgasse

Neustiftgasse

Burggasse

Neubau VII

Oper

Hütteldorfer Str.

Neubau Gürtel

Neubau Gürtel

Schottenfeldgasse

Neubaugasse

Siebensterngasse

Kirchengasse

Westbahnstr.

Seidengasse

Linden-

gasse

Linke Wienzeile

Rechte Wien

Westbahnhof ℹ

Felberstr.

221

Mariahilfer Str.

Kaiserstr.

Mariahilf Str.

Mariahilf VI

Gumpendorfer

Wiede IV

Mariahilfer Gürtel

Mariahilfer Gürtel

Mariahilfer Str.

Sechshauser Gürtel

Linke Wienzeile

Schönbrunner Str.

Wiedner Hauptstr.

Sechshauser Str.

Margareten Str.

Rienprechtsdorfer Str.

← To Schönbrunn

1

Schönbrunner Str.

Mittagasse

Margareten Gürtel

Gaudenzdorfer Gürtel

Margareten V

Siebenbrunneng.

Margareten Gü

Arndtstr.

30

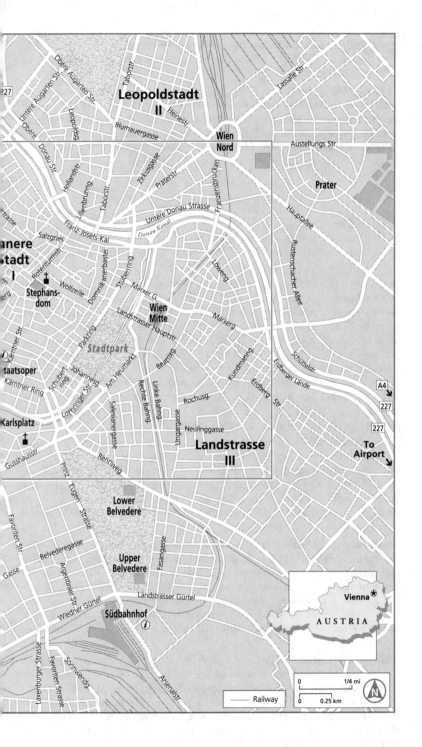

Leopoldstadt
II

Obere Augarten Str.
Untere Augarten Str.
Obere Donau Str.
Leopoldsg.
Taborstr.
Heinestr.
Blumauergasse
Zirkusgasse
Praterstr.
Hollandstr.
Lilienbrunng.
Taborstr.
Franzensbrücken

227

Wien
Nord

Austellungs Str.

Prater

Hauptallee

Unterer Donau Strasse
Donau Kanal
Franz-Josefs-Kai
Salzgries
trasse

anere
tadt
I

Stephans-
dom

Rotenturmstr.
Wollzeile
Dominikanerbastei
Parking
Stubenring
Marxer G.
Landstrasser Hauptstr.

Wien
Mitte

Löweng.

Marxerg.

Rustenschacher Allee

Schüttelstr.

taatsoper

Kärntner Str.

Kärntner Ring

Karlsplatz

Gusshausstr.

Schubertring
Johannesg.
Lothringer Str.
Am Heumarkt
Rechte Bahng.
Linke Bahng.
Salesianergasse
Rennweg
Prinz
Eugen
Strasse

Stadtpark

Beatrixg.
Kundmanng.
Erdberg Str.
Rochusg.
Ungargasse
Neulinggasse

Landstrasse
III

Erdberger Lände

A4
227
227

To
Airport

Lower
Belvedere

Upper
Belvedere

Favoriten Str.
Belvederegasse
Argentinier-Str.
Wiedner Gürtel
Gasse

Fasangasse

Landstrasser Gürtel

Südbahnhof *(i)*

Laxenburger Strasse
Favoriten Strasse
Sonnwendg.
Argenalstr.

Vienna ⊛

AUSTRIA

0   1/4 mi
0   0.25 km

——— Railway

N

goes from high numbers to lower numbers, as determined by the direction of the prevailing traffic: Odd street numbers appear on a driver's left, even numbers on the right.

STREET MAPS   You'll need a very good and detailed map to explore Vienna, as it has some 1,500 miles of streets (many of them narrow). Because so many places, including restaurants and hotels, lie on these alleyways, routine overview maps that are given away at hotels or the tourist office won't do. You'll need a good city map that has an index of streets. These are sold at all major newsstands, bookstores, and often at upscale hotel newsstands. We recommend the **Hallweg** map.

Neighborhoods in Brief

Because visitors spend most of their time in the city center, many of Vienna's hotels and restaurants are conveniently located within or just outside the 1st District. In this section we'll profile the Inner City, or *Innere Stadt,* and the districts that immediately surround it.

Innere Stadt (1st District)   As we mentioned earlier, this compact area, bounded on all sides by the legendary Ring, is at the center of Viennese life. The Inner City has dozens of streets devoted exclusively to pedestrian traffic, including **Kärntnerstrasse,** which bypasses the Vienna State Opera House, and the nearby **Graben,** which backs up to Stephansplatz, home to the famous cathedral. Competing with both the cathedral and the Opera House as the district's most famous building is the **Hofburg,** the famous Habsburg palace that's now a showcase of tourist attractions, including the National Library, the Spanish Riding School, and six museums. Other significant landmarks include the Rathaus (City Hall), Parlament (Parliament), the Universität (University of Vienna), the Naturhistorisches (Natural History) and the Kunsthistorisches (Art History) museums, and Stadtpark.

Leopoldstadt (2nd District)   Once inhabited by Balkan traders, this area doesn't physically border the Ringstrasse, but lies on the eastern side of the Danube Canal, just a short subway ride (U1) from the Inner City. Here you'll find the massive **Prater** park, which boasts an amusement park, miles of tree-lined walking paths, and numerous sports facilities, including a large stadium. Vienna's renowned trade fair exhibition site is also in this district, which has seen a spree of development along the canal in recent years.

Landstrasse (3rd District)   The bucolic **Stadtpark** spreads into this district, where you'll also discover more of Vienna's imperial charm. Streets are dotted with churches, monuments, and palaces, such as the grand **Schwarzenburg Palace** and the looming **Konzerthaus** (concert house). However, the top attraction remains Prince Eugene Savoy's **Belvedere Palace,** an exquisite example of baroque architecture. Several embassies make their home in a small section of Landstrasse that's known as Vienna's diplomatic quarter, and the **Wien Mitte rail station** and the **City Air Terminal** are also located here.

Wieden (4th District)   This small neighborhood extends south from Opernring and Kärtnering, and it's just as fashionable as the 1st District. Most activity centers around **Karlsplatz,** a historical city square that features its domed namesake, Karlskirche. Also seated around this hub are Vienna's **Technical University** and the **Historical Museum of the City of Vienna.** Kärnerstrasse, the main boulevard of the city center, turns into **Wiedner-Hauptstrasse** as it enters this district, and the **Südbahnof,** one of the two main train stations, lies at its southern tip.

The streets of Vienna are surfaced with culture as the streets of other cities with asphalt.
—Karl Kraus (1874–1936)

Margareten (5th District)   Southwest of the 4th district, Wieden, this area does not border the Ring and thus lies a bit farther from the Inner City. You'll start to see more residential neighborhoods, representing the continual growth of Vienna's middle class. The historic homes of composers Franz Schubert and Christoph Gluck still stand here amongst modern apartment complexes and industrial centers.

Mariahilf (6th District)   One of Vienna's busiest shopping streets, **Mariahilfer-strasse,** runs through this bustling neighborhood. The sprawling and lively **Naschmarkt** (Produce Market), selling fresh fruits, vegetables, breads, cheeses, and more, is an ideal scene for people-watching. On Saturdays, the adjacent **Flohmarkt** (Flea Market) adds to the lively but sometimes seedy atmosphere as vendors sell antiques and other junk. The surrounding streets are packed with *Beisls* (small eateries), theaters, cafes, and pubs. As you go farther from the city center, however, you'll find that the landscape becomes more residential.

Neubau (7th District)   Bordering the expansive Museum Quarter of the Inner City, this is an ideal place to stay, as it's easily accessible by public transportation. The picturesque and once neglected **Spittleburg quarter** lies atop a hill just beyond Vienna's most famous museums. It's a vibrant cultural community that's popular with both young and old visitors. The old Spittleburg houses have been renovated into boutiques, restaurants, theaters, and art galleries—a perfect backdrop for an afternoon stroll.

Josephstadt (8th District)   The smallest of Vienna's 23 districts is named after Habsburg Emperor Joseph II and was once home to Vienna's civil servants. Like Neubau, this quiet, friendly neighborhood sits behind the City Hall and the adjacent grand museums of the Ringstrasse. You'll find everything from shady and secluded parks to charming cafes to elaborate monuments and churches. Vienna's oldest and most intimate theater, **Josefstadt Theater,** was built here in 1788 and is still in operation. Josefstadt's shops and restaurants have a varied clientele, from City Hall lawmakers to university students.

Alsergrund (9th District)   This area is often referred to as the academic quarter, not just because of nearby University of Vienna but also because of its many hospitals and clinics. This is Freud territory, and you can visit his home, now the **Freud Museum,** on Berggasse. Here, you'll also stumble upon the **Lichenstein Palace,** one of Vienna's biggest and brightest, which today houses the federal **Museum of Modern Art.** At the northern end of Alsergrund is the **Franz-Josef Bahnhof,** an excellent depot for excursions to Lower Austria.

2 Getting Around

BY PUBLIC TRANSPORTATION

Whether you want to visit the Inner City's historic buildings or the outlying Vienna Woods, **Vienna Transport** (Wiener Verkehrs-betriebe) can take you there. This vast transit network is safe, clean, and easy to use. If you plan on taking full advantage of it, pay the 15AS ($1) fee for a map that outlines the **U-Bahn** (subway), buses, streetcars, and local trains. More detailed than the free maps given out by the city's tourist

---

The Vienna Card

The **Vienna Card** not only buys you 3 days of unlimited public transportation, but helps you save money on some attractions—for example, at Schönbrunn Palace and at the Belvedere museums—as well as concerts, shops, and some restaurants and cafes. Most discounts are in the 10- to- 20% range, but others may range up to one-half the price.

These tickets are available at Tabak-Trafiks, vending machines in underground stations, tourist information offices, the airport's arrival hall (next to baggage claim), the DDSG landing pier (Reichsbrücke), some hotels, and at the travel agencies (Österreichisches Verkehrsbüro) of the two main train stations. Or order one over the phone with a credit card (☎ **01/7984-40028**).

---

officials, it's sold at branch offices of the **Vienna Public Transport Information Center** (Informationdienst der Wiener Verkehrsbetriebe). The five largest locations are in the Opernpassage (an underground passageway adjacent to the State Opera House); the Karlsplatz; the Stephansplatz, near Vienna's cathedral; the Westbahnhof; and the Praterstern. For information about any of these outlets, call ☎ **01/790-9105.**

Vienna maintains a uniform fare that applies to all forms of public transport. Very few buses and streetcars maintain a staff selling tickets on board, having replaced humans long ago with coin-operated machines. A ticket for the bus, the subway, or the tram will cost 17AS ($1.15) if you buy it in advance at a Tabac-Trafiks (a store or kiosk selling tobacco products and newspapers), or 20AS ($1.35) if you buy it aboard the bus or tram. Smart Viennese usually buy their tickets in advance, usually in blocks of at least five at a time, from any of the city's thousands of Tabac-Trafiks or at any of the public transport centers noted above. Remember that no matter what means of transport you use, once a ticket has been stamped (validated) by either a machine or a railway attendant, it's valid for one trip in one direction, anywhere in the city, including transfers.

Discount Tickets

The **Vienna Card** is the best ticket to use when traveling within the city limits. At 210AS ($14.05), it's extremely flexible and functional for tourists because it allows 3 days of unlimited travel, plus various discounts at city museums, restaurants, and shops. You can purchase a Vienna Card at tourist information offices, public transport centers, and some hotels or order one over the phone with a credit card (☎ **01/7984-40028**).

You can also buy tickets that will save you money if you plan to ride a lot on the city's transport system. A ticket valid for unlimited rides during any 24-hour period costs 50AS ($3.35); an equivalent ticket valid for any 72-hour period goes for 130AS ($8.70). There's also a green ticket, priced at 265AS ($17.75), that contains eight individual partitions. Each of these, when stamped, is good for 1 day of unlimited travel. This is great for families, as the partitions can be subdivided among a group of several riders, allowing—for example—two persons 4 days each of unlimited rides; or three persons 2 days each of unlimited rides.

By U-Bahn (Subway)

The U-Bahn is a fast way to get across town or reach the suburbs. It consists of five lines labeled **U1, U2, U3, U4,** and **U6** (there is no U5). Karlsplatz, in the heart of the Inner City, is the most important underground station for visitors as the U4, U2, and

Vienna Public Transport

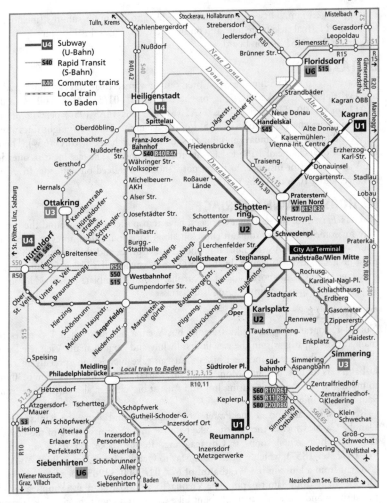

U1 all converge here. The U2 traces part of the Ring, the U4 goes to Schönbrunn, and the U1 stops in Stephansplatz. The U3 also stops in Stephansplatz and connects with the Westbahnof. The underground runs daily from 6am to midnight.

BY TRAM (STREETCAR)

Riding the red and white trams (*Strassenbahn*) is not only a practical way to get around but also a great way to see the city. Tram stops are well marked and lines are labeled as both numbers and letters. Lines 1 and 2 will bring you to all the major sights on the Ringstrasse. Line D skirts the outer Ring and goes to the Südbahnhof, and line 18 goes between the Westbahnof and the Südbahnhof.

BY BUS

Buses traverse Vienna in all directions, and they operate Monday to Saturday from 6am to 10pm and on Sunday from 6am to 8pm. Buses 1A, 2A, and 3A will get you around the Inner City. Convenient night buses are available on weekends and holidays starting at 12:15am. They go from Schwedensplatz to the outer suburbs (including Grinzing). Normal tickets are not valid on these late "N" buses. Instead you pay a special fare of 25AS ($1.70) on board.

BY TAXI

Taxis are easy to find within the city center, but be warned that fares can quickly add up. Taxi stands are marked by signs, or you can call ☎ **01/31300, 60160, 81400, 91011,** or **40100.** The basic fare is 27AS ($1.80), plus 14AS (95¢) per kilometer. There are extra charges of 16AS ($1.05) for luggage in the trunk. For night rides after 11pm and for trips on Sundays and holidays, there is a surcharge of 10AS (65¢). There is an additional charge of 16AS ($1.05) if ordered by phone. The fare for trips outside the Vienna area (for instance, to the airport) should be agreed on with the driver in advance, and a 10% tip is the norm.

BY HORSE-DRAWN CARRIAGE

Vienna's *Fiakers,* or horse-drawn carriages, have transported people around the Inner City for some 300 years. You can clip-clop along for about 30 minutes at a cost of 500AS ($33.50), 800AS ($53.60) for 1 hour. Exact prices and the length of the ride must be negotiated in advance. In the 1st District, you'll find a Fiaker for hire at the following sites: On the north side of St. Stephan's, on Heldenplatz near the Hofburg, and in front of the Albertina on Augustinerstrasse.

BY BICYCLE

Not all European cities are bike friendly, but Vienna has more than 155 miles of marked bicycle paths within the city limits. In July and August, many Viennese leave their cars in the garage and ride bikes. You can take bicycles on specially marked U-Bahn cars for free, but only Monday to Friday from 9am to 3pm and from 6:30pm to midnight. On weekends during July and August bicycles can also carried free from 9am until midnight.

Rental shops abound at the Prater (see chapter 6) and along the banks of the Danube Canal, which is the favorite bike path for most Viennese. One of the best of the many bike rental shops is **Copacagrana,** Reichsbrücke, on the Donauinsel (☎ **01/2365-1857**), which is open from May to October from 9am to 9pm. You can also rent from a kiosk in the **Westbahnhof** (☎ **01/5800-32985**), between May and October daily from 8am to 7pm. The Vienna Tourist Board can also supply a list of rental shops and more information about bike paths throughout the city. Bike rentals begin at around 200AS ($13.40) a day.

BY CAR

A car is useful mainly for trips outside Vienna's city limits. The city is a maze of congested one-way streets, and parking is a problem. Public transportation is so good that there's no need to endure the hassle of driving around Vienna. If you do venture out by car, information on road conditions is available in English 7 days a week from 6am to 8pm from the **Österreichischer Automobil-, Motorrad- und Touringclub (ÖAMTC),** Schubertring 1-3, A-1010 Vienna (☎ **01/711997**). This auto club also maintains a 24-hour emergency road service number. For access, dial ☎ **01/ 120, 123,** or **0660-7500.**

CAR RENTALS   It's always best and less expensive to reserve rental cars in advance before you leave home, but it is possible to rent a car once you've arrived in Vienna. You'll need a passport and a driver's license that's at least 1 year old. Avoid renting a car at the airport as there is an extra 6% tax, in addition to the 21% Value-Added Tax

(VAT) on all rentals. For a 1- to-2-day rental of a small car (Ford Fiesta or Opal) expect to pay around 1,000AS ($67) per day, which includes unlimited mileage and the price of insurance. The government tax is extra. You'll save on the per-day cost if you rent your car for a minimum of 1 week.

Major car-rental companies operating in Vienna include **Avis,** Opernring 1 (☎ **800/331-2112** in the U.S. and Canada, or 01/587-6241 in Vienna); **Budget-Rent-a-Car,** City/Hilton Air Terminal (☎ **800/472-3325** in the U.S. and Canada, or 01/714-6565 in Vienna); and **Hertz,** in the Marriott Hotel, Parkring 12A (☎ **800/654-3001** in the U.S. and Canada, or 01/512-8677 in Vienna).

PARKING   Streetside parking in Vienna's 1st District, site of most of the city's major monuments, is limited almost to the point of being nonexistent. Coin-operated parking meters are not common here. When streetside parking is available at all, it's within any of the city's "blue zones" and is usually restricted to a time limit of 90 minutes or less between 8am and 6pm. If you find an available spot within a blue zone, you'll need to display a *kurtzpark Scheine* (short-term parking voucher) on the dashboard of your car. Valid for time blocks of only 30, 60, or 90 minutes, they're sold at branch offices of Vienna Public Transport offices (see above) and, more conveniently, within tobacco/news shops. You'll have to write in the date and the time of your arrival before displaying the voucher on the right-hand side of your car's dashboard. Be warned that towing of illegally parked cars is not uncommon here. Frankly, it's much easier to simply pay the price of parking in an underground garage and avoid the stress of looking for one of the virtually impossible-to-find street spots.

Parking garages are scattered throughout the city and most charge between 50 and 70AS ($3.35 and $4.70) per hour. Every hotel in Vienna is acutely aware of the location of the nearest parking garage—if you're confused, ask. Some convenient 24-hour garages within the first district include **Parkgarage Am Hof,** am Hof (☎ **01/533-5571**), **Parkgarage Freyung,** Freyung (☎ **01/535-0450**), and **Tiefgarage Kärtner Strasse,** Mahlerstrasse 8 (☎ **01/512-5206**).

DRIVING   Traffic regulations are similar to those in other European cities where you *drive on the right.* The speed limit is 50kmph (31 m.p.h.) in built-up areas within the city limits unless otherwise specified. Out of town, in areas like the Wienerwald, the limit is 130kmph (80 m.p.h.) on motorways and 100kmph (62 m.p.h.) on all other roads.

Fast Facts: Vienna

American Express   The most convenient office in Vienna is at Kärntnerstrasse 21-23 (☎ **01/51540-770**), open Monday to Friday from 9am to 5:30pm and on Saturday 9am to noon.

Baby-Sitters   Most hotels will be able to provide you with the name and number of English-speaking baby-sitters if they do not provide a service of their own. Sitters charge roughly 100 to 150AS ($6.70 to $10.05) per hour. If you plan on utilizing their services beyond 11pm, expect to provide transportation home, most likely via a cab.

Business Hours   Most shops are open Monday to Friday from 9am to 6pm and on Saturday from 9am to noon, 12:30pm, or 1pm, depending on the store. On the first Saturday of every month, shops remain open until 4:30 or 5pm, a tradition known as *langer Samstag.*

Car Rentals   See "Getting Around," earlier in this chapter.

Climate   See "When to Go," in chapter 2.

Crime   See "Safety," below.

Currency Exchange   See "Money," in chapter 2.

Dentist   For dental emergencies at night or on Saturday and Sunday, call ☎ **01/512-2078.** If you dial it, you'll hear either a live person or a recorded announcement telling you the name and phone number of whatever dentist is on 24-hour call for the treatment of dental emergencies.

Doctor   A list of physicians can be found in the telephone directory under *Arzte.* If you have a medical emergency during the night, call ☎ **141** from 7pm to 7am.

Driving Rules   See "Getting Around," earlier in this chapter.

Drug Laws   Penalties are severe and could lead to either imprisonment or deportation. Selling drugs to minors is dealt with particularly harshly.

Drugstores   *Apotheke* (chemist's shops) are open Monday to Friday from 8am to noon and 2 to 6pm, and on Saturday from 8am to noon. Look for a sign outside every shop for the name of the shop that will be open at night and on Sunday. *Note:* These shops fill prescriptions and sell drugs only. For cosmetics and sundries, look for a *Drogerie.*

Electricity   Vienna operates on 220 volts AC, with the European 50-cycle circuit. That means that U.S.-made appliances will need a transformer (sometimes called a converter). Many Viennese hotels stock adapter plugs but not power transformers. Electric clocks, CD players, and tape recorders, however, will not work well even with transformers.

Embassies & Consulates   The main building of the Embassy of the **United States** is at Boltzmanngasse 16, A-1090 Vienna (☎ **01/31339**). However, the consular section is at Gartenbaupromenade 2-4, A-1010 Vienna (☎ **01/31339**). Lost passports, tourist emergencies, and other matters are handled by the consular section. Both the embassy and consulate are open Monday to Friday from 8:30am to noon and 1 to 4pm.

The Embassy of **Canada,** Laurenzerberg 2 (☎ **01/531-380**), is open Monday to Friday from 8:30am to 12:30pm and 1:30 to 3:30pm; the **United Kingdom,** Jauresgasse 12 (☎ **01/71613-0**), is open Monday to Friday 9am to 1pm and 2 to 4pm; **Australia,** Mattiellistrasse 2-4 (☎ **01/512-8580**), is open Monday to Thursday 8:30am to 1pm and 2 to 5:30pm, Friday 8:30am to 1:15pm; and **New Zealand,** Springsiedelgasse 28 (☎ **01/318-8505**), is open Monday to Friday from 8:30am to 5pm, but it's best to call to see if it's actually open. The **Irish Embassy** is at Hilton Center, Landstrasser Hauptstrasse 2 (☎ **01/715-4247**), open Monday to Friday 9 to 11:30am and 1:30 to 4pm.

Emergencies   Call ☎ **122** to report a fire, ☎ **133** for the police, or ☎ **144** for an ambulance.

Holidays   See "When to Go," in chapter 2.

Hospitals   The major hospital is **Allgemeines Krankenhaus,** Währinger Gürtel 18-20 (☎ **01/40400**).

Hot Lines   The Rape Crisis Hot Line is ☎ **01/523-2222,** in service on Monday from 10am to 6pm, Tuesday 2 to 6pm, Wednesday 10am to 2pm, Thursday 5 to 11pm. Threatened or battered women can call an emergency hot line at ☎ **01/71719** around the clock.

Internet Access   In back of the **Amadeus Media Café,** Kärntnerstrasse 19 (☎ **01/514310**), there is free access to the Web. The location is on the fifth floor of Steffi Kaufhaus, one of Vienna's leading department stores. Hours are Monday to Friday from 9:30am to 7pm and Saturday from 9:30am to 5pm. **Café Stein,** Währingerstrasse 6 (☎ **01/319-72-41**), offers Internet access at the rate of 65AS ($4.35) every half hour. The cafe is open daily from 5 to 11pm.

Language   German is the official language of Austria, but because English is taught in the high schools, it's commonly spoken throughout the country, especially in tourist regions. Certain Austrian minorities speak Slavic languages, and Hungarian is commonly spoken in Burgenland.

Another way of communicating if you don't speak German is through KWIK-point, a visual translator, allowing you to point at pictures to communicate. This four-panel brochure contains some 500 color illustrations of everyday items, such as a pay phone or gasoline. You just point to the corresponding picture. Single copies cost $7 and can be ordered from Gaia Communications Inc., P.O. Box 238, Alexandria, VA 22313-0238 (☎ **703/548-8794**).

Legal Aid   The consulate of your country is the place to turn, although consulate officers cannot interfere in the Viennese legal process. They can, however, inform you of your rights and provide a list of attorneys.

Liquor Laws   Wine with meals is a normal part of family life in Vienna. Children are exposed to wine at an early age, and alcohol consumption is not anything out of the ordinary. Eighteen years is the legal drinking age for buying or ordering alcohol.

Luggage Storage/Lockers   All four main train stations of Vienna have lockers available on a 24-hour basis, costing 40AS ($2.70) for 24 hours. It's also possible to store luggage at these terminals daily from 4am to midnight (1:15am at the Westbahnhof) at a cost of 30AS ($2).

Mail   Post offices (*Das Postamt*) in Vienna are located in the heart of every district. If you're unsure of your address in Vienna, correspondence can be addressed in care of a local post office by labeling it either POST RESTANTE or POSTLAGERND. If you choose to do this, it's important to clearly designate the addressee, the name of the town, and its postal code. To claim any correspondence, the addressee must present his or her passport.

Addresses for these can be found in the telephone directory under "Post." Post offices are generally open for mail services Monday to Friday from 8am to noon and 2 to 6pm. The central post office, the **Hauptpostamt,** Fleischmarkt 19 (☎ **01/515090**), and most general post offices, including those within the Westbahnhof, the Sudbahnhof, and the Franz-Josef-Bahnhof, are open 24 hours a day, 7 days a week. Postage stamps are available at all post offices and at tobacco shops, and there are stamp-vending machines outside most post offices.

The postal system in Vienna is, for the most part, efficient and speedy. Mailboxes are painted yellow, and older ones are emblazoned with the double-headed eagle of the Austrian Republic. Newer ones usually have the golden trumpet of the Austrian Postal Service. A blue stripe on a mailbox indicates that mail will be picked up there on a Saturday.

Postcards sent airmail to North America cost 13AS (85¢), as do airmail letters weighing up to 20 grams. Postcards and letters sent airmail to North America will usually take 5 to 7 days to arrive.

As an alternative to having your mail sent *post restante* to post offices, you can have it sent to American Express in Vienna (see above). There's no charge for this service to anyone holding an American Express card or American Express traveler's checks.

Maps   See "Getting Around," earlier in this chapter.

Newspapers & Magazines   Most newsstands at major hotels or news kiosks along the streets sell copies of the *International Herald Tribune* and *USA Today* and also carry copies of the European editions of *Time* and *Newsweek*.

Police   The emergency number is ☎ **133.**

Radio/TV   The Austrian Radio Network (ÖRF) has English-language news broadcasts at 8:05am daily. "Blue Danube Radio" broadcasts daily in English from 7 to 9am, noon to 2pm, and 6 to 7:30pm on 103.8 FM in the Vienna area; the Voice of America broadcasts have news, music, and feature programs at 1197 AM (middle wave, here) from 7am to 1pm and in the midafternoon and early evening. Every Sunday at noon the TV network FSI broadcasts the English-language "Hello, Austria," covering sightseeing suggestions and giving tips about the country. Many first-class and deluxe hotels subscribe to CNN and also certain British channels. Films and programs from the United States and England are often shown in their original language with German subtitles.

Rest Rooms   Vienna has a number of public toilets, labeled WC, scattered at convenient locations throughout the city. Don't hesitate to use them, as they are clean, safe, and well maintained. All major sightseeing attractions also have public facilities.

Safety   In recent years, Vienna has been plagued by purse-snatchers. In the area around St. Stephan's Cathedral, signs (in German only) warn about pickpockets and purse-snatchers. Small foreign children often approach sympathetic adults and ask for money. As the adult goes for his wallet or her purse, full-grown thieves rush in and grab the money, fleeing with it. Unaccompanied women are the most common victims. If you're carrying a purse, do not open it in public.

Taxes   Depending on the object or service, a Value-Added Tax (*Mehrwertsteuer Rückvergütung*, or VAT) of between 7% and 34% is included in the price of items sold. Items such as food, in grocery stores, is taxed at 7%; luxury items such as jewelry are taxed at 34%; many items in between, such as clothing and souvenirs, are taxed at 20%. Austrian residents have no recourse but to pay this tax; short-term visitors from other countries, however, can arrange for a refund of the VAT if they can prove that they carried it out of Austria unused and in nearly new condition and that the purchase was part of a sale totaling more than 1,000AS ($67) per store. To get the refund, you must fill out Form U-34, which is available at most stores (a sign will say "tax-free shopping"). Get one for ÖAMTC quick refund if you plan to get your money at the border. Check whether the store gives refunds itself or uses a service. Sales personnel will help you fill out the form and will affix the store identification stamp. You will show the VAT *(MWSt)* as a separate item or will say that the tax is part of the total price. Keep your U-34 forms handy when you leave the country and have them validated by the Viennese Customs officer at your point of departure.

Know in advance that you'll have to show the articles for which you're claiming a VAT refund. Because of this, it's wise to keep your purchases in a suitcase or carry-on bag that's separate from the rest of your luggage, with all the original tags and

Country & City Codes

The **country code** for Austria is **43.** The **city code** for Vienna is **1;** use this code when you're calling from outside Austria. If you're within Austria but not in Vienna, use **01.** If you're calling within Vienna, simply leave off the code and dial only the regular phone number.

tickets, and the original receipts nearby. Don't check the item within your luggage before you process the paperwork with the Customs agent. In some instances, if your paperwork is in order, you'll receive a tax refund on the spot. If your point of departure is not equipped to issue cash on the spot, you'll have to mail the validated U-34 form or forms back to the store where you bought the merchandise after you return home. It's wise to keep a copy of each form. Within a few weeks, the store will send you a check, bank draft, or international money order covering the amount of your VAT refund. Information and help is available at the Austrian Automobile and Touring Club (ÖAMTC), which has instituted methods of speeding up the refund process. Before you go call the Austrian National Tourist Office for the ÖAMTC brochure "Tax-Free Shopping in Austria."

Taxis   See "Getting Around," earlier in this chapter.

Telegrams/Telex/Fax   The central telegraph office is at Börseplatz 1. As for faxes and telex, virtually every hotel in Austria will have one or both of these and will usually send a message for a nominal charge often less than that of a long-distance phone call.

Telephone   Remember, never dial abroad from your hotel room unless it's an emergency. Place phone calls at the post office or some other location. Viennese hotels routinely add 40% surcharges, and some will add as much as 200% to your call! For help dialing, contact your hotel's operator; or dial ☎ **09** for placement of long-distance calls within Austria or for information about using a telephone company credit card; dial ☎ **1611** for directory assistance; and dial ☎ **08** for help in dialing international long distance. Coin-operated phones are all over Vienna. To make a local call if you don't have a phone card (see below), insert 2AS (15¢) worth of coins (the phone will accept denominations of 1, 5, 10, and 20AS coins in slots designed for each of them), which will give you about 3 minutes of local calling time. Pick up the receiver, then dial the number you want; when your party answers your connection will be made. On some older phones, you'll need to push a clearly indicated button before the connection is made.

Avoid carrying lots of coins by buying a **Wertkarte** at tobacco/news kiosks or at post offices. Each card is electronically coded to provide 50AS ($3.35), 100AS ($6.70), 200AS ($13.40), or 500AS ($33.50) worth of phone calls. Buyers receive a slight discount because cards are priced slightly lower than their face value.

AT&T's USA Direct plan enables you to charge calls to your credit card or to call collect. The access number, ☎ **0800/200-288,** is a local call all over Austria. For **Sprint** dial ☎ **0800/200-236;** for **Worldcom** dial ☎ **0800/200-235;** for **British Telecom** dial ☎ **0800/200-209;** and for **Canada Direct** dial ☎ **0800/200-217.**

The international access code for both the United States and Canada, incidentally, is **001,** followed by the area code and the seven-digit local number.

Time   Vienna operates on central European time, which makes it 6 hours later than U.S. eastern standard time. It advances its clocks 1 hour in summer, however.

Tipping   A service charge of 10% to 15% is included on hotel and restaurant bills, but it's a good policy to leave something extra for waiters and 25AS ($2) per day for your hotel maid.

Railroad station, airport, and hotel porters get 20AS ($1.35) per piece of luggage, plus a 10AS (65¢) tip. Your hairdresser should be tipped 10% of the bill, and the shampoo person will be thankful for a 20AS ($1.35) gratuity. Toilet attendants are usually given 5AS (35¢), and hat-check attendants expect 7 to 15AS (45¢ to $1), depending on the place.

Tourist Offices   See "Visitor Information," in chapter 2.

Transit Information   Information, all types of tickets, and maps of the transportation system are available at Vienna Transport's main offices on Karlsplatz or at the St. Stephan's Square underground station Monday to Friday from 8am to 6pm and on Saturday, Sunday, and holidays from 8:30am to 4pm. Alternatively, you can call ☎ **01/7909,** 24 hours a day for information in German and English about public transport.

Where to Stay 4

Vienna has some of the greatest hotels in Europe, and more than 300 recommendable ones. But finding a room can be a problem, especially in August and September, if you arrive without a reservation. During these peak visiting months you may have to stay on the outskirts of Vienna and commute to the Inner City by streetcar, bus, or subway. But if you're looking to cut costs, staying outside the Inner City is not a bad option. You can expect to pay a fifth to a quarter less for a hotel outside the Ringstrasse.

High season in Vienna encompasses most of the year: from May until October or early November, and during some weeks in midwinter when the city hosts major trade fairs, conventions, and other cultural events. If you're planning a trip around Christmas and New Year's, room reservations should be made at least 1 month in advance. Some rate reductions (usually between 15% and 20%) are available during slower midwinter weeks—it always pays to ask.

Breakfast, usually continental style, is almost always included in the price of a room in Vienna. If you've arrived via car, parking will cost from 350AS ($23.45) per night in upscale hotels or as little as 100AS ($6.70) in hotels that price their parking "promotionally." Most hotel staffs, renowned for their stellar service, are multilingual, which means that they speak English.

ACCOMMODATIONS AGENCIES Any branch of the **Austrian National Tourist Office** (☎ 01/58-86-60), including the Vienna Tourist Board, will help you book a room if you arrive without one. They have branch offices in the arrival halls of the airport, train stations, and major highways that access Vienna (see chapter 3, "Getting to Know Vienna").

If you prefer to deal directly with an Austrian travel agency, three of the city's largest include **Austropa,** Friedrichsgasse 7, A-1010 (☎ 01/588-000); **Austrobus,** Dr. Karl Lueger-Ring 8, A-1010 (☎ 01/534-110); and **Blaguss Reisen,** Wiedner Hauptstrasse 15 A-1040 (☎ 01/50180). Any of them can reserve hotel space in Austria or anywhere else (though you'll have to reserve your own room, so call or write in advance), sell airline tickets both inside and outside of Austria, and procure hard-to-get tickets for music festivals. Many of the employees speak English fluently.

SEASONAL HOTELS Between July and September, some student dormitories are transformed into fully operational hotels. Three of the better of these are the **Academia Hotel,** Pfeilgasse 3A; the **Avis Hotel,** Pfeilgasse 4; and the **Atlas Hotel,** at Lerchenfelderstrasse 1. These dormitory buildings are rather unimaginative, angular buildings from the 1960s, and lodgings will definitely remind you of your own college days. But rooms are comfortable, with phones and private bathrooms, and are priced at relatively reasonable rates. All are within a 20-minute walk west of St. Stephan's Cathedral. Many of them are booked long-term by groups, but individual travelers are welcome if space is available. Depending on the hotel, doubles cost from 820 to 1,080AS ($54.95 to $72.35) a night, and triples run 1,080 to 1,320AS ($72.35 to $88.45) each. Breakfast is included in the rates. Bookings at all three hotels are arranged through the receptionists at the Academia Hotel, which functions as the headquarters for the entire Academia chain. For reservations and information, call ☎ **01/401-76-55** or fax 01/401-76-20. To reach the Academia and Avis hotels, take the U-Bahn to Thalia- strasse, then transfer to tram 46, and get off at Strozzistrasse. For the Atlas Hotel, take the U-Bahn to Lerchenfelderstrasse. Most major credit cards are accepted at these hotels.

PRIVATE HOMES & FURNISHED APARTMENTS For travelers who like to have a home base that is more spacious than an average hotel room, a limited number of private homes and furnished apartments are available. These accommodations can be money-saving options depending on the season and the size of the place. An agency that deals in house rentals is **Mitzwohnzentrale,** Laudongasse 7, A-1080 (☎ **01/ 402-6061**).

Note: Unless otherwise indicated, all accommodations listed here have private bathrooms.

1 Innere Stadt (Inner City)

VERY EXPENSIVE

✪ **ANA Grand Hotel Wien.** Kärnter Ring 9, A-1010 Vienna. ☎ **01/515-800.** Fax 01/515-13-12. www.anagrand.com. E-mail: reservations@anagrand.com. 205 units. A/C MINIBAR TV TEL. 5,100–5,600AS ($341.70–$375.20) double; 9,000AS ($603) suite. AE, DC, MC, V. U-Bahn: Karlsplatz.

Some of the most discerning hotel guests in Europe, often music lovers, prefer this 7-story deluxe hotel to the more traditional and famous Imperial or Bristol. Only a block from the Staatsoper, it's a honey. The luxurious service begins with a doorman ushering you past the columns at the entrance into the stunning lobby and reception area. You enter a world of beveled mirrors, crystal chandeliers, a "Grand Hotel" staircase, marble in various hues, and brass-adorned elevators. Off the lobby is a complex of elegant shops, selling expensive perfumes and pricey clothing. The spacious accommodations are posh, with all the modern amenities, such as data ports, trouser presses, safes, heated floors, hair dryers, beverage makers, phones in the marble bathrooms, and even "anti-fog" mirrors. The more expensive units have more elaborate furnishings and decoration, including delicate stucco work.

Dining/Diversions: The main dining room specializes in both Austrian and international dishes, and there is also a Japanese restaurant that serves the town's best "sushi brunch" on Sunday. There are also two international bars, plus an elaborate afternoon tea service in the lobby lounge.

Amenities: 24-hour room service, baby-sitting, beauty salon, men's hairdresser, business center, coffee shop, concierge, deli, florist, laundry/valet, fitness center and health club.

Hilton International Vienna Plaza. Am Schottenring 11, A-1010 Vienna. ☎ **800/ 445-8667** in the U.S., or 01/31390. Fax 01/31390-22009. www.hilton.com. E-mail: info-viennaplaza@hilton.com. 255 units. A/C MINIBAR TV TEL. 3,200–4,150AS ($214.40–$278.05) double; from 6,400AS ($428.80) suite. AE, DC, MC, V. Free parking. U-Bahn: U2 to Schottentor. Tram: 1 or D. Bus: 40A.

This is Vienna's "other Hilton," and it is a much newer version, having opened in 1989. It rises imposingly for 10 stories, opening onto Ringstrasse just opposite the stock exchange. Its financial district location draws many business clients from around the world, but it's also near many attractions, such as the Burg-theater, City Hall, and the Kunsthistorisches and Naturhistorisches museums. Designed with flair for the modern traveler, the luxury hotel offers spacious guest rooms and suites. Room rates increase with altitude and view; two floors are smoke free. Furnishings tend to be traditional, and many amenities are included, such as electronic locks, three phones, safes, and fluffy robes. Each unit has floor-to-ceiling windows and a large marble bathroom fitted with hair dryers, phone, and radio. The hotel also offers a penthouse floor with balconies.

Dining/Diversions: You shouldn't have trouble finding a place to eat or drink at this hotel as it has three restaurants, a piano bar, a cocktail lounge, and a sidewalk terrace.

Amenities: 24-hour room service, concierge, dry cleaning and laundry service, free airport limo, baby-sitting, business center, health and fitness club (with sauna, massage, gym, whirlpool, solarium, and health bar), car-rental desk.

✪ **Hotel Ambassador.** Kärntnerstrasse 22, A-1010 Vienna. ☎ **01/961-610.** Fax 01/513-29-99. www.ambassador.at. E-mail: reservations@ambassador.at. 105 units. A/C MINIBAR TV TEL. 2,700–4,990AS ($180.90–$334.35) double; 10,000AS ($670) suite. AE, DC, MC, V. Parking 350AS ($23.45). U-Bahn: Stephansplatz.

Until it became a hotel in 1866, the six-story Ambassador was a warehouse for wheat and flour, a far cry from its status today as one of the four or five most glamorous hotels in Vienna. It's no Bristol or Imperial, but it's quite posh, nonetheless. The Ambassador couldn't be better located: It's between the State Opera and St. Stephan's Cathedral, on the square facing the Donner Fountain. Shop-lined Kärntnerstrasse is on the other side. Mark Twain stayed here, as have a host of diplomats and celebrities, including Theodore Roosevelt.

The hotel's trademark color, red, crops up all over: in the silk wall coverings, the bedspreads, the upholstery, or the long carpet that's often unrolled to the limousine of some famous personage. These sumptuous accommodations are an ideal choice for devotees of rococo *fin-de-siècle* decor. Bedrooms are furnished with Biedermeier and art nouveau period pieces. The quieter rooms open onto Neuer Markt, although you'll miss the view of lively Kärntnerstrasse. Comfortable beds with firm mattresses, marble bathrooms with hair dryers and toiletries, and ample closet space add to the hotel's allure. Five rooms are nonsmoking.

Dining/Diversions: The restaurant, Léhar, serves high-quality Austrian and international cuisine. The hotel also has an elegant bar.

Amenities: Room service, laundry, baby-sitting, beauty salon, foreign-currency exchange.

✪ **Hotel Bristol.** Kärntner Ring 1, A-1015 Vienna. ☎ **888/625-5144** (in the U.S.) or 01/515-160. Fax 01/515-16-550. www.westin.com/bristol. E-mail: hotelbristol@westin.com. 146 units. A/C MINIBAR TV TEL. 3,400–5,600AS ($227.80–$375.20) double; 7,000–18,000AS ($469–$1,206) suite. AE, DC, MC, V. Parking 300AS ($20.10). U-Bahn: Karlsplatz. Tram: 1 or 2.

Vienna Inner City Accommodations

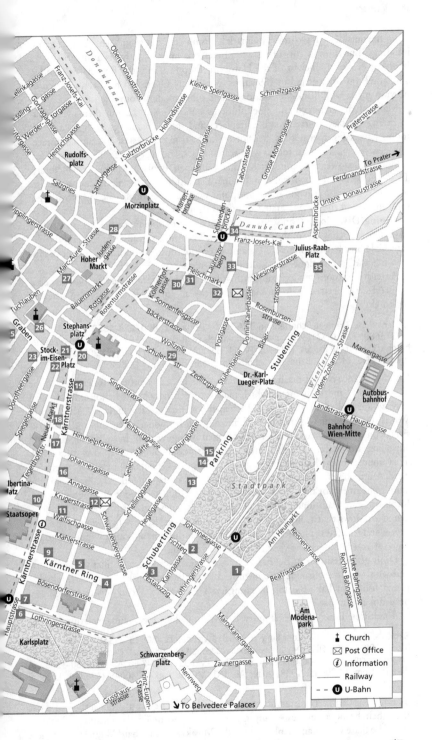

Legend	
†	Church
⊠	Post Office
ⓘ	Information
——	Railway
--- Ⓤ	U-Bahn

↘ To Belvedere Palaces

From the outside, this six-story landmark looks no different from Vienna's other grand buildings. But connoisseurs of Austrian hotels maintain that this is a superb choice. Its decor evokes the height of the Habsburg Empire—only the Imperial is grander. The hotel was constructed in 1894 next to the State Opera but has been updated to provide guests with black-tile bathrooms and other modern conveniences.

Many of the architectural embellishments rank as *objets d'art* in their own right, including the black carved marble fireplaces and the oil paintings in the salons. All rooms have safes, thermostats, bedside controls, firm mattresses, and ample storage, plus generous marble bathrooms with scales, robes, and hair dryers. The Bristol Club Rooms in the tower offer comfortable chairs, an open fireplace, self-service bar, library, TV, video recorder, stereo, deck, and sauna. Each individual accommodation consists of a bedroom with a living-room area, and many have a small balcony providing a rooftop view of the Vienna State Opera and Ringstrasse.

Dining/Diversions: Corkscrew columns of rare marble grace the Korso, Bristol's restaurant, which is one of the best in Vienna. The modern Rôtisserie Sirk and the elegant Café Sirk have an *après-théâtre* ambience; the music room has a resident pianist who fills the ground floor with waltzlike melodies.

Amenities: Room service, baby-sitting, laundry/dry cleaning service, business center, secretarial services, in-room massage, twice-daily maid service, access to a nearby health club.

✪ **Hotel de France.** Schottenring 3, A-1010 Vienna. ☎ **800/223-5652** in the U.S., or 01/313680. Fax 01/315969. www.austria-hotels.co.at/defrance. E-mail: defrance@austria-hotels.co.at. 207 units. A/C MINIBAR TV TEL. 3,900AS ($261.30) double; 5,200AS ($348.40) suite. AE, DC, MC, V. U-Bahn: U2, Schottentor. Tram: 1, 2, 37, or D. Bus: 1A.

Hotel de France is right on the Ring and has long been a favorite. It is neighbor to the university and the Votivkirche, which makes it a centrally located choice. Its chiseled gray facade looks basically as it did when it was first erected in 1872. After World War II, the building was transformed into a hotel. Its modern elements and unobtrusively conservative decor are the result of extensive renovation. In such a subdued and appealing ambience, you often encounter businesspeople from all over the world. They appreciate the high-ceilinged public rooms and Oriental carpets, the generously padded armchairs, and the full-dress portrait of Franz Joseph. The bedrooms are among the finest for their price range in Vienna. Housekeeping is of a high standard; furnishings are traditional, with firm beds, radios, safes, trouser presses, and double-glazed windows that really keep noise pollution down. Roomy bathrooms have hair dryers and toiletries. The best rooms are on the fifth floor, although windows are too high for you to absorb the view unless you're very tall.

Dining/Diversions: At Bel Etage, you can enjoy such dishes as fillet in Roquefort-and-whisky sauce, *tafelspitz* (the favorite dish of the emperor), and *fogas*, the highly prized fish from Lake Balaton in Hungary. There's also a French bistro as well as a beautiful atrium bar.

Amenities: Room service, laundry, baby-sitting, concierge, sauna, solarium.

✪ **Hotel Imperial.** Kärntner Ring 16, A-1015 Vienna. ☎ **800/325-3589** in the U.S., or 01/501100. Fax 01/5011-0410. www.luxurycollection.com/imperial. E-mail: hotel.imperial@luxurycollection.com. 160 units. A/C MINIBAR TV TEL. 5,500–7,600AS ($368.50–$509.20) double; from 14,000AS ($938) suite. AE, DC, MC, V. Parking 400AS ($26.80). U-Bahn: Karlsplatz.

This hotel is definitely the grandest in Vienna. Luminaries from around the world use it as their headquarters, especially musical stars who prefer the location—2 blocks from the State Opera and 1 block from the Musikverein. Richard Wagner stayed here with his family for a few months in 1875 (some scholars claim that he worked out key sections of both *Tannhäuser* and *Lohengrin* during that period). Other artists who have soothed opening-night jitters here over the years include Plácido Domingo, Monserrat Caballé, José Carreras, Eugene Ormandy, and Herbert von Karajan, along with thousands of music lovers who have come to see and hear them.

The hotel was built in 1869 as the private residence of the duke of Württemberg. The Italian architect Zanotti designed the facade, which resembles a massive governmental building with a heroic frieze carved into the pediment below the roofline. It was converted into a private hotel in 1873. The Nazis commandeered it for their headquarters during World War II, and the Russians requisitioned it in 1945, turning it into a ghost of its former self. Massive expenditures have returned it to its former glory.

On the staircase leading up from the glittering salons are archways supported by statues of gods and goddesses, along with two Winterhalter portraits of Emperor Franz Joseph and his wife, Elizabeth. Everything is set against a background of polished red, yellow, and black marble, crystal chandeliers, Gobelin tapestries, and fine rugs. The salons have arched ceilings, intricately painted with garlands of fruit, ornate urns, griffins, and the smiling faces of sphinxes. Some of the royal suites are downright palatial, but even the regular rooms today are soundproof and generally spacious. Accommodations vary greatly in size, as befits a hotel of this era. Those on the mezzanine and first floors are lavishly baroque; as you go higher appointments diminish, as do bathroom sizes. Except for some top-floor rooms, bathrooms are generous in size with marble, heated floors, robes, and hair dryers; beds are frequently renewed with the best mattresses in town. Courtyard rooms are more tranquil but lack the view of the city.

Dining/Diversions: The elegant restaurant, Hotel Imperial Restaurant, has a turn-of-the-century atmosphere, accented by antique silver, portraits of Franz Joseph, and superb service; traditional Austrian dishes are done lightly with excellent flavor. The Imperial Café downstairs plays Viennese music, and the hotel's bar, Maria Theresia, is an intimate rendezvous spot.

Amenities: 24-hour room service, baby-sitting, laundry, hair salon, business center, foreign-currency exchange, access to nearby health club, concierge.

Hotel Inter-Continental Wien. Johannesgasse 28, A-1037 Vienna. ☎ **01/711-22-0.** Fax 01/713-44-89. www.vienna.interconti.com. E-mail: vienna@interconti.com. 453 units. A/C MINIBAR TV TEL. 3,300–4,800AS ($221.10–$321.60) double; from 5,200AS ($348.40) suite. AE, DC, MC, V. Parking: 250AS ($16.75). U-Bahn: Johannesgasse.

Opposite the Stadtpark, and a few minutes from the Ringstrasse, this 5-star deluxe property has forged ahead of the Marriott and the Hilton even though it cloaks its charms in a dull "white tower." Once inside, however, the hotel is inviting and elegant, with a tasteful lobby lit by some of the best hotel chandeliers in Vienna. Many musical stars make this their hotel of choice. The higher the room, the better the view, of course. Rooms are spacious and richly furnished but are not necessarily evocative of Vienna. All the amenities are here: data ports with voice mail, soundproofing, excellent mattresses, and robes and toiletries in combination bathrooms with marble sinks and hair dryers. Three floors are reserved for nonsmokers.

Dining/Diversions: The Four Seasons Restaurant is one of the best for hotel dining in town, serving an international menu with regional specialties featured daily. There is also a spacious brasserie for meals on the run, plus an elegant cafe and lobby bar.

Amenities: Room service, health club, baby-sitting, concierge, laundry/valet, sauna, solarium, and steam room. Tennis arranged nearby.

✪ **Hotel Sacher Wien.** Philharmonikerstrasse 4, A-1010 Vienna. ☎ **01/514560.** Fax 01/512-56-810. www.sacher.com. E-mail: hotel@sacher.com. 106 units. A/C MINIBAR TV TEL. 4,100–9,000AS ($274.70–$603) double; from 14,000AS ($938) suite. AE, DC, MC, V. Parking 390AS ($26.15). U-Bahn: Karlsplatz. Tram: 1, 2, 62, 65, D, or J. Bus: 4A.

The Sacher was built in 1876 and still has an air of Habsburg-era glory. Red velvet, crystal chandeliers, and brocaded curtains in the public rooms evoke Old Vienna. If you want truly grand, we think the Imperial and Bristol are superior, but the Sacher has its diehard admirers. The facade is appropriately elaborate, with neoclassical detailing, a striped awning over the sidewalk cafe, and flags from seven nations displayed near the caryatids on the second floor. Despite its popularity as a setting for spy novels, both the crowned heads of Europe and the deposed heads (especially those of Eastern European countries) have safely dined and lived here.

In addition to intrigue, the Sacher has produced culinary creations that still bear its name. Franz Sacher, the celebrated chef, left the world a fabulously caloric chocolate cake called the Sachertorte.

Most rooms contain antiques or superior reproductions; those facing the opera house have the best views. Rooms near the top are small with cramped bathrooms, but most accommodations are generous in size and often have sitting areas and medium-size marble bathrooms. Inside rooms tend to be dark, however. Mattresses are renewed when the need arises, and thick towels are endlessly supplied by the eagle-eyed house-keeping staff.

Demi-suites and chambers with drawing rooms are more expensive. The reception desk is fairly flexible about making arrangements for salons, apartments, or joining two rooms together, if possible.

Dining/Diversions: Anna Sacher, the elegant coffeehouse, is the music-lover's choice in Vienna. The interior is a splendor of rococo.

Amenities: Concierge (who can probably produce "unobtainable" theater and opera tickets), room service, laundry, baby-sitting, car-rental desk, access to nearby health club.

Radisson/SAS Palais Hotel Vienna. Parkring 16, A-1010 Vienna. ☎ **800/333-3333** in the U.S. or 01/515170. Fax 01/512-2216. www.radisson.com. E-mail: sales@ viezh. rdsas.com. 245 units. A/C MINIBAR TV TEL. 2,700–4,950AS ($180.90–$331.65) double; from 4,900AS ($328.30) suite. AE, DC, MC, V. Parking 350AS ($23.45). U-Bahn: Stadtpark. Tram: 2.

This hotel is one of Vienna's grandest renovations. An unused neoclassical palace was converted into a hotel in 1985 by SAS, the Scandinavian airline; in 1994, another palace next door was added, allowing the hotel to double in size. Near Vienna's most elaborate park (the Stadtpark), the hotel boasts facades accented with cast-iron railings, reclining nymphs, and elaborate cornices. The interior is plushly outfitted with 19th-century architectural motifs, all impeccably restored and dramatically illuminated. The lobby contains arching palms, a soaring ceiling, and a bar with evening piano music. The result is an uncluttered, conservative, and clean hotel that is managed in a breezy, highly efficient manner. Bedrooms are outfitted in either pink or blue and, in the new wing, in summery shades of green and white. Ample closet space is an attractive feature, as are the good beds with firm mattresses, generous-size marble bathrooms with heated floors, trouser presses, makeup mirrors, and hair dryers. Smoke-free units can be arranged. The hotel also offers several duplex suites, or *maisonettes,* conventional suites, and rooms in the Royal Club, which has upgraded amenities and services.

Dining/Diversions: An elegant basement-level restaurant, Le Siècle im Ersten, is decked out with peach-colored upholstery and a white ceramic stove. Here you can enjoy beautifully presented Austrian and Scandinavian dishes while listening to live piano concertos.

Amenities: 24-hour room service, laundry, baby-sitting, plus a business center. Exercise buffs sometimes jog in the Stadtpark before relaxing in the hotel's sauna and whirlpool.

EXPENSIVE

Hotel Amadeus. Wildpretmarkt 5, A-1010 Vienna. ☎ **01/533-87-38.** Fax 01/533-87-38-38. www.tiscover.com/amadeus. 30 units. MINIBAR TV TEL. 2,100AS ($140.70) double. Rates include breakfast. AE, DC, MC, V. Parking 18AS ($1.20). U-Bahn: Stephansplatz.

Cozy and convenient, this hotel is only 2 minutes away from the cathedral and within walking distance of practically everything else of musical or historical note in Vienna. It was built on the site of a once-legendary tavern (Zum roten Igel) that attracted the likes of Johannes Brahms, Franz Schubert, and Moritz von Schwind. Behind a dull 1960s facade, the hotel maintains its bedrooms and carpeted public rooms in tip-top shape. Bedrooms are furnished in a comfortable, modern style, and many open onto views of the cathedral, but ceilings are uncomfortably low. Double-glazing on the windows helps but does not obliterate street noise. Some of the carpeting and fabrics look a little worse for wear. Tiled bathrooms are medium size, but there's not enough room to lay out your toiletries. Eight rooms have showers but no tubs.

Dining/Diversions: The hotel does not have a restaurant; breakfast is the only meal served.

Amenities: Laundry service and baby-sitting (by advance booking only).

Hotel Astoria. Kärntnerstrasse 32-34, A-1015 Vienna. ☎ **01/515770.** Fax 01/515-7782. www.austria-trend.at. E-mail: astoria@austria-trend.at. 118 units. MINIBAR TV TEL. 2,900AS ($194.30) double; 4,000AS ($268) suite. Rates include breakfast. AE, DC, MC, V. Parking 320AS ($21.45). U-Bahn: Stephansplatz.

Hotel Astoria is for nostalgists who want to experience life as it was in the closing days of the Austro-Hungarian Empire. A first-class hotel, the Astoria has an eminently desirable location, lying on the shopping mall near St. Stephan's Cathedral and the State Opera. Decorated in a slightly frayed turn-of-the-century style, the hotel offers well-appointed and traditionally decorated bedrooms. The interior rooms tend to be too dark, and singles are just too cramped. Rooms contain built-in armoires, well-chosen linens and duvets on good beds with firm mattresses, and bathrooms that for the most part are spacious but with old fixtures and such extras as dual basins, heated racks, hair dryers, and bidets. Of course, it has been renovated over the years, but the old style has been preserved, and management seems genuinely concerned about offering high-quality service and accommodation for what is considered a reasonable price in Vienna. The Astoria has long been a favorite with visiting performers like the late Leonard Bernstein.

Dining/Diversions: The restaurant, Astoria, is so special that it deserves (and gets) a special recommendation (see chapter 5, "Where to Dine").

Amenities: Room service, laundry, baby-sitting, car-rental desk.

✪ **Hotel Das Triest.** Wiedner hauptstrasse 12, A-1040 Vienna. ☎ **01/589-18.** Fax 01/589-18-18. www.nethotels.com/das_triest. E-mail: office@vienna.nethotels.com. 73 units. A/C MINIBAR TV TEL. 2,900AS ($194.30) double. Rates include buffet breakfast. AE, DC, MC, V. Parking: 200AS ($13.40). U-Bahn: Stephansplatz.

Sir Terence Conran, the famous English architect and designer, has created the interior decoration for this recently inaugurated hotel in the center of Vienna, a 5-minute walk from St. Stephan's Cathedral. Conran has done for Das Triest what Philippe Starck did for New York's Paramount Hotel—created a stylish address in the heart of one of the world's most important cities. An emerging favorite with artists and musicians, this hip hotel has such grace notes as a courtyard garden. The building was originally used as a stable for horses pulling stagecoaches between Vienna and Trieste—hence its name, "City of Trieste." Its old cross-vaulted rooms, which give the structure a distinctive flair, have been transformed into lounges and suites. Bedrooms are medium size to spacious, tastefully furnished, and comfortable. Amenities such as trouser presses, voice mail with data ports, and excellent mattresses have been installed along with white-tiled bathrooms with heated racks, hair dryers, deluxe toiletries, and vanity mirrors. You're carried to your bedroom by one of two black-glassed elevators. In the afternoon some guests gather for tea in front of the cozy fireplace.

Dining/Diversions: Both Austrian and Italian specialties are served in the formal, tasteful restaurant, with a chic adjoining bar.

Amenities: Room service, laundry/valet, baby-sitting, concierge.

Hotel Europa. Neuer Markt 3, A-1010 Vienna. ☎ **01/515940.** Fax 01/5159-4888. www.austria-trend.at. E-mail: europawien@austria-trend.at. 113 units. A/C MINIBAR TV TEL. 2,600–3,000AS ($174.20–$201) double. Rates include buffet breakfast. AE, DC, MC, V. Parking 320AS ($21.45). U-Bahn: Stephansplatz.

The welcoming parapet of this glass-and-steel hotel extends over the sidewalk almost to the edge of the street. You'll find the 10-story hotel midway between the State Opera and St. Stephan's Cathedral. It offers comfortable bedrooms furnished in Scandinavian modern. Some bedrooms are spacious, with lots of light coming in from the large windows, but nearly all the bathrooms are microscopic.

Dining/Diversions: Europa has a Viennese cafe and a first-class restaurant, Zum Donnerbrunnen, which features zither music at night. The Europa Bar is quite elegant.

Amenities: Dry cleaning and laundry service, secretarial services, concierge, access to nearby health club.

Hotel König Von Ungarn. Schulerstrasse 10, A-1010 Vienna. ☎ **01/515840.** Fax 01/515848. www.kvu.at. E-mail: hotel@kvu.at. 33 units. A/C MINIBAR TV TEL. 2,390AS ($160.15) double; 2,790AS ($186.95) apt.. Rates include breakfast. AE, DC, MC, V. U-Bahn: Stephansplatz.

On a narrow street near St. Stephan's, this hotel occupies a dormered building that dates back to the early 17th century. It has been receiving paying guests for more than 4 centuries and is Vienna's oldest continuously operated hotel—in all, an evocative, intimate, and cozy retreat. It was once a *pied-à-terre* for Hungarian noble families during their stays in the Austrian capital. Mozart reportedly lived here in 1791. He wrote some of his immortal music when he resided in an apartment upstairs, where you'll find a Mozart museum.

The interior abounds with interesting architectural details, such as marble columns supporting the arched ceiling of the King of Hungary restaurant, which is one of Vienna's finest. There's also a mirrored solarium/bar area with a glass roof over the atrium, and a live tree growing out of the pavement. Tall hinged windows overlook the Old Town, and Venetian mirrors adorn some walls. Everywhere you look you'll find low-key luxury, tradition, and modern convenience. Try for the two rooms with balconies. Guest rooms have been newly remodeled with firm mattresses, Biedermeier accents, and traditional furnishings, with safes added as well. Most bathrooms are generous in size with dual basins, hair dryers, and tiled walls. The professional staff is highly efficient, keeping the hotel spotless.

Dining/Diversions: The King of Hungary restaurant is one of the most famous in Vienna.

Amenities: Dry cleaning, laundry service, twice-daily maid service, room service (for breakfast only), baby-sitting.

Hotel Römischer Kaiser. Annagasse 16, A-1010 Vienna. ☎ **800/528-1234** in the U.S., or 01/512-7751. Fax 01/5127-75113. E-mail: info@rkhotel.bestwestern.at. 23 units. A/C MINI-BAR TV TEL. 1,890–3,190AS ($126.65–$213.75) double. Rates include breakfast. AE, DC, MC, V. Parking 320AS ($21.45). U-Bahn: Stephansplatz.

A Best Western affiliate, this hotel is housed in a national trust building that has seen its share of transformations. It's located in a traffic-free zone, between St. Stephan's Cathedral and the Opera House, on a side street off Kärntnerstrasse. It was constructed in 1684 as the private palace of the imperial chamberlain and later housed the Imperial School of Engineering, before becoming a *fin-de-siècle* hostelry. The hotel rents romantically decorated rooms (our favorite has red satin upholstery over a chaise longue). Thick duvets and custom linens make the rooms homelike and inviting, and bathrooms are generous in size, often luxurious, with half tubs, hair dryers, vanity mirrors, and enough shelf space to spread out your toiletries. All rooms have good mattresses, radio clocks, cable TV (with CNN), and room safes. Double-glazing keeps down the noise, and baroque paneling is a nice touch. Some rooms—notably 12, 22, 30, and 38—can accommodate three or four beds, making this a family-friendly place.

Dining/Diversions: The red-carpeted sidewalk cafe has bar service and tables shaded with flowers and umbrellas. It evokes memories of Vienna in its imperial heyday.

Amenities: 24-hour room service, laundry, baby-sitting, twice-daily maid service, bicycle rentals.

K & K Palais Hotel. Rudolfsplatz 11, A-1010 Vienna. ☎ **800/528-1234** in the U.S., or 01/533-1353. Fax 01/5331-35370. www.bestwestern.com. E-mail: kk.palais.hotel@kuk.at. 66 units. A/C MINIBAR TV TEL. 2,520AS ($168.85) double. Rates include breakfast. AE, DC, MC, V. Parking 180AS ($12.05). U-Bahn: Schottenring.

This hotel, with its severely dignified facade, sheltered the affair of Emperor Francis Joseph and his celebrated mistress, Katherina Schratt, in 1890. Occupying a desirable position near the river and a 5-minute walk from the Ring, it remained unused for 2 decades until the Best Western chain renovated it in 1981.

Vestiges of its imperial past remain, in spite of the contemporary but airy lobby and the lattice-covered bar. The public rooms are painted a shade of imperial Austrian yellow, and one of Ms. Schratt's antique secretaries occupies a niche near a white-sided tile stove. The bedrooms are comfortably outfitted and stylish. Rooms have a certain Far East motif, with light wood, wicker, and rattan. Firm mattresses and generous, tiled bathrooms are added attractions, especially the shelf space and state-of-the-art plumbing. Two floors are nonsmoking.

Dining/Diversions: The hotel doesn't have a formal restaurant; however, breakfast is served each morning. A coffee shop serves Austrian fare.

Amenities: Dry cleaning and laundry service, concierge, 17-hour room service, business center and conference rooms.

✪ **Vienna Marriott.** Parkring 12A, A-1010 Vienna. ☎ **800/228-9290** in the U.S., or 01/515180. Fax 01/51518-6736. 347 units. A/C MINIBAR TV TEL. 2,180AS ($146.05) double; 2,900–6,600AS ($194.30–$442.20) suite. AE, DC, MC, V. Parking 400AS ($26.80). Tram: 1 or 2.

The Marriott has a striking exterior and holds its own against SAS, the Palais Hotel, and the Hilton, although the latter two hotels manage to evoke a more Viennese atmosphere. Opposite Stadtpark, the hotel is ideally located for visitors, as it's within walking distance of such landmarks as St. Stephan's Cathedral, the State Opera, and the Hofburg. Its Mississippi-riverboat facade displays expanses of tinted glass set in finely wrought enameled steel. About a third of the building is occupied by the American Consulate offices and a few private apartments.

The hotel's lobby culminates in a stairway whose curved sides frame a splashing waterfall that's surrounded with plants. Many of the comfortably modern bedrooms are larger than those in the city's other contemporary hotels. Spacious mirrored closets are a feature, as are firm mattresses and great bathrooms with large sinks, hair dryers, and (in the better rooms) robes. Furnishings are a bit commercial. There are four smoke-free floors and adequate soundproofing.

Dining/Diversions: Both in-house bars offer live cocktail-hour entertainment, and a pair of restaurants feature appetizing and well-prepared Viennese and international specialties. In the gourmet restaurant, Symphonika, plush pastel-colored banquettes encircle an art nouveau chandelier.

Amenities: 24-hour room service, laundry, baby-sitting, indoor swimming pool, health club with sauna and Jacuzzi, car-rental desk, beauty salon and boutiques, plus secretarial services.

MODERATE

Best Western Hotel Opernring. Opernring 11, A-1010 Vienna. ☎ **800/780-7234** in the U.S., or 01/587-55-18. Fax 01/587-55-18-29. www.bestwestern.com. E-mail: reservation@ opernring.at. 68 units. A/C MINIBAR TV TEL. 1,900–2,200AS ($127.30–$147.40) double; 2,600–3,200AS ($174.20–$214.40) suite. Rates include breakfast. AE, DC, MC, V. U-Bahn: Karlsplatz.

Across from the state opera house, and lying along "the Ring," this 4-star hotel has been much improved under new owners, who have carried out a major rejuvenation of a formerly tired property. Accommodations are fairly large and tastefully furnished with such amenities as data ports, duvet-covered beds with firm mattresses, and spacious tiled bathrooms equipped with hair dryers. Double-glazed windows cut down on the noise in the front bedrooms. Some units are reserved for nonsmokers, and some of the accommodations can sleep three to four family members comfortably. Don't judge the hotel by its rather cramped reception area or its entrance. The third-floor lounge is large and inviting. A bay window opens onto the activity of central Vienna.

Graben Hotel. Dorotheergasse 3, A-1010 Vienna. ☎ **01/512-15-31-0.** Fax 01/ 512-15-31-20. www.kremslehner.hotels.or.at/graben. 41 units. A/C MINIBAR TV TEL. 1,600–2,000AS ($107.20–$134) double; 2,200AS ($147.40) suite. Rates include buffet breakfast. AE, DC, MC, V. U-Bahn: Karlsplatz.

Back in the 18th century, this was called Zum Goldener Jägerhorn; over the years it has attracted an array of "bohemian" writers and artists. The poet Franz Grillparzer was a regular guest, and during the dark days of World War II it was a gathering place for such writers as Franz Kafka, Max Brod, and Peter Altenberg. There aren't too many bohemians around any more, but what's left of them can be seen gathered at the fabled Café Hawelka across the street. The hotel stands on a narrow street off the Kärntnerstrasse, in the very center of the city. One journalist in Vienna wrote that "its staff was lent by Fawlty Towers," but we're sure he meant that lovingly, as they're helpful and bright. Guests gather around the stone fireplace in winter and look at the original postcards left by Altenberg. Rooms are high ceilinged but rather cramped, with rubber floors in the bathrooms. Although there are some art nouveau touches, much of the furniture is a bit drab and spartan for our tastes. If there's any sunlight streaming in, it'll come from the front rooms, not the darker havens in the rear. On site is the excellent trattoria San Stefano, serving some of the best Italian dishes in the area. The Restaurant Altenberg specializes in Austrian dishes. The chef is known for his creamy cake named in honor of Kaiser Franz Josef.

Hotel Am Parkring. Parkring 12, A-1015 Vienna. ☎ **01/514800.** Fax 01/514-8040. www.bestwestern.com. E-mail: parkring@schick-hotels.com. 64 units. A/C MINIBAR TV TEL. 1,900-2,750AS ($127.30–$184.25) double; 3,500–4,500AS ($234.50–$301.50) suite. Rates include breakfast. AE, DC, MC, V. Parking 230AS ($15.40). U-Bahn: Stadtpark or Stebentor. Tram: 1 or 2.

This well-maintained hotel occupies the top 3 floors of a 13-story office building near the edge of Vienna's Stadtpark. A semiprivate elevator services only the street-level entrance and the hotel's floors. There are sweeping views of the city from all of its bedrooms, some of which overlook nearby St. Stephan's Cathedral. Bedrooms are furnished in a conservative but comfortable style and are favored by business travelers and visitors alike, although the atmosphere is a bit sterile if you're seeking nostalgic Vienna. Bedrooms have firm mattresses and well-chosen linens; bathrooms are small but functional (some with showers instead of tubs). Eighteen units were recently equipped with sparkling new bathrooms. This hotel is not the kindest to the lone tourist, as single accommodations tend to be too small, and often sofa beds are used. Rooms here are a standard, reliable choice, but don't expect fireworks. You can dine at the Himmelstube restaurant and relax at the coffee bar, where Vienna's skyline spreads out before you. Room service, baby-sitting, and laundry are available.

✪ **Hotel Am Schubertring.** Schubertring 11, A-1010 Vienna. ☎ **01/717-020.** Fax 01/713-99-66. E-mail: aschu@atnet.at. 39 units. A/C MINIBAR TV TEL. 1,750–2,500AS ($117.25–$167.50) double. AE, DC, MC, V. U-Bahn: Karlsplatz.

In a historic building in the very center of town, this small hotel has a certain charm and style. On the famous Ringstrasse, next to the opera, it has Viennese flair, especially in the use of art nouveau and Biedermeier-style furnishings in its moderate size and comfortable bedrooms with small bathrooms. Rooms are generally quiet, and 8 units are suitable for three guests or more. The top-floor rooms look out over the rooftops of Vienna. At this family-friendly place children under age 6 are housed free if sharing an accommodation with their parents.

Hotel Am Stephansplatz. Stephansplatz 9, A-1010 Vienna. ☎ **01/534-05-0.** Fax 01/534-05-711. E-mail: hotel@stephansplatz.co.at. 60 units. MINIBAR TV TEL. 1,980–2,430AS ($132.65–$162.80) double. Rates include breakfast. AE, DC, MC, V. Parking 350AS ($23.45). U-Bahn: Stephansplatz.

Walk out the door and you'll be facing the front entrance to Vienna's cathedral if you stay here. The location, admittedly, is virtually unbeatable, although a lot of other hotels have more charm and more helpful staffs. Nevertheless, the place has many winning qualities; for example, it receives individual bookings and is not overrun with group package tours. Marble, granite, crystal, and burled woods set the tone for the renovated lobby. Some of the bedrooms contain painted reproductions of rococo furniture and red-flocked wallpaper. All have firm beds. Most rooms, however, are rather sterile and functional, and 10 come with showers only instead of tub baths. Bathrooms tend to be small. Lack of air-conditioning could be a problem in the evening, especially if guests must open their windows onto noisy Stephansplatz. The singles are so plain and cramped that they're hardly recommendable. A typical Viennese coffee shop, the first-floor Dom Café, is a well-known meeting spot.

Hotel Capricorno. Shwedenplatz 3-4, A-1010 Vienna. ☎ **01/5333-1040.** Fax 01/5337-6714. www.hotels-austria.com/Vienna-center/capricorno.htm. E-mail: Capricorno@Schick-Hotels.com. 46 units. A/C MINIBAR TV TEL. 1,580–2,420AS ($105.85–$162.15) double. AE, MC, V. Rates include buffet breakfast. U-Bahn: Stephansplatz.

In the heart of Vienna, this 4-star hotel, a short stroll from St. Stephan's, has more than a convenient location going for it. Next to the Danube Canal, it is solidly commercial and undramatic architecturally on the outside, but rather warm and inviting inside. The reception area is decorated in a modern art nouveau style with tiles and brass trim. Rooms are compact—even cramped in many cases—but they are well furnished and maintained, though a major rejuvenation might be called for in a year or so. Singles are particularly small, mainly because the beds are more spacious than most. Some units, especially those on the lower levels, suffer from noise pollution. The hotel sends its guests to its sibling, the Hotel Stefanie, across the street, for dining in a first-class restaurant, Kronprinz Rudolph, offering both Viennese and international cuisine.

✪ Hotel Kaiserin Elisabeth. Weihburggasse 3, A-1010 Vienna. ☎ **01/515260.** Fax 01/515267. E-mail: kaiserin@ins.at. 63 units. MINIBAR TV TEL. 2,650AS ($177.55) double; 2,950AS ($197.65) suite. Rates include buffet breakfast. AE, DC, MC, V. Parking 350AS ($23.45). U-Bahn: Stephansplatz.

This yellow-stoned hotel is conveniently located near the cathedral. The interior is decorated with Oriental rugs on well-maintained marble and wood floors. The main salon has a pale-blue skylight suspended above it, with mirrors and half-columns in natural wood. The small, quiet rooms have been considerably updated since Wolfgang Mozart, Richard Wagner, Franz Liszt, and Edvard Grieg stayed here, and their musical descendents continue to patronize the place. Polished wood, clean linen, good mattresses, and perhaps another Oriental rug grace the rooms. Bathrooms are a bit cramped with not enough room for your toilet articles, but they are tiled and equipped with half tubs, vanity mirrors, hair dryers, and, in some cases, bidets. In the breakfast area a portrait of Empress Maria Theresa hangs above the fireplace. Room service, laundry, and baby-sitting are available.

Hotel-Pension Arenberg. Stubenring 2, A-1010 Vienna. ☎ **800/528-1234** in the U.S., or 01/512-5291. Fax 01/513-9356. www.bestwestern.com. E-mail: arenberg@ping.at. 23 units. A/C TV TEL. 1,480–1,850AS ($99.15–$123.95) double; 1,780–2,150AS ($119.25–$144.05) triple suite. Rates include breakfast. AE, DC, MC, V. Parking 250AS ($16.75). U-Bahn: Schwedenplatz.

This genteel but unpretentious hotel-pension occupies the second and third floors of a six-story apartment house that was built around the turn of the 20th century. Set in a prestigious neighborhood on Ringstrasse, it offers soundproof bedrooms outfitted in Old World style with Oriental carpets, conservative furniture, and intriguing artwork. The place is rather old-fashioned but has a certain Viennese charm. One enthusiastic reader found it to be a small luxury hotel of Old World charm where the English-speaking staff couldn't have been more delightful or helpful. "On your second visit they treat you like family," the reader wrote. The bedrooms are furnished the way your Viennese grandmother might have found inspiring, although they are a bit small. Many of the mattresses are too soft for many tastes, and the bathrooms are a bit cramped. But in spite of it all, this hotel remains exceptionally appealing to those with a sense of history.

✪ Hotel Royal. Singerstrasse 3, A-1010 Vienna. ☎ **01/515680.** Fax 01/513-9696. 82 units. MINIBAR TV TEL. 1,650–2,000AS ($110.55–$134) double; 2,800AS ($187.60) suite. Rates include breakfast. AE, DC, MC, V. U-Bahn: Stephansplatz.

This dignified, nine-story hotel is on one of the more prestigious streets of the old city, less than a block from St. Stephan's Cathedral. The lobby contains the piano where Wagner composed *Die Meistersinger von Nürnberg.* Each of the good-size rooms is furnished differently, with some good reproductions of antiques and even an occasional original. Built in 1960, the hotel was rebuilt in 1982. Try for a room with a balcony and a view of the cathedral. Corner rooms with spacious foyers are also desirable, although those facing the street tend to be noisy. Bathrooms are of medium size, with mosaic tiles, dual basins, heated towel racks, hair dryers, and, in most cases, a tub bath along with a shower unit. Ristaurante Firenze, under separate management, serves savory Italian food and has the largest selection of Italian wines in Austria. Room service is also available.

Mailberger Hof. Annagasse 7, A-1010 Vienna. ☎ **01/512-0641.** Fax 01/512-0641-10. 46 units. A/C MINIBAR TV TEL. 1,900–2,700AS ($127.30–$180.90) double; from 2,900AS ($194.30) suite. AE, DC, MC, V. U-Bahn: Karlsplatz.

This old palace was built in the 13th century as a mansion for the knights of Malta, and was converted into a hotel about 30 years ago. Off the main drag, Kärntnerstrasse, it lies on a typical Viennese cobblestone street. The two large wooden doors at the entrance still boast a Maltese cross. The vaulted ceiling, the leather armchairs, and maybe the marbleized walls are about all that would remind the knights of their former home. Everywhere the place has been renewed, although a cobblestone courtyard, set with tables in fair weather, remains. A family-run place with a cozy atmosphere, the hotel features moderate-size bedrooms that are often brightened with pastels, each with comfortable beds, plus hair dryers in the small bathrooms. In general, though, the public rooms are more inviting than the private ones. An on-site restaurant begins with a buffet breakfast, then serves Austrian specialties at lunch or dinner. Room service and baby-sitting are available.

INEXPENSIVE

Hotel Austria. Wolfengasse 3A, A-1011 Vienna. ☎ **01/51523.** Fax 01/5152-3506. http://members.ennet.at/hotelans. E-mail: hotelans@ennet.at. 46 units, 42 with bathroom. MINIBAR TV TEL. 1,190AS ($79.75) double without bathroom; 1,800AS ($120.60) double with bathroom; 2,180AS ($146.05) triple with bathroom. Rates include breakfast. AE, DC, MC, V. Parking 250AS ($16.75). U-Bahn: Schwedenplatz. Tram: 1 or 2.

The staff here always seems willing to tell you where to go in the neighborhood for a good meal or a glass of wine, and often distributes typed sheets explaining the medieval origins of this section of the city center. This unpretentious, family-owned hotel sits on a small, quiet street whose name will probably be unfamiliar to many taxi drivers—a corner building on the adjoining street, Fleischmarkt 20, is the point where you'll turn onto the narrow lane. The comfortable furnishings in the lobby and in the chandeliered breakfast room are maintained in tip-top shape. Every year one of the four floors of the hotel is completely renovated with wallpapering, a change of furniture, and a replacement of bedding (you might find the mattresses a bit skimpy even when new). The tiled bathrooms are small but adequate unless you have a lot of toilet articles to spread out. The decor is rather functional, although the hotel is immaculately maintained and inviting nonetheless.

✪ **Hotel Kärntnerhof.** Grashofgasse 4, A-1011 Vienna. ☎ **01/512-1923.** Fax 01/5132-22833. www.karntnerhof.com. E-mail: kaerntnerhof@netway.at. 44 units. 1,270–1,840AS ($85.10–$123.30) double; 2,450–2,950AS ($164.15–$197.65) suite. Rates include buffet breakfast. AE, DC, MC, V. Parking 200AS ($13.40). U-Bahn: Stephansplatz.

Only a 4-minute walk from the cathedral, the Kärntnerhof advertises itself as a *Gutbürgerlich* (bourgeois) family-oriented hotel. The decor of the public rooms is tastefully arranged around Oriental rugs, well-upholstered chairs and couches with cabriole legs, and an occasional 19th-century portrait. The medium-sized units are more up to date, usually with the original parquet floors and striped or patterned wallpaper set off by curtains. Beds are good and renewed whenever necessary. The small private bathrooms glisten with tile walls and floors. The owner is quite helpful, directing guests to the post office and other nearby Vienna landmarks.

Hotel Pension Shermin. Rilkeplatz 7, A-1040 Vienna. ☎ **01/58-66-18-30.** Fax 01/58-66-18-310. www.members.magnet.at/pension.shermin/english.html. 11 units. TV TEL. 1,180–1,480AS ($79.05–$99.15) double. Rates include breakfast. AE, DC, MC, V. Parking 80AS ($5.35). U-Bahn: Karlsplatz.

The Voshmgir family welcomes you into their small, inviting, homelike boarding house in the city center. Bedrooms are big and comfortable, and the combined hotel-pension draws many repeat guests. The location is convenient for such sights as the opera house, Imperial Palace, and the Spanish Riding School, all a 5-minute walk away. Bathrooms are small but have good showers and well-maintained plumbing, plus hair dryers. Furnishings are modern and without much flair, but exceedingly comfortable nonetheless. Room service is offered.

Hotel Post. Fleischmarkt 24, A-1010 Vienna. ☎ **01/51-58-30.** Fax 01/515-83-808. 107 units, 77 with bathroom. TV TEL. 1,370AS ($91.80) double without bathroom, 1,480AS ($99.15) double with bathroom; 1,600AS ($107.20) triple without bathroom, 1,830AS ($122.60) triple with bathroom. Rates include buffet breakfast. AE, DC, MC, V. Parking 220AS ($14.75). Tram: 1 or 2.

Hotel Post lies in the medieval slaughterhouse district, today an interesting section full of hotels and restaurants. The dignified front of this hotel is constructed of gray stone, with a facade of black marble covering the street level. The manager is quick to tell you that both Mozart and Haydn frequently stayed in a former inn at this address. Those composers would probably be amused to hear recordings of their music played in the coffeehouse/restaurant, Le Café/Alte Weinstube, attached to the hotel. Bedrooms, most of which are of medium size, are streamlined and functionally furnished, each well maintained with small tile bathrooms.

Hotel Wandl. Petersplatz 9, A-1010 Vienna. ☎ **01/53-45-50.** Fax 01/53-455-77. E-mail: reservation@hotelwandl.com. 138 units (134 with bathroom). TV TEL. 1,350AS ($90.45) double without bathroom; 1,800–2,200AS ($120.60–$147.40) double with bathroom. Rates include breakfast. AE, DC, MC, V. Parking 250AS ($16.75). U-Bahn: Stephansplatz.

Stepping into this hotel is like stepping into a piece of a family's history—it has been under the same ownership for generations. The Wandl lies in the Inner City and offers views of the steeple of St. Stephan's Cathedral from many of its windows, which often open onto small balconies. The breakfast room is a high-ceilinged, two-toned room with hanging chandeliers and lots of ornamented plaster. The bedrooms usually offer the kind of spacious dimensions that went out of style 60 years ago; bathrooms are small but adequate, tiled, and well maintained. Beds are frequently renewed—all in all, this is a comfortable choice if you're not too demanding. The hotel faces St. Peter's Church. Laundry and baby-sitting are provided.

Pension Dr. Geissler. Postgasse 14, A-1010 Vienna. ☎ **01/533-2803.** Fax 01/533-2635. 30 units, 21 with bathroom. 800AS ($53.60) double without bathroom, 1,200AS ($80.40) double with bathroom. Rates include buffet breakfast. AE, DC, MC, V. Parking 150AS ($10.05). U-Bahn: Schwedenplatz.

Unpretentious lodgings at reasonable prices are offered here, near the well-known Schwedenplatz at the edge of the Danube Canal. The bedrooms in this attractive, informal guesthouse are furnished with simple blond headboards and a few utilitarian pieces. Mattresses are a bit soft but adequate for most sleepers. Hallway bathrooms are generous. so lines are avoided. Most units, however, have their own private bathrooms, which are tiled and well maintained, but a bit cramped.

Pension Neuer Markt. Seilergasse 9, A-1010 Vienna. ☎ **01/512-2316.** Fax 01/513-9105. 36 units. TV TEL. 1,200–1,500AS ($80.40–$100.50) double. Rates include breakfast.

Half board 160AS ($10.70) per person extra. AE, DC, MC, V. Parking 150AS ($10.05). U-Bahn: Stephansplatz.

Near the cathedral, in the heart of Vienna, this pension is housed in a white baroque building that faces a square with an ornate fountain. The carpeted but small rooms are clean and well maintained in an updated motif of white walls and strong colors, with large windows in some. Some of the comfortable, duvet-covered beds are set into niches. Each of the units has central heating. Bathrooms are small, seemingly added as an afterthought, but for Vienna the price is delicious. We recommend reserving 30 days in advance.

Pension Nossek. Graben 17, A-1010 Vienna. ☎ **01/5337-0410.** Fax 01/535-3646. E-mail: pension.nossek@faxvia.net. 26 units (4 with shower only, 22 with bathtub). TEL. 1,350AS ($90.45) double with bathtub or shower; 1,650AS ($110.55) suite with bathtub or shower. Rates include breakfast. No credit cards. Free parking. U-Bahn: Stephansplatz.

Mozart lived in this building in 1781 and 1782, writing the *Haffner* symphony and *The Abduction from the Seraglio.* The pension lies on one of Vienna's best shopping streets, just blocks away from the major sights. In 1909 the building was converted into a guesthouse and has always been a good bet for clean, comfortable accommodations with decent beds—most comfortable. Most of the bedrooms have been renovated, and all but a few singles contain small private bathrooms; 16 rooms offer a minibar.

Pension Pertschy. Habsburgergasse 5, A-1010 Vienna. ☎ **01/534490.** Fax 01/534-4949. 43 units (2 with kitchen). MINIBAR TV TEL. 1,460–1,660AS ($97.80–$111.20) double without kitchen; 1,660AS ($111.20) suite. DC, MC, V. Parking 50–180AS ($3.35–$12.05). U-Bahn: Stephansplatz.

Well-scrubbed and reputable, this simple but historic pension was originally built in the 1700s as the Palais Carviani with a restrained baroque style. Several rooms overlook a central courtyard and are scattered among six or seven private apartments, whose residents are used to foreign visitors roaming through the building. Medium-size bedrooms are high-ceilinged and outfitted in old-fashioned, almost dowdy tones of cream and pink, with good beds and rather cramped bathrooms. Most appealing is its prime location in the heart of Old Vienna (between Habsburgasse and Bräunergasse, just off the Graben).

Zur Wiener Staatsoper. Krugerstrasse 11, A-1010 Vienna. ☎ **01/513-1274.** Fax 01/5131-27415. www.zurwienerstaatsoper.at. E-mail: office@zurweinerstaatsoper.at. 22 units. TV. 1,500–1,700AS ($100.50–$113.90) double. Rates include breakfast. AE, MC, V. Parking 220AS ($14.75). U-Bahn: Karlsplatz. Tram: 1, 2, D, or J; Opernring.

You'll probably stop to admire the elaborately baroque facade of this family-run hotel even if you don't plan to stay here. Rooms are clean and comfortable, although the mattresses are a bit thin and furnishings rather simple and functional. Private bathrooms are bigger than those found on a cruise ship, but not by much. The elevator is convenient as is the hotel's location, near most Inner City monuments.

2 Leopoldstadt (2nd District)

MODERATE

Hotel Stefanie. Taborstrasse 12, A-1020 Vienna. ☎ **800/528-1234** in the U.S., or 01/211500. Fax 01/2115-0160. E-mail: stefanie@schick-hotels.com. 130 units. A/C MINIBAR TV TEL. 1,880–2,520AS ($125.95–$168.85) double. Rates include buffet breakfast. AE, DC, MC, V. Parking 200AS ($13.40). U-Bahn: Schwedenplatz. Tram: 21.

This updated 4-star hotel is across the Danube Canal from St. Stephan's Cathedral, but still easily accessible to the rest of the city. It has had a long and distinguished history, dating back to 1630. A century later, a famous inn, Weisse Rose, stood on this site. Ever since 1870 the hotel has been run by the Schick family. The interior is partially decorated in beautifully finished wall paneling and gilded wall sconces. Upon closer examination much of the decor is reproductions, yet the hotel still emits a hint of 19th-century rococo splendor. The bar area is filled with black leather armchairs on chrome swivel bases, and the concealed lighting throws an azure glow over the artfully displayed bottles. Over the past 20 years all the bedrooms have had major renovations, and today they are well furnished in sleek Viennese styling. Some are a bit small, but they are beautifully maintained with excellent beds and small tiled bathrooms that contain hair dryers, but not enough shelf space. The breakfast served each morning is excellent: an array of rolls, sausages, cheese, bacon, egg dishes, yogurts, cornflakes, and müsli.

3 Landstrasse (3rd District)

VERY EXPENSIVE

✪ **Hotel im Palais Schwarzenberg.** Schwarzenbergplatz 9, A-1030 Vienna. ☎ **01/ 798-4515.** Fax 01/798-4714. www.palais-schwarzenberg.com. E-mail: palais@schwarzenberg. co.at. 42 units. MINIBAR TV TEL. 3,570–5,800AS ($239.20–$388.60) double; from 6,460AS ($432.80) suite. AE, DC, JCB, MC, V. Free parking. Tram: D. U-Bahn: Karlsplatz.

Just outside the Ring, this hotel—more a museum really—is hidden amid 15 acres of manicured gardens. It's an excellent choice if you want a noble and elegant ambience. Unlike the Bristol and the Imperial, this hotel has the aura of a country estate in a formally landscaped and statue-dotted park. The palace was built 300 years ago by Hildebrandt and Fischer von Erlach, masters of baroque architecture, and has held on to its splendid original touches. It was gutted during the Nazi era but was completely reconstructed after the Soviet occupation of Vienna. Today the same striated marble, crystal chandeliers, mythical beasts, oval mirrors, and gilt—lots of it—fill the public rooms between painted murals of festive deities. The posh bedrooms and suites contain exquisite *objets d'art* and antique pieces, although they vary greatly in size. Only a few rooms are air-conditioned. The large marble or tile bathrooms have bidets, robes, and hair dryers.

Dining/Diversions: Guests enjoy the terrace restaurant, Wintergarten, which serves classical French and Viennese cuisine and overlooks the park. The Palais Bar, one of the most elegant in Vienna, is open daily from 10:30am to 2am.

Amenities: 24-hour room service, laundry, baby-sitting, nearby health club, 5 tennis courts, croquet lawn, guest lounges, boutiques, extensive private jogging tracks; courtesy cars are available.

✪ **Vienna Hilton.** Am Stadtpark, A-1030 Vienna. ☎ **800/445-8667** in the U.S., or 01/717000. Fax 01/7170-0339. www.hilton.com. 629 units. A/C MINIBAR TV TEL. 2,900–4,300AS ($194.30–$288.10) double; from 4,900AS ($328.30) suite. AE, DC, MC, V. Parking 250AS ($16.75). The Hilton is attached to the City Air Terminal, the drop-off point for buses coming in at frequent intervals from the airport. U-Bahn: Landstrasse.

This 18-story box overlooks the Danube Canal and offers plush accommodations and elegant public areas. Despite the hotel's modernity, it still manages to provide plenty of Viennese flavor. Its soaring atrium lobby and bustling nightlife make it a vibrant home for business travelers.

The hotel offers well-appointed bedrooms in a range of styles, including Biedermeier, contemporary, baroque, and art nouveau. Regardless of the style, the hotel offers excellent beds with firm mattresses. Because the Hilton towers over the city skyline, it affords great views from the top floors. Its suites and executive floors provide extra comfort for frequent travelers, but standard amenities in all bedrooms include hair dryers in the good-size bathrooms and baskets of toiletries. The adjacent Stadtpark is connected to the hotel and the City Air Terminal by a bridge, which strollers and joggers use during excursions into the landscaped and bird-filled park.

Dining/Diversions: The hotel's main restaurant, Arcadia, is recommended separately (see chapter 5 on "Where to Dine"). Other drinking and dining facilities include the Terminal Pub, offering an express breakfast plus regional specialties throughout the day. The Mangostin Asia Restaurant featuring Thai, Chinese, and Japanese cooking; and the Klimt Bar, open daily from 9am to 2am, is one of the few bars left in Vienna that has live music.

Amenities: 24-hour room service, laundry, baby-sitting, health club with sauna, business center, conference rooms, secretarial services, shopping boutique.

EXPENSIVE

Renaissance Penta Vienna Hotel. Ungargasse 60, A-1030 Vienna. ☎ **01/711750.** Fax 01/711-75-90. www.renaissancehotels.com/VIESE/. E-mail: rhi.viese.sales@renaissancehotel.com. 342 units. A/C MINIBAR TV TEL. 2,200–3,000AS ($147.40–$201) double; from 5,700AS ($381.90) suite. AE, DC, MC, V. Parking 250AS ($16.75).Tram: D to Schloss Belvedere.

In the city's diplomatic quarter, close to the baroque Belvedere Palace, this 7-story hotel is a first-class property with an array of services and amenities. Once it was an imperial military riding school before its successful conversion into a hotel. South of Stadtpark, it is like an impressive Tudor-style castle from the mid-19th century to which a modern glass structure has been added. The lobby sets an elegant tone with its vaulted ceilings, contemporary sculpture, and marble pillars. There are many cozy nooks for retreating here, including a library. Guest rooms found in the hotel's newer building, are each furnished with a certain style and grace and such amenities as hair dryers, tiled bathrooms, and the like. Nonsmoking rooms are available.

Dining/Diversions: The elegant Borromaeus, with its scenic winter garden, offers a fine international cuisine prepared in a classical setting. For informal dining, continental dishes are served at the Arsenal, and the lobby bar is a desired rendezvous.

Amenities: Room service, concierge, airport shuttle, car-rental desk, in-room safes, laundry/valet, baby-sitting, health club, steam room, sauna, solarium, exercise room, Turkish bath, business center, indoor swimming pool.

MODERATE

Biedermeier Hotel. Landstrasser Hauptstrasse 28, A-1030 Vienna. ☎ **800/448/8355** in the U.S., or 01/716710. Fax 01/7167-1503. www.dorint.de/wien. E-mail: hotel.vienna@dorint. 203 units. MINIBAR TV TEL. 2,650AS ($177.55) double; 5,200AS ($348.40) suite. Rates include breakfast. AE, DC, MC, V. Parking 180AS ($12.05). U-Bahn: Rochusgasse.

This hotel was established in 1983 in a renovated late-19th-century apartment house. It boasts a clearly Biedermeier style in both the public areas and the bedrooms. Although the hotel is adjacent to the Wien Mitte bus station and has roaring traffic on all sides, most bedrooms overlook a pedestrian-only walkway lined with shops and cafes. Duvets cover the firm beds, and double-glazing keeps the noise level down. Bathrooms are small and tiled, with fake-marble counters, and hair dryers. On the premises are a formal restaurant, Zu den Deutschmeistern, plus

Vienna Accommodations

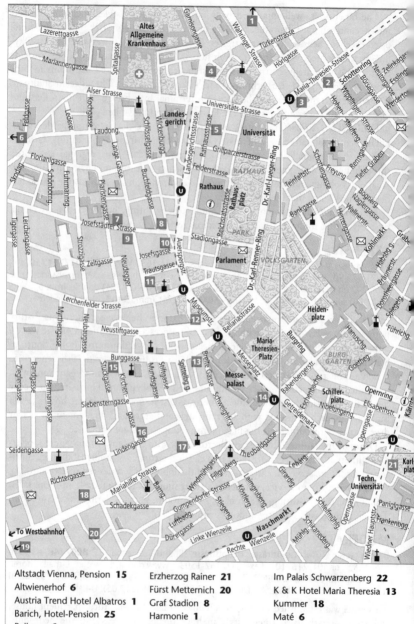

Altstadt Vienna, Pension **15**
Altwienerhof **6**
Austria Trend Hotel Albatros **1**
Barich, Hotel-Pension **25**
Bellevue **1**
Biedermeier **26**
Cordial Theaterhotel Wien **7**
De France **3**

Erzherzog Rainer **21**
Fürst Metternich **20**
Graf Stadion **8**
Harmonie **1**
Hilton International
Vienna Plaza **2**
Hotel-Pension-Museum **12**
Ibis Wien **17**

Im Palais Schwarzenberg **22**
K & K Hotel Maria Theresia **13**
Kummer **18**
Maté **6**
Mercure Josefshof **10**
Novotel Wien Airport **24**
Parkhotel Schönbrunn **19**
President **19**

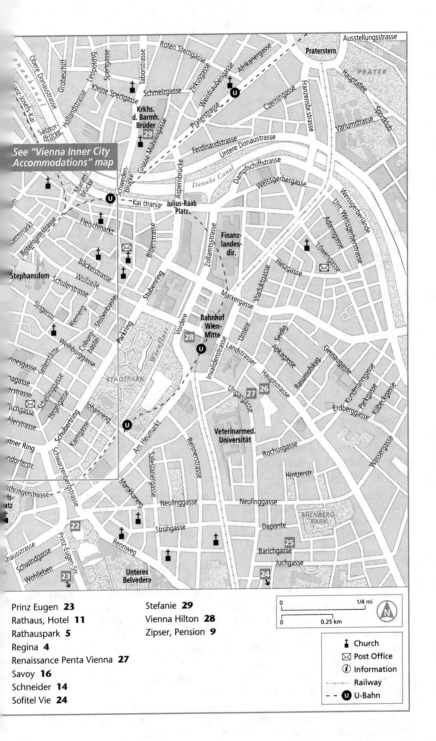

Prinz Eugen **23**
Rathaus, Hotel **11**
Rathauspark **5**
Regina **4**
Renaissance Penta Vienna **27**
Savoy **16**
Schneider **14**
Sofitel Vie **24**

Stefanie **29**
Vienna Hilton **28**
Zipser, Pension **9**

0		1/4 mi
0	0.25 km	

✝	Church
✉	Post Office
ⓘ	Information
⋯⋯	Railway
– – Ⓤ	U-Bahn

the simpler Weissgerberstube. Both are open daily for lunch and dinner. There's also a bar and a cafe terrace overlooking a small garden. Other than that, the hotel has few facilities.

Hotel-Pension Barich. Barichgasse 3, A-1030 Vienna. ☎ **01/712-2275.** Fax 01/7122-27588. www.nethotels.com/barich. E-mail: barich@netway.at. 17 units. MINIBAR TV TEL. 1,380–1,790AS ($92.45–$119.95) double; 2,990AS ($200.35) apt for 5. Rates include buffet breakfast. MC, V. Parking 225AS ($15.10). U-Bahn: Rochusgasse. Bus: 74A.

This spot might be the choice for guests who prefer serene residential surroundings. Northeast of the Südbahnhof, behind an unpretentious facade, this small hotel is quiet and well furnished. The proprietors, Ulrich and Hermine Platz, speak fluent English. All the small bedrooms are soundproofed and have radios, good mattresses, cable TV with CNN, hair dryers, electric trouser presses, tiled bathrooms that are rather tiny, and safes.

4 Wieden & Margareten (4th & 5th Districts)

MODERATE

Hotel Erzherzog Rainer. Wiedner Hauptstrasse 27-29, A-1040 Vienna. ☎ **01/5011-1316.** Fax 01/5011-1350. E-mail: rainer@schick-hotels.com. 84 units. MINIBAR TV TEL. 1,680–2,420AS ($112.55–$162.15) double. Rates include breakfast. AE, MC, V. Parking 220AS ($14.75). U-Bahn: Taubstummengasse.

Popular with groups and business travelers, this 4-star, family-run hotel was built just before World War I and was gradually renovated, room by room, between 1992 and 1994. It's only 5 minutes by foot to the State Opera and Kärntnerstrasse, with a U-Bahn stop just steps away. The bedrooms are well decorated, but come in a variety of sizes; you'll find radios and good beds, but not soundproofing, in all. Bathrooms are tiled and small. Forty rooms contain hair dryers. The singles are impossibly small; on certain days air-conditioning is sorely missed.

An informal brasserie serves Austrian specialties, and the cozy bar is modishly decorated with black and brass. A booking service for opera and theater tickets operates out of the lobby. Other convenient services include 10-hour dry cleaning, babysitting, a car-rental desk, and a helpful concierge.

Hotel Prinz Eugen. Wiedner Gürtel 14, A-1040 Vienna. ☎ **01/505-1741.** Fax 01/5051-74119. www.austria-hotels.co.at. E-mail: prinzeugen@austria-hotels.co.at. 114 units. MINIBAR TV TEL. 2,800AS ($187.60) double or suite. Rates include breakfast. AE, DC, DISC, MC, V. Parking 230AS ($15.40). U-Bahn: Südtiroler Platz or Südbahnhof.

In a section of Vienna favored by diplomats, this hotel is immediately opposite the Belvedere Palace and the Südbahnhof rail station. Subways will carry you quickly to the center of Vienna, and there are good highway connections as well. The hotel was renovated between 1992 and 1996 and has soundproof windows opening onto private balconies. The decor is a mixture of antiques, Oriental rugs, and some glitzy touches like glass walls with brass trim. Suites are nothing more than slightly larger double rooms with an additional bathroom. Bedrooms come in a wide range of sizes, although all are comfortable with firm, duvet-covered beds. Most rooms have safes and trouser presses. Bathrooms, only fair in size, have hair dryers and are well maintained, although 50 rooms have showers only (no tubs). The single accommodations, however, are decidedly small, suitable for one traveling light.

The hotel does not have a restaurant; however, a full breakfast is served each morning, and simple room service is available. There is a cozy, wood-paneled bar, as well. Amenities include room service, baby-sitting, and laundry service.

Family-Friendly Accommodations

- **Hotel Kärntnerhof** *(see page 57)* A family-oriented *Gutbürgerlich* hotel, this establishment lies right in the center of Vienna, and its helpful management welcomes kids.
- **Hotel Graf Stadion** *(see page 69)* Many of the rooms at this hotel—a long-time favorite of families on a tight budget—contain two double beds, suitable for parties of three or four.
- **Hotel Römischer Kaiser** *(see page 53)* The former palace of the imperial chamberlain, this Best Western affiliate offers a glimpse of Imperial Vienna from around 1684. Its staff is extremely hospitable and gracious to visiting families.
- **Hotel Schneider** *(see page 66)* Set between the State Opera and the flower market, this is one of Vienna's better small hotels. Families can rent rooms with kitchenettes to cut down on the high cost of dining in Vienna.

5 Mariahilf (6th District)

MODERATE

Fürst Metternich Hotel. Esterházygasse 33, A-1060 Vienna. ☎ **01/588-70.** Fax 01/ 58-75-268. E-mail: metternich@austrotel.at. 55 units. MINIBAR TV TEL. 1,810AS ($121.25) double. Rates include breakfast. AE, DC, MC, V. Parking 190AS ($12.75). U-Bahn: Zieplergasse.

Pink and gray paint and ornate stone window trim identify this solidly built 19th-century hotel, formally an opulent private home. It's located between the Ring and the Westbahnhof near Mariahilferstrasse, about a 20-minute walk from the cathedral. Many of the grander architectural elements were retained, including a pair of red stone columns in the entranceway and an old-fashioned staircase guarded with griffins. The high-ceilinged bedrooms have a neutral decor, with laminated furnishings, feather pillows, and duvets covering firm mattresses. Bathrooms are partly marbled with modern fixtures and tub baths. They aren't generally roomy, however. Windows in the front units are soundproof in theory, but not in practice. If you want a more tranquil night's sleep, opt for a room in the rear. The Barfly's Club, a popular hangout, is open daily from 6pm to 2am, offering 120 different exotic drinks.

Hotel Kummer. Mariahilferstrasse 71A, A-1060 Vienna. ☎ **01/58895.** Fax 01/587-8133. E-mail: kummer@austria-hotels.co.at. 100 units. MINIBAR TV TEL. 1,810AS ($121.25) double. Rates include buffet breakfast. AE, DC, MC, V. Parking 240AS ($16.10). U-Bahn: Neubaugasse. Bus: 13A or 14A.

Established by the Kummer family in the 19th century, this hotel was built in response to the growing power of the railways as they forged new paths of commerce and tourism through central Europe. A short walk from Vienna's Westbahnhof, the hotel sits in a busy, noisy location, but looks as ornamental as any public monument constructed during those imperial days. The facade is richly embellished with Corinthian capitals on acanthus-leaf bases, urn-shaped balustrades, and representations of four heroic demigods staring down from under the building's eaves. The hotel was restored and renovated in 1994.

The modern public rooms inside are not as delightful as the building's exterior, but they are satisfactory. The bedrooms have soundproof windows and often come with stone balconies. Not all rooms are alike—some feature superior appointments and deluxe furnishings. If possible, opt for a corner room—they are better lit and more spacious. Tiled bathrooms contain tubs in about half the accommodations (otherwise showers), along with hair dryers and vanity mirrors. Some of the singles are so small and dimly lit they aren't recommendable. The hotel contains a restaurant and bar and provides room service, laundry, and baby-sitting.

Hotel President. Wallgasse 23, A-1060 Vienna. ☎ **800/387-8842** or 01/59990. Fax 01/596-7646. 77 units. A/C MINIBAR TV TEL. 2,200AS ($147.40) double; 2,800AS ($187.60) suite. Rates include buffet breakfast. AE, DC, MC, V. Parking 200AS ($13.40). U-Bahn: Gumpendorfer. Bus: 57A.

This 7-story concrete-and-glass hotel was designed in 1975 with enough angles in its facade to give each bedroom an irregular shape. Usually the units have two windows that face different skylines. Aside from the views, each of the decent-size bedrooms has comfortable furnishings, good beds, a radio, and a mini-safe. Bathrooms, though small, are well maintained and brightly lit. Opt for a room—really a studio with a terrace—on the 7th floor, if one is available. The hotel also has a public rooftop terrace where guests sip drinks in summer. The Restaurant Casserole serves above-average Viennese and international cuisine in an informal setting every night until 11pm. Room service, baby-sitting, and laundry are provided.

INEXPENSIVE

✪ **Hotel Schneider.** Getreidemarkt 5, A-1060 Vienna. ☎ **01/588380.** Fax 01/5883-8212. www.best-of-austria.com/hotel/schneider. E-mail: hotel-schneider@netway.at. 70 units. MINIBAR TV TEL. 1,720–2,200AS ($115.25–$147.40) double. Rates include buffet breakfast. AE, DC, MC, V. Parking 250AS ($16.75). U-Bahn: Karlsplatz.

Sitting at the corner of a well-known street, Lehargasse, this hotel is in the center of Vienna between the State Opera and the famous Nasch Market. It's a modern 5-story building with panoramic windows on the ground floor and a red-tile roof. The interior is warmly decorated with some 19th-century antiques and comfortably upholstered chairs. Musicians, singers, actors, and other artists form part of a loyal clientele. This is one of Vienna's better small hotels; families are especially fond of the place as 35 of the accommodations contain kitchenettes. All the small units have cable TV, and some are air-conditioned. Most of the units are at the lower end of the price scale, which barely keeps this hotel in the inexpensive category—that's inexpensive in terms of Vienna.

6 Neubau (7th District)

MODERATE

K + K Hotel Maria Theresia. Kirchberggasse 6-8, A-1070 Vienna. ☎ **800/767-1664** in the U.S., or 01/52123. Fax 01/521-2370. www.kkhotels.com. 123 units. MINIBAR TV TEL. 2,620AS ($175.55) double; 3,020AS ($202.35) suite. Rates include breakfast. AE, DC, MC, V. Parking 140AS ($9.40). U-Bahn: Volkstheater. Bus: 48.

The hotel's initials are a reminder of the empire's dual monarchy (*Kaiserlich und Königlich*—"by appointment to the Emperor of Austria and King of Hungary"). Even the surrounding neighborhood, home to some major museums that lie just outside the Ring, is reminiscent of the days of Empress Maria Theresa. The hotel is in the artists' colony of Spittelberg, within walking distance of the Winter Palace gardens, the Volkstheater, and the famous shopping street Mariahilferstrasse. The hotel, built in the late

1980s, offers amply sized contemporary rooms. The beds (usually twins) are comfortable, and the medium-size bathrooms are attractively tiled.

Its restaurant, Maria Theresia, serves standard continental cuisine, with some regional specialties for variety. Amenities include room service (6:30am to 11pm), dry cleaning and laundry services, and baby-sitting; car-rental and tour desks are also available.

✪ **Pension Altstadt Vienna.** Kirchengasse 41, A-1070 Vienna. ☎ **01/1526-3399.** Fax 01/523-4901. E-mail: hotel@altstadt.at. 28 units. MINIBAR TV TEL. 1,680–1,880AS ($112.55–$125.95) double; 2,180AS ($146.05) suite. AE, DC, MC, V. No parking. U-Bahn: Volkstheater.

A noted connoisseur of modern art, Otto Wiesenthal, converted a century-old private home into this charming and stylish hotel in the mid-1990s. Otto comes from a long line of artists. Grandmother Greta was an avant-garde opera dancer in the 1930s and 1940s and the duenna of a salon frequented by artists and writers. Works by Mr. Wiesenthal's great-great-grandfather Friedrich hang in the Vienna Historic Museum as well as the hotel. Although part of the structure remains a private home, the remainder of the building contains a series of comfortable and cozy bedrooms. Each is outfitted with a different color scheme and contains at least one work of contemporary art, usually by an Austrian painter. Many of the good-size units are a bit quirky in decor, as exemplified by a club chair in leopard prints set against a sponge-painted wall. Nearly all have high ceilings, antiques, parquet floors, double-glazing, and good beds with firm mattresses. The white-tiled bathrooms are medium size, with hair dryers, a second phone, and decent shelf space. About half of the accommodations contain a shower instead of a tub. There's no restaurant on the premises (breakfast is the only meal served), but in view of the dozens of nearby restaurants within the immediate neighborhood, no one seems to mind.

INEXPENSIVE

Hotel Ibis Wien. Mariahilfer Gurtel 22, 1060 Vienna. ☎ **01/599-98.** Fax 01/597-9090. www.hotels-austria.com/Vienna-Westbahnhof/ibis-wien.htm. E-mail: mariahilf@hotel-ibis.co.at. 341 units. A/C MINIBAR TV TEL. 1,090AS ($73.05) double. Parking 130AS ($8.70). U-Bahn: Gumpendorfer.

If you'd like a reasonably priced choice near the Westbahnhof, the main rail station, this is one of your best bets. The station itself is about an eight-minute walk away. Although this is a chain, and its units are no better than a good motel in the United States, for Vienna the price is right. Behind a graceless facade that looks like a small-town department store, the Ibis Wien offers modern comforts. The furnishings, though well maintained, may not always be tasteful. One guest called the upholstery "psychedelic." The bedrooms are bland but snug and inviting with streamlined furnishings and small but tidy private bathrooms. The roof terrace provides a panoramic view of Vienna. Groups are booked in here, and you'll meet all of them in the impersonal restaurant, where reasonably priced meals and wine are served. The bar is a place for a drink—nothing more. Some accommodations are suitable for persons with disabilities, and others are reserved for nonsmokers. Breakfast is served nonstop for 8 hours every day. Room service and baby-sitting, along with laundry, are other amenities.

Hotel-Pension Museum. Museumstrasse 3, A-1070 Vienna. ☎ **01/5234-4260.** Fax 01/5234-42630. www.tiscover.com/hotel.museum. E-mail: Hotel.Museum@surfeu.at. 15 units. TV TEL. 1,450AS ($97.15) double. Rates include breakfast. AE, DC, MC, V. Parking 150AS ($10.05). U-Bahn: Volkstheater.

This hotel was originally built in the 17th century as the home of an aristocratic family. But its exterior was transformed around 1890 into the elegant art nouveau facade it has today. It's across from the Imperial Museums, and there are plenty of palaces, museums, and monuments nearby to keep you busy for days. Bedrooms come in a wide variety of sizes; some are spacious, others a bit cramped. Some of the mattresses have been renewed; some had been slept on by too many guests long before your arrival. Bathrooms are small but tiled, with not much counter space. However, for Vienna the price is right, and this place has its devotees.

Hotel Savoy. Lindengasse 12, A-1070 Vienna. ☎ **01/523-4640.** Fax 01/934640. 42 units. MINIBAR TV TEL. 1,280–1,680AS ($85.75–$112.55) double. Rates include breakfast. AE, DC, MC, V. Free parking. U-Bahn: Neubaugasse.

Built in the 1960s, this well-managed hotel rises 6 stories above one of Vienna's busiest wholesale and retail shopping districts. Within walking distance of Ringstrasse, opposite a recently built station for the city's newest U-Bahn line (the U3), the hotel prides itself on tastefully decorated units with good beds to make you feel at home and get a comfortable night's sleep. Bathrooms are small but tiled. Most units offer picture-window views of the neighborhood. Although the only meal served in the hotel is breakfast, there are dozens of places to eat in the neighborhood.

7 Josefstadt (8th District)

MODERATE

Cordial Theaterhotel Wien. Josefstadter Strasse 22, A-1080 Vienna. ☎ **01/405-3648.** Fax 01/405-1406. www.cordial.co.at/indexns.htm. E-mail: chwien@cordial.co.at. 54 units. MINIBAR TV TEL. 2,070–2,510AS ($138.70–$168.15) double; 2,700–3,400AS ($180.90–$227.80) suite. Rates include breakfast. AE, DC, MC, V. Parking 180AS ($12.05). U-Bahn: Rathaus.

This hotel was created from a 19th-century core that was radically modernized in the late 1980s. Today it's a favorite of Austrian business travelers, who profit from the hotel's proximity to the city's wholesale buying outlets. Each simply furnished room contains its own small but efficient kitchenette, which allows guests to save on restaurant bills. Bedrooms, in a variety of sizes, are well maintained with good beds, plus adequate tiled bathrooms. In addition to a cafe, the hotel maintains a popular bar and restaurant, the Theater-Restaurant, which is especially busy before and after performances next door. Amenities include 24-hour concierge, 15-hour room service, dry cleaning and laundry service, baby-sitting, conference rooms, sauna, and car-rental and tour desks.

Rathauspark Hotel. Rathausstrasse 17, A-1010 Vienna. ☎ **01/404-120.** Fax 01/404-12-761. www.tourist-net.co.at/hotel/austrotel/rathauspark/. E-mail: rathauspark@austria-trend.at. 117 units. A/C MINIBAR TV TEL. 2,300AS ($154.10) double; 2,600AS ($174.20) triple; 2,800AS ($187.60) suite. AE, DC, MC, V. Rates include buffet breakfast. No parking. U-Bahn: Rathaus.

A 5-minute walk from the city center, this 4-star hotel stands behind an elaborate wedding cake facade, installed in an old palace dating back to 1880. The interior doesn't quite live up to the promise of the exterior, but the hotel does tastefully combine the old with the new. Guest rooms vary in size from average to spacious, and all have been updated with contemporary furnishings. Each room has a hair dryer and trouser press. There's a cozy international bar. Only a buffet breakfast is offered, but there are many dining choices nearby.

INEXPENSIVE

Hotel Graf Stadion. Buchfeldgasse 5, A-1080 Vienna. ☎ **01/405-5284.** Fax 01/4050-111. www.graf-stadion.com. E-mail:hotel@graf-stadion.com. 40 units. TV TEL. 1,380AS ($92.45) double; 1,580AS ($105.85) triple; 1,780AS ($119.25) quad. Rates include buffet breakfast. AE, DC, MC, V. Parking 150AS ($10.05). U-Bahn: Rathaus.

This is one of the few genuine Biedermeier-style hotels left in Vienna. It's right behind the Rathaus, a 10-minute walk from most of the central monuments. The facade evokes the building's early 19th-century elegance, with triangular or half-rounded ornamentation above many of the windows. The bedrooms have been refurbished and are comfortably old-fashioned, although you might find the bedding too firm. Bathrooms are small but kept sparklingly clean.

Hotel Rathaus. Lange Gasse 13, A-1080 Vienna. ☎ **01/406-4302.** Fax 01/408-4272. 40 units, 36 with bathroom. TV TEL. 1,150AS ($77.05) double with bathroom. Rates include breakfast. AE, DC, MC, V. Parking 170AS ($11.40). U-Bahn: Lerchenfelderstrasse. Bus: 13.

Located behind a wrought-iron gate, the Hotel Rathaus offers small bedrooms that are simple and functional. Beds are decent, but if you require a firm mattress you might want to book elsewhere. Bathrooms are just adequate, definitely designed for one person at a time; some of the singles lack bathrooms. This is a no-frills place, but because it's so well situated near the university and Parliament, and because its prices are so reasonable, we consider it a worthy choice.

Pension Zipser. Lange Gasse 49, A-1080 Vienna. ☎ **01/404540.** Fax 01/404-5413. www.nethotels.com/zipser. E-mail: zipser@netway.at. 47 units. TV TEL. 1,320–1,480AS ($88.45–$99.15) double. Rates include breakfast. AE, DC, MC, V. Parking 200AS ($13.40). U-Bahn: Rathaus. Bus: 13A.

A 5-minute walk from the Rathaus, this pension offers rooms with wall-to-wall carpeting and central heating, many overlooking a private garden. Much of the renovated interior is tastefully adorned with wood detailing. Generous-size bedrooms are furnished in a functional, modern style, with some opening onto balconies above the garden. Bathrooms are small, but housekeeping rates high marks.

8 Alsergrund (9th District)

MODERATE

Austria Trend Hotel Albatros. Liechtensteinstrasse 89, A-1090 Vienna. ☎ **01/317-35-08.** Fax 01/317-35-08-85. www.hotels-austria.com/Vienna-josefstadt/albatros.htm. E-mail: albatros@austria-trend.at. 70 units. A/C MINIBAR TV TEL. 1,840AS ($123.30) double. Rates include breakfast. AE, DC, MC, V. Parking: 150AS ($10.05). U-Bahn: Friedensbrücke.

A 10-minute ride from the center, this 4-star choice is dull on the outside but lively inside. The well-furnished bedrooms were completely renovated in 1998. Bedrooms are medium in size, with comfortable upholstery and quality mattresses, along with small but efficient bathrooms with hair dryers. The hotel also offers a recreation area with sauna, steam bath, and solarium, as well as a cozy lobby bar. Start the day in the inviting breakfast room where delicious Viennese coffee is served 24 hours a day.

Harmonie. Harmoiegasse 5-7, A-1090 Vienna. ☎ **800/780-7234** in the U.S., or 01/317-66-040. Fax 01/317-66-04-55. www.webtourist.ch/travel/europe/austria/vienna/bestwesternharmonie.htm. E-mail: hotel-harmonie@telenetz.com. 126 units. MINIBAR TV TEL. 1,450–2,100AS ($97.15–$140.70) double; 2,000–2,550AS ($134–$170.85) triple. AE, DC, MC, V. Parking 150AS ($10.05). Tram: D to Schlickgasse.

Although it's beginning to show its age and some areas could use some sprucing up, the hotel enjoys a tranquil setting near the university. Sigmund Freud trod these same streets, and his office and famous couch were nearby. A vine-covered rowhouse, this 4-star hotel is part of the Best Western chain. A dusty orange marble coats the lobby crowned by a sculptured ceiling. Most rooms are small to medium in size but are tidily maintained and furnished like a home. Ask for one of the more gracious and slightly larger rooms in the rear. A few rooms come only with shower (no bathtub). A paneled restaurant serves both a buffet breakfast and standard Austrian meals at other times of day.

Hotel Bellevue. Althanstrasse 5, A-1091 Vienna. ☎ **01/31348.** Fax 01/3134-8801. E-mail: bellevue@austria-hotels.co.at. 173 units. MINIBAR TV TEL. 1,810–2,400AS ($121.25–$160.80) double; 2,800–3,600AS ($187.60–$241.20) suite. Rates include breakfast. AE, DC, MC, V. Parking 100AS ($6.70). U-Bahn: Friedensbrücke. Tram: 5 or D.

This hotel, with its ornate sandstone facade and Italianate embellishments, was built in 1873, at about the same time as the Franz-Josefs Bahnhof, which lies a short walk away and whose passengers it was designed to house. Its wedge-shaped position on the acute angle of a busy street corner is similar to the Flatiron Building in Manhattan.

Most of the antique details have been stripped from the public rooms, leaving a clean series of lines and a limited handful of antiques. At least 100 of the hotel's bedrooms are in a new wing added in 1982. All bedrooms are clean, functional, and well maintained. Rooms are decorated in monochromatic color schemes of brown or blue and contain comfortable low beds and utilitarian desks and chairs. Bathrooms are of medium size. Facilities include laundry, baby-sitting, and room service. The hotel maintains its own restaurant and cafe, serving standard Viennese and international cuisine.

Hotel Mercure Josefshof. Josefsgasse 4, A-1090 Vienna. ☎ **01/404-190.** Fax 01/ 404-191-50. www.llmembver_members.chello.at/hotel.josefshof.gmbh/intro-e.htm. E-mail: johof@netway.at. 48 units. A/C MINIBAR TV TEL. 1,680–2,270AS ($112.55–$152.10) double; 1,900–2,690AS ($127.30–$180.25) suite. AE, DC, MC, V. U-Bahn: Rathaus.

Close to the Parliament and next to the English Theater, this Biedermeier mansion is located down a narrow cobblestone street. The hotel's gilded touches include a baroque lobby with marble checkerboard floors and a lounge brimming with antiques. Standard-size bedrooms have double-glazed windows, and a few accommodations come with kitchenettes, great for families. The corner rooms are the most spacious; bathrooms are small, however, and a dozen come with showers (no tubs). Several rooms are suitable for persons with disabilities. A lavish breakfast buffet is served in the morning and can be enjoyed in summer in an inner courtyard with plants and flowers. Room service is also available until midnight. There's also a solarium and sauna.

Hotel Regina. Rooseveltplatz 15, A-1090 Vienna. ☎ **01/404460.** Fax 01/408-8392. 135 units. MINIBAR TV TEL. 2,000AS ($134) double. Rates include breakfast. AE, DC, MC, V. Parking 260AS ($17.40). U-Bahn: Schottenring. Tram: 1, 2, 38, 40, or 41.

Established in 1896 near the Votive Church, this hotel has a structure that every Viennese would instantly recognize—the "Ringstrasse" style. The facade is appropriately grand, reminiscent of a French Renaissance palace. The tree-lined street is usually calm, especially at night. The Regina is an Old World hotel with red salons and interminable corridors. Bedrooms are well maintained and traditionally furnished, some with half-canopied beds and elaborate furnishings. Despite variation in style and size, all have comfortable beds and small, well-maintained bathrooms. The Regina was fully renovated in 1993. There's a restaurant, a cafe, and a bar on-site.

9 Near Schönbrunn

EXPENSIVE

✪ **Parkhotel Schönbrunn.** Hietzinger Hauptstrasse 10-20, A-1131 Vienna. ☎ **01/ 87804.** Fax 01/8780-43220. www.austria-trend.at. E-mail: parkhotel.schoenbrunn@austria-trend.at. 399 units. MINIBAR TV TEL. 1,900–2,800AS ($127.30–$187.60) double; 3,500AS ($234.50) suite. Rates include breakfast. AE, DC, JCB, MC, V. Parking 200AS ($13.40). U-Bahn: Hietzing. Tram: 58 or 60.

Called the "guest house of the kaisers," this 4-star hotel—1½ miles from the Westbahnhof, 3 miles from the City Air Terminal—is today part of the Steigenberger reservations system. It has had a long history since Franz Joseph I ordered its construction in 1907. The first performances of *Loreleyklänge* by Johann Strauss, and of *Die Schönbrunner,* the famous Josef Lanner waltz, took place here. During its heyday, guests ranged from Thomas Edison to Walt Disney.

Today the hotel complex is modern and updated. The original part of the building is used for public rooms, which have lost some of their past elegant. Contemporary wings and annexes include the Stöckl, Residenz, and Maximilian (which has the most boring and cramped rooms), together with a villa formerly inhabited by Van Swieten, the personal doctor of Empress Maria Theresa. Rooms are generally spacious and well appointed, and all accommodations have good beds. The well-furnished guest rooms are done in a variety of styles ranging from classical to modern. Each accommodation is equipped with a small private bathroom, radio, and TV/VCR. Opposite the magical Schönbrunn Castle and its park, the hotel is only a 10-minute tram ride from the Inner City.

Dining/Diversions: Inside is a coffeehouse, along with a series of lavishly outfitted public salons. The Jagerstubl is traditionally decorated in forest colors. There's also a French restaurant, plus a winter-garden restaurant, a gypsy tavern, and two bars.

Amenities: Room service, laundry, baby-sitting, pool, fitness center, sauna, solarium.

INEXPENSIVE

✪ **Altwienerhof.** Herklotzgasse 6, A-1150 Vienna. ☎ **01/892-6000.** Fax 01/ 892-60-00-8. www.altwienerhof.at. E-mail: altwienerhof@netwav.at. 27 units. TV TEL. 1,200AS ($80.40) double; 1,800AS ($120.60) suite. Rates include breakfast. AE, DC, MC, V. Parking 150AS ($10.05). U-Bahn: Gumpendorferstrasse. Tram: 6, 8, or 18.

This is mainly a highly acclaimed restaurant, one of the finest and most expensive in the city. But it's also a reasonably priced hotel, with traditionally furnished bedrooms, many of which were renovated in 1993. Its Old World charm is carefully nurtured by the owners, Rudolf and Ursula Kellner, and their helpful and welcoming staff. Bedrooms are quite large, with good firm mattresses, along with luxurious bathrooms with separate toilets. Bathrooms are equipped with mirrors, hair dryers, towel warmers, double bathtubs, and showers with an aquamassage. (See chapter 5, "Where to Dine," for a complete description of the restaurant.)

10 Elsewhere in Vienna

INEXPENSIVE

Hotel Maté. Ottakringer Strasse 34-36, A-1170 Vienna. ☎ **01/404550.** Fax 01/ 4045-5888. 126 units. MINIBAR TV TEL. 1,680AS ($112.55) double; 1,980AS ($132.65) suite. Rates include breakfast. AE, DC, MC, V. Parking 100AS ($6.70). Tram: 44.

Built in 1973 by members of the Matejovsky family, this 7-story hotel has rows of decorative geometric designs along a streamlined facade. The handcrafted hardwood in the public rooms creates an unusual visual effect. There's a bar area lined with marble and an indoor swimming pool under a barrel vault roof. The bedrooms are cozy, with soundproof windows and comfortable beds. They benefit from a renovation completed in 1994. Bathrooms are adequate in size and tiled. The hotel is classified 4-star by the Austrian government, in spite of its relatively low prices.

A short walk from the hotel is a less expensive three-star hotel, **Maté Dependence,** Bergsteiggasse 22 (☎ **01/40466**), under the same management. It has 47 rooms, each with TV and telephone, and was built in the 1960s. Breakfast is the only meal served. A double costs 1,380AS ($92.45), including breakfast.

11 Airport Hotels

EXPENSIVE

Hotel Sofitel Vie. Flughafen Wien, A-1300 Vienna. ☎ **01/701-510.** Fax 01/706-2828. www.hotelsaustria.com/vienna/sofitel_vie/. E-mail: sofitel@atnet.at. 142 units. A/C MINIBAR TV TEL. 2,350–3,300AS ($157.45–$221.10) double; 4,500AS ($301.50) suite. AE, DC, MC, V. Free parking.

If you have an early morning flight, this 5-star hotel is your best bet at the airport. Directly opposite the arrivals and departure hall, it's a tasteful, comfortable stopover for those between flights or late arrivals. It's so close that you can walk right to the airport. Standard Sofitel comforts mean spacious, well-furnished, and sound-insulated bedrooms with either one king-size or two queen-size beds, plus well-equipped though small bathrooms with hair dryers. Some rooms are suitable for persons with disabilities, and others are set aside for nonsmokers.

Dining/Diversions: Both Italian specialties and an international menu are offered in Don Giovanni. The Leoporello Bar serves drinks both night and day.

Amenities: Room service, concierge, laundry/valet, baby-sitting, fitness club, sauna, solarium, steam room.

MODERATE

Novotel Wien Airport Hotel. Flughafen Wien, A-1300 Vienna. ☎ **01/70-107-0.** Fax 01/707-3239. www.novotel.at/adress.htm. E-mail: novotel@atnet.at. 183 units. 1,850–2,150AS ($123.95–$144.05) double. AE, DC, MC, V. Free parking.

Far less desirable than its more prestigious neighbor, the Sofitel, this is nevertheless a fine, convenient, reasonably priced alternative, right at the airport, next to the World Trade Center. This 5-story, standard chain hotel offers laminated furnishings, good beds, sofas that can convert to beds, soundproofing, and tiny bathrooms. Two of the floors are nonsmoking, and there are accommodations suitable for those with disabilities. Children are especially welcome, and B&B is free for 2 children under 16 years of age sharing a room with their parents. There is a standard restaurant and international bar, with room service offered daily from 5am to midnight.

5

Where to Dine

In Vienna, eating out is a local pastime. Besides Austrian and French cuisine, you'll find restaurants serving Serbian, Slovenian, Slovakian, Hungarian, and Czech food, along with Chinese, Italian, and Russian. Before dining out, refer to the section on Austrian cuisine, "A Taste of Vienna," in Appendix A.

Vienna's so-called Bermuda Triangle is a concentration of restaurants and bars a short walk north of Stephansplatz. This restaurant district is bordered by Schwedenplatz, Rotenturmstrassem, Hohermarkt, and Marcus Aurelius Strasse.

MEALS & DINING CUSTOMS Although Viennese meals are traditionally big and hearty, innovative chefs throughout the city are now turning out lighter versions of the old classics. Even so, the Viennese still love to eat, often as many as six times a day. Breakfast usually consists of bread with butter, jam, or cheese along with milk and coffee. Around 10am it's time for *Gabelfrühstück* (snack breakfast) when diners usually savor some type of meat, perhaps little finger sausages. Lunch at midday is normally a filling meal, and the afternoon *Jause* consists of coffee, open-face sandwiches, and the luscious pastries that the Viennese make so well. Dinners may also be hearty, although many locals prefer a light meal then.

Because Vienna cherishes its theaters, concert halls, and opera houses, many locals choose to dine after a performance. *Après-théâtre* is all the rage in this city, and many restaurants and cafes stay open late to cater to cultural buffs.

Unlike many Western European capitals, Vienna's restaurants still stick to Sunday closings (marked by SONNTAG RUHETAG signs). Also beware of those summer holiday closings, when chefs would rather rush to nearby lake resorts than cook for Vienna's tourist hordes. Sometimes vacation closings are announced only a week or two before the restaurant actually shuts down.

1 Restaurants by Cuisine

ASIAN
East-West (p. 81)

AUSTRIAN
Altes Jägerhaus (p. 87)
Altwienerhof (p. 93)
Augustinerkeller (p. 84)

Glacisbeisel (p. 91)
Griechenbeisl (p.81)
Gulaschmuseum (p. 85)
Hietzinger Brau (p. 94)
Hotel Astoria Restaurant
 (p. 82)
Kardos (p. 82)

Leupold's Kupferdachl (p. 79)
Motto (p. 89)
Palmenhaus (p. 83)
Piaristenkeller (p. 93)
Plutzer Bräu (p. 92)
Restaurant Salzamt (p. 86)
Sacher Hotel Restaurant (p. 78)
Sailer (p. 94)
Schlossgasse 21 (p. 89)
Steirereck (p. 88)
Wein-Comptoir (p. 83)
Zu Den 3 Hacken (p. 86)
Zum Kuchldragoner (p. 87)

BALKAN

Dubrovnik (p. 84)
Kardos (p. 82)

COFFEEHOUSES, TEAROOMS & CAFES

Café Central (p. 95)
Café Demel (p. 95)
Café Diglas (p. 95)
Café Dommayer (p. 95)
Café Frauenhuber (p. 96)
Café Imperial (p. 96)
Café Landtmann (p. 96)
Café Mozart (p. 96)
Café Sperl (p. 97)
Café Tirolerhof (p. 97)
Café/Restaurant Prückel (p. 97)
Demmer's Teehaus (p. 97)

CONTINENTAL

Dö & Co. (p. 79)
Blau Stern (p. 94)
Gasthaus Lux (p. 91)
Kunsthallenrestaurant (p. 85)
MAK Café (p. 82)

CROATIAN

Dubrovnik (p. 84)

DELI

Buffet Trzesniewski (p. 84)
Dö & Co. (p. 80)

FRENCH

Altwienerhof (p. 93)

GAME

Altes Jägerhaus (p. 87)
Sailer (p. 94)

HUNGARIAN

Alte Backstube (p. 92)
Gulaschmuseum (p. 85)
Kardos (p. 82)

INTERNATIONAL

Amerlingbeisl (p. 91)
Arcadia Restaurant (p. 88)
Bohème (p. 91)
Café Cuadro (p. 90)
Dö & Co. (p. 79)
Drei Husaren (p. 78)
Hansen (p. 85)
Hotel Astoria Restaurant (p. 82)
König von Ungarn (p. 75)
Korso bei Der Oper (p. 78)
Niky's Kuchlmasterei (p. 88)
Restaurant Taubenkobel (p. 94)
Sacher Hotel Restaurant (p. 78)
Schlossgasse 21 (p. 89)
Wiener Rathauskeller (p. 80)
Wein-Comptoir (p. 83)
Zum Finsteren Stern (p. 86)
Zum Schwarzen Kameel (p. 80)

ITALIAN

A Tavola (p. 84)
Cantinetta Antinori (p. 80)
Firenze Enoteca (p. 81)
Motto (p. 89)

MEDITERRANEAN

Hansen (p. 85)

RUSSIAN

Abend-Restaurant Feuervogel (p. 93)

SEAFOOD

Kervansaray und Hummer Bar (p. 75)

SLOVENIAN

Kardos (p. 82)

SOUTH AMERICAN

Taverna La Carabela/La Carabelita (p. 82)

THAI

Motto (p. 89)

VEGETARIAN
Siddhartha (p. 86)

VIENNESE
Alfi's Goldener Spiegel (p. 90)
Alte Backstube (p. 92)
Bohème (p. 91)
Drei Husaren (p. 78)
Dubrovnik (p. 84)
Glacisbeisel (p. 91)
Gösser Bierklinik (p. 85)
Hauswirth (p. 90)
König von Ungarn (p. 75)
Korso bei Der Oper (p. 78)
Leupold's Kupferdachl (p. 79)

Niky's Kuchlmasterei (p. 88)
Ofenloch (p. 83)
Plachutta (p. 79)
Raimundstüberl (p. 90
Restaurant at Palais Schwarzenberg
    (p. 87)
Sacher Hotel Restaurant (p. 78)
Sailer (p. 94)
Silberwirt (p. 89)
Steirereck (p. 88)
Wiener Rathauskeller (p. 80)
Zum Weissen Rauchfangkehrer
    (p. 83)
Zwölf-Apostelkeller (p. 87)

2 Innere Stadt (Inner City)

VERY EXPENSIVE

✪ **Kervansaray und Hummer Bar.** Mahlerstrasse 9. ☎ **01/512-8843.** Reservations recommended. Main courses 265–355AS ($17.75–$23.80). AE, DC, MC, V. Restaurant Mon–Sat noon–midnight. Bar Mon–Sat 6pm–midnight. U-Bahn: Karlsplatz. Tram: 1 or 2. Bus: 3A. SEAFOOD.

Here you'll sense the historic link between the Habsburgs and their 19th-century neighbor, the Ottoman Empire. This is actually a three-in-one place. In addition to the two restaurants, there's also a deli. The Kervansaray and the Hummer Bar (Lobster Bar) occupy two different floors, but each serves an array of delectable seafood flown in frequently from the North Sea or the Bosphorus.

On the ground floor, in the Kervansaray, polite waiters, many of whom are Turkish, announce a changing array of daily specials and serve tempting salads from a hors d'oeuvre table. Upstairs, guests enjoy the bounties of the sea at the Lobster Bar.

The menu has a short list of meat dishes like filet mignon with Roquefort sauce, but most main courses feature seafood, including grilled fillet of sole with fresh asparagus, Norwegian salmon with a horseradish and champagne sauce, and, of course, lobster. Appetizers include a lobster and salmon caviar cocktail. If shellfish is your weakness, tabs can run very high indeed.

König von Ungarn (King of Hungary). Schulerstrasse 10. ☎ **01/512-5319.** Reservations required. Main courses 190–320AS ($12.75–$21.45); fixed-price menu 390AS ($26.15) at lunch, 490AS ($32.85) at dinner. AE, DC, MC, V. Mon–Fri noon–2:30pm and 6–10:30pm. U-Bahn: Stephansplatz. Bus: 1A. VIENNESE/INTERNATIONAL.

Housed in the famous hotel of the same name, this restaurant offers a rich atmosphere with crystal chandeliers, antiques, marble columns, and vaulted ceilings. The service here is superb and the menu appealing. If you're unsure of what to order, try the *tafelspitz*, a savory boiled-beef specialty, elegantly dispensed from a trolley. Other choices, which change seasonally, include a ragoût of seafood with fresh mushrooms, tournedos of beef with a mustard-and-horseradish sauce, and an array of appetizers like scampi in caviar sauce. Chefs balance flavors, textures, and colors to create a meal long favored by locals, who often bring out-of-town guests here.

Vienna Dining

Abend-Restaurant
  Feuervogel **18**
A Tavola **44**
Alfi's Goldener Spiegel **2**
Altes Jägerhaus **38**
Arcadia **37**
Augustinerkeller **48**
Amerlingbeisl **4**
Bohéme **5**
Buffet Trzesniewski **33**
Café Central **11**
Café Cuadro **4**
Café Demel **13**
Café Diglas **29**
Café Frauenhuber **46**
Café Imperial **56**
Café Landtmann **8**
Café Mozart **49**
Café Sperl **3**
Café Tirolerhof **51**
Café/Restaurant Prückel **25**
Cantinetta Antinori **31**
Demmer's Teehaus **9**
Dö & Co. **32**
Dö & Co. (deli) **54**
Drei Husaren **45**
Dubrovnik **47**
East-West **41**
Firenze Enoteca **43**
Gasthaus Lux **4**
Glacisbeisl **6**
Gösser Bierklinik **15**
Griechenbeisl **26**
Gulaschmuseum **40**
Hansen **17**
Hauswirth **4**
Hotel Astoria Restaurant **50**
Kardos **35**
Kervansary und
  Hummer Bar **55**
König von Ungarn **34**
Korso bei der Oper **53**
Kunsthallenrestaurant **1**
Leupold's Kupferdachl **10**
MAK Café **36**
Motto **4**
Niky's Kuchlmasterei **24**
Ofenloch **16**
Palmenhaus **12**
Plachutta **39**
Plutzer Braü **4**
Raimundstüberl **4**
Restaurant at Palais
  Schwarzenberg **57**
Restaurant Salzamt **20**
Sacher Hotel Restaurant **52**
Schlossgasse 21 **4**
Siddhartha **28**

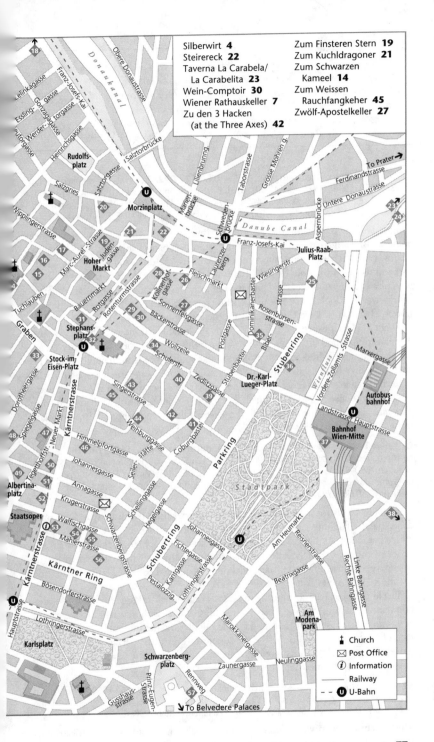

Silberwirt **4**
Steirereck **22**
Taverna La Carabela/
La Carabelita **23**
Wein-Comptoir **30**
Wiener Rathauskeller **7**
Zu den 3 Hacken
(at the Three Axes) **42**

Zum Finsteren Stern **19**
Zum Kuchldragoner **21**
Zum Schwarzen
Kameel **14**
Zum Weissen
Rauchfangkeher **45**
Zwölf-Apostelkeller **27**

Church
Post Office
Information
Railway
U-Bahn

Impressions

The people of Vienna are completely different from western and alpine Austrians, with a different set of morals and attitudes from the rest of the country. They regard their city as incomparable as indeed it is, after a fashion. No European capital has such a stately, imperial air . . . the double-headed eagle still broods overhead wherever you go and no other European capital has such delightful surroundings.
    —Richard Bassett, *The Austrians—Strange Tales from the Vienna Woods,* 1988

✪ **Drei Husaren.** Weihburggasse 4. ☎ **01/512-1092.** Reservations required. Main courses 250–500AS ($16.75–$33.50); menu dégustation (6 courses) 920AS ($61.65); 4-course fixed-price business lunch 440AS ($29.50). AE, DC, MC, V. Daily noon–3pm and 6pm–1am. Closed mid-July to mid-Aug. U-Bahn: Stephansplatz. VIENNESE/INTERNATIONAL.

This restaurant is an enduring favorite for inventive and classic Viennese cuisine. Some consider it as much an institution as St. Stephan's Cathedral, which looms nearby. Over the years it has entertained the famous (the duke and duchess of Windsor) and the not-so-famous. Just off Kärntnerstrasse, it has a large plate-glass window with plaster mannequins of the Hungarian officers who established the restaurant after World War I. A look inside reveals Gobelin tapestries, antiques, fine rugs, and lots of flowers. The owner, Uwe Kohl, is perhaps the most gracious host in Vienna.

Drei Huseran is expensive and select, with a delectable cuisine rated by most as the best traditional food in Vienna. Enjoy Gypsy melodies while you savor lobster-cream soup with tarragon, freshwater salmon with pike soufflé, or breast of guinea fowl. The chef specializes in veal, including his deliciously flavored *kalbsbrücken Metternich.* A renowned repertoire of more than 35 hors d'oeuvres is served from a roving trolley, but, if you choose to indulge, your bill is likely to double. Finish with the *Husaren pfannkuchen* (Hussar's pancake), or the cheese-filled crêpe topped with chocolate sauce, a secret recipe that's been a favorite since the 1960s.

✪ **Korso bei Der Oper.** In the Bristol Hotel, Kärntneering 1. ☎ **01/5151-6546.** Reservations required. Main courses 250–400AS ($16.75–$26.80); fixed-price menu 480AS ($32.15) at lunch, 890–940AS ($59.65–$63) at dinner. AE, DC, MC, V. Sun–Fri noon–2pm; daily 6–11pm. Closed 3 weeks in Aug and for Sun lunch in July. U-Bahn: Karlsplatz. Tram: 1 or 2. VIENNESE/INTERNATIONAL.

This citadel of gastronomic chic is decorated with expensive paneling, sparkling chandeliers, and—flanking either side of a baronial fireplace—two of the most breathtaking baroque columns in Vienna. Set in the elegant Bristol Hotel, the restaurant has its own entrance directly across from the State Opera, which helps explain its legendary clientele of opera stars, including the late Leonard Bernstein, Plácido Domingo, and Agnes Baltza.

The kitchen concocts an alluring mixture of traditional and modern cuisine for discriminating palates. Your meal may feature fillet of char with a sorrel sauce, saddle of veal with cèpe mushrooms and homemade noodles, or the inevitable *tafelspitz.* The rack of lamb is excellent, as are the medallions of beef with a shallot-flavored butter sauce and Roquefort-flavored noodles. The wine list here is extensive, and the service, as you'd expect, is impeccable.

✪ **Sacher Hotel Restaurant.** Philharmonikerstrasse 4. ☎ **01/514560.** Reservations required. Main courses 180–610AS ($12.05–$40.85). AE, DC, MC, V. Daily noon–3pm and 6–11:30pm. U-Bahn: Karlsplatz. AUSTRIAN/VIENNESE/INTERNATIONAL.

Most celebrities who visit Vienna eventually make their way to this scarlet dining room for the restaurant's most famous dish, *tafelspitz.* The chef at Sacher prepares the boiled beef with a savory, herb-flavored sauce that is truly fit for the emperor's table. Other delectable dishes include fish terrine and veal steak with morels. For dessert, the Sachertorte—a chocolate sponge cake that's sliced in half and filled with apricot jam—enjoys world renown. The most famous pastry in Vienna, the torte was supposedly created in 1832 by Franz Sacher while he served as Prince Metternich's apprentice.

Wear your finest dining attire, and make sure to show up before 11pm, even though the restaurant officially closes at 1am. The hotel does have tables in the adjoining and less formal Red Bar, where the menu is available every day from noon to 11:30pm (last order). The Sacher has always been a favorite for either before or after the opera.

EXPENSIVE

✪ **Dö & Co.** In the Haas & Haas, Stephansplatz 4. ☎ **01/512-26-66.** Reservations recommended. Main courses 255–285AS ($17.10–$19.10). V. Daily noon–3pm and 6pm–midnight. U-Bahn: Stephansplatz. CONTINENTAL/INTERNATIONAL.

Stylish, upscale, and rather expensive, this restaurant attracts a purely Viennese clientele and very few visitors. Perhaps this results from its inconvenient location on the 7th floor of one of central Europe's most controversial buildings, the aggressively ultramodern Haas Haus, which stands in jarring proximity to Vienna's cathedral. You'll navigate your way through somewhat claustrophobic passageways past a vigilant maître d'hotel, who will lead you to tables with views of an immaculate "showcase" kitchen on one side and the city's historic core on the other. The restaurant takes immense pride in the freshness of its meats, fish, and produce, some of which are displayed like valued art objects in glass cases. The menu changes with the season but is always esoteric, rare, and unusual. Examples include Uruguayan beef, Austrian venison, grilled baby turbot from the coast of Norway, deep-fried monkfish, and carpaccio Parmigiana, as well as such traditional Austrian specialties as *tafelspitz* and Wiener schnitzel. There's also a repertoire of Thai dishes, including crispy pork salad, red curried chicken, and sweet-and-sour red snapper. At the "wok buffet," you assemble the ingredients for your meal on a plate, then deliver it to a uniformed chef who will quick-sear it with whatever sauces you want.

Leupold's Kupferdachl. Schottengasse 7. ☎ **01/533-9381.** Reservations recommended. Main course 200–260AS ($13.40–$17.40). AE, DC, MC, V. Mon–Fri 10am–3pm; Mon–Sat 6pm–midnight. U-Bahn: Schottentor. Tram: 2, 43, or 44. VIENNESE/AUSTRIAN.

Run by the Leupold family since the 1950s, this eatery serves "new Austrian" cuisine, although the chef also prepares traditional dishes. The menu includes beef tenderloin (Old Viennese style) with dumplings boiled in a napkin, lamb loin breaded and served with potatoes, and chicken breast Kiev. The interior is both rustic and elegant, decorated with Oriental rugs and cozy banquettes with intricate straight-back chairs. Leupold also operates a beer pub with good music and better prices. The pub is open daily from 10am to midnight with main courses ranging from 40 to 175AS ($2.70 to $11.75).

✪ **Plachutta.** Wollzeile 10. ☎ **01/512-1577.** Reservations recommended. Main courses 200–500AS ($13.40–$33.50). DC, MC, V. Daily 11:30am–11:15pm. U-Bahn: Stubentor. VIENNESE.

Few restaurants have built such a fetish around one dish as Plachutta has done with *tafelspitz,* offering 10 different variations of the boiled beef dish that was the favorite of Emperor Franz Josef throughout his prolonged reign. The differences between the versions are a function of the cut of beef you request. We recommend *Schulterscherzel* (shoulder of beef) and *Beinfleisch* (shank of beef), but if you're in doubt, the waitstaff is endlessly knowledgeable about one of the most oft-debated subjects in Viennese cuisine. Hash brown potatoes, chives, and an appealing mixture of horseradish and chopped apples accompany each. There's more on the menu here than boiled beef. Other Viennese staples include goulash soup, grilled or sautéed fish, calves' liver, fried Viennese chicken, and braised pork with cabbage.

⭘ **Wiener Rathauskeller.** Rathausplatz 1. ☎ **01/4051-2190.** Reservations required. Main courses 250–450AS ($16.75–$30.15); Vienna music evening with dinner (Tues–Sat at 8pm) 450AS ($30.15). AE, DC, MC, V. Mon–Sat 11:30am–3pm and 6–11pm. U-Bahn: Rathaus. VIENNESE/INTERNATIONAL.

City halls throughout the Teutonic world have traditionally maintained restaurants in their basements, and Vienna is no exception. Although its famous Rathaus was built between 1871 and 1883, its cellar-level restaurant wasn't added until 1899. Today, in half a dozen richly atmospheric dining rooms, with high vaulted ceilings and stained-glass windows, you can enjoy good and reasonably priced food. The chef's specialty is a *Rathauskellerplatte* for two, consisting of various cuts of meat, including a veal schnitzel, lamb cutlets, and pork medallions. One section of the cellar is devoted every evening to a Viennese musical soirée beginning at 8pm. Live musicians ramble through the world of operetta, waltz, and *Schrammel* ("evergreen") music, as you dine.

Zum Schwarzen Kameel (Stiebitz). Bognergasse 5. ☎ **01/533-8125.** Main courses 160–350AS ($10.70–$23.45). AE, DC, MC, V. Mon–Fri 8:30am–3pm; Sat 8:30am–4pm; Mon–Sat 6–10:30pm. U-Bahn: Schottentor. Bus: 2A or 3A. INTERNATIONAL.

This restaurant has remained in the same family since 1618. A delicatessen against one of the walls sells wine, liquor, and specialty meat items, although most of the action takes place in the cafe. On a Saturday morning the cafe section is packed with chic weekend Viennese trying to recover from a late night. Uniformed waiters will bring you a beverage, and you can select open-face sandwiches from the trays on the black countertops. Beyond the cafe is a perfectly preserved art deco dining room with jeweled copper chandeliers hanging from beaded strings. The 11 tables are surrounded by polished paneling, yellowed ceramic tiles, and a dusky plaster ceiling frieze of grape leaves. The hearty and well-flavored cuisine features herring fillet Oslo, potato soup, tournedos, Roman *saltimbocca* (veal with ham), and an array of daily fish specials.

MODERATE

Cantinetta Antinori. 3–5 Jasomirgottstrasse. ☎ **01/533-7722.** Reservations required. Main courses 180–300AS ($12.05–$20.10). AE, DC, MC, V. Daily 11:30am–11pm. U-Bahn: Stephansplatz. ITALIAN.

This is one of three European restaurants established and maintained by the Antinori family, owners of sprawling and well-respected Tuscan vineyards whose name is nearly synonymous with Chianti. The traditions and aesthetics of the original in Florence were duplicated during the mid-1990s in both Zürich and Vienna as a means of show-casing Antinori wines and Tuscan cooking. Within a 140-year-old building overlook-ing the Stephansplatz and Vienna's cathedral, you'll find a high-ceilinged dining room, as well as a greenhouse-style "winter garden." Your meal might begin with a sophisti-cated medley of "antipasti tipico," including marinated vegetables and seafood. This might be followed by a drop-dead ravioli stuffed with porcini mushrooms and sum-mer truffles or perfectly grilled lamb with sun-dried tomatoes and Mediterranean herbs. A simple but flavorful dessert is *panna cotta,* a creamy flan. A huge selection of wines is served by the glass.

Dö & Co. Akademiestrasse 3. ☎ **01/512-6474.** Reservations recommended for one of the tables. Main courses 170–250AS ($11.40–$16.75). AE, DC, MC, V. Mon–Fri 10:30am–7:30pm; Sat 10am–6pm. U-Bahn: Karlsplatz. DELI.

Located next to the State Opera, this sophisticated delicatessen is connected by a corridor to the Kervansaray und Hummer Bar (see above). Sprawling glass display cases are filled with pâtés, seafood salads, quiches, Viennese pastries, and more. Try one of the three shrimp platters or a portion of Norwegian lobster Thermidor.

Customers can take their foodstuffs with them or sit at one of the tiny, somewhat cramped tables near the entrance. The place is likely to be packed, especially at lunchtime, with demanding gastronomes willing to sacrifice space and ambience for a taste of the good life.

East-West. Seilerstätte 14. ☎ **01/512-9149.** Reservations recommended. Main courses 129–280AS ($8.65–$18.75). AE, DC, MC, V. Daily 11:30am–2:30pm and 5:30–11pm. U-Bahn: Stephansplatz.ASIAN.

Opened in 1999, this is the first pan-Asian restaurant ever established within Vienna's Ring. As such, it's favored by business travelers interested in impressing their Asian clients with a place distinctly missing the prevalent sense of *Mittel-Europa*. In a streamlined, monochromatic, wood-trimmed design, East-West offers a sophisticated menu, which divides its food into dishes from North, South, West, and East Asia, as well as sections devoted to the mountains of Central Asia, plus traditional Chinese dishes well known to most Western diners. Unusual, relatively modern dishes include gingerpepper chicken in rice wine sauce; "Malaysian triangle" (three different preparations of pork in a satay sauce); glass noodles salad with cucumbers, chicken, and sesame; the "Golden Age of Siam" (chicken with red and green peppers and red coconut curry); and Marco Polo beef (spicy beef with scallions served on a hot stone).

✪ **Firenze Enoteca.** Singerstrasse 3. ☎ **01/513-4374.** Reservations recommended. Main courses 110–350AS ($7.35–$23.45). AE, DC, MC, V. Daily noon–2pm and 6–11pm. U-Bahn: Stephansplatz. ITALIAN.

This is Vienna's premier Italian restaurant. In the heart of the monument quarter, near St. Stephan's Cathedral and next to the Royal Hotel, it's furnished in Tuscan Renaissance style, with copies of frescoes by Benozzo Gozzoli. The kitchen specializes in homemade pasta served with zesty sauces. According to the chef, the cuisine is "80% Tuscan, 20% from the rest of Italy." Start with selections from the antipasti table, then choose among dishes like spaghetti with "fruits of the sea"; penne with salmon; veal cutlet with ham, cheese, and sardines; or perhaps filet mignon in a tomato-garlic sauce. Be sure to complement any meal here with a classic bottle of Chianti.

Griechenbeisl. Fleischmarkt 11. ☎ **01/533-1941.** Reservations required. Main courses 145–265AS ($9.70–$17.75); fixed-price menu 270–445AS ($18.10–$29.80). AE, DC, MC, V. Daily 11am–1am (last orders at 11:30pm). Tram: N or Z. AUSTRIAN.

Griechenbeisl was established in 1450 and is still one of the city's leading restaurants, although locals come here for the atmosphere and not necessarily culinary finesse. There's a maze of dining areas on three different floors, all with low vaulted ceilings, smoky paneling, and wrought-iron chandeliers. Watch out for the Styrian-vested waiters who scurry around the building with large trays of food. As you enter from the street, look down at the grate under your feet for an illuminated view of a pirate counting his money. As you go in, be sure to look for the so-called inner sanctum, with signatures of former patrons like Mozart, Beethoven, and Mark Twain.

The Pilsen beer is well chilled, and the food is *Gutbürgerlich*—hearty, ample, and solid home cooking. Dishes include deer stew, Hungarian and Viennese *gulasch*, sauerkraut, and venison steak. You can also sample such dishes as spinach strudel with feta cheese, spit-roasted pike perch in pepper sauce, brochette of salmon, and escalope of turkey stuffed with spinach. As an added treat, the restaurant features nighttime accordion and zither music.

Dining on the Danube

In summer the Viennese flock to the Danube to dine in one of 20 or 30 restaurants on the river. Our pick of the lot is **Taverna La Carabela/La Carabelita,** Donauinsein (no phone).

Designed like an octagonal, rough-hewn *bohio* you might see beside a beach in Mexico, it floats on pontoons in the Danube, connected to the "mainland" by a rustic-looking gangplank. No one will mind if you just hang out for a cocktail—perhaps a "Danube Waltz" made from gin, Blue Curaçao, and seltzer. But if you're hungry, the South American menu lists calamari, chicken wings with Mexican-style red sauce, chili con carne, tacos, and burgers. Staff here is an engaging blend of Austrian and Hispanic (usually from Venezuela and Colombia); and recorded versions of salsa and merengue help you forget, at least for the moment, that you're actually deep in the heart of Central Europe. Most cocktails cost from 60 to 100AS ($4 to $6.70). Reservations are not accepted and main courses go from 85 to 115AS ($5.70 to $7.70). Hours are May to September only, Monday to Friday from 6pm to 4am and Saturday and Sunday from 4pm to 5am. U-Bahn: Reichsbrücke.

✪ **Hotel Astoria Restaurant.** Kärntnerstrasse 32 (entrance at Führichgasse 1). ☎ **01/ 5157-7172.** Reservations recommended. Main courses 185–275AS ($12.40–$18.45). Fixed-price menu 300–540AS ($20.10–$36.20). AE, DC, MC, V. Mon–Fri 7–10am, noon–3pm, and 6–9pm. Closed July 1–Aug 24. U-Bahn: Karlsplatz or Stephansplatz. AUSTRIAN/ INTERNATIONAL.

The first-floor restaurant inside the Hotel Astoria (see chapter 4, "Where to Stay") dates from 1911 and remains the premier authentic Jugendstil dining room in Vienna. The foyer is lined with portraits of opera stars, and a handsome marble fireplace enhances the grandiose decor. A varied opera menu is served both before and after performances at the nearby Staatsoper. Typical dishes include *tafelspitz,* saddle of veal, and tournedos with morel sauce. The recipes are tried and true from the Old Vienna kitchen, so don't expect much in the way of innovation here. It's great value, however.

✪ **Kardos.** Dominikaner Bastei 8. ☎ **01/512-6949.** Reservations recommended. Main courses 90–240AS ($6.05–$16.10). AE, DC, MC, V. Mon–Sat 11am–2:30pm and 6pm–midnight. Closed Aug. U-Bahn: Schwedenplatz. BALKAN/HUNGARIAN/SLOVENIAN/AUSTRIAN.

This folkloric restaurant specializes in the strong flavors and traditions that developed in different parts of what used to be known as the Austro-Hungarian Empire. In a setting that celebrates the idiosyncratic folklore of various regions of the Balkans and the Great Hungarian Plain, this restaurant welcomes newcomers with *grammel*—piquant little rolls seasoned with minced pork and spices—and a choice of grilled meats. Other specialties include Hungarian *fogosch,* a form of pike-perch that's baked with vegetables and parsley potatoes, in addition to Hungarian goulash, and braised cabbage. The cellar is filled with pinewood accents and brightly colored Hungarian accessories that create an atmosphere of Gypsy *schmaltz.* During the winter, you're likely to find a strolling violinist. Start your meal with a glass of *barack,* an aperitif made from fermented apricots.

MAK Café. In the Österreichisches Museum für Angewandte Kunst (MAK), Stubenring 5. ☎ **01/714-0121.** Reservations not necessary. Main courses 90–120AS ($6.05–$8.05) lunch, 100–240AS ($6.70–$16.10) dinner. No credit cards. Tues–Sun 10am–midnight. U-Bahn: Stubentor. CONTINENTAL.

Of the many restaurants within Vienna's museums, this is the most unusual and the most sought-after. It occupies an enormous and echoing room on the MAK museum's street level, beneath an elaborately coffered and painted late-19th-century ceiling. In deliberate contrast, the restaurant's tables, chairs, and accessories are artfully minimalist and avant-garde. You can opt for Czech, Swedish, Hungarian, or Austrian dishes. Examples include a savory *bollito misto* (a medley of boiled meats); stuffed breast of chicken with spinach; carpaccio with Parmesan cheese; roast duck with orange sauce; and an unusual selection of *pierogies,* the stuffed potato dumplings native to Poland and Russia.

Ofenloch. Kurrentgasse 8. ☎ **01/533-8844.** Reservations required. Main courses 128–255AS ($8.60–$17.10). AE, DC, MC, V. Daily 11:30am–10:45pm. U-Bahn: Stephansplatz. Bus: 1A. VIENNESE.

The Viennese have known about this spot since the 1600s, when it functioned as a simple tavern. At this old-fashioned eating house, waitresses wear classic Austrian regalia and will give you a menu that looks more like a magazine, with some amusing mock-medieval illustrations inside. The hearty soup dishes are popular, as is the schnitzel. For smaller appetites, the menu offers a variety of salads and cheese platters, plus an entire page devoted to one-dish meals, all of which go well with wine and beer. For dessert, choose from an array of old-style Viennese specialties.

✪ **Palmenhaus.** In the Burggarten. ☎ **01/533-1033.** Reservations recommended for dinner. Main courses 95–240AS ($6.35–$16.10), pastries 39–48AS ($2.60–$3.20). AE, DC, MC. V. Daily 10am–2am. U-Bahn: Opera. AUSTRIAN.

Many architectural critics consider the *Jugendstil* glass canopy of this greenhouse the most beautiful in Austria. Overlooking the formal terraces of the Burggarten, it was built between 1901 and 1904 by the Habsburg's court architect, Friedrich Ohmann, as a graceful architectural transition between the Albertina and the National Library. Damaged during wartime bombings and left abandoned for years, it was restored in 1998 by trend-setting architects Christian Knechtl and Gregor Eichinger. Today, its central section functions as a chic cafe with extended opening hours and, despite the lavishly historic setting, an appealingly informal atmosphere. No one will mind if you drop in just for a drink and one of the voluptuous pastries displayed near the entrance. The sophisticated menu changes monthly and might include fresh Austrian goat cheese with stewed peppers and zucchini salad; young herring with sour cream, horseradish, and deep-fried beignets stuffed with apples and cabbage; and breast of chicken layered with goose liver and served with a port-flavored mango glaze, plus grilled fish.

✪ **Wein-Comptoir.** Bäckerstrasse 6. ☎ **01/512-1760.** Reservations recommended. Main courses 130–250AS ($8.70–$16.75). AE, DC, MC, V. Mon–Sat 5pm–1am (last orders). U-Bahn: Stephansplatz. AUSTRIAN/INTERNATIONAL.

This is one of the most charming and unpretentious wine taverns in Old Vienna. Sample from a wide selection of wines, mostly Austrian, while relaxing at the street-level tables or in the brick-vaulted cellar dining room. Because most dishes are cooked to order, prepare yourself for a long wait. Full meals might include breast of venison in a goose-liver sauce, *tafelspitz,* or breast of pheasant with bacon. For an appetizer, try either the rich potato soup flavored with bacon bits or a terrine of pike and zander. The cooking is robust and flavorful.

Zum Weissen Rauchfangkehrer. Weihburggasse 4. ☎ **01/512-3471.** Reservations required. Main courses 110–350AS ($7.35–$23.45). AE, DC, MC, V. Daily 5pm–1am. U-Bahn: Stephansplatz. VIENNESE.

Established in the 1860s, this dinner-only place is the former guildhall for Vienna's chimney sweeps. In fact, the name, translated as the "white chimney sweep," comes from the story of a drunken and blackened chimney sweep who fell into a kneading trough and woke up the next day covered in flour. The dining room here is rustic, with deer antlers, fanciful chandeliers, and pine banquettes that vaguely resemble church pews. A piano in one of the inner rooms provides music and adds to the comfortable ambience. Big street-level windows let in lots of light and pieces of stained glass are also scattered among the woodwork. The hearty, flavorful menu offers Viennese fried chicken, both Tyrolean schnitzel and Wiener schnitzel, wild game, veal goulash, bratwurst, and several kinds of strudel. You'll certainly want to finish with the house specialty, a fabulously rich chocolate cream puff.

INEXPENSIVE

✪ **A Tavola.** Weihburggasse 3–5. ☎ **01/512-7955.** Reservations required. Main courses 120–195AS ($8.05–$13.05). AE, DC, MC, V. Mon–Sat 12–3pm and 6–11pm. U-Bahn: Stephansplatz. ITALIAN.

Located at a 14th-century site, this well-managed and likable restaurant was once the home of a much-venerated restaurant (Stadtkrug), which had for generations been favored by visiting artists, such as Leonard Bernstein. Today, a duet of dining rooms presents an informal but well-rehearsed setting for Tuscan cuisine. You might begin your meal with a selection of well-rounded vegetable and seafood antipasti. Favorite pastas include penne with eggplant and tomatoes, risotto with mushrooms, gnocchi with four cheeses, entrecôte of beef, and a well-prepared version of sea bass.

Augustinerkeller. Augustinerstrasse 1. ☎ **01/533-1026.** Main courses 110–180AS ($7.35–$12.05). AE, DC, MC, V. Daily 11am–midnight. U-Bahn: Stephansplatz. AUSTRIAN.

Since 1857, the Augustinerkeller has served wine, beer, and food from the basement of one of the grand Hofburg palaces. It attracts a lively and diverse group that gets more and more boisterous as the *Schrammel* music plays late into the night. The long, narrow room with brick vaulting, worn pine-board floors, and wooden banquettes is usually packed, often with roaming accordion players. An upstairs room has a smaller crowd and no music. This place offers one of the best values for wine tasting in Vienna. The ground-floor lobby lists prices of vintage local wines by the glass. Tasters can sample from hundreds of bottles. Aside from wine and beer, simple food, including roast chicken on a spit, schnitzel, and *tafelspitz*, is served.

✪ **Buffet Trzesniewski.** Dorotheergasse 1. ☎ **01/512-3291.** Reservations not accepted. Sandwiches 10AS (65¢). No credit cards. Mon–Fri 8:30am–7:30pm; Sat 9am–5pm. U-Bahn: Stephansplatz. SANDWICHES.

Everyone in Vienna knows about this spot, from the most hurried office worker to the most elite hostess. Franz Kafka lived next door and used to come here for sandwiches and beer. It's unlike any buffet you've seen, with six or seven cramped tables and a rapidly moving queue jostling for space next to the glass countertops. Indicate to the waitress the kind of sandwich you want; if you can't read German, just point. Most people devour the delicious finger sandwiches, which come in 18 different combinations of cream cheese, egg, onion, salami, mushroom, herring, green and red peppers, tomatoes, lobster, and many other tasty ingredients. You can also order small glasses of fruit juice, beer, or wine with your snack. If you do order a drink, the cashier will give you a rubber token, which you'll present to the person at the far end of the counter.

Dubrovnik. Am Heumarkt 5. ☎ **01/713-7102.** Reservations recommended. Main courses 80–220AS ($5.35–$14.75). AE, DC, MC, V. Daily 11am–11pm. U-Bahn: Stadtpark. CROATIAN/ BALKAN/VIENNESE.

Dubrovnik's allegiance is to the culinary (and cultural) traditions of Croatia. The restaurant, founded in 1965, is composed of three dining rooms on either side of a central vestibule filled with busy waiters in Croat costume. The menu lists a lengthy choice of Balkan dishes, including a savory bean soup; homemade sausages; stuffed cabbage; fillet of veal with boiled potatoes, sour cream, and sauerkraut; and grilled pork kidney. Among the fish dishes, the most exotic is *fogosch* (a whitefish) served with potatoes and garlic. For dessert, try the baklava or an assortment of Bulgarian cheeses. Live piano entertainment is presented nightly from 7:30 to 11pm.

Gösser Bierklinik. Steindlgasse 4. ☎ **01/535-6897.** Reservations recommended for parties of 3 or more. Main courses 100–225AS ($6.70–$15.10). DC, MC, V. Mon–Sat 10am–11pm. U-Bahn: Stephansplatz. Tram: 31 or 32. VIENNESE.

Also known as the *Güldene Drache* (Golden Dragon), this restaurant serves the Styrian-brewed Gösser, reportedly the finest beer in the city. It's a sudsy and rustic institution in a building that, according to tradition, dates from Roman times. An inn operated here in the early 16th century, when Maxmillian I ruled the empire, so the decor is strictly medieval. The rushed and harried waitresses are usually carrying ample mugs of Gösser beer. When you finally get their attention, order up some hearty Austrian fare like veal chops with dumplings.

✪ **Gulaschmuseum.** Schulerstrasse 20. ☎ **01/512-1017.** Reservations recommended. Main courses 80–155AS ($5.35–$10.40). AE, DC, MC, V. Mon–Fri 9am–midnight; Sat–Sun 10am–midnight. U-Bahn: Wollzeile or Stephansplatz. AUSTRIAN/HUNGARIAN.

If you thought that goulash was available in only one form, think again. This restaurant celebrates at least 15 varieties of it, each an authentic Hungarian version and each redolent with the country's most distinctive spice, paprika. The Viennese adopted the Hungarian dish from their former "colony" centuries ago and have made it part of their own culinary repertoire. You can order goulash with roast beef, veal, pork, fried chicken livers, and even all-vegetarian versions made with potatoes, beans, or mushrooms. Boiled potatoes and rough-textured brown or black bread will usually accompany your choice. An excellent appetizer is the "national crêpe of the Magyars," *Hortobágy palatschinken,* stuffed with minced beef and paprika-flavored cream sauce. If you prefer an Austrian dish, there's *tafelspitz* (boiled beef), Wiener schnitzel, fresh fish, and such dessert specialties as house-made *apfelstrudel* and Sachertorte.

✪ **Hansen.** In the cellar of the Börsegebäude (Vienna Stock Exchange), Wipplingerstrasse 34 at the Schottenring. ☎ **01/532-05-42.** Reservations recommended. Main courses 85–215AS ($5.70–$14.40). AE, DC, MC, V. Mon–Fri 9am–8pm (last order); Sat 9am–3pm (last order). U-Bahn: Schottenring. MEDITERRANEAN/INTERNATIONAL.

One of the most intriguing and stylish restaurants in Vienna opened as a partnership between a time-tested culinary team and one of Austria's most famous horticulturists and gardening stores (Lederleitner, GmbH). You'll find them cheek-by-jowl in the deep and dramatic-looking vaulted cellars of Vienna's stock exchange, a *beaux-arts* pile that was designed in the 1890s by the restaurant's namesake, Theophile Hansen. The contrast of the cold gray granite of the cellars, the urban congestion outside, and an indoor similar to a greenhouse is especially alluring. The movers and shakers of corporate Vienna keep the place filled during lunch and relatively early dinners. Choose from a small but savory menu that changes every week. Examples include a spicy bean salad with strips of chicken breast served in a summer broth; lukewarm vegetable salad with curry and wild greens; clear salmon soup with tofu; risotto with cheese and sour cherries; and pork fillet with butter beans and wild-berry relish.

Kunsthallenrestaurant. Treitlstrasse 2. ☎ **01/586-9864.** Reservations not necessary. Main courses 90–135AS ($6.05–$9.05). No credit cards. Daily 10am–2am. U-Bahn: Karlsplatz. CONTINENTAL.

There's nothing particularly beautiful about this restaurant, but it's associated with one of Vienna's most respected repositories of modern art. The building that contains it might remind you of an oversized shoebox painted florescent orange-yellow. Inside, the decor resembles a prefabricated mess hall in an army barracks. The food, however, is well prepared, staff is congenial, and you never really know who might drop in for coffee, a drink, or any of the simple but well-prepared dishes, including wurst with potatoes and salad, braised breast of chicken with mashed potatoes, roasted pork with fresh vegetables, pastas, soups, and salads.

✪ **Restaurant Salzamt.** Ruprechtsplatz 1. ☎ **01/533-5332.** Reservations recommended. Main courses 95–225AS ($6.35–$15.10). V. Daily 5pm–2am (bar) and 6pm–midnight (restaurant). U-Bahn: Schwedenplatz. AUSTRIAN.

This is the best restaurant in the "Bermuda Triangle" neighborhood. It evokes a turn-of-the-century Viennese bistro, replete with Weiner Werkstatte–inspired chairs and lighting fixtures, cream-colored walls, and dark tables and banquettes where you're likely to see an arts-involved, sometimes surprisingly prominent clientele of loyal diners. Sit within its vaulted interior or—if weather permits—move out to any of the tables on the square, each overlooking the venerable walls of Vienna's oldest church, St. Ruprecht's. Well-prepared items include a terrine of broccoli and artichoke hearts; light-textured pastas; fillets of pork with a Gorgonzola-enriched cream sauce; roast beef with wild lettuce salad; several kinds of goulash; and fresh fish.

Siddhartha. Fleischmarkt 16. ☎ **01/513-1197.** Reservations recommended for parties of 3 or more. Main courses 98–156AS ($6.55–$10.45). AE, MC, V. Daily 11:30am–3pm and 6–11pm. U-Bahn: Schwedenplatz. VEGETARIAN.

At the end of a covered arcade in Old Vienna, this place is crowded but clean with white stucco, candlelight, fresh flowers, and vaulted ceilings. The walls are adorned with Hindu and Buddhist art and artifacts. Only vegetarian food is served here, and it's so popular you'll be lucky to get a seat during peak hours. House specialties include ratatouille, quiche Lorraine, the "Siddhartha" combination plate for two, Roquefort crêpes, and mushrooms Romanoff. There are far better vegetarian restaurants around the world, but in Vienna, this one's the best.

Zu den 3 Hacken (at the Three Axes). Singerstrasse 28. ☎ **01/512-5895.** Reservations recommended. Main courses 86–220AS ($5.75–$14.75). AE, DC, MC, V. Mon–Sat 12:30pm–midnight. U-Bahn: Stephansplatz. AUSTRIAN.

This cozy and charming restaurant was established 350 years ago and today is the oldest tavern (*gastehaus*) in Vienna. In 1827, Franz Schubert had an ongoing claim to one of its tables, where he entertained his cronies. Today, the Three Axes has green-painted lattices and potted ivy on tables that jut onto the sidewalk of a historic street (Singerstrasse) near the cathedral. Inside, small wooden tables fill three paneled dining rooms. The old-fashioned menu is replete with *tafelspitz*, *zwiebelrostbraten*, goulash, mixed grills, and desserts that include Hungarian-inspired *palatschinken* (crêpes) with chocolate-hazelnut sauce. The Czech and Austrian beer seems to taste especially good here.

Zum Finsteren Stern. 3–5 Sterngasse. ☎ **01/535-8152.** Reservations accepted. Daily special 135–160AS ($9.05–$10.70). Mon–Sat 3:30pm–2am. MC, V. U-Bahn: Schwedenplatz. INTERNATIONAL.

This is one of the simplest and least pretentious restaurants in Vienna, with a clientele who enjoys the utter lack of glamour and the workaday approach to food and wine. "To the Dark Star," on a small cobbled street in the old Jewish quarter, is part of a wine bar and wine store. Your hostess, Ella Peneder, prepares one platter per day on a hot plate. Depending on her mood, it might be a ragoût of lamb with green salad or crêpes stuffed with a mixture of sautéed porcini mushrooms and cubed veal. Wine, depending on its vintage, sells for between 25 and 55AS ($1.70 and $3.70) a glass. If you don't want wine, ask for a glass of elderberry juice instead. There's no coffee served, and only four tables in the joint, which you'll probably share with other diners.

Zum Kuchldragoner. Seitenstettengasse 3 or Ruprechtsplatz 4–5. ☎ **01-533-83-71.** Reservations recommended. Main courses 85–135AS ($5.70–$9.05). MC, V. Daily 11am–12:30am. U-Bahn: Schwedenplatz. AUSTRIAN.

Some aspects of this place will remind you of an old-fashioned Austrian tavern, perched high in the mountains, far from any congested city neighborhood. But this place has a bustling, irreverent, and sometimes jaded approach to feeding old-fashioned, flavorful cuisine to large numbers of diners, usually late into the night after everyone has had more than a drink or two. You can grab a table inside, but we prefer the outdoor tables, immediately adjacent to the Romanesque foundation of Vienna's oldest church, St. Ruprecht's. Come here for steins of beer and such staples as Wiener schnitzel, baked eggplant layered with ham and cheese, and grilled lamb cutlets.

Zwölf-Apostelkeller. Sonnenfelsgasse 3. ☎ **01/512-6777.** Main courses 70–150AS ($4.70–$10.05). AE, DC, MC, V. Daily 4pm–midnight. Closed July. U-Bahn: Stephansplatz. Tram: 1, 2, 21, D, or N. Bus: 1A. VIENNESE.

Sections of this old wine tavern's walls predate 1561. Rows of wooden tables stand under vaulted ceilings, with lighting partially provided by the streetlights that are set into the masonry floor. It's so deep that you feel you've entered a dungeon. This place is popular with students because of its low prices and proximity to St. Stephan's. In addition to beer and wine, hearty Austrian fare is served. Specialties include Hungarian goulash soup, meat dumplings, and a *Schlachtplatte* (a selection of hot black pudding, liverwurst, pork, and pork sausage with a hot bacon-and-cabbage salad). The cooking is hardly refined, but it's very well prepared. For those seeking a taste of old Vienna, this is the place.

3 Leopoldstadt (2nd District)

INEXPENSIVE

Altes Jägerhaus. Freudenau 255. ☎ **01/7289-5770.** Reservations recommended. Main courses 90–198AS ($6.05–$13.25). No credit cards. Daily 11:30am–11:30pm. U-Bahn: Schlachthausgasse; then take Bus 77A. AUSTRIAN/GAME.

The decor here hasn't changed much since 1899. Located 1 mile from the entrance to the Prater, in a verdant park, the place is a welcome escape from the more crowded restaurants of the Inner City. Select a seat in any of the four old-fashioned dining rooms. Seasonal game dishes like pheasant and venison are the house specialty, but you'll also find an array of well-prepared seafood dishes that might include freshwater and saltwater trout, zander, or salmon. The menu also features a delicious repertoire of Austrian staples like *tafelspitz* (boiled beef) and schnitzel.

4 Landstrasse (3rd District)

VERY EXPENSIVE

✪ **Restaurant at Palais Schwarzenberg.** Schwarzenbergplatz 9. ☎ **01/798-4515.** Reservations required. Main courses 300–400AS ($20.10–$26.80); fixed-price lunch 420AS ($28.15); 5-course fixed-price dinner 820AS ($54.95). AE, DC, MC, V. Daily 6–10:30am, noon–2:30pm, and 6:30–10pm. U-Bahn: Karlsplatz. Tram: D. CLASSICAL VIENNESE.

In one of Vienna's premier hotels (see chapter 4), Restaurant at Palais Schwarzenberg has one of the most distinguished backgrounds of any restaurant in the city. It's owned by Prince Karl Johannes von Schwarzenberg, scion of one of Austria's most aristocratic families. Take your time over an aperitif in the deluxe cocktail lounge. In summer you can dine Habsburg-style on a magnificent terrace. The cuisine is refined, with many French dishes, and the chef adjusts his menu seasonally. His many specialties include fillet of catfish on a ragoût of potatoes and morels with leek, medallions of venison roasted with fresh morels, and, for dessert, a chocolate-mint soufflé with passion fruit. Service is first class, and the wine cellar is nothing less than superb.

✪ **Steirereck**. Rasumofskygasse 2. ☎ **01/713-3168.** Reservations required. Main courses 248–395AS ($16.60–$26.45); 3-course fixed-price lunch 425AS ($28.50); 5-course fixed-price dinner 930AS ($62.30). AE, DC, MC, V. Mon–Fri 10:30am–2pm and 7pm–midnight. Closed holidays. Tram: N. Bus: 4. VIENNESE/AUSTRIAN.

Steirereck means "corner of Styria," which is exactly what Heinz and Margarethe Reitbauer have created in this intimate, rustic restaurant on the Danube Canal between Central Station and the Prater. The Reitbauers transplanted original beams and archways from an old castle in Styria to enhance the ambience. You'll find both traditional Viennese dishes and "new Austrian" selections on the menu. Appetizers include a caviar-semolina dumpling, roasted turbot with fennel, or goose-liver Steirereck. Some enticing main courses include asparagus with pigeon, saddle of lamb for two, prime Styrian roast beef, or red-pepper risotto with rabbit. The menu is wisely limited and well prepared, changing daily depending on what's fresh at the market. The restaurant is popular with after-theater diners, and patrons are invited to inspect the large wine cellar, which holds some 35,000 bottles.

EXPENSIVE

Arcadia Restaurant. In the Vienna Hilton, Am Stadtpark. ☎ **01/717000.** Reservations recommended for dinner. Main courses 165–340AS ($11.05–$22.80); breakfast buffet 300AS ($20.10); lunch buffet 410AS ($27.45); Sun brunch 480AS ($32.15). AE, DC, MC, V. Daily 6:30am–11pm. U-Bahn: Stadtpark. INTERNATIONAL.

Everything from an early business breakfast to an after-theater dinner is served here. The breakfast buffet is the most lavish in town, and at lunch a large selection of hot and cold specials, including delectable desserts and Viennese pastries, is spread out before you. In summer guests try for one of the tables on the outdoor terrace. One section of the dinner menu is reserved for lamb, which this restaurant does exceptionally well. Other main courses include pan-fried fillet of Norwegian salmon with chive sauce and grilled veal T-bone served with lime butter. Enjoy the famous summer barbecue for 480AS ($32.15), prepared on the terrace with a charwood grill.

Niky's Kuchlmasterei. Obere Weissgerberstrasse 6. ☎ **01/712-9000.** Reservations recommended. Main courses 300–450AS ($20.10–$30.15); fixed-price menu 394AS ($26.40) for 3-course lunch, 695AS ($46.55) for 7-course dinner. AE, DC, MC, V. Mon–Sat noon–midnight. U-Bahn: Schwedenplatz. VIENNESE/INTERNATIONAL.

After a long and pleasant meal, your bill will arrive in an elaborate jewel box, along with an amusing message in German that offers a tongue-in-cheek apology for cashing your check. The decor features old stonework with some modern architectural innovations, and the extensive menu boasts well-prepared dishes. The lively crowd of loyal habitués adds to the welcoming ambience, making Niky's a good choice for an evening meal, especially in summer when you can dine on its unforgettable terrace.

⊕ Family-Friendly Dining

- **A Tavola** *(see p. 84)*   This is an informal and reasonably priced Italian restaurant offering mainly Tuscan specialties. Your kids will adore the pastas; each dish could be a meal unto itself. The vegetable and seafood antipasti is also one of the best in town.
- **Glacisbeisel** *(see page 91)*   Housed in what was once the imperial stables, this restaurant might be the best place to introduce your child to Viennese food. We recommend ordering *tafelspitz,* boiled beef with potato rösti, followed by a milk-and-cream strudel with vanilla sauce.
- **Gulaschmuseum** *(see p. 85)*   If your kids think ordering hamburgers in a foreign country is adventurous eating, here is a great place to introduce them to goulash—it comes in at least 15 delicious varieties. Few kids will turn down the homemade apfelstrudel.

5 Wieden & Margareten (4th & 5th Districts)

MODERATE

Motto. Schönbrunnerstrasse 30 (the entrance is on Rudigergasse). ☎ **01/587-0672.** Reservations recommended. Main courses 92–228AS ($6.15–$15.30). No credit cards. Daily 6pm–4am. U-Bahn: Pilgramgasse. THAI/ITALIAN/AUSTRIAN.

This is Austria's premier gay restaurant, a cavernous red-and-black interior, a busy bar area, and a crowd that has included many international glam celebs (Thierry Mugler, John Galliano, and lots of theater people). Even Helmut Lang worked here briefly as a waiter. It's set behind green doors with a sign that's so small and discreet as to be nearly invisible. In summer, tables are set up in a garden. No one will mind if you pop in just for a drink; it's a busy nightspot in its own right. But if you're hungry, cuisine is about as eclectic as it gets, ranging from sushi and Thai-inspired curries to hearty Austrian classics.

Schlossgasse 21. Schlossgasse 21. ☎ **01/544-0767.** Reservations recommended. Main courses 88–248AS ($5.90–$16.60). V. Daily 6pm–3am. U-Bahn: Pilgramgasse. AUSTRIAN/INTERNATIONAL.

This cozy restaurant is in a turn-of-the-century building, decorated in a pleasant mishmash of old and new furnishings, much like you would find in someone's home. There's classic Austrian fare as well as some interesting and palate-pleasing Asian dishes, such as Indonesian satay and Chinese stir-frys. An enduring favorite is the steak.

INEXPENSIVE

Silberwirt. Schlossgasse 21. ☎ **01/544-4907.** Reservations recommended. Main courses 90–250AS ($6.05–$16.75). V. Daily noon–midnight. U-Bahn: Pilgramgasse. VIENNESE.

Despite the fact that it opened a quarter of a century ago, this restaurant resembles the traditional *Beisl* (bistro) with its copious portions of conservative, time-honored Viennese food. You can dine within the pair of dining rooms or move into the beer garden. The menu includes stuffed mushrooms, *tafelspitz,* schnitzels, and fillets of zanderfish, salmon, and trout. Silberwirt shares the same building and address as Schlossgasse 21, listed above.

6 Mariahilf (6th District)

MODERATE

Raimundstüberl. Liniengasse 29. ☎ **01/596-7784.** Reservations recommended. Main courses 95–240AS ($6.35–$16.10). DC, MC, V. Daily 10:30am–2pm and 5:30pm–midnight. U-Bahn: Gumpen-dorferstrasse or Westbahnhof. VIENNESE.

Emphasizing Old World decor and time-tested cuisine, this restaurant is also a good value, in a neighborhood loaded with simpler, and usually less worthy, choices. Established around the turn of the 20th century, it features a pair of wood-sheathed dining rooms, a garden, and copious portions of schnitzels, goulashes, and beefsteaks, which are smothered in mushrooms. The staff is polite and the ambience pure Viennese.

INEXPENSIVE

Alfi's Goldener Spiegel. Linke Wienzeile 46 (entrance on Stiegengasse). ☎ **01/586-6608.** Reservations not necessary. Main courses 90–150AS ($6.05–$10.05). No credit cards. Wed–Mon 7pm–2am. U-Bahn: Kettenbruckengasse. VIENNESE.

By everyone's accounts, this is the most reputable and most enduring gay restaurant in Vienna, with a cuisine and an ambience that might remind you of a simple Viennese bistro in a working-class district. There's a congenial bar area crowded with locals. If you sit down in the restaurant, expect large portions of traditional Viennese specialties, such as Wiener schnitzel, Rouladen of beef, fillet steaks with pepper sauce, and *tafelspitz.*

Café Cuadro. Margarethenstrasse 77. ☎ **01/544-7550.** Reservations not necessary. Breakfasts 56–66AS ($3.75–$4.40); main courses 42–48AS ($2.80–$3.20) lunch, 42–185AS ($2.80–$12.40) dinner. V. Mon–Sat 8am–midnight; Sun 9am–11pm. U-Bahn: Pilgramgasse. INTERNATIONAL.

Trendy, counterculture, and arts-oriented, this cafe and bistro is little more than a long glassed-in corridor with vaguely Bauhaus-inspired detailing. There are clusters of industrial-looking tables, but many clients opt for a seat at the long, luncheonette-style counter above a plexiglas floor with four-sided geometric patterns illuminated from below. In keeping with the establishment's name (Cuadro), the menu features four of everything. That includes four salads (including a very good seafood salad), four kinds of juicy burgers, four kinds of spaghetti, four homemade soups, four kinds of steak, and—if you're an early riser—four different breakfasts.

7 Neubau (7th District)

EXPENSIVE

✪ **Hauswirth.** Otto-Bauer-Gasse 20. ☎ **01/587-1261.** Reservations recommended. Main courses 185–310AS ($12.40–$20.75); 3-course fixed-price menu 485AS ($32.50); 4-course fixed-priced menu 875AS ($58.65). AE, DC, MC, V. Daily 11:30am–3pm; Mon–Sat 6pm–midnight. Closed Dec 23–Jan 8. U-Bahn: Zieglerstrasse. Tram: 52 or 58. VIENNESE.

The imposing leaded-glass door to this restaurant is under a rectangular corridor. Inside is an art nouveau enclave, which has become a stomping ground of the well-dressed and well-to-do. The summertime gardens are lovely, but in winter you'll eat in a paneled room accented by dark wood and crystal chandeliers. The chef adjusts his menu seasonally, obtaining whatever is fresh at local markets. Offerings might include quail, venison, asparagus, fresh berries, goose liver, sweetbreads, well-prepared steaks, seafood specialties, and a tempting array of homemade pastries. The kitchen has great finesse, and everything arrives fresh and appetizing. The cellar holds not only a large variety of the finest Austrian wines but also a well-chosen selection from some of the best European vineyards.

MODERATE

Bohème. Spittelberggasse 19. ☎ **01/523-3173.** Reservations recommended. Main courses 98–222AS ($6.55–$14.85). AE, DC, MC, V. Mon–Sat 6–11:30pm. Closed Dec 24–Jan 7. U-Bahn: Volkstheater. VIENNESE/INTERNATIONAL.

The carefully maintained house occupied by this restaurant won a municipal award in 1992 for the authenticity of its historic restoration. Originally built in 1750 in the baroque style, it once functioned as a bakery. Today, its historic street is an all-pedestrian walkway loaded with shops.

Since opening in 1989, Bohème has attracted a clientele well versed in the nuances of wine, food, and the endless range of opera music that reverberates through the two dining rooms. Even the decor is theatrical—it looks like a cross between a severely dignified stage set and an artsy, turn-of-the-century cafe. The menu is separated into opera movements, with overtures (aperitifs), prologues (appetizers), and first and second acts (soups and main courses, respectively). Some tempting items include thinly sliced cured ham with melons, Andalusian gazpacho, platters of mixed fish fillets with tomato risotto, *tafelspitz* with horseradish, gourmet versions of bratwurst and sausages on a bed of ratatouille, and an array of vegetarian dishes.

Glacisbeisl. Messepalast. ☎ **01/526-6795.** Reservations required. Main courses 120–265AS ($8.05–$17.75). AE, DC, MC, V. Daily 10am–midnight. Closed Dec 24–Feb 1. Bus: 48A. VIENNESE/AUSTRIAN.

Near the English Theater, inside a maze of palatial buildings whose entrances lie on Museumsstrasse, this restaurant is within the walls of the former imperial stables. To reach it, you'll have to traverse a series of courtyards. Climb one flight above ground level to a wood-sheathed dining room filled with tin cake molds and regional pottery. The restaurant serves Wiener schnitzel, *tafelspitz* (boiled beef with potato rösti), plus a milk-and-cream strudel with vanilla sauce. In summer, it seats more than 200 diners on an open-air terrace. Don't expect imaginative cooking here, but you do get a reliable, filling, and imminently satisfying meal.

INEXPENSIVE

Amerlingbeisl. Stiftgasse 8. ☎ **01/526-1660.** Reservations not necessary. Main courses 68–123AS ($4.55–$8.25). No credit cards. Daily 9am–2am. U-Bahn: Volkstheater. INTERNATIONAL.

There's a modern sensibility here, the result of a hip clientele, an occasionally blasé staff, and a minimalist, somewhat industrial-looking decor. But if you get nostalgic, you can opt for a table set out on the cobblestones of the early 19th-century building's glassed-in courtyard, beneath a grape arbor, where horses used to be stabled. Come to this neighborhood spot for simple but good food and a glass of beer or wine. The menu ranges from sandwiches and salads to more elaborate fare such as Argentinean steak with rice, vegetarian empanadas with chile sauce, turkey or pork schnitzels with potato salad, and dessert crêpes stuffed with marmalade.

Gasthaus Lux. Schrankgasse 4 or Spittelberggasse 3. ☎ **01/526-9491.** Reservations not necessary. Main courses 78–222AS ($5.25–$14.85). Daily 10am–2am. U-Bahn: Volkstheater. CONTINENTAL.

Dark, labyrinthine, and reminiscent of turn-of-the-century Vienna, this place attracts an artsy crowd who appreciate the well-flavored food and the conspiratorial atmosphere. Check out the variety of seating options before sitting down. Most of the rooms are rich and jewel-toned with dog-eared newspapers lying around; there's also a glassed-in area within what used to be an open-air courtyard. This is a nice spot for a drink, coffee, or any of about a dozen kinds of tea. But if you're hungry, there's simple portions of goat cheese with balsamic-flavored tomatoes as well as more elaborate fare, such as a sauté of venison with exotic mushrooms, marinated char with carrots

Picnics & Street Food

Picnickers will find that Vienna is among the best-stocked cities in Europe for food supplies. The best—and least expensive—place is the ☉ **Naschmarkt,** an open-air market that's only a 5-minute stroll from Karlsplatz (the nearest U-Bahn stop). Here you'll find hundreds of stalls selling fresh produce, breads, meats, cheeses, flowers, tea, and more. There are also fast-food counters and other stands peddling ready-made foods like grilled chicken, Austrian and German sausages, even sandwiches and beer. The market is open Monday to Friday from 6am to 6:30pm and on Saturday from 6am to 1pm. You can also buy your picnic at one of Vienna's many delis, like **Demel Vis à Vis** (opposite the main shop) at Kohlmarkt 11 (☎ **01/533-6020**). Other possibilities are **Kurkonditorei Ober-laa,** Neuer Markt 16 (☎ **01/513-2936**) and **Gerstner** at Kärntnerstrasse 15 (☎ **01/5124-9630**).

With your picnic basket in hand, head for such ideal settings as the Stadtpark or the Volksgarten, both on the famous Ring. Even better, if the weather is right, plan an excursion into the Vienna Woods.

On street corners throughout Vienna you'll find one of the city's most popular snack spots, the **Würstelstand.** These small stands sell frankfurters, bratwurst, curry wurst, and other Austrian sausages, which are usually served on a roll *mit senf* (with mustard). Try the *Käsekrainer,* a fat frankfurter with tasty bits of cheese. Conveniently located stands are on Seilergasse (just off Stephansplatz) and Kupferschmiedgasse (just off Kärntnerstrasse). Beers and soda are also sold.

in jelly and orange-flavored vinaigrette, and spaghetti with calamari. Vegetarians appreciate such dishes as salsify cake (made from the edible root of the salsify plant) with lemon-flavored cream sauce and green salad or truffled risotto with chanterelles and Parmesan cheese.

☉ **Plutzer Bräu.** Schrankgasse 4. ☎ **01/526-12-15.** Reservations not necessary. Main courses 72–156AS ($4.80–$10.45); 2-course set-price lunch served daily 11:30am–3pm, 76AS ($5.10). MC, V. Daily 11am–11:45pm. U-Bahn: Volkstheater. AUSTRIAN.

This is one of the best examples in Vienna of the explosion of hip and trendy restaurants within the city's 7th District, just to the southeast of the city's inner core. Maintained by the Plutzer Brewery, it occupies the cavernous cellar of an imposing 19th-century building. Any antique references are quickly lost once you're inside, thanks to an industrial-looking decor with exposed heating ducts and burnished stainless steel. The food is excellent and includes veal stew in beer sauce with dumplings, "brewmaster's style" pork steak, and pasta with herbs and feta cheese. Everything tastes better accompanied by a fresh-brewed Plutzer beer. Dessert might include curd dumplings with poppy seeds and sweet breadcrumbs,

8 Josefstadt (8th District)

MODERATE

Alte Backstube. Lange Gasse 34. ☎ **01/406-11-01.** Reservations required. Main courses 120–290AS ($8.05–$19.45). AE, MC, V. Mon–Sat 11am–midnight; Sun 5pm–midnight. Closed Aug. U-Bahn: Rathaus. Go east along Schmidgasse to Lange Gasse. VIENNESE/HUNGARIAN.

This spot is worth visiting just to admire the baroque sculptures that crown the top of the doorway. The building was originally designed as a private home in 1697, and 4 years later it was transformed into a bakery, complete with wood-burning stoves. For over 2 centuries the establishment served the baking needs of the neighborhood. In 1963, the owners added a dining room and a dainty front room for beer and tea.

Wholesome, robust specialties include braised pork with cabbage, Viennese-style goulash, and roast venison with cranberry sauce and bread dumplings. There's an English-language menu if you need it. Try the house dessert, cream-cheese strudel with hot vanilla sauce.

Piaristenkeller. Piaristengasse 45. ☎ **01/405-9152.** Reservations recommended. Main courses 150–280AS ($10.05–$18.75). AE, DC, MC, V. Daily 6pm–midnight. U-Bahn: Rathaus. AUSTRIAN.

Erich Emberger has successfully renovated this wine tavern originally founded in 1697 by Piarist monks. The kitchen, which once served the cloisters, serves traditional Austrian specialties in a vast cellar room with centuries-old vaulted ceilings. The most expensive item on the menu is a mixed grill, with four different kinds of meat. Zither music is played from 7:30pm on, and in summer the garden at the church square is open from 11am to midnight. Wine and beer are available whenever the cellar is open. Advance booking is required for a guided tour of the cloister's old wine vaults. Tours of six or more pay 150AS ($10.05) per person.

9 Alsergrund (9th District)

MODERATE

Abend-Restaurant Feuervogel. Alserbachstrasse 21. ☎ **01/317-5391.** Reservations recommended. Main courses 110–190AS ($7.35–$12.75); 5-course fixed-price menu 400AS ($26.80); 3-course fixed-price menu 295AS ($19.75). AE, DC, MC, V. Mon–Sat 6pm–1am. Closed July 15–Aug 15. U-Bahn: Friedensbrücke. Bus: 32. RUSSIAN.

Since World War I, this restaurant, across from the palace of the prince of Liechtenstein, has been a Viennese landmark. Gypsy violinists play Russian and Viennese music in romantically Slavic surroundings. Specialties include chicken Kiev, beef Stroganoff, veal Dolgoruki, and borscht. For an hors d'oeuvre try *Sakkuska*, a variety platter popular in Russia. Be sure to sample the Russian ice cream, *plombier.*

10 Near Schönbrunn

VERY EXPENSIVE

✪ **Altwienerhof.** Herklotzgasse 6. ☎ **01/892-6000.** Reservations recommended. Main courses 275–395AS ($18.45–$26.45); fixed-price lunch 385–450AS ($25.80–$30.15); menu dégustation (dinner only) 880AS ($58.95) for 6 courses, 1,200AS ($80.40) for 8 courses. AE, DC, MC, V. Mon–Sat 11:15am–2pm and 6:30–10:30pm. Closed first 3 weeks in Jan. U-Bahn: Gumpendorferstrasse. AUSTRIAN/FRENCH.

A short walk from Schönbrunn Palace, this is one of the premier dining spots in Vienna. Rudolf and Ursula Kellner bring sophistication and charm to a wood-paneled series of dining rooms that retain many Biedermeier embellishments from the original 1870s building. The chef prepares a cuisine moderne, using only the freshest and highest-quality ingredients. Because the menu changes frequently, we can't recommend specialties, but the maître d' is always willing to assist. Each night the chef prepares a *menu dégustation,* which is a sampling of the kitchen's best nightly dishes. The wine list consists of well over 700 items. The cellar houses about 18,000 bottles; each of the wines is selected by Mr. Kellner himself. The Kellners also run a small (25-room) budget hotel on the premises (see chapter 4, "Where to Stay").

MODERATE

Hietzinger Brau. Auhofstrasse 1. ☎ **01/877-7087-0.** Reservations not necessary. Main courses 170–268AS ($11.40–$17.95). DC, MC, V. Daily 11:30am–3pm and 6–11:30pm. U-Bahn: Hietzing. AUSTRIAN.

Established in 1743, this is the most famous restaurant in the vicinity of Schönebrunn Palace. Everything about it evokes a sense of Viennese bourgeois stability—wood paneling, a staff in folk costume, and platters heaped high with hearty cuisine. The menu lists more than a dozen preparations of beef, including the time-tested favorite, *tafelspitz*, as well as mixed grills, lobster, salmon, crabmeat, and zander. Franz-Joseph himself would enjoy the very large Wiener schnitzels, the creamy goulash, even the braised calf's head. Wine is available, but by far the most popular beverage here is the local brew, Hietzinger.

11 In the Outer Districts

EXPENSIVE

✪ **Sailer.** Gersthoferstrasse 14. ☎ **01/4792-1210.** Reservations required. Main courses 200-300AS ($13.40–$20.10). AE, DC, MC, V. Daily noon–3pm and 6pm–midnight. Tram: 9, 40, or 41. Bus: 10A. VIENNESE/AUSTRIAN/GAME.

Located near the Türkenschanzpark, this restaurant is tastefully decorated in Old Vienna style, with wood paneling, Biedermeier portraits, and, in one of the cellar rooms, hand-carved antique chairs. The restaurant, and the house it's in, were established in 1892 by the ancestors of the present owners. Their specialties include deer, elk, wild boar, pheasant, and partridge, each prepared according to time-honored Viennese recipes. The owners have given in to demands for an updated lighter cuisine with daily specials.

INEXPENSIVE

Blau Stern. Döblinger Gürtel 2. ☎ **01/369-6564.** Reservations not necessary. Main courses 75–165AS ($5.05–$11.05). No credit cards. Daily 9am–2am. U-Bahn: Nussdorfer Strasse. CONTINENTAL.

It's well managed, hip, and stylish, but because of its location in Vienna's outlying 19th District, it's almost exclusively patronized by local residents. High-ceilinged and streamlined, it looks like a postmodern hybrid of a typical Austrian coffeehouse and an American-style bar. Sunday morning the place is mobbed with a breakfast crowd that might include local celebrity and racecar champ Niki Lauda. Expect bacon and eggs, light fare such as pastas and salads, and daily specials that include braised scampi with vegetable beignets and avocado sauce. The name comes from the *blau stern* (blue star) that used to adorn sacks of coffee imported into Austria from South America by the restaurant's owners.

12 On the Outskirts

EXPENSIVE

✪ **Restaurant Taubenkobel.** Hauptstrasse 33, Schützen. ☎ **0268/42297.** Reservations recommended. Main courses 220–310AS ($14.75–$20.75); set menus 590–890AS ($39.55–$59.65). AE, DC, MC, V. Wed–Sun noon–3pm and 4pm–midnight. From Vienna, take the A2 highway, then the A3 highway, heading south. Exit at the signs for Schützen. INTERNATIONAL.

This is an increasingly well-known restaurant that lies beside the main street of the hamlet of Schützen, about 25 miles southeast of Vienna. Within a solidly built, white-fronted, 200-year old *maison bourgeoise,* with a quintet of small and tastefully rustic dining rooms, the artful and idiosyncratic cuisine of hardworking self-taught chef and owner, Wazlter Eselböck, is served. Past clients have included high-placed government officials and a scattering of artists. Mr. Eselböck was designated Austrian Chef of the Year in 1995.

The menu items change by the season and by Eselböck's whim. You can expect a meal that's more sophisticated and upscale than anything else in the region. Dishes may include veal cutlets with mustard sauce, herbs, and eggplant slices; a summer salad of marinated salmon trout and eel; Asian-style corn soup with sweetwater crab; lamb served with pumpkin, wild greens, and natural juices; and Austrian Angus steak served with mushrooms and butter-enriched mashed potatoes with fresh truffles.

13 Coffeehouses & Cafés

⭐ **Café Central.** Herrengasse 14. ☎ **01/533-3763.** Desserts 28–45AS ($1.90–$3); coffee 26–70AS ($1.75–$4.70). Mon–Sat 7am–8pm; closed Sun and holidays. U-Bahn: Herrengasse.

Café Central stands in the center of Vienna just across from the Hofburg (the imperial winter palace) and the Spanish Riding School. This grandly proportioned cafe offers a glimpse into 19th-century Viennese life—it was once the center of Austria's literati and the meeting place of the country's best-known writers. Even Vladimir Lenin, under an assumed name, is said to have met his colleagues here. The cafe offers a variety of Viennese coffees and a vast selection of desserts and pastries, as well as Viennese and provincial dishes.

⭐ **Café Demel.** Kohlmarkt 14. ☎ **01/533-5516.** Coffee 50AS ($3.35); desserts begin at 50AS ($3.35). Daily 10am–7pm. U-Bahn: Herrengasse. Bus: 1A or 2A.

The windows of this venerated cafe are filled with fanciful spun-sugar creations of characters from folk legends. Inside this splendidly baroque Viennese landmark are black marble tables, embellished plaster walls, elaborate half paneling, and crystal. Dozens of different pastries are available every day, including Pralinentorte, Senegal torte, truffle torte, Sandtorte, and Maximiliantorte, as well as cream-filled horns (Gugelhupfs). If you're not in the mood for sweets, Demel also serves a mammoth variety of tea sandwiches made with smoked salmon, egg salad, caviar, or shrimp. If you want to be traditional, ask for a Demel-Coffee, which is filtered coffee served with milk, cream, or whipped cream.

Café Diglas. Wollzeile 10. ☎ **01/512-5765.** Coffee 28–86AS ($1.90–$5.75). Mon–Wed 7am–midnight, Thurs–Sat 7am–2am; Sun 9am–midnight. U-Bahn: Stephansplatz.

Café Diglas evokes between-the-wars Vienna better than many of its competitors, thanks to a decor that retains some of the original accessories from when it opened in 1934. The cafe prides itself on its long-ago association with Franz Lehár. It offers everything in the way of run-of-the-mill caffeine fixes as well as more elaborate, liqueur-enriched concoctions, such as a Biedermeier (with apricot schnapps and cream).

Café Dommayer. Dommayergasse 1. ☎ **01/877-5465.** Coffee, tea, and pastries 28–66AS ($1.90–$4.40). Daily 7am–midnight. U-Bahn: Schönbrunn.

This cafe is most closely associated with visits to Schönbrunn Palace, with a reputation for courtliness that goes back to 1787. In 1844, Johann Strauss Jr. made his musical debut here, and beginning in 1924, this has been the place for tea dancing every day after 5pm. Today, Dommayer is revered by many Viennese. During clement weather, a garden with seats for 300 people opens in back. Many clients, some of them elderly, opt to spend an entire afternoon here, watching the world and conversing with friends. Every Saturday afternoon between 2 and 4pm, a pianist and violinist perform;

every third Saturday, an all-woman orchestra plays mostly Strauss. Most people come
here for coffee, tea, and pastries, but if you have a more substantial appetite, there's
Wiener schnitzels, rostbratens, and fish.

Café Frauenhuber. Himmelpfortgasse 6. ☎ **01/512-4323.** Small coffee 26AS ($1.75).
Daily 8am–11pm. U-Bahn: Stephansplatz.

Even the Viennese debate when this place opened: Opinion is divided between 1824
and 1788. Regardless, it still has a justifiable claim to being the oldest continuously
operating coffeehouse in the city. Management does its best to keep the legend alive:
They stock newspapers in at least four languages that become increasingly dog-eared
and battered as the day progresses, much as the place itself has become a bit battered
and more than a bit smoke-stained over the years. Besides the coffee, Wiener schnitzel,
served with potato salad and greens, is a good bet here, as are any of the ice cream
dishes and pastries.

✪ **Café Imperial.** Karntner Ring 16. ☎ **01/5011-0389.** Coffee 55AS ($3.70); pastries
from 50AS ($3.35). Daily from 7am–11pm. U-Bahn: Karlsplatz.

Housed in the deluxe Hotel Imperial (see chapter 4, "Where to Stay"), this place was
a favorite of Gustav Mahler and a host of other celebrated cultural figures. The "Imperial Toast" is a mini-meal in itself: white bread with veal, chicken, and leaf spinach
that's gratinéed in the oven and served with hollandaise sauce. A daily
breakfast/brunch buffet for 395AS ($26.45) is served all day on Sunday from 7am
until closing at 11pm.

✪ **Café Landtmann.** Dr.-Karl-Lueger-Ring 4. ☎ **01/532-0621.** Large coffee 44AS
($2.95); fixed-price lunch 115AS ($7.70). Daily 8am–midnight; lunch 11:30am–3pm; dinner
5–11pm. Tram: 1, 2, or D.

One of the Ring's great coffeehouses, this spot has a history dating to the 1880s. Overlooking the Burgtheater, it has traditionally drawn a mixture of politicians, journalists,
and actors. It was also Freud's favorite. The original chandeliers and the prewar chairs
have been refurbished. We highly suggest spending an hour or so here, perusing the
newspapers, sipping on coffee, or planning the day's itinerary.

Café Mozart. Albertinaplatz 2. ☎ **01/5130-88115.** Small coffee 30AS ($2); main courses
110–280AS ($7.35–$18.75). Daily 8am–midnight. U-Bahn: Karlsplatz.

Like many other establishments throughout Austria, this one celebrates an association
with Mozart, who stopped here for a dose of gossip and *ein kleiner brauner* (small
black coffee). Don't expect the 18th-century trappings that originally graced this
200-year-old place; they were replaced long ago by a more contemporary and neutral
decor. You'll probably stay just for coffee or perhaps some ice cream or a drink. But if
you're hungry, full meals are available.

○ **Café Sperl.** Gumpendorferstrasse 11. ☎ **01/586-4158.** Coffee 26–38AS ($1.75–$2.55); main courses 38–140AS ($2.55–$9.40). Mon–Sat 7am–11pm; Sun 3–11pm; July–Aug closed Sun. U-Bahn: Karlsplatz.

The gilded-age panels and accessories that were installed on the day of Sperl's opening in 1880 are still in place, which contributed to Sperl winning the 1998 Austrian Tourism Award for "Austria's best coffeehouse of the year." Composer and conductor Franz Lehár came here almost every weekday for years. Besides coffee, there is more substantial fare, including salads, toasts, omelets, steaks, and Wiener schnitzels. Its staff still practices a world-weary and bemused kind of courtliness, but in a concession to modern tastes, there's a billiards table and some dartboards on the premises.

Café Tirolerhof. Fürichgasse 8. ☎ **01/512-7833.** Coffee to 60AS ($4); strudel 40AS ($2.70); Viennese breakfast 69AS ($4.60). Tues–Sat 7am–midnight; Sun 7am–2pm. U-Bahn: Stephansplatz or Karlsplatz.

This coffeehouse, which has been under the same management for decades, makes for a convenient sightseeing break, particularly during a tour of the nearby Hofburg complex. One coffee specialty is the Maria Theresa, a large cup of mocha flavored with apricot liqueur and topped with whipped cream. If coffee sounds too hot, try the tasty milkshakes. You can also order a Viennese breakfast of coffee, tea, or hot chocolate, two Viennese rolls, butter, jam, and honey.

Café/Restaurant Prückel. Stubenring 24. ☎ **01/512-6115.** Coffee to 72AS ($4.80); main courses 59–125AS ($3.95 to $8.40). Daily 9am–10pm. U-Bahn: Stubentor.

This place was built in the early 1900s and renovated in 1955, just after Austria regained its independence. The spot plays host to offbeat, artsy patrons who lounge in the Sputnik-era chairs among piles of dog-eared newspapers. The owner offers 20 different kinds of coffee, including the house favorite, Maria Theresa, a large black coffee with orange liqueur and whipped cream.

Demmer's Teehaus. Mölkerbastei 5. ☎ **01/533-5995.** Teas begin at 30AS ($2). Mon–Fri 10am–6:30pm. U-Bahn: Schottentor.

Thirty different kinds of tea are served here, along with dozens of pastries, cakes, toasts, and English sandwiches. Demmer's is managed by the previously recommended restaurant, Buffet Trzesniewski; the teahouse offers you a chance to sit down, relax, and enjoy your drink or snack.

6

Exploring Vienna

"**A**sia begins at Landstrasse," remarked Austria's renowned statesman Prince von Metternich to suggest the power and influence of the far-flung Austrian Empire, whose destiny was controlled by the Habsburg dynasty from 1273 to 1918.

Viennese prosperity under the Habsburgs reached its peak under the long reign of Maria Theresa in the late 18th century. Many of the sights described below are traced directly to the great empress who escorted Vienna through the Age of Enlightenment. She welcomed Mozart, the child prodigy, to her court at Schönbrunn when he was just 6 years old.

With the collapse of the Napoleonic Empire, Vienna took over Paris's long-held position as "the center of Europe." At the far-reaching Congress of Vienna (1814– 15), the crowned heads of Europe met to restructure Europe's political boundaries. But so much time was devoted to galas that Prince de Ligne remarked, "The Congress doesn't make progress, it dances."

In this chapter we'll explore the many sights of Vienna. It's possible to spend a week here and only touch the surface of this multifaceted city. We'll take you through the highlights, but even this venture will take more than a week of fast-paced walking.

Suggested Itineraries

Many readers will not have time to see Vienna as it really deserves to be seen. Some visitors will have only a day or two; with those people in mind, we've compiled a list of the major attractions a first-time visitor will not want to miss, as well as additional sights for those with more time. To help your touring strategies, we've outlined some suggested itineraries below based on the length of your stay. Regardless of time, no one should miss the Inner City, Schönbrunn Palace, Hofburg Palace, Belvedere Palace, Kunsthistorisches Museum, and St. Stephan's Cathedral. You also might consider one of our three city walking tours mapped out in chapter 7.

If You Have 1 Day

Begin at **St. Stephan's Cathedral** where you can climb the south tower of the cathedral for a panoramic view of the city (you can also take an elevator to the top). From here, branch out for a tour of the **Inner City,** or Old Town. Stroll down **Kärntnerstrasse,** the main shopping artery, and enjoy the 11am ritual of coffee in a grand cafe, such as the Café Imperial. In the afternoon, visit **Schönbrunn Palace,** the magnificent summer seat of the Habsburg dynasty. Have dinner in a Viennese wine tavern.

If You Have 2 Days

On Day 2, explore other major attractions of Vienna, including the **Hofburg,** the **Imperial Crypts,** and the **Kunsthistorisches Museum.** In the evening, attend a performance of the **opera** or perhaps a concert in the famous **Konzerthaus.**

If You Have 3 Days

Try to work two important performances into your schedule: the **Spanish Riding School** (Tuesday to Saturday) and the **Vienna Boys' Choir** (singing at masses on Sunday). Also be sure to visit the **Belvedere Palace** and its fine-art galleries. Take a stroll through the **Naschmarkt,** the city's major open-air market, and finish the day with our **walking tour** of Imperial Vienna (see chapter 7, "Vienna Walking Tours").

If You Have 4 Days or More

On Day 4, take a tour of the **Vienna Woods** and then visit **Klosterneuburg Abbey,** Austria's most impressive abbey (see chapter 10, "Side Trips from Vienna"). Return to Vienna for an evening of fun at the **Prater** amusement park.

On Day 5, "mop up" all the attractions you missed on your first 4 days. These might include a visit to the **Sigmund Freud Museum** or a walk through the **Stadtpark,** at Parkring.

Or if these less important attractions don't interest you, take a **Danube boat cruise** (available May to September only). End your travels at a *heurige,* a typically Viennese wine cellar in Grinzing or Heiligenstadt.

1 The Hofburg Palace Complex

Once the winter palace of the Habsburgs, the vast and impressive Hofburg sits in the heart of Vienna. To reach it (you can hardly miss it), head up Kohlmarkt to Michaelerplatz 1, Burgring (☎ **01/587-5554** for general information), where you'll stumble across two enormous fountains embellished with statuary. You can also take the **U-Bahn** to Stephansplatz, Herrengasse, or Mariahilferstrasse, or else **Tram** 1, 2, D, or J to Burgring.

This complex of imperial edifices, the first of which was constructed in 1279, grew with the empire, so that today the palace is virtually a city within a city. The earliest parts were built around a courtyard, the **Swiss Court,** named for the Swiss mercenaries who performed guard duty here. This most ancient section of the palace is at least 700 years old.

The Hofburg's complexity of styles, which are not always harmonious, is the result of each emperor opting to add to or take away some of the work done by his or her predecessors. The Hofburg, which has withstood three major sieges and a great fire, is called simply *die Burg,* or "the palace," by Viennese. Of its more than 2,600 rooms, fewer than 2 dozen are open to the public.

✪ **Schatzkammer (Imperial Treasury).** Hofburg, Schweizerhof. ☎ **01/533-7931.** Admission 100AS ($6.70) adults; 70AS ($4.70) children, seniors, and students. Wed–Mon 10am–6pm.

Reached by a staircase from the Swiss Court, the Schatzkammer is the greatest treasury in the world. It's divided into two sections: the Imperial Profane and the Sacerdotal Treasuries. The first displays the crown jewels and an assortment of imperial riches, and the other, of course, contains ecclesiastical treasures.

The Hofburg

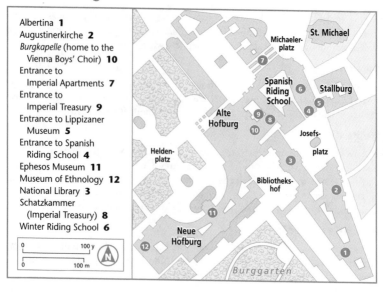

Albertina **1**
Augustinerkirche **2**
Burgkapelle (home to the
    Vienna Boys' Choir) **10**
Entrance to
    Imperial Apartments **7**
Entrance to
    Imperial Treasury **9**
Entrance to Lippizaner
    Museum **5**
Entrance to Spanish
    Riding School **4**
Ephesos Museum **11**
Museum of Ethnology **12**
National Library **3**
Schatzkammer
    (Imperial Treasury) **8**
Winter Riding School **6**

St. Michael
Michaeler-
platz
Spanish
Riding
School
Stallburg
Alte
Hofburg
Josefs-
platz
Helden-
platz
Bibliotheks-
hof
Neue
Hofburg
Burggarten

The most outstanding exhibit in the Schatzkammer is the imperial crown of the
Holy Roman Empire, which dates from 962. It's so big that, even though padded, it
probably slipped down over the ears of the imperial incumbents. Studded with emer-
alds, sapphires, diamonds, and rubies, this 1,000-year-old symbol of sovereignty is a
priceless treasure, a fact recognized by Adolf Hitler, who had it taken to Nürnberg in
1938 (the American army returned it to Vienna after World War II ended). Also on
display is the imperial crown of Austria, worn by the Habsburg rulers from 1804 to
the end of the empire. Be sure to have a look at the coronation robes, some of which
date from the 12th century.

You can also view the 8th-century saber of Charlemagne and the 9th-century Holy
Lance. The latter, a sacred emblem of imperial authority, was thought in medieval
times to be the weapon that pierced the side of Christ on the cross. Among the great
Schatzkammer prizes is the Burgundian Treasure. Seized in the 15th century and
brought to Vienna, it is rich in vestments, oil paintings, robes, and gems. Highlight-
ing this collection of loot are artifacts connected with the Order of the Golden Fleece,
a medieval order of chivalry.

✪ **Kaiserappartements (Imperial Apartments).** Michaeler Platz 1 (inside the Ring,
about a 7-minute walk from Stephansplatz; entrance via the Kasertor in the Inneren Burghof).
☎ **01/533-7570.** Admission 95AS ($6.35) adults, 75AS ($5.05) students under 25, 50AS
($3.35) children 6–15, free for children 5 and under. Daily 9am–4:30pm. U-Bahn: U-1 or U-3
to Stephansplatz. Tram: 1, 2, 3, or J to Burgring.

The Kaiserappartements, on the first floor, is where the emperors and their wives and
children lived. To reach these apartments, enter through the rotunda of Michaelerplatz. The apartments are richly decorated with tapestries, many from Aubusson in
France. Unfortunately, you can't visit the quarters once occupied by Empress Maria
Theresa—they are now used by the president of Austria. The court tableware and silver are outrageously ornate, reflecting the pomp and splendor of a bygone era. The
Imperial Silver and Porcelain Collection, from the Hapsburg household of the 18th
and 19th centuries, provides a window into their court etiquette.

The Imperial Apartments seem to be most closely associated with the long reign of Franz Joseph. A famous, full-length portrait of his beautiful wife, Elisabeth of Bavaria (Sissi), hangs in the apartments. You'll see the "iron bed" of Franz Joseph, who claimed he slept like his own soldiers. Maybe that explains why his wife spent so much time traveling!

✪ **Die Burgkapelle (Home of the Vienna Boys' Choir).** Hofburg (entrance on Schweizerhof). ☎ **01/533-9927.** Mass: Seats 70–380AS ($4.70–$25.45); standing room free. Concerts 400–550AS ($26.80–$36.85). Masses (performances) held only Jan–June and mid-Sept until the end of Dec, Sun and holidays at 9:15am. Concerts May–June and Sept–Oct Fri at 4pm.

Construction of this Gothic chapel began in 1447 during the reign of Emperor Frederick III, but it was later massively renovated. From 1449 it was the private chapel

Sissi—Eternal Beauty

Empress Elisabeth of Austria, affectionately known to her subjects as "Sissi," is remembered as one of history's most tragic and fascinating women. An "empress against her will," she was at once a fairy-tale princess and a liberated woman. It's not surprising that she has frequently been compared to Britain's late Princess Diana—both were elegant women, dedicated to social causes, who suffered through unhappy marriages. Both were "people's" princesses, who succeeded in winning a special place in the hearts of their subjects.

Elisabeth was born in Munich on Christmas Day 1837. She grew up away from the ceremony of court and developed an unconventional, freedom-loving spirit. When Emperor Franz Joseph of Austria met the 15-year-old, he fell in love at once, although he was supposed to marry her sister, Helene. Franz Joseph and Elisabeth were married on April 24, 1854, in Vienna.

With her beauty and natural grace, Elisabeth soon charmed the public, but in her private life there were serious problems. Living under a strict court regime and her domineering aunt and mother-in-law, the Grand Duchess Sophie, she felt constrained and unhappy. She saw little of her husband—"I wish he were not emperor," she once declared.

She was liberal and forward-minded, and in the nationality conflict with Hungary, she was decisively for the Hungarians. The respect and affection with which she was regarded in Hungary has lasted until the present day.

Personal blows left heavy marks on Sissi's life. But her most terrible tragedy was the suicide of her son, Rudolf, in 1889. She was never able to get over it. From that time on, she dressed only in black and stayed far from the pomp and ceremony of the Viennese court.

On September 10, 1898, as she was walking along the promenade by Lake Geneva, a 24-year-old anarchist stabbed her to death. To the assassin, Elisabeth represented the monarchic order that he despised; ironically, he was unaware that Elisabeth's contempt for the monarchy, which she considered a "ruin," matched his own.

Even a century after her death, Sissi's hold on the popular imagination remains undiminished. A TV series about her life achieved unprecedented popularity, and the musical "Elisabeth" has run for years in Vienna. On the 100th anniversary of her death, celebrated in 1998, she was memorialized in a special exhibition: Elisabeth—Eternal Beauty.

of the royal family. Today the Burgkapelle hosts the Hofmusikkapelle, an ensemble of the Vienna Boys' Choir and members of the Vienna State Opera chorus and orchestra, which performs works by classical and modern composers. Written applications for reserved seats should be sent at least 8 weeks in advance. Use a credit card; do not send cash or checks. For reservations, write to Verwaltung der Hofmusikkapelle, Hofburg, A-1010 Vienna. If you failed to reserve in advance, you may be lucky enough to secure tickets from a block sold at the Burgkapelle box office every Friday from 11am to 1pm or 3 to 5pm, plus Sunday 8:15 to 8:45am. The line starts forming at least half an hour before that. If you're willing to settle for standing room, it's free.

The Vienna Boys' Choir boarding school is at Palais Augarten, Obere Augartenstrasse.

Neue Burg. Heldenplatz. ☎ **01/525-24-484.** Admission to Hofjagd and Rüstkammer, Musikinstrumentensammlung, and Ephesos Museum, 60AS ($4) adults, 40AS ($2.70) children. Mon, Wed, and Sun 10am–6pm.

The most recent addition to the Hofburg complex is the Neue Burg, or New Château. Construction was started in 1881 and continued through 1913. The palace was the residence of Archduke Franz Ferdinand, the nephew and heir apparent of Franz Joseph, whose assassination at Sarajevo was the spark that led to World War I.

The **arms and armor collection** is second only to that of the Metropolitan Museum of Art in New York. It's in the Hofjagd and Rüstkammer, on the second floor of the New Château. On display are crossbows, swords, helmets, pistols, and armor, mostly the property of Habsburg emperors and princes. Some of the exhibits, such as the scimitars, were captured from the Turks as they fled the battlefield outside Vienna in 1683. Don't miss the armor worn by the young (and small) Habsburg princes.

Another section, the **Musikinstrumentensammlung** (☎ **01/52524**, ext. 471), is devoted to old musical instruments, mainly from the 17th and 18th centuries, but with some from the 16th century. Some of the instruments, especially the pianos and harpsichords, were played by Brahms, Schubert, Mahler, Beethoven, and the Austrian emperors, who fancied themselves to be musicians.

In the **Ephesos Museum** (Museum of Ephesian Sculpture), Neue Burg 1, Heldenplatz, with an entrance behind the Prince Eugene monument (☎ **01/52524**), you'll see high-quality finds from Ephesus in Turkey and the Greek island of Samothrace. Here the prize exhibit is the Parthian monument, the most important relief frieze from Roman times ever found in Asia Minor. It was erected to celebrate Rome's victorious conclusion of the Parthian wars (A.D. 161–65).

Visit the **Museum für Völkerkunde** (Museum of Ethnology), Neue Burg, Hofburg (☎ **01/53430**) for no other reason than to see the rare Aztec feather headdress. Also on display are Benin bronzes, Cook's collections of Polynesian art, and Indonesian, African, Eskimo, and pre-Columbian exhibits. Admission is 80AS ($5.35) for adults, 40AS ($2.70) for children. The museum is open daily from 10am to 4pm.

Österreichische Nationalbibliothek (Austrian National Library). Josefplatz 1. ☎ **01/5341-0202.** Summer admission 60AS ($4) adults, 40AS ($2.70) children, students, and seniors; winter admission 40AS ($2.70) adults, 20AS ($1.35) children, students, and seniors. Nov–Apr Mon–Sat 10am–2pm; May–Oct Mon–Wed and Fri–Sat 10am–4pm, Thurs 10am–7pm, and Sun and public holidays 10am–1pm.

The royal library of the Habsburgs dates back to the 14th century, and the library building, developed at the court from 1723 on, is still expanding to the Neue Hofburg. The Great Hall of the present-day library was ordered by Karl VI and designed by those masters of the baroque, the von Erlachs. Its splendor is captured in the frescoes of Daniel Gran and the equestrian statue of Joseph II. The complete collection of Prince Eugene of Savoy is the core of the precious holdings shelved in front of the library building. With its manuscripts, rare autographs, globes, maps, and other memorabilia, it's among the finest libraries in the world.

Albertina. Augustinerstrasse 1. ☎ **01/53483.** Admission 45AS ($3) adults, 20AS ($1.35) students, free for children under 11. Tues–Sun 10am–5pm.

Currently closed for a major renovation; check status before heading here. The development of graphic arts since the 14th century is explored at this Hofburg museum, which has gathered one of the world's greatest graphics collections. The most outstanding treasure is the Dürer collection, especially *Praying Hands*, although what you'll usually see are copies—the originals are shown only on special occasions. The 20,000-plus drawings and more than 250,000 original etchings and prints include work by such artists as Poussin, Fragonard, Rubens, Rembrandt, Michelangelo, and Leonardo da Vinci.

Augustinerkirche (Church of the Augustians). Augustinerstrasse 3. ☎ **01/533-7099.** Guided tour 10AS (65¢) contribution. Mon, Thurs, Fri 10am–noon and Wed and Sat 10am–6pm.

This 14th-century church was built to serve as the parish church of the imperial court. In the latter part of the 18th century it was stripped of its baroque embellishments and its original Gothic features were restored. The Chapel of St. George, dating from 1337, is entered from the right aisle. The tomb of Maria Christina, the favorite daughter of Maria Theresa, is housed in the main nave near the rear entrance, but there's no body in it. (The princess was actually buried in the Imperial Crypt, which is described later in this section.) The richly ornamented tomb is one of Canova's masterpieces. A small room in the Loreto Chapel is filled with urns containing the hearts of the imperial Habsburg family. They can be viewed through a window in an iron door. The Chapel of St. George and the Loreto Chapel are only open to the public by asking for a guided tour.

This church is as much a place of life as it is death. Hapsburg weddings here have included Maria Theresa to Francis Stephen of Lorraine in 1736, Marie Antoinette to Louis XVI of France in 1770, Marie-Louise of Austria to Napoléon in 1810 (by proxy—he didn't show up), and Franz Joseph to Elisabeth of Bavaria in 1854.

The most convenient—and perhaps the most dramatic—time to visit the church is on Sunday at 11am, when a high mass is celebrated with choir, soloists, and orchestra. On selected Sundays of the church year and in July and August, beautiful organ masses are presented during services. Admission for the masses is free, but donations are most welcome. On Friday at 7:30pm from the end of May until the end of September—and on certain selected Fridays throughout the year—organ recitals and concerts are also presented here. Tickets range from 80 to 200AS ($5.35 to $13.40), depending on the event.

✪ **Spanische Reitschule (Spanish Riding School).** Michaelerplatz 1, Hofburg. ☎ **01/533-9032.** Regular performances 250–900AS ($16.75–$60.30) seats, 200AS ($13.40) standing room. Classical art of riding with music 250AS ($16.75) adults, free for children 3–6 with an adult, children under age 3 not admitted. Training session 100AS ($6.70) adults, 30AS ($2) children. Regular shows Mar–June and Sept to mid-Dec, most Suns at 10:45am and some Weds at 7pm. Classical dressage with music performances Apr–June and Sept, most Sats at 10am. Training sessions Mar–June, first 2 weeks in Sept, and mid-Oct to mid-Dec Tues–Sat 10am–noon.

This riding school is a reminder that horses were an important part of everyday Vienna life for many centuries, particularly during the imperial heyday. The school is housed in a white, crystal-chandeliered ballroom in an 18th-century building. You'll marvel at the skill and beauty of the sleek Lippizaner stallions as their adept trainers put them through their paces in a show that hasn't changed for 4 centuries. These are the world's most famous, classically styled equine performers. Many North Americans have seen them in the States, but to watch the Lippizaners prance to the music of Johann Strauss or a Chopin polonaise in their home setting is a pleasure you shouldn't miss.

Reservations for performances must be made in advance, as early as possible. Order your tickets for the Sunday and Wednesday shows by writing to Spanische Reitschule, Hofburg, A-1010 Vienna (fax 01/535-0186 within Austria; 43/535-0186 elsewhere), or through a travel agency in Vienna. (Tickets for Saturday shows can be ordered only through a travel agency.) Tickets for training sessions with no advance reservations can be purchased at the entrance.

Lippizaner Museum. Reitschulgasse 2, Stallburg. ☎ **01/533-7811.** Admission 50AS ($3.35) adults, 35AS ($2.35) children. Daily 9am–6pm.

The latest attraction at Hofburg Palace is this newly opened museum near the stables of the famous white stallions. This permanent exhibition begins with the historic inception of the Spanish Riding School in the 16th century and extends to the stallions' near destruction in the closing weeks of World War II. Paintings, historic engravings, drawings, photographs, uniforms and bridles, plus video and film presentations, bring to life the history of the Spanish Riding School, offering an insight into the breeding and training of these champion horses. Visitors to the museum are able to see through a window into the stallions' stables while they are being fed and saddled.

2 Other Top Attractions

THE INNER CITY

✪ **Domkirche St. Stephan (St. Stephan's Cathedral).** Stephansplatz 1. ☎ **01/515-52563.** Free admission Cathedral; tour of catacombs 40AS ($2.70) adults, 15AS ($1) children under 15. Guided tour of cathedral 40AS ($2.70) adults, 15AS ($1) children under 15. North Tower 40AS ($2.70) adults, 15AS ($1) children under 15; South Tower 30AS ($2) adults, 20AS ($1.35) students, 10AS (65¢) children under 15. Evening tours, including tour of the roof, 130AS ($8.70) adults, 50AS ($3.35) children under 15. Cathedral, daily 6am–10pm except times of service. Tour of catacombs, Mon–Sat at 10, 11, and 11:30am, and 1:30, 2, 2:30, 3:30, 4, and 4:30pm; Sun at 2, 2:30, 3:30, 4, and 4:30pm. Guided tour of cathedral, Mon–Sat at 10:30am and 3pm; Sun at 3pm. Special evening tour Sat 7pm (June–Sept). North Tower, Oct–Mar daily 8:30am–5pm; Apr–Sept daily 9am–6pm. South Tower, daily 9am–5:30pm. Bus: 1A, 2A, or 3A. U-Bahn: Stephansplatz.

A basilica built on the site of a Romanesque sanctuary, this cathedral was founded in the 12th century in what was, even in the Middle Ages, the town's center.

Stephansdom was virtually destroyed in a 1258 fire that swept through Vienna, and toward the dawn of the 14th century the basilica's ruins were replaced by a Gothic building. The cathedral suffered terribly during the Turkish siege of 1683, but then experienced peace until Russian bombardments in 1945. Destruction continued as the Germans fired on Vienna as they fled the city at the close of World War II. Restored and reopened in 1948, the cathedral is today one of the greatest Gothic structures in Europe, rich in wood carvings, altars, sculptures, and paintings. The 450-foot steeple has come to symbolize the very spirit of Vienna.

The 352-foot-long cathedral is inextricably entwined with Viennese and Austrian history. It was here that mourners attended Mozart's "pauper's funeral" in 1791, and it was on the cathedral door that Napoléon posted his farewell edict in 1805.

The **pulpit** of St. Stephan's is the enduring masterpiece of stonecarver Anton Pilgrim. But the chief treasure of the cathedral is the carved, wooden **Wiener Neustadt altarpiece** that dates from 1447. The richly painted and gilded altar depicts the Virgin Mary between St. Catherine and St. Barbara and can be viewed in the left-hand chapel of the choir. In the Apostles' Choir look for the curious tomb of Emperor Frederick III. Made of a pinkish Salzburg marble in the 17th century, the carved tomb depicts hideous little hobgoblins trying to enter and wake the emperor from his eternal sleep. The entrance to the catacombs or crypt is on the north side next to the Capistran pulpit. Here you'll see the funeral urns that contain the entrails of 56 members of the Habsburg family. (As we noted earlier, the hearts are interned in St. George's Chapel of the Augustinerkirche, and the bodies are entombed in the Imperial Crypt of the Kapuziner Church.)

You can climb the 343-step South Tower of St. Stephan's for a view of the Vienna Woods. Called *Alter Steffl* (Old Steve), the tower, marked by its needlelike spire, dominates the city's skyline. It was originally built between 1350 and 1433 but was reconstructed after heavy damage in World War II. The North Tower (*Nordturm*), reached by elevator, was never finished to match the South Tower, but was crowned in the Renaissance style in 1579. From here you get a panoramic sweep of the city and the Danube.

✪ **Staatsoper (State Opera).** Opernring 2. ☎ **01/5144-42960.** Tours daily year-round, 2 to 5 times a day, depending on demand. Tour times are posted on a board outside the entrance. Tours 60AS ($4) per person. U-Bahn: Karlsplatz.

This is one of the most important opera houses in the world. When it was originally built in the 1860s, critics apparently so upset one of the architects, Eduard van der Null, that he killed himself. In 1945, at the end of World War II, despite other pressing needs, such as public housing, Vienna started restoration work on the theater, finishing it in time to celebrate the country's independence from occupation forces in 1955. It's so important to the Austrians that they don't seem to begrudge the some million schillings a day its operation costs taxpayers. (See also chapter 9, "Vienna After Dark.")

Gemäldegalerie der Akademie der Bildenden Künste (Gallery of Painting and Fine Arts). Schillerplatz 3. ☎ **01/58816.** Admission 50AS ($3.35) adults and children, 20AS ($1.35) students. Tues–Sun 10am–4pm. U-Bahn: Karlsplatz.

When in Vienna, always make at least one visit to this painting gallery to see the *Last Judgment* triptych by the incomparable Hieronymus Bosch. In this masterpiece, the artist conjured up all the demons of Hell for a terrifying view of the suffering and sins that humankind must endure. You'll also be able to view many Dutch and Flemish paintings, some from as far back as the 15th century, although the academy is noted for its 17th-century art. The gallery boasts works by van Dyck, Rembrandt, and a host of other artists. There are several works by Lucas Cranach the Elder, the most outstanding being his *Lucretia*, completed in 1532. Some say it's as enigmatic as *Mona Lisa*. Rubens is represented here by more than a dozen oil sketches. You can see Rembrandt's *Portrait of a Woman* and scrutinize Guardi's scenes from 18th-century Venice.

✪ **Kunsthistorisches Museum (Museum of Fine Arts).** Maria-Theresien-Platz, Burgring 5. ☎ **01/52524-0.** Admission 102AS ($6.85) adults, 80AS ($5.35) students and seniors, free for children under 6. Daily 10am–6pm. Thurs until 9pm. U-Bahn: Mariahilfer-strasse. Tram: 52, 58, D, or J.

Across from the Hofburg Palace, this huge building houses many of the fabulous art collections gathered by the Habsburgs as they added new territories to their empire. One highlight is the fine collection of ancient Egyptian and Greek art. The museum also has works by many of the great European masters, such as Velásquez and Titian.

On display here are Roger van der Weyden's *Crucifixion* triptych, a Memling altarpiece, and Jan van Eyck's portrait of Cardinal Albergati. But it's the works of Pieter Brueghel the Elder for which the museum is renowned. This 16th-century Flemish

Vienna Attractions

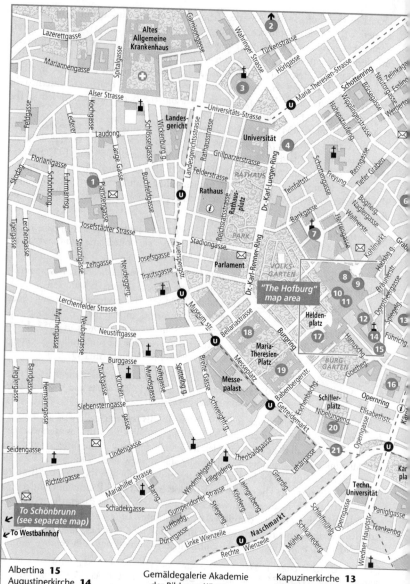

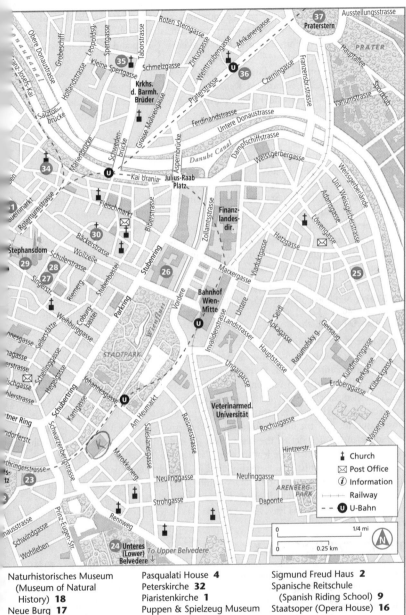

master is known for his sensitive yet vigorous landscapes. He did many lively studies
of peasant life, and his pictures today seem almost an ethnographic study of his time.
Don't leave without a glimpse of Brueghel's *Children's Games* and his *Hunters in the
Snow,* one of his most celebrated works.

Don't miss the work of van Dyck, especially his *Venus in the Forge of Vulcan,* nor
Peter Paul Rubens's *Self-Portrait* and *Woman with a Cape,* for which he is said to have
used the face of his second wife, Helen Fourment. The Rembrandt collection includes
two remarkable self-portraits as well as a moving portrait of his mother and one of his
son, Titus.

A highlight of any trip to Vienna is the museum's Albrecht Dürer collection. The
Renaissance German painter and engraver (1471–1528) is known for his innovative
art and his painstakingly detailed workmanship. *Blue Madonna* is here as are some of
his realistic landscapes, such as the *Martyrdom of 10,000 Christians.*

The glory of the French, Spanish, and Italian schools is also visible, having often
come into Habsburg hands as "gifts." Titian is represented by *A Girl with a Cloak,*
Veronese by an *Adoration of the Magi,* Caravaggio by his *Virgin of the Rosary,* Raphael
by *The Madonna in the Meadow,* and Tintoretto by his painting of Susanna caught off
guard in her bath. One of our all-time favorite painters is Giorgione, and here visitors
can gaze at his *Trio of Philosophers.*

Secession Building. Friedrichstrasse, 12 (on the western side of Karlsplatz). ☎ **01/
587-53070.** Admission 50AS ($3.35) adults, 30AS ($2) children. Special exhibitions 60AS
($4) adults, 40AS ($2.70) children. Tues–Wed 10am–6pm, Thurs 10am–8pm, Sat–Sun
10am–4pm. U-Bahn: Karlsplatz.

Come here if for no other reason than to see Gustav Klimt's *Beethoven Frieze,* a
30-meter-long visual interpretation of Beethoven's *Ninth Symphony.* This building—
a virtual art manifesto proclamation—stands south of the Opernring, beside the
Academy of Fine Arts. The Secession building was the home of the Viennese avant-garde,
which extolled the glories of *Jugendstil* or art nouveau. A young group of painters and
architects launched the Secessionist movement in 1897 in rebellion against the strict,
conservative ideas of the official Academy of Fine Arts. Gustav Klimt was a leader of
the movement, which defied the historicism favored by the Emperor Franz Joseph.
The works of Kokoschka were featured here, as was the "barbarian" Paul Gauguin.

Today the Secessionist artists are displayed in the Belvedere Palace, and this building is used for substantial contemporary exhibits. It was constructed in 1898 and is
crowned by a dome once called "outrageous in its useless luxury." The empty dome—
covered in triumphal laurel leaves—echoes that of the Karlskirche on the other side of
Vienna.

OUTSIDE THE INNER CITY
✪ **Schönbrunn Palace.** Schönbrunner Schlossstrasse. ☎ **01/81113.** Admission 125AS
($8.40) adults, 65AS ($4.35) children 6–15, free for children under 6. Gardens free. Apartments, Apr–Oct daily 8:30am–5pm; Nov–Mar daily 9am–4:30pm. U-Bahn: U-4 to Schönbrunn.

The 1,441-room Schönbrunn Palace was designed for the Habsburgs by those masters
of the baroque, the von Erlachs. It was built between 1696 and 1712, at the request
of Emperor Leopold I for his son, Joseph I. Leopold envisioned a palace whose
grandeur would surpass that of Versailles. However, Austria's treasury, drained by the
cost of wars, would not support the ambitious undertaking, and the original plans
were never carried out.

Schönbrunn Park & Palace

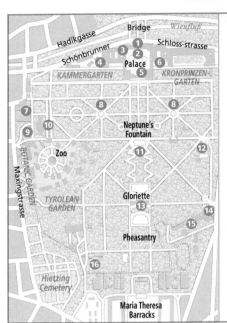

THE PARK

1 Main Gate
2 Courtyard
3 Theater
4 Mews
5 Chapel
6 Restaurant
7 Hietzing Church
8 Naiad's Fountains
9 Joseph II Monument
10 Palm House
11 Neptune's Fountain
12 Schöner Brunnen
13 Gloriette
14 Small Gloriette
15 Spring
16 Octagonal Pavilion

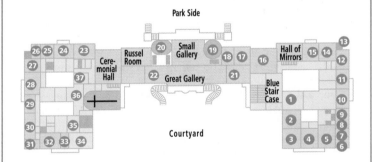

THE PALACE

1 Guard Room
2 Billiard Room
3 Walnut Room
4 Franz Joseph's Study
5 Franz Joseph's Bedroom
6 Cabinet
7 Stairs Cabinet
8 Dressing Room
9 Bedroom of Franz Joseph I & Elisabeth
10 Empress Elisabeth's Salon
11 Marie Antoinette's Room

12 Nursery
13 Breakfast Room
14 Yellow Salon
15 Balcony Room
16 17 18 Rosa Rooms
19 20 Round and Oval Chinese Cabinets
21 Lantern Room
22 Carousel Room
23 Blue Chinese Salon
24 Vieux-Laque Room
25 Napoleon Room
26 Porcelain Room

27 Millions Room
28 Gobelin Tapestry Room
29 Archduchess Sophie's Study
30 Red Drawing Room
31 East Terrace Cabinet
32 Bed-of-State Room
33 Writing Room
34 Drawing Room
35 Wild Boar Room
36 Passage Chamber
37 Bergl-Zimmer

An Evening with Mozart

Schönbrunn Palace's greatest summer attraction is the **Mozart Festival,** presented from June to September, with the majority of concerts in July and August. This open-air festival, set in the Imperial Gardens, was initiated in 1992. It attracts top-notch international artists and is bound to include a performance of the opera *Don Giovanni.* Among recent additions was an all-new staging of *Die Zauberflöte,* perhaps Mozart's most enigmatic opera. Under the starry summer sky, a night of enchantment awaits visitors in a city renowned for its charmed musical progeny. Concerts begin at 9:30pm and last for 90 minutes, with ticket prices ranging from 64 to 94AS ($5.10 to $7.50). For more information on the **Festival Mozart in Schönbrunn,** 24 Fleischmarkt, A-1010 Vienna, call ☎ **01/512-0100.**

When Maria Theresa became empress, she changed the original plans, and Schönbrunn looks today much as she conceived it. Done in "Maria Theresa ochre," with delicate rococo touches designed for her by Austrian Nikolaus Pacassi, the palace is in complete contrast to the grim, forbidding Hofburg. Schönbrunn was the imperial summer palace during Maria Theresa's 40-year reign, and it was the scene of great ceremonial balls, lavish banquets, and fabulous receptions held during the Congress of Vienna. At the age of 6, Mozart performed in the Hall of Mirrors before Maria Theresa and her court. The empress's secret meetings with her chancellor, Prince Kaunitz, were held in the round Chinese Room.

Franz Joseph was born within the palace walls. It was the setting for the lavish court life associated with his reign, and he spent the final years of his life here. The last of the Habsburg rulers, Karl I, signed a document here on November 11, 1918, renouncing his participation in affairs of state—not quite an abdication, but tantamount to one. Allied bombs damaged the palace during World War II, but restoration has obliterated the scars.

The **Imperial Gardens** of the palace are embellished by the Gloriette, a marble summerhouse topped by a stone canopy with an imperial eagle. The so-called Roman Ruins, dating from the late 18th century when it was fashionable to simulate the ravaged grandeur of Rome, consist of a collection of marble statues and fountains. The park was laid out by Adria van Steckhoven and contains many fountains and heroic statues, often depicting Greek mythological characters. It can be visited until sunset daily.

The **State Apartments** are the most stunning display in the palace. Much of the interior ornamentation is in the rococo style, with red, white, and gold (real 23½ karat gold) predominating. Of the 40 rooms that you can visit, particularly fascinating is the "Room of Millions," decorated with Indian and Persian miniatures—a truly grand rococo salon. Guided tours of many of the palace rooms, lasting 50 minutes, are narrated in English every half hour beginning at 9:30am. (You should tip the guide.)

Also on the grounds is the baroque **Schlosstheater** (Palace Theater; ☎ **01/ 876-4272**), which has summer performances. Marie Antoinette appeared on its stage in pastorals during her happy youth, and Max Reinhardt, the theatrical impresario, launched an acting school here.

The **Wagenburg** or Carriage Museum (☎ **01/877-3244**) is also worth a visit. It contains a fine display of imperial coaches from the 17th through the 20th century. The museum is open from April to October, Tuesday to Sunday from 9am to 6pm; and November to March, Tuesday to Sunday, 10am to 5pm. Admission is 60AS ($4) for adults and 40AS ($2.70) for seniors and children age 10 and under.

Österreichische Galerie Belvedere. Prinz-Eugen-Strasse 27. ☎ **01/79557.** Admission 90AS ($6.05) adults, free for children 16 and under. Tues–Sun 10am–6pm. Tram: D to Schloss Belvedere.

Southeast of Karlsplatz, the Belvedere sits on a slope above Vienna. The approach to the palace is memorable—through a long garden with a huge circular pond that reflects the sky and the looming palace buildings. Designed by Johann Lukas von Hildebrandt, who was the last major Austrian baroque architect, the Belvedere was built as a summer home for Prince Eugene of Savoy. It consists of two palatial buildings, made up of a series of interlocking cubes. The interior is dominated by two great, flowing staircases. The Gold Salon in Lower Belvedere is one of the most beautiful rooms in the palace. A regal French-style garden lies between the two buildings.

Unteres Belvedere (Lower Belvedere), with its entrance at Rennweg 6A, was constructed from 1714 to 1716. **Oberes Belvedere** (Upper Belvedere) was started in 1721 and completed in 1723. Anton Bruckner, the composer, lived in one of the buildings until his death in 1896. The palace was the residence of Archduke Franz Ferdinand, whose assassination sparked World War I. In May 1955, the peace treaty recognizing Austria as a sovereign state was signed in Upper Belvedere by the Allied powers. The treaty is on display in a large salon decorated in red marble.

The Lower (Unteres) Belvedere houses the **Barockmuseum** (Museum of Baroque Art). The original sculptures from the Neuer Markt fountain (replaced now by copies), the work of Georg Raphael Donner, who died in 1741, are displayed here. During his life, Donner dominated the development of Austrian sculpture. The fountain's four figures represent the four major tributaries of the Danube. Works by Franz Anton Maulbertsch, an 18th-century painter, are also exhibited here. Maulbertsch, strongly influenced by Tiepolo, was the greatest and most original Austrian painter of his day. He was best known for his iridescent colors and flowing brushwork.

Museum Mittelalterlicher Kunst (Museum of Medieval Art) is located in the Orangery at Lower Belvedere. Here you'll see art from the Gothic period as well as a Tyrolean Romanesque crucifix that dates from the 12th century. Outstanding works include Rueland Frueauf's seven panels depicting scenes from the life of the Madonna and the Passion of Christ.

Upper (Oberes) Belvedere houses the **Galerie des 19. and 20. Jahrhunderts** (Gallery of 19th- and 20th-Century Art). Here you also find the works by the artists of the 1897 Secessionist movement. Most outstanding are those by Gustav Klimt (1862–1918), one of the movement's founders. Klimt's highly decorative painting uses a geometrical approach, blending figures with their backgrounds. Witness the extraordinary *Judith.* Other notable works by Klimt are *The Kiss, Adam and Eve,* and five panoramic lakeside landscapes from Attersee. Sharing almost equal billing with Klimt is Egon Schiele (1890–1918), whose masterpieces here include *The Wife of an Artist.* Schiele could be both morbid, as exemplified by *Death and Girl,* or cruelly observant, as in *The Artist's Family.* Works by Vincent van Gogh, Oskar Kokoschka, James Ensor, and C. D. Freidrich are also represented.

Hundertwasserhaus. Löwengasse and Kegelgasse 3. No phone. U-Bahn: Landstrasse. Tram: N.

In a city filled with baroque palaces and numerous architectural adornments, this sprawling public-housing project in the rather bleak 3rd District is visited—or at least seen from the window of a tour bus—by about a million visitors annually. Completed in 1985, it was the work of self-styled "eco-architect" Friedensreich Hundertwasser. The complex, which has a facade like a gigantic black-and-white game board, is relieved with scattered splotches of red, yellow, and blue. Trees stick out at 45° angles from apartments designed to accommodate human tenants among the foliage.

There are 50 apartments here, and signs warn not to go inside. However, there's a tiny gift shop at the entrance where you can buy Hundertwasser posters and postcards, plus a coffee shop on the first floor. With its irregular shape, its turrets, and its "rolling meadows" of grass and trees, the Hundertwasserhaus is certainly the most controversial building in Vienna.

Museum Moderner Kunst Stiftung Ludwig Wien (Museum of Modern Art). Arsenalstrasse 1 and Fürstengasse 1. ☎ **01/317-6900** or 01/799-6900. Admission 60AS ($4) adults for 1 house, 80AS ($5.35) for both houses; 40AS ($2.70) students and seniors for 1 house, 60AS ($4) for both houses; free for children under 11. Both houses Tues–Sun 10am–6pm. U-Bahn: Südtirolerplatz for Museum des 20. Jahrhunderts. Tram: D to Fürstengasse for Palais Liechtenstein.

This museum comprises two exhibition buildings, the Museum des 20. Jahrhunderts, which was first opened to the public in 1962, and the Palais Liechtenstein, a building rented in 1979 to add more exhibition space. The **Museum des 20. Jahrhunderts** at the Schweizer Garten is housed in a pavilion originally constructed for the world exposition in Brussels in 1958. On the first floor of the museum, large alternating exhibitions are presented. The international collection is exhibited on the second floor, featuring the works of such artists as Donald Judd, Lawrence Weiner, Bertrand Lavier, and Jannis Kounellis. In the sculpture gardens, you'll discover works by Henry Moore, Fritz Wotruba, and Alberto Giacometti.

The baroque **Palais Liechtenstein,** built between 1698 and 1711, displays a cross section of 20th-century international art. Special rooms are dedicated to various art movements from expressionism (Jawlensky, Pechstein) to cubism (Léger, Gleizes) to futurism (Balla), and on and on, ranging from surrealism (Magritte, Ernst) to Vienna Actionism (Nitsch, Rainer), and ending with pop art (Warhol, Rauschenberg).

3 Churches

See also section 1 of this chapter for the Burgkapelle, where the Vienna Boys' Choir performs, and the Augustinerkirche. Section 2, "Other Top Attractions," contains the description of St. Stephan's Cathedral.

THE INNER CITY

✪ **Kapuzinerkirche.** With the Kaisergruft (Imperial Crypt). Neuer Markt. ☎ **01/512-6853.** Admission 40AS ($2.70) adults, 30AS ($2) children. Daily 9:30am–4pm. U-Bahn: Stephansplatz.

The Kapuziner Church (just inside the ring behind the Opera) has housed the Imperial Crypt, the burial vault of the Habsburgs, for some 3 centuries. Capuchin friars guard the family's final resting place, where 12 emperors, 17 empresses, and dozens of archdukes are entombed. But only their bodies are here. Their hearts are in urns in the Loreto Chapel of the Augustinerkirche in the Hofburg complex, and their entrails are similarly enshrined in a crypt below St. Stephan's Cathedral.

Most outstanding of the imperial tombs is the double sarcophagus of Maria Theresa and her consort, Francis Stephen (François, duke of Lorraine or, in German, Franz von Lothringen, 1708–65), the parents of Marie Antoinette. Before her own death, the empress used to descend into the tomb often to visit the gravesite of her beloved Francis. The "King of Rome," the ill-fated son of Napoléon and Marie-Louise of Austria, was buried here in a bronze coffin after his death at age 21. (Hitler managed to anger both the Austrians and the French by having the remains of Napoléon's son transferred to Paris in 1940.) Although she was not a Habsburg, Countess Fuchs, the governess who practically reared Maria Theresa, also lies in the crypt.

Emperor Franz Joseph was interred here in 1916. He was a frail old man who out-lived his time and died just before the final collapse of his empire. His wife, Empress Elis-abeth, was also buried here after her assassination in Geneva in 1898, as was their son, Archduke Rudolf, who allegedly committed suicide at Mayerling (see box in chapter 10).

Die Deutschordenkirche (Church of the Teutonic Order). Singerstrasse 7. ☎ 01/512-1065. Free admission to the church; treasury, 50AS ($3.35) adults, 30AS ($2) children under 11. Church daily 9am–6pm. Treasury Mon–Tues and Thurs 10am–noon; Wed and Fri–Sat 3–5pm. U-Bahn: Stephansplatz.

The Order of the Teutonic Knights was a German society founded in 1190 in the Holy Land. The order came to Vienna in 1205, but the church they built dates from 1395. The building never fell prey to the baroque madness that swept the city after the Counter-Reformation, so you see it pretty much in its original form, a Gothic church dedicated to St. Elizabeth. The 16th-century Flemish altarpiece standing at the main altar is richly decorated with wood carving, gilt, and painted panel inserts. Many knights of the Teutonic Order are buried here, their heraldic shields still mounted on some of the upper walls.

In the knights' treasury, on the second floor of the church, you'll see mementos such as seals and coins illustrating the history of the order, as well as a collection of arms, vases, gold, crystal, and precious stones. Also on display are the charter given to the Teutonic Order by Henry IV of England and a collection of medieval paintings. A curious exhibit is the Viper Tongue Credenza, said to have the power to detect poison in food and render it harmless.

Maria Am Gestade (St. Mary's on the Bank). At Passauer Platz. ☎ 01/5339-5940. Free admission. Daily 7am–7pm. U-Bahn: Stephanplatz.

This church, also known as the Church of Our Lady of the Riverbank, was once just that. With an arm of the Danube flowing by, it was a favorite place of worship for fish-ermen. But the river was redirected, and now the church relies on its own beauty to draw people. A Romanesque church on this site was rebuilt in the Gothic style between 1394 and 1427. The western facade is flamboyant, with a remarkable seven-sided Gothic tower surmounted by a dome that culminates in a lacelike crown.

Michaelerkirche (Church of St. Michael). Michaelerplatz. ☎ 01/533-8000. Free admis-sion. Mon–Sat 6:45am–8pm; Sun 8am–6:30pm. U-Bahn: Herrengasse. Bus: 1A, 2A, or 3A.

Over its long history, this church has felt the hand of many architects and designers, resulting in a medley of styles, not all harmonious. Some of the remaining Romanesque sections can be traced to the early 1200s. The exact date of the chancel is not known, but it's probably from the mid-14th century. The catacombs remain as they were in the Middle Ages.

Most of St. Michael's as it appears today dates from 1792, when the facade was redone in neoclassical style; however, the spire is from the 16th century. The main altar is richly decorated in baroque style, and the altarpiece, entitled *The Collapse of the Angels* (1781), was the last major baroque work completed in Vienna.

Minoritenkirche (Church of the Minorites). Minoritenplatz 2A. ☎ 01/533-4162. Free admission. Apr–Oct Mon–Sat 9am–6pm; Nov–Mar Mon–Sat 9am–5pm. U-Bahn: Herrengasse.

If you're tired of baroque ornamentation, visit this church of the Friar Minor Conven-tual, a Franciscan order also called the Minorite friars (inferior brothers). Construction of this church began in 1250 but was not completed until early in the 14th century. Its tower was damaged by the Turks in their two sieges of Vienna, and it later fell prey to baroque architects and designers in the 18th century. But in 1784, Ferdinand von Hohenberg ordered the baroque additions removed, and the simple lines of the

This is one of the most perplexing cities that I was ever in. It is extensive, irregular, crowded, dusty, dissipated, magnificent, and to me disagreeable. It has immense palaces, superb galleries of paintings, several theatres, public walks, and drives crowded with equipages. In short, everything bears the stamp of luxury and ostentation; for here is assembled and concentrated all the wealth, fashion, and nobility of the Austrian empire.
Washington Irving, letter to his sister, from *Tales of a Traveller (1824)*

original Gothic church returned, complete with Gothic cloisters. Inside you'll see a mosaic copy of da Vinci's *The Last Supper.* Masses are held on Sunday at 8:30 and 11am.

Peterskirche (St. Peter's Church). Peterplatz. ☎ **01/533-6433.** Free admission. Daily 9am–6:30pm. U-Bahn: Stephansplatz.

This is the second-oldest church in Vienna, but the spot on which it stands may well be Vienna's oldest Christian church site. It's believed that a place of worship stood here in the second half of the 4th century. Charlemagne is credited with having founded a church on the site during the late 8th or early 9th century.

The present St. Peter's, the most lavishly decorated baroque church in Vienna, was designed in 1702 by Gabriel Montani. Hildebrandt, the noted architect who designed the Belvedere Palace, is believed to have finished the building in 1732. The fresco in the dome is a masterpiece by J. M. Rottmayr depicting the coronation of the Virgin. The church contains many frescoes and much gilded carved wood, plus altarpieces done by well-known artists of the period.

Ruprechtskirche (St. Rupert's Church). Ruprechtsplatz. ☎ **01/553-6003.** Free admission. Mon–Thurs 9:30–11:30am; Fri 9:30am–1pm. U-Bahn: Schwedenplatz.

The oldest church in Vienna, Ruprechtskirche has stood here since 740, although much that you see now, such as the aisle, is from the 11th century. Beautiful new stained-glass windows, the work of Lydia Roppolt, were installed in 1993. It's believed that much of the masonry from a Roman shrine on this spot was used in the present church. The tower and nave are Romanesque; the rest of the church is Gothic. St. Rupert is the patron saint of the Danube's salt merchants.

Universitätskirche (Church of the Jesuits). Dr.-Ignaz-Seipel-Platz 1. ☎ **01/512-1335** or 01/5125-2320. Free admission. Daily 8am–7pm. U-Bahn: Stephansplatz or Stubentor. Tram: 1 or 2. Bus: 1A.

Built at the time of the Counter-Reformation, this church is rich in baroque embellishments. This was the university church, dedicated to the Jesuit saints Ignatius of Loyola and Franciscus Xaverius. The high-baroque decorations—galleries, columns, and the *trompe-l'oeil* painting on the ceiling, which gives the illusion of a dome—were added from 1703 to 1705. The embellishments were the work of a Jesuit lay brother, Andrea Pozzo, at the orders of Emperor Leopold I. Look for Pozzo's painting of Mary behind the main altar. Choir and orchestra services (mostly classical) are celebrated on Sunday and Holy Days at 10am.

OUTSIDE THE INNER CITY

✪ **Karlskirche (Church of St. Charles).** Karlsplatz. ☎ **01/504-6187.** Free admission. Self-guided tours, 10AS (65¢) adults, 5AS (35¢) children. Mon–Fri 7:30am–7pm; Sat 8:30am–7pm; Sun 9am–7pm. Bus: 4.

Construction on Karlskirche, dedicated to St. Charles Borromeo, was begun in 1716 by order of Emperor Charles VI. The Black Plague swept Vienna in 1713, and the emperor made a vow to build the church if the disease would abate. The master of the baroque, Johann Bernard Fischer von Erlach, did the original work on the church from 1716 to 1722, and his son, Joseph Emanuel, completed it between 1723 and 1737. The lavishly decorated interior stands as a testament to the father-and-son duo. J. M. Rottmayr painted many of the frescoes inside the church from 1725 to 1730.

The green copper dome of Karlskirche is 236 feet high, a dramatic landmark on the Viennese skyline. Two columns, spin-offs from Trajan's Column in Rome, flank the front of the church, which opens onto Karlsplatz. There's also a sculpture by Henry Moore in a little pool.

Piaristenkirche (Church of the Piarist Order). Piaristeng 54. ☎ **01/405-9553.** Free admission. Mon–Fri 2:30–6pm; Sat 10am–noon. U-Bahn: Rathaus.

Work on the Piaristenkirche, more popularly known as Piaristenplatz, was launched in 1716 by a Roman Catholic teaching congregation known as the Piarists (fathers of religious schools). The church, however, was not consecrated until 1771. Some of the designs submitted during that long period are believed to have been drawn by von Hildebrandt, the noted architect who designed the Belvedere Palace, but many builders had a hand in its construction. This church is noteworthy for its fine classic facade as well as the frescoes by F. A. Maulbertsch, which adorn the inside of the circular cupolas.

Votivkirche. Rooseveltplatz 8. ☎ **01/406-1192.** Free admission. Tues–Sun 9am–1pm and 4–6:30pm. U-Bahn: Schottenor.

After a failed assassination attempt on Emperor Franz Joseph, a collection was taken for the construction of the Votive Church, which sits across from the site where the attempt was made. Heinrich von Ferstel began work on the neo-Gothic church in 1856, but it was not consecrated until 1879. The magnificent facade features awesome lacy spires and intricate sculpture. Most noteworthy is the Renaissance sarcophagus tomb of Niklas Salm, who commanded Austrian forces during the Turkish siege in 1529.

4 Museums & Galleries

THE INNER CITY

Naturhistorisches Museum (Natural History Museum). Maria-Theresien Platz, Burgring 5. ☎ **01/521770.** Admission 50AS ($3.35). Wed 9am–9pm; Thurs–Mon 9am–6:30pm. U-Bahn: Volkstheater. Tram: 52, 58, D, or J.

In a handsome neo-Renaissance building near the Museum of Fine Arts, this museum has important collections of early Stone Age artifacts, anthropological and zoological materials, and meteorites. The notable exhibit here is the Stone-Age figure called Venus of Willendorf, whose discovery in 1906 attests to the area's ancient habitation.

Österreichisches Museum für Angewandte Kunst (Museum of Applied Art). Stubenring 5. ☎ **01/711360.** Admission 90AS ($6.05) adults, 45AS ($3) children 6–18, free for children 5 and under. Tues 10am–midnight; Wed–Sun 10am–6pm. U-Bahn: Stubentor. Tram: 1, 2.

Of special interest here is a rich collection of tapestries, some from the 16th century, and the most outstanding assemblage of Viennese porcelain in the world. Look for a Persian carpet depicting *The Hunt* as well as the group of 13th-century Limoges enamels. Biedermeier furniture and other antiques, glassware and crystal, and large collections of lace and textiles are also displayed. An entire hall is devoted to art nouveau. There are outstanding objects from the Wiener Werkstatte (Vienna Workshop), founded in 1903 by architect Josef Hoffman. In the workshop, large numbers of well-known artists and craftsmen created a variety of objects—glass, porcelain, textiles, wooden articles, and jewelry.

Uhrenmuseum der Stadt Wien (Municipal Clock Museum). Schulhof 2. ☎ **01/ 533-2265.** Admission 50AS ($3.35) adults, 20AS ($1.35) children. Tues–Sun 9am–4:30pm. U-Bahn: Stephansplatz.

A wide-ranging group of timepieces—some ancient, some modern—are on view here. Housed in what was once the Obizzi town house, the museum dates from 1917 and attracts clock collectors from all over Europe and North America. Check out Rutschmann's 18th-century astronomical clock. There are several interesting cuckoo clocks and a gigantic timepiece that was once mounted in the tower of St. Stephan's.

OUTSIDE THE INNER CITY

Heeresgeschichtliches Museum (Museum of Military History). Arsenal 3. ☎ **01/ 79561.** Admission 70AS ($4.70) adults, 45AS ($3) children. Sat–Thurs 9am–5pm. Closed Jan 1, Easter, May 1, Nov 1, Dec 24–25 and 31. Tram: 18 or D.

The oldest state museum in Vienna, this building was constructed from 1850 to 1856, a precursor to the Ringstrasse style. Inside, Habsburg military history—defeats as well as triumphs—is delineated.

A special display case in front of the Franz-Josef Hall contains the six orders of the House of Habsburg that Franz Joseph sported on all public occasions. The Sarajevo room is fascinating—it contains mementos of the assassination of Archduke Franz Ferdinand and his wife on June 28, 1914, the event that sparked World War I. The archduke's bloodstained uniform is displayed, along with the bullet-scarred car in which the royal couple rode. Many exhibits focus on the Austro-Hungarian navy, and frescoes depict important battles, including those fought against the Turks in and around Vienna.

Historisches Museum der Stadt Wien (Historical Museum of Vienna). Karlsplatz 4. ☎ **01/505-8747.** Admission 50AS ($3.35) adults, 20AS ($1.35) children. Tues–Sun 9am–6pm. U-Bahn: Karlsplatz.

History buffs should seek out this fascinating but little-visited collection. Here the full panorama of Old Vienna's history unfolds, beginning with the settlement of prehistoric tribes in the Danube basin. Roman relics, artifacts from the reign of the dukes of Babenberg, and a wealth of leftovers from the Habsburg sovereignty are on display, as well as arms and armor from various eras. A scale model shows Vienna as it looked in the Habsburg heyday. You'll see pottery and ceramics dating from the Roman era, 14th-century stained-glass windows, mementos of the Turkish sieges of 1529 and 1683, and Biedermeier furniture. There's also a section on Vienna's art nouveau.

Sigmund Freud Haus. Berggasse 19. ☎ **01/319-1596.** Admission 60AS ($4) adults, 40AS ($2.70) seniors and students, 25AS ($1.70) children 10–15, free for children under 10. Daily 9am–6pm. Tram: D to Schlickgasse.

Walking through this museum, you can almost imagine the good doctor ushering you in and telling you to make yourself comfortable on the couch. The study and waiting room he used during his residence here from 1891 to 1938 are filled with antiques and mementos, including his velour hat and dark walking stick with ivory handle.

The museum also has a bookshop with a variety of postcards of the apartment, books by Freud, posters, prints, and pens.

5 Parks & Gardens

When the weather is fine, Vienna's residents shun city parks in favor of the **Wiener-wald (Vienna Woods),** a wide arc of forested countryside that surrounds northwestern and southwestern Vienna (for more details, see chapter 10, "Side Trips from Vienna"). But if you love parks, you'll find some magnificent ones in Vienna, where there are more than 4,000 acres of gardens and parks within the city limits and no fewer than 770 sports fields and playgrounds. You can, of course, visit the grounds of **Schönbrunn Park** and **Belvedere Park** when you tour those once-royal palaces. Below, we highlight only the most popular parks of Vienna.

THE INNER CITY

✪ **Stadtpark**. Parkring. Tram: 1, 2, J, or T. U-Bahn: Stadtpark.

This lovely park lies on the slope where the Danube used to overflow into the Inner City before the construction of the Danube Canal. Many memorial statues stand in the park; the best known depicts Johann Strauss Jr., composer of operettas and waltzes like "The Blue Danube Waltz." Here, too, are monuments to Franz Schubert and Hans Makart, a well-known artist whose work you'll see in churches and museums throughout Vienna. These monuments are surrounded by verdant squares of grass, well-manicured flower gardens, and plenty of benches. The park is open 24 hours daily.

From Easter to October, **Café Maierei am Stadtpark** (☎ **01/714-61-590**), built in 1867, is an old-world schmaltzy cafe with occasional bouts of waltz music. You can sit at a garden table and often enjoy live music as you sip the local wine.

Burggarten. Operning-Burgring, next to the Hofburg. Tram: 1, 2, 52, 58, or D.

These are the former gardens of the Habsburg emperors. They were laid out soon after the Volksgarten (see below) was completed. Look for the monument to Mozart as well as an equestrian statue of Francis Stephen, Maria Theresa's beloved husband. The only open-air statue of Franz Joseph in all Vienna is also here, and there's a statue of Goethe at the park entrance.

Volksgarten (People's Park). Dr.-Karl-Renner-Ring, between the Hofburg and the Burgtheater. Tram: 1, 2, or D.

Laid out in 1820 on the site of the old city wall fortifications, Vienna's oldest public garden can be entered from Dr.-Karl-Lueger-Ring. It's dotted with monuments, including a 1907 memorial to assassinated Empress Elisabeth and the so-called Temple of Theseus, a copy of the Theseion in Athens.

OUTSIDE THE INNER CITY

✪ **Praterverband (The Prater)**. Prater 9. ☎ **01/728-05-16**. Free admission, but you'll pay for various rides and amusements. May–Sept daily 9am–midnight; Oct–Nov daily 10am–10pm; Nov 4–Dec 1 daily 10am–6pm. U-Bahn: Praterstern.

This extensive tract of woods and meadowland in the 2nd District has been Vienna's favorite recreation area since 1766, when Emperor Joseph II opened it to the public. Before it became a public park, it had been used as a hunting preserve and riding ground for the aristocracy.

The Prater is an open fairground, without barricades and without an entrance gate. Its attractions are independently operated and maintained by individual entrepreneurs, who determine their own hours, prices, and, to a large extent, their own policies and priorities. The Prater is probably the most loosely organized amusement park in Europe, more a public park or garden that happens to have rides and food kiosks sprouting from the flowerbeds and statuary. Few other spots in Vienna convey such a sense of the decadent end to the Habsburg empire—it's turn-of-the-century nostalgia, with a touch of 1950s-era tawdriness thrown in.

The Prater is the birthplace of the waltz, first introduced here in 1820 by Johann Strauss (I) and Josef Lanner. However, it was under Johann Strauss (II), "the king of the waltz," that this musical form reached its greatest popularity.

Tales of the Vienna Woods

The Vienna Woods (*Wienerwald* in German) weren't simply dreamed up by Johann Strauss (II) to enliven his musical tales told in waltz time. The Wiener-wald is a delightful hilly landscape of gentle paths and trees that borders Vienna on its southwestern and northwestern sides. If you stroll through this area, a weekend playground for the Viennese, you'll be following in the footsteps of Strauss and Schubert. Beethoven, when his hearing was failing, claimed that the chirping birds, the trees, and leafy vineyards of the Wienerwald made it easier for him to compose.

A round-trip through the woods takes about 3½ hours by car, a distance of some 50 miles (80km). Even if you don't have a car, the woods can be visited relatively easily. Board tram no. 1 near the State Opera, going to Schottentor; here, switch to tram no. 38 (the same ticket is valid) going out to the village of **Grinzing,** home to the famous heurigen (wine taverns). If you can resist the heurigen, board bus no. 38A, which goes through the Wienerwald up the hill to **Kahlenberg,** on the northeasternmost spur of the Alps (1,585 feet/483m). The whole trip takes about 1 hour each way.

If the weather is fair and clear, from Kahlenberg you can see all the way to Hungary and Slovakia. At the top of the hill is the small Church of St. Joseph, where King John Sobieski of Poland stopped to pray before leading his troops to the defense of Vienna against the Turks. For one of the best views of Vienna, go to the right of the Kahlenberg restaurant. From the terrace you'll have a panoramic sweep, including the spires of St. Stephan's.

Many Austrian visitors from the country, a hardy lot, walk along a footpath to the suburbs of **Nussdorf** and **Heiligenstadt.** At Nussdorf, it's possible to take tram D back to the center of Vienna.

For more about the Wienerwald, see chapter 10, "Side Trips from Vienna."

The best-known part of the huge park is at the end nearest the entrance from the Ring. Here you'll find the **Riesenrad,** the giant 220-foot Ferris wheel, which was constructed in 1897. Erected at a time when European engineers were showing off their "high-tech" abilities, the wheel was designed by Walter Basset, a British engineer following in the footsteps of Alexandre Eiffel, who had constructed his tower in Paris a decade earlier. It was designed for the Universal Exhibition (1896–97), marking the golden anniversary of Franz Joseph's coronation as emperor in 1848. Like the Eiffel Tower, it was intended only as a temporary exhibition. But except for World War II damage, the Ferris wheel has been rotating without interruption since 1897.

In 1997, the Ferris wheel celebrated its 100th anniversary, and it remains (after St. Stephan's Cathedral tower) the second most famous landmark in Vienna. It was immortalized in the 1951 film *The Third Man* with Joseph Cotten and Orson Welles. To ride the Ferris wheel costs 55AS ($3.70) for adults, 20AS ($1.35) for youths age 4 to 14, and 5AS (35¢) for ages 1 to 3.

Just beside the Riesenrad is the terminus of the **Lilliputian railroad,** the 2.6-mile narrow-gauge line that operates in summer using vintage steam locomotives. The amusement park, right behind the Ferris wheel, has all the typical entertainment facilities—roller coasters, merry-go-rounds, tunnels of love, game arcades. Rides usually cost from 40 to 50AS ($2.70 to $3.35) each. There are also swimming pools, riding schools, and racecourses. International soccer matches are held in the Prater stadium.

If you drive here, don't forget to observe the NO ENTRY and NO PARKING signs, which apply after 3pm daily. The place is frequently jammed on Sunday afternoons in summer.

Botanischer Garten (Botanical Garden of the University of Vienna). Rennweg 14. ☎ **01/4277-54100.** Free admission. Apr and Oct daily 9am–5pm; May and Sept daily 9am–7pm; June–Aug daily 9am–7:30pm. Tram: 71 to Unteres Belvedere.

These lush gardens contain exotic (and sometimes rare) plants from all over the world. Located in Landstrasse (3rd District) right next to the Belvedere Park, the Botanical Garden developed on a spot where Maria Theresa once ordered medicinal herbs to be planted. Always call in advance if the weather is doubtful.

Donaupark. Wagramer Strasse. U-Bahn to Reichsbrücke.

This 247-acre park, located in the 22nd District between the Danube Canal and the Alte Donau (Old Danube), was converted in 1964 from a garbage dump to a recreation park. Within the park you'll find flower- and shrub-filled grounds, a bee house, a bird sanctuary with native and exotic specimens, a small-animal paddock, a horse-riding course, playgrounds, and games.

An outstanding feature of the park is the **Donauturm** (Danube Tower), Donauturmstrasse 4 (☎ **01/2633-5720**), an 828-foot tower with two rotating cafe-restaurants. One restaurant is at 528 feet, the other at 561 feet; both offer a panoramic view of the city and serve international and Viennese specialties. There's also a sightseeing terrace at 495 feet. Two express elevators take people up the tower, which in summer is open daily from 9am to midnight, and in winter, daily from 10am to midnight. The charge for the elevator ride is 65AS ($4.35) for adults and 45AS ($3) for children.

6 Especially for Kids

The greatest attraction for kids is the **Prater Amusement Park,** but there's much more in Vienna that children find amusing, especially the performances at the **Spanish Riding School.** They also love climbing the tower of **St. Stephan's Cathedral.** The **Natural History Museum** has a children's room as well as other collections the kids will enjoy. And nothing quite tops a day like a picnic in the **Vienna Woods.**

Other worthwhile museums for children include the **Zirkus und Clownmuseum (Circus and Clown Museum),** Karmelitergasse 9 (☎ **01/369-1111**), a tribute to clowns and circus performers throughout the centuries; and the **Wiener Straasenbahnmuseum (Streetcar Museum),** Ludwig-Koessler-Platz (☎ **01/7909-44900**), which commemorates the public conveyances that helped usher Vienna and the Habsburg Empire into the Industrial Age.

Below, we list other fun-filled attractions that you and your children will love. (See also "Sports & Active Pursuits" at the end of this chapter.)

Schönbrunner Tiergarten. Schönbrunn Gardens. ☎ **01/8779-2940.** Admission 120AS ($8.05) adults, 55AS ($3.70) students, 30AS ($2) children 3–6. Mar–Sept daily 9am–6:30pm; Oct–Feb daily 9am–5pm. U-Bahn: Hietzing.

The world's oldest zoo was founded by the husband of Empress Maria Theresa. Maria Theresa liked to have breakfast here with her brood, favoring animal antics with her eggs. The baroque buildings in the historical park landscape present a unique setting for modern animal keeping; the tranquility makes for a relaxing, yet interesting outing.

Puppen & Spielzeug Museum (Doll and Toy Museum). Schulhof 4. ☎ **01/535-6860.** Admission 60AS ($4) adults, 30AS ($2) children. Tues–Sun 10am–6pm. U-Bahn: Stephansplatz or Herrengasse.

Located near the Clock Museum (see section 4, "Museums & Galleries" above), this is a museum for all ages. Its collection of dolls and dollhouses is one of the most remarkable in the world, ranging from the 1740s to the 1930s. Some of the most outstanding dolls are from Germany, which has a rich doll-making heritage.

7　Musical Landmarks

If you're a fan of Mozart, Schubert, Beethoven, Strauss, or Haydn, you've landed in the right city. While in town, not only will you be able to hear their music in the concert halls and palaces where they performed, but you can also visit the houses and apartments in which they lived and worked as well as the cemeteries where they were buried.

Haydns Wohnhaus. Haydngasse 19. ☎ **01/596-1307.** Admission 25AS ($1.70) adults, 10AS (65¢) students and children. Tues–Sun 9am–12:15pm and 1–4:30pm. Tram: 52 or 58.

This is where Franz Josef Haydn conceived and wrote his magnificent later oratorios *The Seasons* and *The Creation.* He lived in this house from 1797 until his death in 1809. Haydn gave lessons to Beethoven here. There's also a room in this house, which is a branch of the Historical Museum of Vienna, honoring Johannes Brahms.

Johann-Strauss-Memorial Rooms. Praterstrasse 54. ☎ **01/214-0121.** Admission 25AS ($1.70) adults, 10AS (65¢) children. Tues–Sun 9am–12:15pm and 1–4:30pm. U-Bahn: Nestroyplatz.

"The King of the Waltz," Johann Strauss (II), lived at this address for a number of years, composing "The Blue Danube Waltz" here in 1867. The house is now part of the Historical Museum of Vienna.

Mozart-Wohnung/Figarohaus (Mozart Memorial). Domgasse 5. ☎ **01/513-6294.** Admission 25AS ($1.70) adults, 10AS (65¢) students and children. Tues–Sun 9am–6pm. U-Bahn: Stephansplatz.

This 17th-century house is called the House of Figaro because Mozart composed his opera *The Marriage of Figaro* here. The composer resided here from 1784 to 1787, a relatively happy period in what was otherwise a rather tragic life. It was here that he often played chamber-music concerts with Haydn. Over the years he lived in a dozen houses in all, which became more squalid as he aged. He died in poverty and was given a pauper's blessing at St. Stephan's Cathedral in 1791, then buried in St. Marx Cemetery. The Domgasse apartment has been turned into a museum.

Pasqualati House. Mölker Bastei 8. ☎ **01/535-8905.** Admission 25AS ($1.70) adults, 10AS (65¢) children. Tues–Sun 9am–12:15pm and 1–4:30pm. U-Bahn: Schottentor.

Beethoven lived in this building on and off from 1804 to 1814. It's likely that either the landlord was tolerant or the neighbors were deaf. Beethoven is known to have composed his Fourth, Fifth, and Seventh Symphonies here, as well as his only opera, *Fidelio,* and other works.

There isn't much to see except some family portraits and the composer's scores, but Beethoven lovers may feel it's worth the climb to the fourth floor (there's no elevator).

Schubert Museum. Nussdorferstrasse 54. ☎ **01/317-3601.** Admission 25AS ($1.70) adults, 10AS (65¢) students and children. Tues–Sun 9am–12:15pm and 1–4:30pm. S-Bahn: Canisiusgasse.

The son of a poor schoolmaster, Schubert was born here in 1797 in a house built earlier in that century. Many Schubert mementos are on view. You can also visit the house at Kettenbrückengasse 6, where he died at age 31.

You Paid What?

47,000 hotels, 700 airlines, 50 rental car companies. And a few million ways to save money.

Travelocity.com
A Sabre Company

Go Virtually Anywhere.

AOL Keyword: Travel

Will you have enough stories to tell your grandchildre

©2000 Yahoo! Inc.

Yahoo! Travel

8 Organized Tours

Wiener Rundfahrten (Vienna Sightseeing Tours), Stelzhamergasse 4-11 (☎ **01/ 7124-6830**), offers many tours, ranging from the evening "Viennese Serenade and Grinzing" trip to a 1-day excursion by motorcoach to Budapest costing 1,300AS ($87.10) per person.

The **historical city tour** costs 400AS ($26.80) for adults and is free for children age 12 and under. It's ideal for visitors who are pressed for time and yet want to be shown the major (and most frequently photographed) monuments of Vienna. It takes you past the historic buildings of Ringstrasse—the State Opera, Hofburg Palace, museums, Parliament, City Hall, Burgtheater, the University, and the Votive Church—into the heart of Vienna. Tours. The bus leave the State Opera daily at 9:30 and 10:30am and at 2:30pm. The tour lasts 3½ hours.

"Vienna Woods–Mayerling," another popular bus excursion, lasting about 4 hours, leaves from the State Opera and takes you to the towns of Perchtoldsdorf and Modling, and also to the Abbey of Heiligenkreuz, a center of Christian culture since medieval times. The village of Mayerling is linked to the tragic suicide of Crown Prince Rudolf, only son of Emperor Franz Joseph. The tour also takes you for a short walk through Baden, the spa that was once a favorite summer resort of the aristocracy. Tours cost 500AS ($33.50) for adults and 200AS ($13.40) for children.

A **"Grand City Tour,"** which includes visits to the Schönbrunn and Belvedere palaces, leaves the State Opera daily at 9:30am and again at 2:30pm, lasting about 3 hours and costing 400AS ($26.80) for adults and 200AS ($13.40) for children.

A variation on the city tour includes an optional visit to the Spanish Riding School, where the world-renowned Lippizaner stallions are trained and showcased. This tour is offered Tuesday to Saturday, leaving from the State Opera building at 9:30am. In addition to driving in a bus past the monuments of Vienna, with guided commentary, the tour includes a half-hour performance by the Lippizaners on their home turf. Adults pay 500AS ($33.50) and children are charged 200AS ($13.40); free for children under age 12.

Information and booking for these tours are possible either through Vienna Sightseeing Tours (see above) or through their affiliate, **Elite Tours,** Operngasse 4 (☎ **01/ 513-2225**).

Vienna Tourist Guides offer guided 2-hour walks through the old city, plus themed walks on the history of Jews in the city; famous musicians who have lived in Vienna, including Mozart; and tours of wine cellars, crypts, and excavations. Available at the tourist office, a brochure, *Walks in Vienna,* supplies details, times, and departure points of these tours, none of which requires an advance reservation. Including entrance fees, tours cost 150AS ($10.05) for adults, and 75AS ($5.05) for those age 17 and under.

9 Sports & Active Pursuits

ACTIVE SPORTS

BIKING   Vienna maintains almost 200 miles of bike lanes and paths, some of which meander through the most elegant parks in Europe. Depending on their location, they'll be identified either by a yellow image of a cyclist stenciled directly onto the pavement, or by the rows of red brick set amid the cobblestones or concrete of the busy boulevards in the city center.

You can rent a bike for 90 to 150AS ($6.05 to $10.05) per hour. You'll usually be asked to leave either your passport or a form of ID as a deposit. One rental shop is

Pedal Power, Ausstellungsstrasse 3 (☎ **01/729-7234**). There are others at the Prater and along the banks of the Danube Canal. You can also rent from a kiosk in the **Westbahnhof** (☎ **01/5800-32985**). Also see "Getting Around" in chapter 3.

An unusual, almost uninterrupted bike path goes around the long and skinny island that separates the Danube from the Neue Donau Canal, which parallels it. Low-lying and occasionally marshy, but with paved paths along most of its length, it provides clear views of central Europe's industrial landscape and the endless river traffic that flows by on either side. The most exciting villages and stopovers along the Danube, including Melk and Dürnstein, are linked by a riverside bike trail between Vienna and Naarn. You'll pass castles of yesteryear, medieval towns, and latticed vineyards.

BOATING   Wear a straw boating hat and hum a few bars of a Strauss waltz as you paddle your way around the quiet eddies of the Alte Donau. This gently curving stream bisects residential neighborhoods to the north of the Danube, and is preferable to the muddy and swift-moving currents of the river itself.

At **An der Obere** along the Danube, you'll find some kiosks in summer where you can rent a boat, perhaps a canoe or a kayak. There are, of course, organized tours of the Danube, but it's more fun to do it yourself.

GOLF   If you're even considering it, think again. The two golf courses in or near Vienna are chronically overbooked, forcing even long-term members to be highly flexible about their starting times. The busier of the two courses is in the Prater, at **Golfplatz Wien-Freudenau,** Freudenau 65a (☎ **01/728-9564**). More distant, and more likely to perhaps have a weekday tee time (but almost never on a weekend) is **Föhrenwald,** Bodenstrasse 54 (☎ **02622/29171**), an 18-hole course about 30 miles south of Vienna, in the suburb of Wiener Neustadt.

HEALTH CLUBS   Even if you're not registered there, you are welcome to use the popular health club **Fitness Center Pyron** in the Vienna Hilton, Am Stadtpark (☎ **01/712-0955**), on the third floor of the deluxe hotel. After registering at the desk, you'll be given a locker key, a towel, and access to the sauna, cold baths, and showers; women and men share the facilities equally. Admission to the sauna and gym is 200AS ($13.40) for nonresidents, 180AS ($12.05) for hotel guests. The club is open daily from 11am to 10pm September to May, and 2 to 10pm June to August. Women who prefer to have their sauna alone are directed to a private room.

HIKING   You're likely to expend plenty of shoe leather simply walking from one of Vienna's museums and palaces to another, but if you yearn for a more isolated setting, the city tourist offices will provide information about its eight **Stadt-Wander-Wege.** These marked hiking paths usually originate at a stop for the city's far-flung network of trams.

You can also head east of town into the vast precincts of the **Lainzer Tiergarten,** where hiking trails meander amid forested hills, colonies of deer, and abundant bird life. To get there, first take the U-Bahn to the Kennedy Brücke/Heitzing station, which lies a few steps from the entrance to Schönbrunn Palace. A trek among the formal gardens of Schönbrunn might provide exercise enough, but if you're hungry for more, from here you can take tram 60, then bus 60B into the distant but verdant confines of the Lainzer Tiergarten.

ICE-SKATING   There's a public rink, the **Wiener Eislaufverein,** Lothringer Strasse 22 (☎ **01/713-6353**), within a 20-minute walk southeast of the cathedral. Located just outside the famous Am Stadtpark, near the Inter-Continental Hotel, and especially crowded on weekends, the rink rents skates and is open daily from 8am to 8pm between late October and early March. Monday to Saturday the charge is 80AS ($5.35) for adults, 65AS ($4.35) for children age 7 to 18. On Sunday the price goes

Cruising the Danube

Its waters aren't as idyllic as the Strauss waltz would lead you to believe, and its color is usually muddy brown rather than blue. But despite these drawbacks, many visitors to Austria view a day cruise along the Danube as a highlight of their trip. Until the advent of railroads and highways, the Danube played a vital role in Austria's history, helping build the complex mercantile society that eventually begat the Habsburg empire.

The most professional cruise line is the **DDSG Blue Danube Steamship Co.** (Donau-Dampfschiffahrts-Gesellschafts "Blue Danube," or DDSG Blue Danube), whose main offices are at Fredrickstrasse 7, A-1010 Vienna (☎ **01/588800**). The most appealing cruise sails through the Wachau region east of Vienna, from April to October between Vienna and Dürnstein. The cruise departs every Sunday at 8:30am from the company's piers at Handelskai 265, 1020 Vienna, arriving in Dürnstein 6 hours later. The cost each way is 200AS ($13.40) for adults, half-price for children age 15 and under. To reach the Vienna piers, take U-Bahn no. 1 to Vorgartenstrasse, about 4½ miles from St. Stephansplatz.

An alternative route takes passengers to Melk Abbey every Sunday, leaving at 8:30am between April and October from the same location and arriving at Melk at 1:40pm. The cost is 190AS ($12.75) each way for adults, half-price for children age 15 and under. If you want to go by boat to Melk during the week, you'll have to take a train to the railway station in Krems, where you can board a boat at Schiffstation Krems, about a 15-minute walk from the station. Three river cruises depart daily at 10:15am, 1pm, and 3:45pm for the 3-hour trip between Krems and Melk. One-way fare costs 95AS ($6.35) per person. Frankly, most travelers find the one-way trip to either Dürnstein or Melk adequate exposure to the glories of riverboat travel, so we advise taking one of the many trains back to Vienna after your visit.

A final note: Between April and October, DDSG operates a daily hydrofoil that departs from the Vienna piers at 9am and arrives in Budapest at 2:30pm. One-way transit costs 780AS ($62.40) for adults, half-price for children age 15 and under.

up to 95AS ($6.35) for adults, 75AS ($5.05) for children. Skates rentals are 75AS ($5.05) per pair. The rest of the year (from April to September), the site is transformed into seven public tennis courts, available to anyone who wants to play. Courts cost 100AS ($6.70) for daily sessions between 8am and noon; 130AS ($8.70) for sessions between noon and 5pm, and 200AS ($13.40) for sessions between 5 and 8pm.

SKIING   Limited skiing is available on the **Hohe Wand,** west of town. To reach it, ride the U4 subway to the Hütteldorf station, then take bus 49B to the city's 14th District. The area around the Semmering (about an hour from the city) is a favorite of Viennese looking for a quick skiing getaway. For information on skiing in Austria, contact the Austrian National Tourist Office, Margaretenstrasse 1, A-1040 (☎ **01/58866**).

SWIMMING   Despite the popularity of certain beaches on islands in the Alte Donau Canal in summer, swimming in either the Danube or any of its satellite canals is not recommended because of pollution and a dangerous undertow in the main river.

To compensate, Vienna has dozens of swimming pools. Your hotel's receptionist can tell you about options in your neighborhood. One of the most modern is in the Prater. For pool locations and information, contact Rathaus (City Hall), Friedrich Schmidt-Platz (☎ **01/40005**).

TENNIS   You'll find that many of the tennis courts in Vienna are almost constantly booked. Your hotel might have connections with one, but if not, contact the city's largest tennis agency, **Sportservice Wien-Sport,** Bacherplatz 14 (☎ **01/545-3131** or 01/545-1201). They have ties to dozens of indoor and outdoor tennis courts throughout Vienna, and can guarantee playing time at some for a modest fee.

SPECTATOR SPORTS

HORSE RACING   It all takes place at the **Prater,** at Trabbrennplatz (☎ **01/ 218-9535**). The season runs from April to November and includes both sulky and flat racing. The Vienna Derby, one of the season's highlights, takes place on the third Sunday in June.

SOCCER   Football, as it's called in Europe, tends to draw a less impassioned response in Austria than in Germany or Italy. Most of the city's matches are played in the Prater's **Weiner Stadion,** Meiereistrasse 7 (☎ **01/728-0854**). Smaller matches or those played during midwinter or during unfavorable weather usually take place under the protective roof of the **Stadthalle,** Vogelweidplatz 14 (☎ **01/98100**).

Tickets to any of these events are usually available at the gate on the day of the match, although it's usually wiser to reserve tickets through one of Vienna's ticket agencies. These can be picked up at the **Kartenbüro Flamm,** Kärntner Ring 3 (☎ **01/512-4225**), or ordered through the mail several weeks in advance from the **Vienna Ticket Service,** Borscgasse 1, A-1010 Vienna (☎ **01/534-1363;** fax 01/534-1328).

7

Vienna Walking Tours

Vienna's architecture is a rich and evocative treasure trove that includes buildings erected during virtually every period of the city's history. Although there was extensive damage to the city during World War II, Vienna retained many of its important buildings, and reconstruction has been meticulous. All this makes Vienna a natural for rewarding walking tours.

Each of the three walking tours below is geared toward a different kind of Viennese experience. Note that many of the streets in the revered 1st District are now pedestrian malls, and cars have been banished except for early morning deliveries; however, on the streets where there's still traffic, beware of cars, because drivers sometimes roar through narrow streets at relatively high speeds.

Walking Tour 1: Imperial Vienna

Start: Staatsoper (State Opera House).
Finish: Staatsoper (State Opera House).
Time: 3 hours.
Best Time: During daylight hours or at dusk.
Worst Time: Rainy days.

Although there are dozens of potential paths through Vienna's historic center, this meandering tour will give you at least an exterior view of the Habsburgs' urban haunts. This tour also reveals lesser-known sights best seen from the outside on foot. Later, you can pick and choose the attractions you most want to revisit. (For details on many of these sights, see chapter 6.)

Our tour begins at the southernmost loop of **Ringstrasse,** the beltway that encircles most of the historic core of the city, within the shadow of the very symbol of Austrian culture itself, the:

1. **Staatsoper (State Opera House).** Built between 1861 and 1865 in a style inspired by the French Renaissance (and faithfully reconstructed after World War II), it was so severely criticized when it was unveiled that one of its architects, Eduard van der Null, committed suicide. (See Walking Tour 2 for a more extensive discussion.)

On Opernring, walk 1 block northward on Austria's most famous pedestrian street, **Kärntnerstrasse**. We'll eventually walk past the glamorous shops and famous houses, but for the moment, turn left behind the arcaded bulk of the State Opera onto Philhar-monikerstrasse. On the right-hand side, you'll see the lushly carved caryatids and globe lights of Vienna's best-known hotel, the:

2. Hotel Sacher. If you're interested, a confectionery store with a separate streetside entrance sells the hotel's namesake, Sachertorte, which can be shipped anywhere in the world.

A few steps later you'll find yourself amid the irregular angles of Alberti-naplatz, where you'll be able to plunge into the purely Viennese experience of the *Kaffeehaus.*

🥃 **TAKE A BREAK**   If you'd rather indulge in heartier fare than the coffee-houses offer, try the **Augustinerkeller,** Augustinerstrasse 1 (☎ **01/533-1026**), in the basement of the Hofburg palace sheltering the Albertina collection. This popular wine tavern, open daily from 11am to midnight, offers wine, beer, and Austrian food.

In the same building as your rest stop is the:

3. Albertina Collection. A monumental staircase in the building's side supports the equestrian statue that dominates the square. Its subject is Field Marshal Arch-duke Albrecht, in honor of a battle he won in 1866.

Adjacent to Albertinaplatz, at Lobkowitzplatz 2, lies one of the many baroque jewels of Vienna, the:

4. Lobkowitz Palace. (Its position is confusing because of the rows of buildings partially concealing it. To get here, walk about 50 paces to the right of the Albertina Collection.) This privately owned building existed in smaller form at the time of the second Turkish siege of Vienna. After the Turks were driven from the outskirts of the city, the palace was enlarged by the reigning architect of his day, Fischer von Erlach. In 1735 it passed into the hands of Prince Lobkowitz and still bears his name. The prince was a great patron of the arts; Beethoven's Third Symphony premiered here in 1803.

At the far end of Lobkowitzplatz, take Gluckgasse past a series of antiques shops filled with art deco jewelry and silverware. At the end of the block, at Tegetthoffstrasse, go left. About 50 paces later you'll be in front of the deceptively simple facade of the:

5. Church of the Capuchin Friars. Originally constructed in the 1620s, its facade was rebuilt along a severely simple design following old illustrations in 1935. Despite its humble appearance, the church contains the burial vaults of every Habsburg ruler since 1633. The heavily sculpted double casket of Maria Theresa and her husband, Francis, is flanked with weeping nymphs and skulls but capped with a triumphant cherub uniting the couple once again in love.

The portal of this church marks the beginning of the Neuer Markt, whose perimeter is lined with rows of elegant baroque houses. The square's centerpiece is one of the most beautiful works of outdoor art in Austria, the:

6. Donner Fountain. Holding a snake, the gracefully undraped Goddess of Provi-dence is attended by four laughing cherubs struggling with fish. Beside the waters flowing into the basin of the fountain are four allegorical figures representing nearby tributaries of the Danube. The fountain is a copy of the original, which was moved to the Baroque Museum in the Belvedere Palace. The original was commissioned by the City Council in 1737, executed by Georg Raphael Donner, but judged obscene and immoral when viewed for the first time by Maria Theresa. Today it's considered a masterpiece.

Walking Tour 1: Imperial Vienna

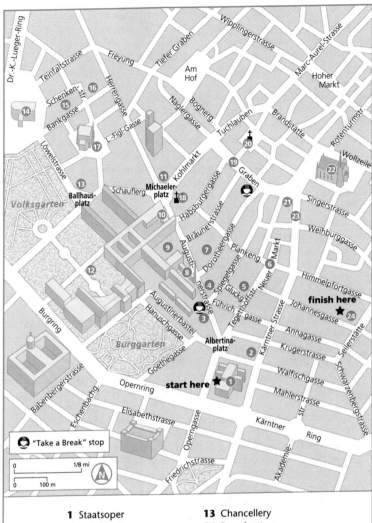

1 Staatsoper
2 Hotel Sacher
3 Albertina Collection
4 Lobkowitz Palace
5 Church of the
   Capuchin Friars
6 Donner Fountain
7 Dorotheum
8 Hofburg
9 Josefsplatz
10 Spanish Riding School
11 Loos House
12 Heldenplatz

13 Chancellery
14 Burgtheater
15 Palais Liechtenstein
16 Hungarian Embassy
17 Church of the Minorites
18 St. Michael's Church
19 Plague Column
20 Peterskirche
21 Stock-im-Eisen
22 St. Stephen's Cathedral
23 Kärntnerstrasse
24 Savoy Foundation for
   Noble Ladies

Now take the street stretching west from the side of the fountain, Planken-gasse, where a yellow baroque church fills the space at the end of the street. As you approach it, you'll pass an array of shops filled with alluringly old-fashioned merchandise. Even the pharmacy at the corner of Spiegelgasse has a vaulted ceiling and rows of antique bottles. The store at Plankengasse 6, as well as its next-door neighbor at the corner of Dorotheergasse, is well stocked with museum-quality antique clocks. Turn left when you reach Dorotheergasse, past the turn-of-the-century Italianate bulk of no. 17. Therein lies one of the most historic auction houses of Europe, the:

7. Dorotheum, established in 1707, and rebuilt in the neo-baroque style in 1901. Here, Austria's impoverished aristocracy could discreetly liquidate their estates.

About half a block later, turn right onto Augustinerstrasse, which borders the interconnected labyrinth of palaces, museums, and public buildings known as the:

8. Hofburg. The grime-encrusted grandeur of this narrow street is usually diminished by the traffic roaring past its darkened stone walls. Despite that modern intrusion, this group of buildings is the single most impressive symbol of the former majesty and might of the Habsburgs.

In about half a block you'll arrive at:

9. Josefsplatz, where a huge equestrian statue of Joseph II seems to be storming the gate of no. 5, the Palffy Palace, originally built around 1575 with a combination of classical and Renaissance motifs. Two pairs of relaxed caryatids guard the entrance. Next door, at no. 6, is another once-glittering private residence, the Palavicini Palace, which was completed in 1784 for members of the Fries family and later purchased by the family whose name it bears today. A few steps later, a pedestrian tunnel leads past the:

10. Spanish Riding School (Spanische Reitschule). The district becomes increasingly filled with slightly decayed vestiges of a vanished empire whose baroque monuments are flanked by outmoded, too-narrow streets and thundering traffic. Michaelerplatz now opens to your view. Opposite the six groups of combative statues is a streamlined building with rows of unadorned windows, known as the:

11. Loos House, Michaelerplatz 3. Designed in 1910, it immediately became the most violently condemned building in town. That almost certainly stemmed from the unabashed (some would say provocative) contrast between the lavishly ornamented facade of the Michaelerplatz entrance to the Hofburg and what contemporary critics compared to "the gridwork of a sewer." Franz Joseph himself hated the building so much that he used the Michaelerplatz exit as infrequently as possible so that he wouldn't have to look at the building that faced it.

A covered tunnel that empties both pedestrians and automobiles into the square takes you beneath the Hofburg complex. Notice the passageway's elaborate ceiling where spears, capes, and shields crown the supports of the elaborate dome. This must be one of the most heavily embellished traffic tunnels in the world. As you walk through the tunnel, an awesomely proportioned series of courtyards reveal the Imperial Age's addiction to conspicuous grandeur.

When you eventually emerge from the tunnel, you'll find yourself surrounded by the magnificent curves of:

12. Heldenplatz. Its carefully constructed symmetry seems to dictate that each of the stately buildings bordering it, as well as each of its equestrian statues and ornate lampposts, have a well-balanced mate.

Gardens stretch out in well-maintained splendor. Enjoy the gardens if you want, but to continue the tour, put the rhythmically spaced columns of the

Hofburg's curved facade behind you and walk catercorner to the far end of the palace's right-hand wing. At Ballhausplatz, notice the:

13. Chancellery, at no. 2. It's an elegant building, yet its facade is modest in comparison with the ornamentation of its royal neighbor. The events that transpired within have influenced the course of European history hundreds of times since the building was erected in 1720. Here, Count Kaunitz plotted with Maria Theresa to expand the influence of her monarchy. Prince Metternich used these rooms as his headquarters during the Congress of Vienna (1814–15). Many of the decisions made here were links in the chain of events leading up to World War I. In 1934, Dollfuss was murdered here by Austrian Nazis. Four years later, Hermann Göring, threatening a military attack, forced the ouster of the Austrian cabinet with telephone calls made to an office in this building. Rebuilt after the bombings of World War II, this battle-scarred edifice has housed Austria's Foreign Ministry and its Federal Chancellor's office since 1945.

Walk along the side of the Chancellery's adjacent gardens, along Lowelstrasse, until you reach the:

14. Burgtheater, the national theater of Austria. Notice the window trim of some of the buildings along the way, each of which seems to have its own ox, satyr, cherub, or Neptune carved above it.

At the Burgtheater, make a sharp right-hand turn onto Bankgasse. The ornate beauty of the:

15. Palais Liechtenstein, completed in the early 18th century, is on your right, at no. 9. A few buildings farther on, stone garlands and glimpses of crystal chandeliers are visible at the:

16. Hungarian Embassy, at no. 4–6.

Now retrace your steps for about half a block until you reach Abraham-a-Sancta-Clara-Gasse. At its end you'll see the severe Gothic facade of the:

17. Church of the Minorites, on Minoritenplatz. Its 14th-century severity contrasts sharply with the group of stone warriors struggling to support the gilt-edged portico of the baroque palace facing it.

Walk behind the blackened bulk of the church to the curve of the building's rear. At this point some maps of Vienna might lead you astray. Regardless of the markings on your particular map, look for Leopold-Figl-Gasse and walk down it. You'll pass between two sprawling buildings, each of which belongs to one or another of the Austrian bureaucracies linked by an above-ground bridge. A block later, turn right onto Herrengasse. Within a few minutes, you'll be on the now-familiar Michaelerplatz. This time you'll have a better view of:

18. St. Michael's Church. Winged angels carved by Lorenzo Mattielli in 1792 fly above the entranceway, and a single pointed tower rises. Turn left (north) along Kohlmarkt, noticing the elegant houses along the way: no. 14 houses Demel's, the most famous coffeehouse of Vienna; no. 9 and no. 11 bear plaques for Chopin and Haydn, respectively.

At the broad pedestrian walkway known as the Graben, turn right. The baroque:

19. Plague Column in the center has chiseled representations of clouds piled high like whipped cream. It's dotted profusely with statues of ecstatic saints fervently thanking God for relief from an outbreak of the Black Plague that erupted in Vienna in 1679 and may have killed as many as 150,000 people. Carved between 1682 and 1693 by a team of the most famous artists of the era, this column eventually inspired the erection of many similar monuments throughout Austria.

A few feet before the Plague Column, turn left onto Jungferngasse and enter our favorite church in Vienna:

20. Peterskirche. Believed to be on the site of a crude wooden church built during the Christianization of Austria around A.D. 350 and later (according to legend) rebuilt by Charlemagne, it was lavishly upgraded during the 1700s by baroque artists, including the famous painter J. M. Rottmayr.

Return to the Graben, passing the Plague Column. A few steps beyond it, pass the bronze statue of a beneficent saint leading a small child in the right direction. You might, after all this, enjoy a sandwich. Leave the Graben at one of the first intersections on the right, Dorotheergasse, where you'll find a fine choice.

TAKE A BREAK Despite its functional simplicity, **Buffet Trzes- niewski,** Dorotheergasse 1 (☎ 01/512-3291), has satisfied the hunger pangs of everyone who was anyone in Vienna in the last century. For more information, see chapter 5, "Where to Dine."

After your break, continue in a southeasterly direction down the Graben to its terminus. Here you'll find a vaguely defined section of pavement that signs will identify as:

21. Stock-im-Eisen. Here two pedestrian thoroughfares, the Graben and Kärntner- strasse, meet at the southernmost corner of Stephansplatz. To your right, notice the sheet of curved plexiglas bolted to the corner of an unobtrusive building at the periphery of the square. Behind it are the preserved remains of a tree. In it, 16th-century blacksmiths would drive a nail for luck each time they left Vienna. Today the gnarled and dusty log is covered with an almost uninterrupted casing of angular, hand-forged nails.

By now, it will be difficult to avoid a full view of Vienna's most symbolic building:

22. St. Stephan's Cathedral. Newcomers should circumnavigate the building's exte- rior to check out its 12th- and 13th-century stonework before going inside. When you exit, turn left after passing through the main portal and head down the most famous street in Vienna's Inner City, the pedestrian-only:

23. Kärntnerstrasse. As you wander through the street, don't miss the mini-museum of glassmaking that decorates the second floor of the world-famous glassmaker, **Lobmyer,** at no. 26.

If you still have the energy, make a detour off Kärntnerstrasse, turning left on Johannesgasse. You'll pass some old and very interesting facades before reaching the baroque carvings and stone lions that guard the 17th-century portals of the:

24. Savoy Foundation for Noble Ladies (Savoysches Damenstift), at no. 15. Countless generations of well-born Austrian damsels struggled to learn "the gen- tle arts of womanhood" here. Established by the duchess of Savoy-Carignan and originally built in 1688, its facade is adorned with a lead statue by the baroque sculptor F. X. Messerschmidt.

As you retrace your steps back to the shops and the pedestrian crush of Kärnt- nerstrasse, you might hear strains of music cascading into the street from the Vienna Conservatory of Music, which occupies several buildings on Johannes- gasse. Turn left as you reenter Kärntnerstrasse, enjoying the sights until you even- tually return to your point of origin, the State Opera House.

Walking Tour 2: South of the Ring

Start: Staatsoper (State Opera House).
Finish: Gumpendorferstrasse (on Saturdays, Flohmarkt).
Time: 3½ hours, not counting visits to museums.
Best Time: Saturday morning, when the Flohmarkt is open.
Worst Time: After dark, or in the rain.

The temptation is strong, especially for first-time visitors to Vienna, to limit their exploration only to those monuments within the Ring—the city's medieval core, the 1st District.

You'll discover a different side of Vienna by following this tour, which incorporates the sometime surreal manifestations of *fin-de-siècle* Habsburg majesty a short distance south of the Ring. The tour also includes less celebrated late-19th-century buildings that don't seem as striking today as when they were designed, but which, for their era, were almost revolutionary.

Regrettably, parts of the 6th District, the area of this tour, were heavily damaged, then rebuilt, after the horrors of World War II, and will require navigating beside less-than-inspiring boulevards that contain heavy traffic. Fortunately, a network of underground walkways, designed by city planners as part of Vienna's subway system, will make navigating the densest traffic a lot easier.

Begin your tour near the southern facade of:

1. **The Staatsoper (Vienna State Opera).** This was the first of the many monuments built during the massive Ringstrasse project begun around 1850 by Franz Joseph on land reclaimed from the razing of Vienna's medieval fortifications. This French Renaissance construction was plagued by controversy and cost overruns from the moment its foundations were laid. Notice how, on the building's southern edge, bad overall planning resulted in the roaring traffic of the nearby Ringstrasse to be several feet higher than the building's foundation. This error, coupled with an offhand—but widely reported—criticism of the situation by Franz Joseph, is believed to have contributed to the suicide (by hanging) of one of the building's architects, van der Null, and the death by stroke, a few weeks later, of its other architect, von Sicardsburg. The roof and much of the interior were largely rebuilt after a night bombing on March 12, 1945, sent the original building up in flames. Ironically, the last performance before its near-destruction had been a rousing version of Wagner's *Götterdammerung*, with its immolation scene.

   Since its reconstruction, the Staatsoper has nurtured such luminaries as Bruno Walter and Herbert von Karajan, who survived some of the most Byzantine and convoluted political intrigue of any concert house in the world.

   Across the avenue, on your left as you face the Ring, at the intersection of the Kärntner Ring and the Kärntnerstrasse, is one of Europe's grandest hotels, the:

2. **Hotel Bristol,** Kärntner Ring 1. Ornate and socially impeccable, the Bristol reigns alongside the Sacher and the Imperial as the grande dames of Viennese hotels. A deceptively unpretentious lobby might disappoint, as the most impressive reception areas are concealed in a labyrinth of upstairs corridors. Consider returning later for a mid-afternoon coffee or a drink in one of the bars.

   Take a deep breath before descending into the depths of an underground passageway that begins at the corner of the Kärnerstrasse and the Kärntner Ring, just south of the Opera House. (You'll find it's a lot easier and safer than trying to cross the roaring traffic of the Ring as an unarmed pedestrian.) You'll bypass some underground boutiques before climbing out on the southern edge of the Opernring.

Walk west along the Opernring, using another of those underground tunnels to cross beneath the Operngasse, until you reach the Robert-Stolz-Platz, named after an Austrian composer who died nearby in 1975. If you glance north, across the Opernring, you'll see a faraway statue of Goethe, brooding in a bronze chair, usually garnished with a roosting pigeon. The Robert-Stolz-Platz opens southward into the Schillerplatz, where, as you'd expect, an equivalent statue features an image of Schiller. The building on Schillerplatz's southern edge (Schillerplatz 3) is the:

3. **Akademie der Bildenden Künste (Fine Arts Academy).** It was erected between 1872 and 1876 by the Danish architect Theophil Hansen in a mix of Greek Revival and Italian Renaissance styles. It was here that the artistic dreams of 18-year-old Adolf Hitler were dashed, in 1907 and 1908, when he failed twice to gain admission to what was at the time the ultimate arbiter of the nation's artistic taste and vision. Ironically, a few years later, painter Egon Schiele, an artist of Hitler's age, eventually seceded from the same academy because of its academic restrictions and pomposity. For details about the exhibits in this building, refer to chapter 6.

Now, walk east for a half block along the Niebelungengasse, then south along the Makartgasse, skirting the side of the Academy. Makartgasse was named after Hans Makart, the most admired and sought-after painter in 19th-century Vienna, the darling of the Academy you've just visited. The soaring and artfully cluttered studio he occupied was subsidized by Franz Joseph himself and transformed into a salon every afternoon at 4pm to receive every prominent newcomer in town. Exhibitions of his huge historical canvases attracted up to 34,000 people at a time. Young Adolf Hitler is said to have idolized Makart's grandiloquent sense of flamboyance; Klimt and Schiele of the Secessionist school at first admired him, then abandoned his presuppositions and forged a bold new path of their own. Rumor and innuendo swirled about the specific identities of the models who appeared as artfully undressed figures within the handsome and promiscuous artist's paintings. He fell from social grace after defying upper-class conventions by marrying a ballet dancer, then contracted a case of syphilis that killed him at age 44.

At the end of Makartgasse, turn left (east) for a half block. Then turn right onto the Friedrichstrasse. Before the end of the block, at Friedrichstrasse 12, is the *Jugendstil* facade of a building that launched one of the most admired and envied artistic statements of the early 20th century:

4. **The Secession.** At the time of its construction in 1898, its design was much more controversial than it is today, and as such attracted hundreds of passersby who would literally gawk. Its severe cubic lines, Assyrian-looking corner towers, and gilded dome caused its detractors to refer to it as "the Gilded Cabbage," and "Mahdi's Tomb." It was immediately interpreted as an insult to bourgeois sensibilities. Despite the controversy that surrounded it (or perhaps because of it), 57,000 people attended the inaugural exhibition of Secessionist works. The Secession's location, within a short walk of the organization it defied (the previously visited Academy of Fine Arts), was an accident, only prompted by the availability of real estate. Inside, a roster of innovative display techniques—revolutionary for their time—included movable panels, unadorned walls, and natural light pouring in from skylights. The inscription above the door, *Jeder Zein sein Kunst, Jeder Kunst sein Freiheit,* translates as "To every age its art, to every art its freedom." Damaged during World War II and looted in 1945, it lay derelict until 1973, when it was bought and later restored as a municipal treasure.

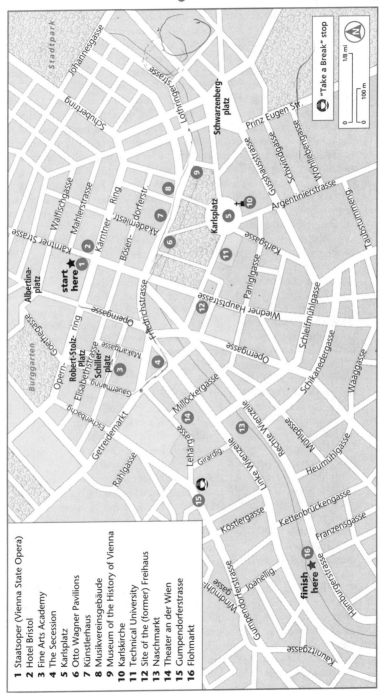

1 Staatsoper (Vienna State Opera)
2 Hotel Bristol
3 Fine Arts Academy
4 The Secession
5 Karlsplatz
6 Otto Wagner Pavilions
7 Künstlerhaus
8 Musikvereinsgebäude
9 Museum of the History of Vienna
10 Karlskirche
11 Technical University
12 Site of the (former) Freihaus
13 Naschmarkt
14 Theater an der Wien
15 Gumpendorferstrasse
16 Flohmarkt

"Take a Break" stop

start here

finish here

From here, retrace your steps in a northeasterly direction beside the dense traffic of the Friedrichstrasse for 2 blocks. At the corner of the Niebelungengasse and the Friedrichstrasse (which forks gently into the Operngasse nearby) you'll find the entrance to an underground tunnel, part of Vienna's subway network, that will lead you safely beneath roaring traffic for several blocks to your next point of interest. Follow the underground signs to the subway and to the Wiedner Hauptstrasse. Turn right at the first major underground intersection, again following signs to the Wiedner Hauptstrasse. After what might seem a rather long walk, you'll ascend into daylight near the sprawling and sunken perimeter of the:

5. Karlsplatz. For many generations, this sunken bowl contained Vienna's fruit and vegetable markets. Too large to be called a square and too small to be a park, it's an awkward space that's valued today mainly as a means of showcasing the important buildings that surround it. Climb from the Karlsplatz up a flight of stone steps to the platform that skirts the Karlsplatz's northern edge, and walk east for a minute or two. The small-scale pair of *Jugendstil* pavilions you'll notice are among the most famous of their type in Vienna, the:

6. Otto Wagner Pavilions. Originally designed by Otto Wagner as a station for his *Stadtbahn* (the subway system he designed around the turn of the century), they are gems of applied Secessionist theory and preserved as monuments by the city. After their construction, many of their decorative adornments were copied throughout other districts of the Austro-Hungarian Empire as part of their respective late-19th-century building booms. Regrettably, many were later demolished as part of the Soviet regime's control of the Iron Curtain countries during the Cold War. Art historians consider them Vienna's response to the art nouveau metro stations of Paris built around the same time.

From here, continue walking eastward. The first building across the avenue on your left, at Friedrichstrasse 5, is the:

7. Künstlerhaus. Around 1900 its name was rigidly associated with conservative art, and as such tended to enrage the iconoclastic rebels who later formed the Secessionist movement. Completed in 1868, this not particularly striking building functioned for years as the exhibition hall for students at the Fine Arts Academy. Today, it's used for temporary exhibitions, and devotes some of its space to film and theater experiments.

Immediately to the right (east) of the Künstlerhaus is the Renaissance-inspired:

8. Musikvereinsgebaude (Friends of Music Building), Karlsplatz 13, home of the Vienna Philharmonic and site of concerts that are often sold out years in advance through fiercely protected private subscriptions. Constructed between 1867 and 1869, and designed by the same Theophil Hansen who built the previously visited Fine Arts Academy, it's another example of the way architects dabbled in the great historical styles of the past during the late-19th-century revitalization of the Ringstrasse.

Within the confines of the Karlsplatz, at Karlsplatz 4, a short walk to the southeast from the Musikverein, is a monument that serves, better than any other, to bind together the complicated worlds, subcultures, and historic periods that form the city of Vienna:

9. Historisches Museum der Stadt Wien (Museum of the History of Vienna). Its holdings are so vast, it deserves to be saved for a separate visit. Continue your clockwise circumnavigation of the Karlsplatz to the majestic confines of the:

10. Karlskirche (Church of St. Charles). Built by Emperor Charles VI, father of Maria Theresa, who mourned the loss of Austria's vast domains in Spain, this church was conceived as a means of recapturing some of Vienna's imperial glory.

It is almost always cited as the monument for which the baroque architect Fischer von Erlach the Elder is best remembered today and the most impressive baroque building in Austria. Built between 1716 and 1737, nominally in thanks for Vienna surviving another disastrous bout with the plague, it manages to combine aspects of a votive church with images of imperial grandeur. At the time of its construction, the Ringstrasse was not yet in place, and it lay within an easy and unrestricted stroll from the emperor's residence in the Hofburg. Rather coyly, Charles didn't name the church after himself but after a Milanese prelate (St. Charles Borromeo), although the confusion that ensued was almost certainly deliberate. To construct the skeleton of the church's dome, 300 massive oak trees were felled. The twin towers in front, although not strictly synchronized with the theories of baroque architecture, were inspired by Trajan's Column in Rome, the Pillars of Hercules (Gibraltar) in Spain, and Mannerist renderings of what contemporary historians imagined as the long-lost Temple of Jerusalem. The reflecting fountain in front of the church, site of a parking lot in recent times, contains a statue donated by Henry Moore in 1978.

Now, continue walking clockwise around the perimeter of the square to the southern edge of the Karlsplatz. A short side street running into the Karlsplatz here is the Karlsgasse. At Karlsgasse 4, you'll see a plaque announcing that in a building that once stood here, Johannes Brahms died in 1897. The next major building you'll see is the showcase of Austria's justifiably famous reputation for scientific and engineering excellence, the:

11. **Technische Universität (Technical University).** Its Ionic portico overlooks a public park with portrait busts of the great names associated with this treasure trove of Austrian inventiveness. Josef Madersperger, original inventor of the sewing machine in 1815, who died impoverished while others, such as the Singer family, profited from his invention; and Siegfried Marcus, inventor of a crude version of the gasoline-powered automobile in 1864, were graduates of the school. Other Austrians associated with the school are Ernst Mach, for whom the speed at which an aircraft breaks the sound barrier is named; and Josef Weineck, whose experiments with the solidification of fats laid the groundwork for the cosmetics industry.

Continue walking west along the southern perimeter of the Karlsplatz, past the Resselpark, and across the Wiedner Hauptstrasse, a modern manifestation of an ancient road that originally linked Vienna to Venice and Trieste. Urban historians consider this neighborhood to be Vienna's first suburb, although wartime damage from as early as the Turkish sieges of 1683 has largely destroyed its antique character. Sprawling annexes of the Technical University and not particularly interesting modern buildings now occupy the neighborhood to your left, stretching for about 4 blocks between the Wiedner Hauptstrasse and the Naschmarkt (which you'll soon visit). But historians value it as the 18th-century site of one of the largest communal housing projects in Europe, the now demolished:

12. **Freihaus.** In the 18th century, more than 1,000 people inhabited apartments here. In 1782, the *Theater auf der Wieden,* where Mozart's *Magic Flute* premiered, opened in a wing of the building. During the 19th century, when the Freihaus degenerated into an industrial slum and became a civic embarrassment in close proximity to the Karlskirche and the State Opera House, much of it was demolished to make room for the Operngasse. World War II bombings finished off the rest.

Continue walking along the Treitlstrasse, which is the logical westward extension of Resselpark, until you reach the Rechte Wienzeile, a broad boulevard that once flanked the quays of the Danube before the river was diverted as part of 19th-century urban renewal. Within the filled-in riverbed, you'll see the congested booths and labyrinthine stalls of Vienna's largest food and vegetable market, the:

13. Naschmarkt. Wander through the produce, meat, and dairy stalls. If you want to buy, there are more appealing and more expensive shops near the Naschmarkt's eastern end. The center is devoted to housewares and less glamorous food outlets, including lots of butcher shops.

After exploring the food market, walk along the market's northern fringe, the Linke Weinzeile. At the corner of the Millöckergasse, you'll see a historic theater that, during the decade-long renovation of the State Opera House, functioned as Vienna's primary venue for the performing arts, the:

14. Theater an der Wien, Linke Weinzeile 6. Despite its modern facade (the result of an unfortunate demolition and rebuilding around 1900 as well as damage during World War II), it's the oldest theater in Vienna, dating back to 1801. To get an idea of the age of this place, bypass the front entrance, and walk northwest along Millöckergasse— named after an overwhelmingly popular composer of Viennese operettas, Karl Millöcker (1842–99). At no. 8 is the theater's famous *Pappagenotor,* a stage door entrance capped with a homage to Pappageno, the Panlike character in Mozart's *Magic Flute.* The likeness was deliberately modeled after Emanuel Schikaneder, the first actor to play the role, author of most of the libretto, and the first manager, in 1801, of what was at the time a new theater. Attached to the wall near the *Pappagenotor* is a plaque recognizing that Beethoven lived and composed parts of his Third Symphony and the *Kreuzer* sonata inside. An early—later rewritten—version of Beethoven's *Fidelio* premiered at this theater, but after an uncharitable reception by the Viennese, it was revised by its composer into the form it bears today.

Continue walking northwest along Millöckergasse, then turn left onto the Lehárgasse. (The massive building on the Lehárgasse's north side is yet another annex of the Technical University.) Within about 3 blocks, Lehárgasse merges into the:

15. Gumpendorferstrasse. The street is lined with the same sort of historically eclectic houses, on a smaller scale, that you'll find on the Ringstrasse. Previously the medieval village of Gumpendorf, the neighborhood was incorporated into the city of Vienna as the 6th District in 1850. Modern Viennese refer to the neighborhood as Mariahilf. At this point, it's time to:

☕ **TAKE A BREAK** Café Sperl, Gumpendorferstrasse 11 (☎ **01/ 586-4158**), is one of the most historic cafes in the district. From the time of its establishment in the mid-1800s until renovations in the 1960s ripped away some of its once-ornate interior, it functioned as a hub of social and intellectual life in this monument-rich district. The artists who initiated the Secession maintained a more or less permanent table in the cafe. The Sperl is open Monday to Saturday from 7am to 11pm, Sunday from 3 to 11pm. Closed Sunday in July and August. Coffee costs from 30 to 42AS ($2 to $2.80); generous *tagestellers* (plates of the day) of Viennese food range from 95 to 110AS ($6.35 to $7.35).

After your break, walk southwest along Gumpendorferstrasse, admiring the eclectic Ringstrasse-style houses and apartment buildings that line the sidewalks. At Köstlergasse, turn left and stroll for about a block past more of the same ornate 19th-century architecture. At the end of Köstlergasse (at nos. 1 and 3) are apartment houses designed by Otto Wagner. Around the corner at Linke Weinzeile no. 40, you'll see yet another of his designs, an apartment house referred to by architecture students around the world as the Majolikahaus. Adjacent to the Majolikahaus, at 38 Linke Weinzeile, is the **Medallion House,** with a Secession-style floral display crafted from tiles set into its facade. It was designed by turn-of-the-century Secessionist Koloman Moser, creator of the stained-glass windows in the Am Steinhof church. Your tour is about over, unless it happens to be Saturday, between 7am and around 4pm. If so, continue southwest along Linke Wienzeile (cross over the Kettenbruckengasse) toward the enchantingly seedy site of one of Europe's most nostalgic flea markets, the:

16. **Flohmarkt.** Don't expect glamour, or even merchants who are particularly polite. But scattered amid the racks of cheap clothing, kitchenware, and hardware, you're likely to find plenty of imperial kitsch: porcelain figures of Franz Joseph, medallions of Empress Maria Theresa, drawings of the Hofburg, soldier figurines of the Imperial Guard, paintings of St. Stephan's Cathedral, and faded portraits of the Empress Elisabeth.

Walking Tour 3: Vienna's Back Streets

Start: Maria am Gestade.
Finish: St. Stephan's Cathedral.
Time: 2½ hours (not counting visits to interiors).
Best Time: Daylight hours, when you can visit shops and cafes en route.
Worst Time: In the rain and between 4 and 6pm.

In 1192, the English king Richard I (the Lion-Hearted) was captured trespassing on Babenburg lands in the village of Erdberg (now part of Vienna's 3rd District) after his return to England from the Third Crusade. The funds handed over from the English for his ransom were used for the enlargement of Vienna's fortifications that eventually incorporated some of the neighborhoods you'll cover on this walking tour. In horrified response, the pope excommunicated the Babenburg potentate who held a Christian crusader, but not before some of medieval London was mortgaged to pay the ransom and, eventually, pay for Vienna's city walls.

Much of this tour focuses on smaller, individual buildings and lesser-known landmarks on distinctive streets whose historic pavements have been trod by some of the most influential characters of Viennese history. Prepare yourself for a labyrinth of medieval streets and covered passages and insights into the age-old Viennese congestion that sociologists claim helped catalyze the artistic output of the Habsburg Empire.

Begin your promenade slightly northwest of Stephansplatz with a visit to one of the least frequently visited churches of central Vienna:

1. **Maria am Gestade ("Maria-Stiegen-Kirche"/Church of St. Mary on the Strand),** Salvatorgasse 1. Designated centuries ago as the Czech national church in Vienna, it replaced an older, wooden church, erected in the 800s, with the 14th-century stonework you'll see today. Restricted by the narrowness of the medieval streets around it, the church's unusual floor plan is only 30 feet wide, but it's capped with an elaborate pierced Gothic steeple that soars above the district as one of the neighborhood's most distinctive features. Since the early 19th century, when the first of at least five subsequent renovations were conducted, the church has been held by art historians as one of the most distinctive but underrated buildings in town.

From here, walk south along the alleyway that flanks the church's eastern edge, turning left (east) at the Wipplingerstrasse for an eventual view of the:

2. Altes Rathaus, Wipplingerstrasse 3. The building was confiscated by the Habsburg ruler, Duke Frederick the Fair, in 1316 from the leader of an anti-Habsburg revolt and subsequently donated to the city. In 1700, it was embellished with a baroque facade and a courtyard fountain (1740–41) that's famous for being one of Raphael Donner's last works. The building functioned as Vienna's Town Hall until 1885, when the city's municipal functions were moved to grander, neo-Gothic quarters on the Ring. Today, the Altes Rathaus contains a minor museum dedicated to the Austrian resistance to the Turks.

Wipplingerstrasse runs east into the:

3. Hoher Markt, the city's oldest market place. Until the early 1700s, it was the location of a public gallows, and until the early 1800s, it was the site of a pillory used to punish and humiliate dishonest bakers. Hoher Markt was originally the forum of the ancient Roman settlement of Vindobona. There are some excavations of what's believed to be a Roman barracks visible within the courtyard of the building at no. 3. It's likely, according to scholars, that Marcus Aurelius died of the plague here in A.D. 180. In the 1700s, the instruments of torture that dominated the square were replaced with several different generations of plague columns (columns erected in thanksgiving for deliverance from the Turks and from the plague). The present version was designed by Josef Emanuele von Ehrlach in 1732 and sculpted by Italian-born Antonio Corradini. An important scene from the film *The Third Man* was filmed at the base of the Hoher Markt's famous clock, the Ankeruhr, which—to everyone's amazement—escaped destruction during the square's aerial bombardments in 1945.

From here, walk a short block east along the Liechtensteingasse, then turn left and walk northeast along one of Vienna's most prominent shopping streets, the Rotenturmstrasse, for 2 blocks. Then turn right (east) onto the:

4. Griechengasse. The construction of this narrow street in the 1100s was representative of the almost desperate need for expansion away from the city's earlier perimeter, which more or less followed the ancient configuration of the Roman settlement of Vindobona. Griechengasse's name comes from the influx of Greek merchants that arrived during the 18th century, precursors of the waves of immigrants flooding into modern Vienna from Eastern Europe and the Middle East today. At Griechengasse 5, notice the unpretentious exterior of the local Greek Orthodox church, built in 1805 with the plain facade that was legally required of all non-Catholic churches up until the 19th century. At Griechengasse 7, occupying the point where the street turns sharply at an angle, stands a 14th-century watchtower, one of the few medieval vestiges left from the old city walls, that was incorporated long ago into the antique architecture that surrounds it.

The Griechengasse will narrow at this point and in some places be spanned with buttresses supporting the walls of the buildings on either side. Griechengasse soon intersects with a thoroughfare where, during the 12th century, you'd have been affronted with the stench of rancid blood from the nearby slaughterhouses.

Turn right and head to:

5. Fleischmarkt. Notice the heroic frieze above the facade of the antique apartment house at no. 18 ("The Tolerance House"), which depicts in symbolic form Joseph II, son of Maria Theresa, granting freedom of worship to what was at the time a mostly Greek Orthodox neighborhood. Number 9, begun in the 1400s and progressively improved and enlarged during the next 300 years, was used as an inn (or more likely, a flophouse) and warehouse for traders from the Balkans and the Middle East during the age of Mozart.

Walking Tour 3: Vienna's Back Streets

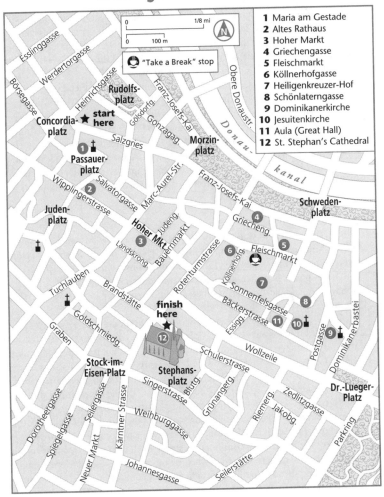

0   1/8 mi
0   100 m

🥤 "Take a Break" stop

1 Maria am Gestade
2 Altes Rathaus
3 Hoher Markt
4 Griechengasse
5 Fleischmarkt
6 Köllnerhofgasse
7 Heiligenkreuzer-Hof
8 Schönlaterngasse
9 Dominikanerkirche
10 Jesuitenkirche
11 Aula (Great Hall)
12 St. Stephan's Cathedral

🥤 **TAKE A BREAK**   at an inn named for the many Greeks who made it their regular dining spot for hundreds of years, **Griechenbeisl,** Fleischmarkt 11 (**☎ 01/533-1941**). Established in 1450 and divided into a warren of cozy dining rooms, it's described more fully in chapter 5, "Where to Dine."

Adjacent to the Greichenbeisl rise the walls of another Greek Orthodox church. It was embellished in 1858 by Theophil Hansen, the Danish-born architect of many of the grand buildings of the Ringstrasse, an ardent advocate of the Greek Revival style as shown by his recent design for the Austrian Parliament.

At Fleischmarkt 15, notice the baroque facade of the birthplace of a not-very-well-known Biedermeier painter, Moritz von Schwind, whose claim to fame lies in his membership in the circle of friends who attended the *Schubertiades,* evenings of music and philosophy organized by Franz Schubert in Vienna during the early 19th century.

A branch of the Vienna post office lies at no. 19, within the premises of a monastery confiscated from the Dominicans by Joseph II as part of his campaign to secularize the Austrian government. Ironically, the only ecclesiastical trappings left in this bureaucratic setting are the skeletons of dozens of dead brethren, buried in the building's crypt many generations ago.

The uninspired modern facade of the building at no. 24 Fleischmarkt was the long-ago site of a now-defunct hotel, Zur Stadt London, whose musical guests included the family of young Mozart as well as Franz Liszt, Richard Wagner (when he wasn't fleeing his creditors), and the Polish exile Chopin. The building at no. 14 Fleischmarkt shows a rich use of *Jugendstil* detailing, and a plaque commemorating it as the birthplace of one of the directors of the Court Opera in the latter days of the Habsburg dynasty. At Fleischmarkt 1, residents will tell you about the birth here of a later director of the same opera company, after its reorganization into the State Opera.

Turn left onto the:

6. **Köllnerhofgasse** and walk for about a half block. No. 1–3 functioned long ago as the headquarters of a group of merchants, based on the Rhine in Cologne, who set up a trading operation in Vienna in response to fiscal and legal perks and privileges granted to merchants during medieval times. The building you'll see today—remarkable for the number of windows that pierce its facade—dates from 1792.

At this point, turn left into a cul-de-sac that funnels through a wide gate into a courtyard that's always open to pedestrians. The cul-de-sac is Grashofgasse, at the end of which is a wall painted with a restored fresco of the Stift Heiligenkreuz (Holy Cross Abbey), a well-known 12th-century Cistercian monastery 15 miles west of town. A covered arcade, which is usually open, pierces the wall of Grashofgasse 3 and leads into the cobble-covered public courtyard of the:

7. **Heiligenkreuz-Hof,** an ecclesiastical complex that incorporates a 17th-century cluster of monks' apartments, lodging for an abbot, and the diminutive baroque chapel of St. Bernard, which is usually closed to the public except for wedding ceremonies. The courtyard's continued existence in the heart of Vienna is unusual: Many equivalent tracts formerly owned by other abbeys were converted long ago into building sites and public parks after sale or confiscation by the government.

Exit the monastery's courtyard from its opposite (southeastern) edge onto the:

8. **Schönlanterngasse.** Its name derives from the ornate wrought-iron street lamp that adorns the facade of the 16th-century building at no. 6. What hangs there now is a copy; the original has been moved to the Historical Museum of Vienna. This well-maintained street is part of a designated historic preservation district. Renovation loans to facilitate such preservation were issued at rock-bottom interest rates, and have been referred to ever since as *Kultur Schillings*. The neighborhood you're in is a prime example of these loans in action.

At no. 7 on the Schönlanterngasse lies the **Basilikenhaus,** a 13th-century bakery supported by 12th-century foundations. When foul odors began emanating from the building's well, the medieval residents of the building assumed that it was sheltering a basilisk (a mythological reptile from the Sahara Desert whose breath and gaze were fatal). The building's facade incorporates a stone replica of the beast, who was killed, according to a wall plaque, by a local baker who bravely showed the creature its own reflection in a mirror. A modern interpretation of what happened involves the possibility of methane gas or subterranean sulfurous vapors seeping out of the building's well.

The house at no. 7A on the Schonlanterngasse was the home of Robert Schumann from 1838 to 1839, the winter he rediscovered some of the unpublished compositions of Franz Schubert. Schumann, basking in the glory of a successful musical and social career, did more than anyone else to elevate Schubert to posthumous star status. The groundwork for the renaissance of Schubert's music was laid at this spot.

The building at no. 9 on the same street has functioned as a smithy (*Die Alte Schmiede*) since the Middle Ages. From its outside, you can glimpse a collection of antique blacksmith tools. Continue walking eastward along the Schönlanterngasse, where you'll see the back of a church you'll visit in a moment, the Jesuit Church. Continue walking (the street will make a sharp turn to the right) until it widens into the broad plaza of the Postgasse, where you turn right. The monument that rises in front of you, at Postgasse 4, is the:

9. Dominikanerkirche. This is the third of three Dominican churches to be built on this site. The earliest, constructed around 1237, burned down. The second, completed around 1300, was demolished by the Turks during their siege of 1529. The building you'll see today was completed in 1632 and is the most important early baroque church in Vienna. The rather murky-looking frescoes in the side chapels are artistically noteworthy, in some cases, as they are the 1726 statement of baroque artist Françoise Roettiers. However, it's mainly attractive as an example of baroque architecture and for the pomp of its high altar. Elevated to the rank of what the Viennese clergy refers to as a "minor basilica" in 1927, it's officially referred to as the "Rosary Basilica ad S. Mariam Rotundam." Incidentally, don't confuse the Dominikanerkirche with the less architecturally significant Greek Orthodox Church of St. Barbara, a few steps to the north, whose simple facade and elaborate liturgical rituals are sited at Postgasse 10. Incidentally, Beethoven lived for about a year in a building adjacent to St. Barbara's, Postgasse 8.

Now, walk south along the Postgasse to its dead end, and turn right into an narrow alley interspersed with steps. The alley will widen within a few paces into the Bäckerstrasse, a street noted for its imposing 18th-century architecture. Architects of such minor palaces as the ones at nos. 8 and 10 have adorned their facades with unusual details that could be appreciated from close up. Long ago, no. 16 contained an inn (*Schmauswaberl—"The Little Feast Hive"*) favored at the time by university students because of its habit of serving food left over from the banquets at the Hofburg at discounted prices. Other buildings of architectural note include nos. 7, 12, and 14, whose statue of Mary in a niche above the door shows evidence of the powerful effect of the Virgin on the everyday hopes and dreams of Vienna during the baroque age.

Follow Bäkerstrasse for about a block until you reach the confines of the square that's referred to by locals as the Universitätsplatz but by virtually every map in Vienna as the Dr. Ignaz Seipel-Platz (named for a theologian/priest who functioned twice as chancellor of Austria between the two world wars). The building that dominates the square is the:

10. Jesuitenkirche/Universitätskirche (Jesuit Church/University Church). It was built between 1623 and 1627 and adorned with twin towers and an enhanced baroque facade in the early 1700s by those workhorses of the Austrian Counter-Reformation, the Jesuits. The Jesuits were invited to Vienna by Ferdinand, the Spanish-born and fervently Catholic emperor, at a time when about three-quarters of the population had converted to Protestantism. It was estimated that only four Catholic priests remained at their posts within the entire city. From this building, the Jesuits spearheaded the 18th-century reconversion of Austria back to Catholicism and more or less dominated the curriculum at the nearby university. For such a stern group of academics, the Jesuits' church is amazingly ornate, with allegorical frescoes and all the aesthetic tricks that make its visitors believe they've entered a transitional world midway between earth and heaven.

The western edge of Dr. Ignaz Seipel-Platz is flanked by one of the showcase buildings of Vienna's university, the:

11. Aula (Great Hall) is Vienna's premier rococo attraction and a precursor of the great concert halls that dot the landmark of Austria today. In the 1700s, musical works were presented in halls such as this one, or in private homes or the palaces of wealthy patrons. The premiere of Haydn's oratorio *The Creation* happened here, as well as the first performance of Beethoven's Seventh Symphony.

Exit from the Dr. Ignaz Seipel-Platz by its northwestern corner and walk along the Sonnenfelsgasse. Flanked with 15th- and 16th-century houses (which until recently received complaints because of the number of bordellos they housed), the street is architecturally noteworthy. The building at Sonnenfelsgasse 19, dating from 1628, once was home to the proctor (administrator) of the nearby university. Other buildings of noteworthy beauty include nos. 3, 15, and 17. The street, incidentally, was named after one of the few advisors who could ever win an argument with Maria Theresa, Josef von Sonnenfels. Sonnenfels was descended from a long line of German rabbis and was the son of a Viennese Christian convert. He learned a dozen languages while employed as a foot soldier in the Austrian army and later used his influence to abolish torture in the prisons and particularly cruel methods of capital punishment. Beethoven dedicated his Piano Sonata in D major to him.

Walk to the western terminus of the Sonnenfelsgasse, then turn left and fork sharply back to the east along the Bäkerstrasse. You will, in effect, have circumnavigated an entire medieval block.

After your exploration of Bakerstrasse, turn south into a narrow alleyway, the Essigstrasse (Vinegar Street), and cross over the Wollzeile, centerpiece of the wool merchants and weavers' guild during the Middle Ages and now a noted shopping district. Continue your southward trek along the Stroblgasse, which will lead into the Schulerstrasse. Turn right onto the Schulerstrasse, which will lead within a block to a sweeping view of the side of:

12. St. Stephan's Cathedral. Built over a period of 400 years, and the symbol of Vienna itself, it's one of the most evocative and history-soaked monuments of Vienna. (See "Other Top Attractions," in chapter 6.)

Shopping 8

Visitors can spend many happy hours shopping or just browsing in Vienna's shops, where handicrafts are produced according to a long-established tradition of skilled workmanship. Popular for their beauty and quality are petit-point items, hand-painted Wiener Augarten porcelain, gold and silver work, ceramics, enamel jewelry, wrought-iron articles, and leather goods, among others.

1 The Shopping Scene

The main shopping streets are in the city center (1st District). Here you'll find **Kärntnerstrasse,** between the State Opera and Stock-im-Eisen-Platz; the **Graben,** between Stock-im-Eisen-Platz and Kohlmarkt; **Kohlmarkt,** between the Graben and Michaelerplatz; and **Rotensturmstrasse,** between Stephansplatz and Kai. There are also **Mariahilferstrasse,** between Babenbergerstrasse and Schönbrunn, one of the longest streets in Vienna; **Favoritenstrasse,** between Südtiroler Platz and Reumannplatz; and **Landstrasser Hauptstrasse.**

The **Naschmarkt** is a vegetable and fruit market with a lively scene every day. To visit it, head south of the opera district. It's at Linke and Rechte Wienzeile. (See "Open-Air Markets," later in this chapter).

SHOPPING HOURS

Shops are normally open Monday to Friday from 9am to 6pm and on Saturday from 9am to 1pm. Small shops close between noon and 2pm for lunch. Railroad-station shops in the Westbahnhof and the Südbahnhof are open daily from 7am to 11pm, offering groceries, smoker's supplies, stationery, books, and flowers.

A SHOPPING CENTER

Ringstrassen Galleries. In the Palais Corso and in the Kärntnerringhof, Kärntner Ring 5-13. ☎ **01/512-518.**

Rental fees for shop space in central Vienna are legendarily expensive. In response to the high rents, about 70 boutique-ish emporiums selling everything from hosiery to key chains to evening wear have pooled their resources and moved to labyrinthine quarters near the State Opera House, midway between the Bristol Hotel and the Anna Hotel. The prominent location guarantees a certain glamour, although the cramped dimensions of many of the stores might be a turn-off. But the selection is broad, and no one can deny the gallery's easy-to-find location. Each shop is operated independently, but virtually all of them conduct business Monday to Friday 10am to 7pm and Saturday 10am to 5pm. Three stores here of particular interest to fashion hounds include Yves St. Laurent, Casselli, and Agatha Paris, all recommended separately below.

2 Shopping A to Z

ANTIQUES

Vienna's antiques shops constitute a limitless treasure trove. You can find valuable old books, engravings, etchings, and paintings in secondhand shops, bookshops, and picture galleries.

✪ **Dorotheum.** Dorotheergasse 17. ☎ **01/5156-0449.**

Dating from 1707, this is the oldest auction house in Europe. Emperor Joseph I established the auction house so that impoverished aristocrats could fairly (and anonymously) get good value for their heirlooms. Today the Dorotheum holds many art auctions. If you're interested in an item, you give a small fee to a *sensal,* one of the licensed bidders, and he or she will bid in your name. The objects for sale cover a vast array of items, including exquisite furniture and carpets, delicate *objets d'art,* and valuable paintings, as well as decorative jewelry. If you're unable to attend an auction, you can still browse through the sales rooms at your own pace, selecting items you wish to purchase directly to take home with you the same day. Approximately 31 auctions are held in July alone; over the course of a year, these auctions are responsible for the exchange of some 250,000 pieces of art and antiques.

Es Brennt. Freisingergasse 1. ☎ **01/532-0900.**

Just a few steps from the Graben, a thoroughfare lined with shops, this is an antiques store whose tastes are funkier, more counterculture, and more iconoclastic than the grander purveyors of antiques nearby. Its specialties includes art deco, French and English antiques, Austrian Bauhaus–inspired pieces, and old furniture from the 1920s to the 1960s. There's a lot of retro stuff here from the age of Sputnik, and a lot of kitsch, whose origins in socialist Hungary or the former Czechoslovakia render them all the more fascinating. Haven't you always wanted a Czech chrome toaster?

Glasgalerie Kovacek. Spiegelgasse 12. ☎ **01/512-9954.**

Its ground floor is devoted to antique glass collected from estate sales and private collections throughout Austria. The majority of these items date to the 19th and early 20th centuries, although some 17th-century pieces are displayed as well. The most appealing antique pieces boast heraldic symbols, sometimes from branches of the Habsburgs themselves. There's also a collection of cunning glass paperweights imported from Bohemia, France, Italy, and other parts of Austria.

The upper floor is devoted to the kind of classical paintings against which the Secessionists revolted. Look for canvases by Franz Makart, foremost of the 19th-century historic academics, as well as some Secessionist works, including two by Kokoscha.

Flohmarkt. Linke Wienzeille. No phone.

You may find a little of everything at this flea market, which is located near the Naschmarkt and the Kettenbrückengasse U-Bahn Station. It runs every Saturday from 8am to 6pm except on public holidays. The Viennese have perfected the skill of haggling, and the Flohmarkt is one of their favorite arenas for this ritual battle of wills. It takes a trained eye to spot the antique treasures that are scattered among the junk. Everything you've ever wanted is here, especially if you're seeking those chunky Swiss

---

Vat Refunds

Fortunately for visitors to Austria, the country's Value-Added Tax (VAT), which can be as high as 35% on some luxury goods, is refundable. See "Taxes" under the section "Fast Facts" in chapter 3 to learn the proper refund procedure.

---

watches from the 1970s, glassware from the Czech Republic (sold as "Venetian glassware"), and even Russian icons. Believe it or not, some of this stuff is original, other merchandise merely the knockoff.

ART
✪ **Ö.W. (Österreichische Werkstatten).** Kärntnerstrasse 6. ☎ **01/512-2418.**

This three-floor, well-run store sells hundreds of handmade art objects. Leading artists and craftspeople throughout the country organized this cooperative to showcase their wares. The location is easy to find, only half a minute's walk from St. Stephan's Cathedral. There's an especially good selection of pewter, along with modern jewelry, glassware, brass, baskets, ceramics, and serving spoons fashioned from deer horn and bone. Take some time to wander through this place; you never know what treasure is hidden in a nook of this cavernous outlet. Even if you skip every other store in Vienna, check this one out.

BOOKS
The British Bookshop. Weihburggasse 24-26. ☎ **01/512-1945.**

This is the largest and most comprehensive emporium of English-language books in Austria, with a sprawling ground-floor showroom loaded with American, Australian, and English books. There are no periodicals, and no cute displays devoted to sales of such gift items as English marmalade or tea cozies. All you'll find is enough reading material to last you for the rest of your life and educational aids for teaching English as a second language.

Gerold & Co. Graben 31. ☎ **01/533-5014.**

This is a good bookstore for English-language publications. The sales personnel are helpful, and you can often pick up many titles not available elsewhere. Established in 1775, Gerold has a reputation for foreign-language books (Portuguese, Spanish, French, Italian, and English), especially those on art, architecture, psychology, and teaching foreign languages.

Morawa. Wollzeile 11. ☎ **01/51562.**

It's huge and rambling, occupying a labyrinth of vaulted rooms a short walk from St. Stephan's Cathedral. This outlet sells both English- and German-language books.

Shakespeare & Company. Sterngasse 2. ☎ **01/535-5053.**

This store carries an especially good selection of English-language magazines.

CHANDELIERS
✪ **J. & L. Lobmeyr.** Kärntnerstrasse 26. ☎ **01/512-0508.**

If during your exploration of Vienna you should happen to admire a crystal chandelier, there's a good chance that it was made by this company. Designated purveyor to the Imperial Court of Austria in the early 19th century, it has maintained an elevated position ever since. The company is credited with designing and creating the first electric chandelier in 1883. It has also designed chandeliers for the Vienna State Opera,

Vienna Shopping

A.E. Köchert **24**
Agatha Paris **8**
Albin Denk **31**
Altmann & Kühne **28**
Arcadia Opera Shop **1**
Augarten Porzellan **26**
The British Bookshop **16**
Casselli **10**
Da Caruso **5**
Dorotheum **25**
Es Brennt **34**
Flohmarkt **6**
Gerold & Co. **30**
Gerstner **13**
Glasgalerie Kovacek **20**
Helmut Lang **17**
J. & L. Lobmeyr **18**
Kober **32**
Lanz **12**
Loden Plankl **3**
Mary Kindermoden **33**
Morawa **35**
Naschmarkt **7**
Niederösterreichisches **1**
Ö.W. (Österreichische
  Werkstatten) **15**
Pawlata **22**
Petit Point Kovacec **19**
Popp & Kretschmer **23**
Ringstrasse Galleries **11**
Rozet & Fischmeister **2**
Shakespeare & Co. **36**
Sportalm Trachtenmoden **27**
Steffl Kaufhaus **21**
Wein & Co. **4**
Yves St. Laurent Rive Gauche **9**
Zur Schwabischen Jungfrau **29**

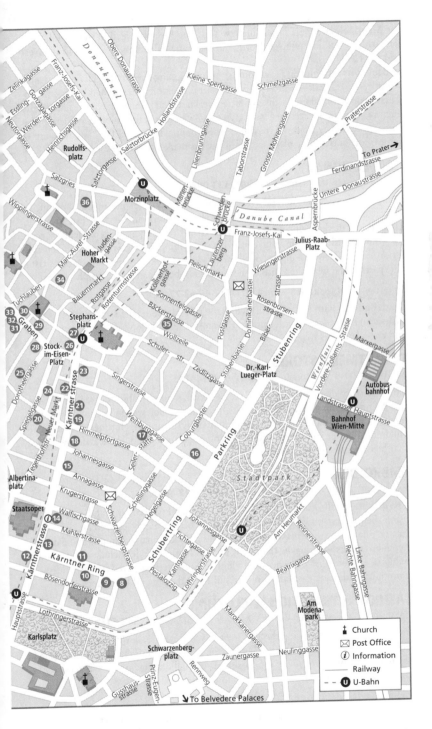

Church
Post Office
Information
Railway
U-Bahn

the Metropolitan Opera House in New York, the Assembly Hall in the Kremlin, the new concert hall in Fukuoka, Japan, and for many palaces and mosques in the Near and Far East.

Behind its art nouveau facade on the main shopping street of the city center, you'll see at least 50 chandeliers of all shapes and sizes. The store also sells hand-painted Hungarian porcelain, along with complete breakfast and dinner services. They'll also engrave your family crest on a wine glass or sell you one of the uniquely modern pieces of sculptured glass from the third-floor showroom. The second floor is a museum of some of the outstanding pieces the company has made since it was established in 1823.

CONFECTIONARY

Altmann & Kühne. Graben 30. ☎ **01/533-0927.**

Many Viennese adults we asked have detailed memories of marzipan, hazelnut, or nougat bought for them by parents during strolls along the Graben. Established in 1928, this is the kind of cozy shop where virtually nothing inside is particularly good for your waistline or for your teeth, but everything is positively and undeniably scrumptious. The visual display of all things sweet is almost as appealing as their taste. The pastries and tarts filled with fresh seasonal raspberries are, quite simply, delectable.

Gerstner. Kärntnerstrasse 13-15. ☎ **01/512-49-63-77.**

This competes with Café Demel (see chapter 5) as one of the city's greatest pastry-makers and *chocolatiers,* with some of the most delectable-looking cakes, petits-fours, and chocolate anywhere.

DEPARTMENT STORES

Steffl Kaufhaus. Kärntnerstrasse 19. ☎ **01/514310.**

This five-story department store is one of Vienna's most visible and well advertised. You'll find rambling racks of cosmetics, perfumes, a noteworthy section devoted to books and periodicals, housewares, and thousands of garments for men, women, and children. If there's something you forgot to pack for your trip, chances are very good that Steffl Kaufhaus will have it.

EMBROIDERY

Petit Point Kovacec. Kärntnerstrasse 16. ☎ **01/512-4886.**

The delicate, small-scale art of *petit point,* where floral patterns are hand-embroidered using the smallest possible stitches, has always been a highly prized craft for which Austria is famous. All items were completed using traditional techniques and patterns, by embroiderers working in their own homes. Items for sale include purses, bookmarkers, key holders, brooches, and rings set into sterling silver frames, and more ambitious works, such as framed pictures of floral themes and landscapes.

FASHION & TRADITIONAL CLOTHING

Casselli. In the Ringstrassen Galleries, Kärntner Ring 5-7. ☎ **01/512-5350.**

You might enjoy rummaging through the racks of this store, devoted to the tastes and budgets of hip younger women. Many of the garments are Italian made or inspired, the remainder Austrian; young shop assistants throughout downtown Vienna swear by the place for both casual street clothes and experimental evening wear.

Helmut Lang. Seilergasse 6. ☎ **01/513-2588.**

Although Helmut Lang's earliest creative years were spent in his hometown of Vienna, his real fame didn't come until after many years in Paris and New York. In 1996, this "designer of the moment" returned, with fanfare, to open a boutique within Vienna's medieval core. Since then, it has done a booming business. Fashions here are for both men and women. Want something funky? Check out his underwear inspired by the pre-AIDS 1970s.

Lanz. Kärntnerstrasse 10. ☎ **01/512-2456.**

A well-known Austrian store, Lanz specializes in Austrian dirndls and other folk clothing. This rustically elegant shop's stock is mostly for women, although they do offer a limited selection of men's jackets, neckties, and hats. Clothes for toddlers begin at sizes appropriate for a 1-year-old; women's apparel begins at size 36 (American size 7).

☯ Loden Plankl. Michaelerplatz 6. ☎ **01/533-8032.**

Established in 1830 by the Plankl family, this store is the oldest and most reputable outlet in Vienna for traditional Austrian clothing. You'll find Austrian loden coats, shoes, trousers, dirndls, jackets, lederhosen, and suits for men, women, and children. The building, located opposite the Hofburg, dates from the 17th century. Children's clothing usually begins with items for 2-year-olds, and women's sizes range from 7 to 20 (American). Large or tall men won't be ignored either, as sizes go up to 60.

Mary Kindermoden. Graben 14. ☎ **01/533-6097.**

Here's a store specializing in children's clothing with a regional twist. If you've thought about buying a pair of lederhosen for your nephew or a dirndl for your niece, this is the place to go. In the heart of the Old Town, near St. Stephan's Cathedral, the store has two floors stocked with well-made garments, including lace swaddling clothes for christenings. Most garments are for children aged 10 months to 14 years. The staff speaks English and seems to deal well with children.

Niederösterreichisches Heimatwerk. Herrengasse 6. ☎ **01/533-3495.**

This is one of the best-stocked clothing stores in Vienna if you're looking for traditional garments that men, women, and children still wear with undeniable style in Austria. The inventory covers three full floors and includes garments inspired by the folk traditions of Styria, the Tyrol, Carinthia, and virtually every other Austrian province. If you're looking for a loden coat, a dirndl, a jaunty alpine hat (with or without a pheasant feather), or an incredibly durable pair of lederhosen, this is the place. You'll also find handcrafted gift items (pewter, breadboards and breadbaskets, crystal, and tableware) laden with alpine charm.

Popp & Kretschmer. Kärntnerstrasse 51. ☎ **01/512-7801.**

The staff here is usually as well dressed and elegant as the clientele, and if you appear to be a bona fide customer, the sales clerks will offer coffee, tea, or champagne as you scrutinize the carefully selected merchandise. The store contains three floors of dresses for women, along with shoes, handbags, belts, and a small selection of men's briefcases and travel bags. You'll find it opposite the State Opera, near many of the grand old hotels of Vienna.

Sportalm Trachtenmoden. In the Haas Haus, Stephansplatz 12. ☎ **01/535-5289.**

This stylish women's store stocks a staggering collection of dirndls. Many are faithful replicas of designs that haven't been altered for generations; others take greater liberties in meeting modern tastes. Children's sizes fit girls ages 1 to 14. You'll find the store within the jarringly modern Haas Haus, across the plaza from Vienna's cathedral.

Yves St. Laurent Rive Gauche. In the Ringstrassen Galleries, Kärntner Ring 5-7. ☎ **01/512-5202.**

Looking for an evening gown (*Abendkleide*) or cocktail dress (*Cocktailkleide*) that's as divine as the Wagnerian opus you're about to hear at the State Opera? Head for the only distributor of Yves St. Laurent in Austria, a stylish, well-stocked boutique with a discerning sales staff. They carry virtually every piece of *prêt-à-porter* the French master has created this season. The only menswear in the shop is a collection of neckties.

JEWELRY

✪ **A. E. Köchert.** Neuer Markt 15. ☎ **01/512-5828.**

Here the sixth generation of the family that served as court jewelers until the end of the Habsburg Empire continues their tradition of fine workmanship. The store, founded in 1814, is in a 16th-century, landmark-status building. The firm has designed many of the crown jewels of Europe, but the staff still gives equal attention to the customers looking only at charms for a bracelet.

Agatha Paris. In the Ringstrassen Galleries, Kärntner Ring 5-7. ☎ **01/512-4621.**

The concept here is small scale and intensely decorative, with jewelry that manages to be both exotic and tasteful at the same time. Many pieces are inset with semi-precious (i.e., affordable) gemstones; others combine gold and silver into attractive ornaments, which are sometimes based on antique models.

Rozet & Fischmeister. Kohlmarkt 11. ☎ **01/533-8061.**

Few jewelry stores in Austria attain the prestige of this 200-year-old emporium of good taste and conspicuous consumption. Owned by the same family since it was established in 1770, it specializes in gold jewelry, gemstones set in artful settings, and both antique and modern versions of silver tableware. If you're looking for flawless copies of Biedermeier silverware or pieces, this is where you want to go. If you opt to buy an engagement ring here or a bauble for a friend, you'll be following in the footsteps of Franz Joseph I. Staff here will even quietly admit that he made several discreet purchases for his legendary mistress, actress Katharina Schratt.

LACE AND NEEDLEWORK

Zur Schwabischen Jungfrau. Graben 26. ☎ **01/402-6301.**

This is one of the most illustrious shops in Austria, with a reputation that goes back almost 300 years. Here, Maria Theresa bought her first handkerchiefs, thousands of debutantes have shopped for dresses, Middle Eastern oil billionaires have cornered the shop's supply of hand-embroidered silk sheets, and costume designers from Vienna's operas and theaters have rummaged through the racks of material for their flounces and bodices. Come here for towels, bed linens, lace tablecloths, and some of the most elaborate needlepoint and embroidery anywhere. Service is courtly, cordial, Old World, and impeccable.

MUSIC

✪ **Arcadia Opera Shop.** Wiener Staatsoper, Kärntnerstrasse 40. ☎ **01/513-9568.**

This respected record store is one of the best for classical music. The well-educated staff knows the music and its practitioners (as well as the availability of recordings) and is usually eager to share that knowledge with customers. It's located on the street level of the Vienna State Opera, with a separate entrance opening onto Kärntnerstrasse. The shop also carries books on art, music, architecture, and opera, as well as an assortment of musical memorabilia. Any of these would make a worthwhile souvenir for the Mozart buff back home. Guided tours of the splendid opera house end here, as well.

Open-Air Markets

Since the Middle Ages Viennese merchants have thrived by hauling produce, dairy products, and meats in bulk from the fertile farms of Lower Austria and Burgenland into the city center. The tradition of buying the day's provisions directly from street stalls is so prevalent that there's a strong disincentive, even today, for the establishment of modern supermarkets within the city center. A walk through Vienna's open-air markets—the Naschmarkt, the Rochusmarkt, or the Brunnenmarkt—will quickly convince you of the allure of this kind of shopping.

The largest of the city's outdoor food markets is the **Naschmarkt,** Wienzeile, in the 6th District (U-Bahn: Karlsplatz), just south of the Ring. It occupies what was originally the riverbed of a branch of the Danube that was diverted and paved over during the massive public works projects of the 19th century. It's the most popular and colorful of the bunch and the most comprehensive.

Entire books have been written about the subcultures and linguistic dialects that flourish among the Naschmarkt's denizens. Observe the following unwritten rules if you want to avoid the wrath of the notoriously short-tempered women selling their goods: Never touch merchandise unless you intend to buy something. Don't try to buy less than a half-kilo (about a pound) of potatoes. And—even if your German is good—don't even try to understand the raunchy Viennese patois. The market is often compared to the old (and now defunct) Les Halles of Paris.

Get there early in the morning and wander through the labyrinth of outdoor food stands where Vienna's restaurants and hotels stock up on provisions for the day. At the end of your tour, head for the nearby **Coffeehouse Drechsler** for breakfast or an early morning cup of coffee.

Somewhat smaller and less varied are the **Rochusmarkt,** at Landstrasser Hauptstrasse at the corner of the Erdbergstrasse, in the 3rd District (U-Bahn: Rochusgasse), a short distance east of the Ring; and the **Brunnenmarkt,** on the Brunnengasse, in the 16th District (U-Bahn: Josefstädterstrasse), a subway ride west of the center and a short walk north of Vienna's Westbahnhof. Even if you don't want to return to your hotel with bushels of carrots or potatoes, the experience is colorful enough—and in some cases, kitschy enough—to be a highlight of your trip to Vienna.

Most merchants in these markets maintain approximately the same hours: Monday to Friday from 8am to 6pm, Saturday from 8am to noon.

Da Caruso. Operngasse 4. ☎ **01/513-1326.**

Set almost adjacent to the Vienna State Opera, this store is known to music fans and musicologists worldwide for its inventory of rare and unusual recordings of historic performances by the Vienna Opera and the Vienna Philharmonic. If you're looking for a magical or particularly emotional performance by Maria Callas, Herbert von Karajan, or Bruno Walter, chances are you can get it here, redigitalized on a CD. There's also a collection of taped films. The staff is hip, alert, and obviously in love with music.

PORCELAIN & POTTERY
✪ **Albin Denk.** Graben 13. ☎ **01/512-4439.**

Albin Denk is the oldest continuously operating porcelain store in Vienna, doing business since 1702. Its clients have included Empress Elizabeth, and the shop you see today looks almost the same as it did when she visited. The three low-ceilinged rooms are beautifully decorated with thousands of objects from Meissen, Dresden, and other regions. With such a wealth of riches, it can be hard to make a selection.

Augarten Porzellan. Stock-im-Eisenplatz 3-4. ☎ **01/512-1494.**

Established in 1718, Augarten porcelain is, after Meissen, the oldest manufacturer of porcelain in Europe. This multi-tiered shop is the most visible and well-stocked outlet in the world. Virtually anything can be shipped anywhere. The tableware—fragile dinner plates with traditional or contemporary patterns—is elegant and much sought after. Also noteworthy are porcelain statues of the Lippizaner horses.

Pawlata. Kärntnerstrasse 14. ☎ **01/512-1764.**

A short walk from St. Stephan's Cathedral, this shop contains a diverse collection of Gmunden stoneware and pottery. The pottery is based on patterns developed centuries ago. The vases, plates, soup tureens, casseroles, and water pitchers usually have background colors of white or cream and either stripes or country-rustic floral patterns in fresh shades of green, blue, black, yellow, and red.

TOYS
Kober. 14-15 Graben. ☎ **01/533-6019.**

Kober has been a household name, especially at Christmastime in Vienna, for more than 100 years. There are old-fashioned wooden toys, teddy bears straight out of a Styrian storybook, go-carts (assembly required), building sets, and car and airplane models. The occasional set of toy soldiers is more *Nutcracker Suite* than G.I. Joe.

WINE
Wein & Co. Habsburgerstrasse 3. ☎ **01/535-0916.**

Since the colonization of Vindobona by the ancient Romans, the Viennese have always taken their wines seriously. Wein & Co. is Vienna's largest wine outlet, a sprawling cellar-level ode to the joys of the grape and the bounty of Bacchus. The layout resembles a supermarket, its shelves loaded with Rheinrieslings, Blauburgunder, Blaufrankischer, Grüner Veltliners, Zweigelts, and a roster of obscurer Austrian wines. You'll also find wines from around the world, including South Africa and Chile.

9

Vienna After Dark

Whatever nightlife scene turns you on, Vienna has a little bit of everything. You can dance into the morning hours, attend a festival, go to the theater, hear a concert, gamble, or simply indulge in Vienna's legendary spirits at a local tavern.

The best sources of information about what's happening on the cultural scene is **"Wien Monatsprogramm,"** which is distributed free at tourist information offices and at many hotel reception desks. *Die Presse,* the Viennese daily, publishes a special magazine in its Thursday edition outlining the major cultural events for the coming week. It's in German but still might be helpful.

Except for students, ticket discounts are usually not offered in Vienna. However, "Wien Monatsprogramm" lists outlets where you can purchase tickets in advance and cut down on the surcharge imposed by travel agencies. These agencies routinely add about 22% to what may already be an expensive ticket.

If you'd rather not go broke attending a performance at the Staatsoper or the Burgtheater, you can purchase standing-room tickets for about 50AS ($3.35). Bona fide students with valid IDs are eligible for many discounts if they're under age 27. For example, the Burgtheater, Akademietheater, and the Staatsoper will sell student tickets for just 90AS ($6.05) on the night of the performance. Theaters almost routinely grant students about 20% off the regular ticket price.

Vienna is the home of four major symphony orchestras, including the world-acclaimed **Vienna Symphony** and the **Vienna Philharmonic,** as well as the **ÖRF Symphony Orchestra** and the **Niederösterreichische Tonkünstler.** There are literally dozens of others, ranging from smaller orchestras to chamber orchestras.

1 The Performing Arts

Music is at the heart of Vienna's cultural life. This has been true for a couple of centuries or so, and the city continues to lure composers and librettists, musicians and music lovers. You can find places to enjoy everything from chamber music to pop, from waltzes to jazz. You'll find small discos and large concert halls, as well as musical theaters. If somehow you should tire of aural entertainment, you'll find no shortage of theater, from classical to modern to avant-garde. Below we'll describe just a few of the better-known spots for cultural recreation—if you're in Vienna long enough, you'll find many other delights on your own.

A NOTE ON EVENING DRESS   Vienna is still not quite as informal as North America or the rest of Europe. Many people still dress well for concerts and theaters. For especially festive occasions, such as opera premieres, receptions, and balls, tails or dinner jackets and evening dresses still appear. Younger people and visitors, however, no longer adhere to these customs, and informal dress is accepted almost everywhere. If you want to dress up, however, you can rent evening wear (as well as carnival costumes) from several places in Vienna, which you'll find in the telephone directory classified section (the Yellow Pages in the United States) under *Kleiderleihanstalten.*

OPERA & CLASSICAL MUSIC

✪ Staatsoper (State Opera). Opernring 2. ☎ **01/5144-42960.** Tickets 150–2,500AS ($10.05–$167.50). Tours cost 45AS ($3) per person; times are posted on a board outside the entrance. U-Bahn: Karlsplatz.

This is the world's legendary opera house. Opera is sacred in Vienna—when World War II was over, the city's top priority was the restoration of the heavily damaged Staatsoper. With the Vienna Philharmonic Orchestra in the pit, the leading opera stars of the world perform here. In their day, Richard Strauss and Gustav Mahler worked as directors. Daily performances are given from the first of September until the end of June. Tickets are hard to get but worth the effort. (Also see "Other Top Attractions," in chapter 6.)

Wiener Konzerthaus. Lothringerstrasse 20. ☎ **01/712-1211.** Ticket prices depend on the event. Box office open Mon–Fri 9am–7:30pm; Sat 9am–1pm. U-Bahn: Stadtpark.

This major concert hall, built in 1912, is home to the Wiener Sympohniker. With three auditoriums, it's the venue for a wide spectrum of musical events, including orchestral concerts, chamber music recitals, choir concerts, piano recitals, and opera stage performances.

Musikverein. Karlsplatz 6. ☎ **01/505-8190** for the box office. Tickets 55AS ($3.70) for standing room, up to 1,300AS ($87.10) for seats. Box office open Mon–Fri 9am–6pm; Sat 9am–noon. U-Bahn: Karlsplatz.

Consider yourself lucky if you get to hear the Vienna Philharmonic here. One of the Musikverein's two concert halls, the Golden Hall, has often served as the setting for various TV productions. Out of the 600 or so concerts that are presented per season, (September to June), only 10 to 12 are played by the Vienna Philharmonic. These are usually subscription concerts, sold out long in advance. Standing room is available at almost any concert, but you must line up hours before the show.

Theater an der Wien. Linke Wienzeile 6. ☎ **01/58885** for tickets. Tickets 400–1,350AS ($26.80–$90.45). Box office open daily 9am–1pm and 2–6pm. U-Bahn: Karlsplatz.

Since opening on June 13, 1801, this theater has been offering excellent opera and operetta presentations. This was the site of the premiere of Beethoven's *Fidelio* in 1805; in fact, the composer once lived in the building. The world premiere of Johann Strauss II's *Die Fledermaus* was also performed here. Invariably, an article appears every year in some newspaper proclaiming that the Theater an der Wien was the site of the premiere of Mozart's *The Magic Flute*—a neat trick, considering that the first performance of that great work was in 1791, 10 years before the theater opened. During the years of occupation after World War II, when the Staatsoper was being restored after heavy damage, the Vienna State Opera played here.

Volksoper. Währingerstrasse 78. ☎ **01/5144-43318.** Tickets 90–900AS ($6.05–$60.30), standing room 30–50AS ($2–$3.35). Box office opens 1 hour before showtime. U-Bahn: Volksoper.

The Toughest Ticket in Town

Reservations and information for the four state theaters—the **Staatsoper** (State Opera), **Volksoper**, **Burgtheater** (National Theater), and the **Akademietheater**—can be obtained by calling the office that handles reservations and schedule information for all four theaters (☎ **01/5144-42959**), Monday to Friday from 8am to 5pm. The line is often busy. The major performance season is from September until June, with more limited presentations in summer. Many tickets are sold by subscription before the box office opens. For all four theaters, box office sales begin 1 month before each performance at the **Bundestheaterkasse,** Goethegasse 1 (☎ **01/51-44-40**), open Monday to Friday from 8am to 6pm, on Saturday and Sunday from 9am to noon. Credit-card sales can be arranged by telephone within 6 days of a performance by calling ☎ **01/513-1513**, Monday to Friday from 10am to 6pm and on Saturday and Sunday from 10am to noon. Tickets for all state theater performances, including the opera, are also available by writing to the **Österreichischer Bundestheaterverband,** Goethegasse 1, A-1010 Vienna. Information and ticket requests can be faxed to **01/5144-42969**. Orders must be received at least 3 weeks in advance of the performance.

The single most common complaint of music lovers in Vienna is the unavailability of tickets. As a last chance, you have the option of consulting a ticket broker. Their surcharge usually won't exceed 25%, except for extremely rare tickets when that surcharge might be doubled or tripled. At least half a dozen ticket agencies maintain offices in the city, but one of the most reputable is **Liener Brünn** (☎ **01/533-09-61**). Their tickets are sometimes available months in advance or as little as a few hours before an event.

As a final resort, remember that the concierges at virtually every upscale hotel in Vienna long ago learned sophisticated tricks for acquiring hard-to-come-by tickets. A gratuity might work wonders and will be expected anyway for the phone work. You'll pay a hefty surcharge as well.

This opera house presents lavish productions of Viennese operettas, light opera, and other musicals from the first of September until the end of June on a daily schedule. Tickets go on sale at the Volksoper itself only 1 hour before performance.

Schönbrunner Palace Theater. At Schönbrunn Palace, Schönbrunner Schlossstrasse. ☎ **01/512-01-00.** Tickets 250–650AS ($16.10–$43.55). U-Bahn: Schönbrunn.

This gem of a theater opened in 1749 for the entertainment of Maria Theresa's court. The architecture is a mixture of baroque and rococo, and there's a large, plush box where the imperial family used to sit. The theater is used for performances of the Max Reinhardt Seminar (theater productions) and opera productions throughout the year. Operettas and comic operas are presented in July and August. Many different groups, each responsible for its own ticket sales, perform here. Performances are given nightly, Tuesday to Saturday, in July and August.

THEATER

Burgtheater (National Theater). Dr.-Karl-Lueger-Ring 2. ☎ **01/5144-4145.** Tickets 60–600AS ($4–$40.20) for seats, 80AS ($5.35) for standing room. Tram: 1, 2, or D to Burgtheater.

The Burgtheater produces classical and modern plays in German. Work started on the original structure in 1776, but the theater was destroyed in World War II and later reopened in 1955. It's the dream of every German-speaking actor to appear here.

Vienna's Own Playwright

If your German is halfway passable, try to see a play by **Arthur Schnitzler,** if one is being staged during your visit. This mild-mannered playwright, who died in 1931, was the quintessential Viennese writer. Through his works he gave the imperial city the charm and style one more often associates with Paris. Whenever possible we attend a revival of one of his plays, such as *Einsame Weg* (*The Solitary Path*) or *Professor Bernhardi*. Our favorite is *Reigen,* on which the film *La Ronde* was based. Schnitzler's plays are often performed at the Theater in der Josefstadt.

Akademietheater. Lisztstrasse 3. ☎ **01/5144-42656.** Tickets 70–550AS ($4.70–$36.85) for seats, 30AS ($2) standing room. U-Bahn: Stadtpark.

This theater specializes in both classic and contemporary works, from Brecht to Shakespeare. The Burgtheater Company often performs here, as it's the second, smaller house for this world-famous company.

Theater in der Josefstadt. Josefstadterstrasse 26. ☎ **01/42700.** Tickets 80–850AS ($5.35–$56.95). Box office open daily 9am–6pm. U-Bahn: Rathaus. Tram: J. Bus: 13A.

One of the most influential theaters in the German-speaking world, this theater reached legendary heights of excellence under the aegis of Max Reinhardt beginning in 1924. It was built in 1776 and presents a variety of comedies and dramas.

Vienna's English Theatre. Josefsgasse 12. ☎ **01/402-1260-0.** Tickets 190–490AS ($12.75–$32.85). Box office open Mon–Fri 10am–5pm; Sat 10am–4pm. U-Bahn: Rathaus. Tram: J. Bus: 13A.

This English-speaking theater was established in 1963 and proved to be so popular that it has been around ever since. Many international actors and celebrities have appeared on the stage of this neo-baroque theater. Princess Grace of Monaco once played here in a performance to raise money for charity. Works by American playwrights are occasionally presented.

Volkstheater. Neustiftgasse 1. ☎ **01/524-7263.** Tickets 70–500AS ($4.70–$33.50). Box office open daily 10am–8pm. Tram: 1, 2, 49, D, or J. Bus: 48A.

Built in 1889, this theater presents classical works of European theater. Some of the pieces produced here are videotaped for distribution throughout the German-speaking world, and include original versions and translations of works by Nestroy, Raimund, and Strindberg. Modern plays and comedies are also presented. The theater's season runs from September to June.

2 The Club & Music Scene

AN ENTERTAINMENT COMPLEX

Volksgarten. Entrances from the Heldenplatz and from Burgring 1. ☎ **01/5330-5180.** Cover 50AS ($3.35) for the show (9pm–2am), 75–140AS ($5.05–$9.40) for the disco (11pm–4am). U-Bahn: Volkstheatre.

This is the largest and most diverse entertainment complex within Vienna's Ring. It was established in 1946 in a building very close to the Hofburg. It's a labyrinth of rooms and outdoor spaces, a kind of happy-go-lucky maze. Tyrolean oom-pah-pah music alternates here with classic rock 'n' roll. A restaurant, open from 11am to midnight, serves steins of beer, wine, and main courses priced from 75 to 165AS ($5.05

to $11.05). A disco (a bit jarring when played simultaneously with the evergreen music) is open every night from 11pm, although it's pretty empty before midnight.

CABARET
First Floor. Seitenstettengasse 5. ☎ **01/533-7866.** No cover. U-Bahn: Schwedenplatz.

As its name implies, this hip and worldly nightclub is one floor above street level in an antique building in the city's historic Jewish district. Most of the people in this metallic-looking, mostly blue space range in age from 25 to 45 years old. There's a long and very active bar area along with a vast, artfully illuminated aquarium. Mixed drinks cost 90 to 130AS ($6.05 to $8.70) each. There's live music—usually only a piano and bass—on Monday night. Hours are Monday to Saturday 7pm to 4am, Sunday 7pm to 3am.

Moulin Rouge. Walfischgasse 11. ☎ **01/512-2130.** Cover 75AS ($5.05). U-Bahn: Karlsplatz.

Established prior to World War II, this spot has been known for many years as the leading risqué nightclub of Vienna. It's modeled after the original Moulin Rouge in Paris and is just to the right of the opera house, with curved walls, clapboard siding, and a reconstruction of the Moulin Rouge trademark, a windmill. If you're window-shopping, you can see pictures of the "artists," presented stark naked, so there won't be many surprises if you decide to go in. It's a lavishly decorated club with two tiers of seating. The club opens nightly at 10pm, presenting one show, at 11pm. Once inside, a beer costs 200AS ($13.40); a whisky goes for 250AS ($16.75).

U-4. Schönbrunner Strasse 222. ☎ **01/815-8307.** Cover varies from nothing to 100AS ($6.70). U-Bahn: Pilgramgasse.

Although the origins of this club go back to the 1920s, it continues to reinvent itself with each generation of nightclubbers. Today, it's always cited as one of the trendiest and most innovative clubs in Vienna. Depending on the schedule, there may be Italian night, salsa/Latino night, and—every Thursday—gay night. It's open nightly from 9pm to around 3am.

ROCK, JAZZ & BLUES
✪ **Jazzland.** Franz-Josefs-Kai 29. ☎ **01/533-2575.** Cover 180AS ($12.05). U-Bahn: Schwedenplatz.

This is the most famous jazz bar in Austria, noted for the quality of its U.S. and Central European–based performers. It's in a deep, 200-year-old cellar, with exposed brick walls and dim lighting. Beer—which seems to be the thing to order here—costs 50AS ($3.35). Platters of Viennese food cost from 70 to 100AS ($4.70 to $6.70). The place is open nightly from 8pm to 1am. There are three sets nightly beginning at 9pm.

Papa's Tapas. Schwarzenbergplatz 10. ☎ **01/505-0311.** Cover 50–150AS ($3.35–$10.05), depending on the event. U-Bahn: Karlsplatz.

This place attracts a rock 'n' roll crowd. It's at the same location as the Atrium disco (see below). In a corner is the Würlitzer Bar, with an American-made jukebox playing vintage '50s stuff, including Elvis. Papa's plays host to a changing roster of visiting rock stars, whose arrival is always noted in the Vienna newspapers. When there's no live music, there's still beer, with a large one costing 42AS ($2.80). The club is open Monday to Thursday from 8pm to 2am and on Friday and Saturday from 8pm until 3:30am.

Rockhaus. Adalbert-Stifter-Strasse 73. ☎ **01/332-46-41.** Cover charge 200–380AS ($13.40–$25.45). Tram: 31 or 32.

Rockhaus is a direct competitor of the also-recommended Tunnel. As such, it attracts much the same crowd, and—with perhaps a higher percentage of folk singers, reggae, soca, and new wave artists—some of the same musicians. It's also about twice as large as the Tunnel, which means larger crowds and louder volumes. About half of the bands that play here are Austrian; the remainder fly in from other parts of Europe and, on occasion, from such Asian music centers as the Philippines. Rockhaus rocks and rolls every Tuesday to Sunday, with the bar drawing a heavy after-work crowd beginning around 6pm and live music beginning sometime after 8:30pm.

Tunnel. Florianigasse 39. ☎ **01/405-3465.** Cover 50–90AS ($3.35–$6.05). U-Bahn: Rathaus.

In a smoke-filled cellar near Town Hall, Tunnel showcases bands from virtually everywhere. You'll never know quite what to expect, as the only hint of who's playing is a recorded, German-language message and occasional advertisements in local newspapers. But if you're willing to take a chance, this is a pretty cool spot. It's open daily from 8pm to 2am, with live music beginning around 9pm.

DANCE CLUBS

Atrium. Schwarzenbergplatz 10 (Schwindgasse 1). ☎ **01/505-3594.** Cover 40AS ($2.70). U-Bahn: Karlsplatz.

Vienna's first disco caters to a young crowd that gathers here Thursday and Sunday from 8:30pm to 2am and Friday and Saturday from 8:30pm to 4am. Every Thursday and Sunday drinks are two-for-one for the first hour of business. Otherwise, a large beer costs 40AS ($2.70).

P1 Discothek. Rotgasse 9. ☎ **01/535-9995.** Cover 65AS ($4.35) Tues–Thurs; 90AS ($6.05) Fri–Sat. U-Bahn: Stephansplatz.

Vienna's hottest disco is filled with locals and visitors alike, most in their mid-20s. In what used to be a film studio, the club has a spacious floor that can hold as many as 2,000 dancers. Two DJs alternate nightly. Once or twice a month, there's live music. The club is open Tuesday to Saturday from 8pm to 6am. Beer costs 45AS ($3) and up.

Queen Anne. Johannesgasse 12. ☎ **01/512-0203.** Cover Fri–Sat 90AS ($6.05), including first drink. U-Bahn: Stadtpark.

The fabulous people come to this nightclub and disco—David Bowie, German playboy Gunther Sachs, the princess of Auersperg, and the 1970s heavy-metal band Deep Purple. Occasional musical acts range from Mick Jagger look-alikes to imitations of Watusi dancers. The brown doors with brass trim are open daily from 10pm to 6am. A scotch and soda goes for 95AS ($6.35); beer starts at 80AS ($5.35).

Scotch Club. Parkring 10. ☎ **01/512-9417.** No cover. U-Bahn: Stadtpark or Stubentor.

Except for the whisky, there's not much that's Scottish about this disco and coffeehouse in Vienna's most fashionable area, a 5-minute walk from the Hilton, Marriott, Radisson/SAS, Parkring, and Imperial. It's a popular meeting place for society figures and has in the past attracted such celebs as Austrian pop singer Uta Jürgens and Harry Belafonte. There's a disco in the cellar, a bistro and supper restaurant on the street level, and a cocktail bar above. The plush disco has a hydraulic stage, an artificial waterfall, and fancy lights. Main courses in the bistro range from 190 to 250AS ($12.75 to $16.75); beer costs 110AS ($7.35). The disco pulsates daily from 9pm to 5am, the restaurant every evening from 7pm to 4am.

Titanic. Theobaldgasse 11. ☎ **01/587-4758.** 30AS ($2) cover charge. U-Bahn: Mariahilferstrasse.

A sprawling dance club that has thrived since the early 1980s, Titanic has two different dance floors and a likable upstairs restaurant where Mexican, Italian, and international dishes provide bursts of quick energy for further rounds of dancing. A mirrored world with strobe lights and no seating, this club is designed for dancing, drinking, and mingling, sometimes aggressively, throughout the evening. It's popular with American students and athletes. As for the music, you're likely to find everything that's playing in London or New York—soul, funk, hip-hop, house, disco—with the notable exception of techno and rave music, which is deliberately avoided. The restaurant serves dinner every Wednesday to Saturday from 7pm to 2am, with main courses priced at 80 to 140AS ($5.35 to $9.40). The dancing areas are open nightly from 10pm to around 4am, depending on business. Beer costs from 29 to 47AS ($1.95 to $3.15).

3 The Bar Scene

Viennese bars range from time-honored upscale haunts to loud, trendy lounges that stay open until dawn. Vienna's blossoming bar scene is located in the **Bermuda Triangle,** an area roughly bordered by Judengasse, Seitenstättengasse Rabensteig, and Franz-Josefs-Kai. You'll find everything from intimate watering holes to large bars with live music. The closest U-Bahn stop is Schwedenplatz. Below is just a sampling of the bars you'll find in Vienna.

Barfly's Club. In the Hotel Fürst Metternich, Esterházygasse 33. ☎ **01/586-0825.** U-Bahn: Kirchengasse. Tram: 5.

This is the most urbane and sophisticated cocktail bar in town, frequented by journalists, actors, and politicians. It's got a laissez-faire ambience set in a paneled room lined with rows of illuminated bottles, reminiscent of the bars found on transatlantic oceanliners in the 1930s. A menu lists about 250 cocktails priced from 90 to 130AS ($6.05 to $8.70) each. The only food served is "toast" (warm sandwiches) for 80AS ($5.35). Open daily from 8pm (6pm October to April) to between 2 and 4am, depending on the night.

Esterházykeller. Haarhof 1. ☎ **01/533-3482.** U-Bahn: Stephansplatz.

The ancient bricks and scarred wooden tables of this famous drinking spot are permeated with the aroma of endless pints of spilled beer. An outing here isn't recommended for everyone, but if you decide to chance it, choose the left-hand entrance (facing from the street) and begin your descent into its endless recesses and labyrinthine passages. Wine, a specialty, starts at 24 to 34AS ($1.60 to $2.30) a glass. Order a bottle if you plan to stay a while. Open Monday to Friday from 10:30am to 11pm and on Saturday and Sunday from 4 to 10pm.

Kleines Café. Franziskaner Platz. No phone. U-Bahn: Stephansplatz.

Virtually every painter and sculptor in modern-day Vienna seems to be intimately familiar with this cramped but cozy two-room bar and cafe. In summer, tables are set up on the Franziskanerplatz outside, overlooking the votive fountain dedicated to Moses. The rest of the year, people nestle beneath the 18th-century vaults of an antique building that was "modernized" around 1830 with a Biedermeier facade. Its popularity rests on Hammo Poeschl, a well-known entrepreneur and cult of personality whose interest in the arts is legendary. Sandwiches cost 20 to 65AS ($1.35 to $4.35); main courses range from 65 to 80AS ($4.35 to $5.35). The place is open Monday to Saturday from 10am to 2am; Sunday from 1pm to 2am. No credit cards accepted.

Krah Krah. Rabensteig 8. ☎ **01/533-8193.** U-Bahn: Schwedenplatz.

This place is the most animated and well-known meat market in the area. Every day an attractive, and sometimes available, after-work crowd fills this woodsy, somewhat battered space. Beer is the drink of choice here, with more than 35 kinds available, many of them on tap, from 39 to 47AS ($2.60 to $3.15) each. Simple food, such as open-face sandwiches, cost 55 to 95AS ($3.70 to $6.35). It's open Monday to Saturday from 11am to 2am, Sunday from 11am to 1am.

✪ **Loos American Bar.** Kärntnerdurchgang 10. ☎ **01/512-3283.** U-Bahn: Stephansplatz.

One of the most interesting and unusual bars in Vienna, this dark bar was designed by the noteworthy architect Adolf Loos in 1908. At the time, it functioned as the drinking room of a private men's club; today, it's more democratic—its arts-and-media crowd tends to be hip, single, and bilingual. Walls, floors, and ceilings sport layers of dark marble and black onyx, making this one of the most expensive small-scale decors in the city. No food is served, but the bar specializes in 15 kinds of martinis, plus 11 Manhattans, each for 90AS ($6.05). Beers cost 25 to 45AS ($1.70 to $3) each. From June to September, it's open Monday to Thursday from 6pm to 4am, Friday to Sunday until 5am. The rest of the year, hours are Sunday to Thursday from noon to 4am, Friday and Saturday to 5am.

Onyx Bar. In the Haas Haus, Stephansplatz 12. ☎ **01/535-3969.** U-Bahn: Stephansplatz.

One of the most appealing, if crowded, bars near the Stephensplatz is on the sixth (next-to-uppermost) floor of one of Vienna's most controversial buildings—the ultramodern, glass-fronted Haas Haus, whose facade reflects the turrets and medieval stonework of St. Stephan's Cathedral. Expect live or recorded music, usually beginning after 8:30pm, when some of the more exuberant folks in the crowd might actually get up and dance. Between 6pm and 2am the staff serves a long and varied cocktail menu, including strawberry margaritas and caipirinhas, each priced from 110 to 200AS ($7.35 to $13.40). Lunch is served from noon to 3pm daily, dinner from 6pm to midnight

Rhiz Bar Modern. Llerchenfeldergürtel, 37-38 Stadtbahnbögen. ☎ **01/409-2505.** No cover. U-Bahn: Josefstädterstrasse.

Hip, multicultural, and electronically sophisticated, this bar is nested into the vaulted, turn-of-the-century niches created by the trusses of the U-6 subway line, a few blocks west of the Ring. In a once-grimy industrial-age space, stainless-steel ventilation ducts, a green plastic bar, and a sophisticated stereo system have been installed. A TV camera broadcasts images of the crowd over the Internet every night between 10pm and 3am. (Its home page is www.rhiz.org.) Artists to investment bakers sip Austrian wines, Scottish whisky, and beer from everywhere in Europe. A large beer costs 38AS ($2.55). Open Monday to Saturday 6pm to 4am, Sunday to 2am.

✪ **St. Urbani-Keller.** Am Hof 12. ☎ **01/533-9102.** U-Bahn: Stephansplatz or Fahnenpasse.

Named after the patron saint of winemaking, this cellar is one of the most historic in Vienna. Carl Hipfinger first renovated the cellar as a public gathering place in 1906. Much of the decor, from the German Romantic-style paneling to the wrought-iron lighting fixtures, was designed by one of Austria's most famous architects, Walcher von Molthein, who rebuilt Vienna's Kreuzenstein Castle at the beginning of the 20th century. The cellar has brick vaulting dating from the 13th century and sections of Roman walls.

The most popular room is down on the lowest level. Thick oak tables are surrounded by a large collection of art, including numerous crucifixes and a Renaissance chandelier of St. Lucretia. Folk music wafts through. Many kinds of wine are served, but the featured vintage comes from the owner's family vineyards. In the past, this wine has been presented to everybody from Hitler's North Africa commander, General Rommel (the Desert Fox), to the president of Austria. It's open daily from 6pm to 1am, with hot food served until midnight. Meals begin at 65AS ($4.35) for goulash. Watch your step on the way up or down.

GAY & LESBIAN BARS

Alfi's Goldener Spiegel. Linke Wienzeile 46. ☎ **01/586-6608.** U-Bahn: Kettenbruckengasse.

The most enduring gay restaurant in Vienna, already recommended in chapter 5, is also the most popular gay bar. The place is very meat-markety, and the bar is open Wednesday to Monday from 7pm to 2am.

Eagle Bar. Blümelgasse 1. ☎ **01/587-26-61.** U-Bahn: Neubaugasse.

This is one of the premier leather and denim bars for gay men in Vienna. There's no dancing, but virtually every gay male in town has dropped in at least once or twice for a quick look around. It's open daily from 9pm to 4am. Large beers begin at 38AS ($2.55).

Frauencafé. Langegasse 11. ☎ **01/406-37-54.** U-Bahn: Lerchenfelderstrasse.

Frauencafé is a politically conscious cafe for gay and (to a lesser degree) heterosexual women. Established in 1977, in cramped quarters in a century-old building, it's filled with magazines, newspapers, and modern paintings, and caters to locals and foreigners alike. Next door is a feminist bookstore with which the cafe is loosely affiliated. Open Tuesday to Saturday, in summer from 8:30pm to 2am, in winter from 7pm to 2am. Glasses of wine begin at 17AS ($1.15).

4 The Heurigen

✪ These wine taverns on the outskirts of Vienna have long been celebrated in operetta, film, and song. Grinzing is the most visited district, but other Heurigen neighborhoods include Sievering, Neustift, Nussdorf, or Heiligenstadt.

Grinzing lies at the edge of the Vienna Woods, a short distance northwest of the center. Once it was a separate village, now overtaken by the ever-increasing city boundaries of Vienna. Much of Grinzing remains unchanged, looking the same as it did when Beethoven lived nearby. It's a district of crooked old streets and houses, their thick walls built around inner courtyards where grape arbors shelter wine drinkers. The sound of zithers and accordions lasts long into the summer night.

Which brings up another point. If you're a motorist, don't drive out to the Heurigen. Police patrols are very strict, and you're not allowed to be driving with more than 0.8% alcohol in your bloodstream. It's much better to take public transportation. Most Heurigen are reached in 30 to 40 minutes.

Take tram no. 1 to Schottentor, and change there for tram no. 38 to Grinzing; no. 41 to Neustift am Wald; and no. 38 to Sievering, which is also reached by bus no. 39A. Heiligenstadt is the last stop on U-Bahn line U-4.

We'll start you off with some of our favorites.

Alter Klosterkeller im Passauerhof. Cobenzigasse 9, Grinzing. ☎ **01/320-6345.**

One of Vienna's well-known wine taverns, this spot maintains an old-fashioned ambience little changed since the turn of the 20th century. Some of its foundations date from the 12th century. Specialties include such familiar fare as *tafelspitz* (boiled beef), an array of roasts, and plenty of strudel. You can order wine by the glass or bottle. Main courses range from 90 to 150AS ($6.05 to $10.05). Drinks begin at 30AS ($2). Open daily from 6pm to midnight. Live music is played from 6 to 11pm. Closed in February.

Altes Presshaus. Cobenzlgasse 15, Grinzing. ☎ **01/320-0203.**

The oldest heurige in Grinzing has been open since 1527. Ask to see their authentic cellar. The wood paneling and antique furniture give the interior character. The garden terrace blossoms throughout the summer. Meals cost 150 to 350AS ($10.05 to

$23.45); drinks begin at 30AS ($2). Open daily from 4pm to midnight; closed January and February.

✪ **Der Rudolfshof.** Cobenzlgasse 8, Grinzing. ☎ **01/32-21-08.**

One of the most appealing wine restaurants in Grinzing dates back to 1848, when it was little more than a shack within a garden. Its real fame came around the turn of the century, when Crown Prince Rudolf, son of Emperor Franz Josef, adopted it as his favorite watering hole. An articulate liberal whose revolutionary dialogues alarmed most of his father's cabinet, he might have developed some of his more incendiary ideas here. A verdant garden, scattered with tables, is favored by Viennese apartment dwellers on warm summer evenings. Inside, portraits of Rudolf decorate a setting that evokes an old-fashioned hunting lodge. Come here for pitchers of the fruity white wine *Gruner Veltliner* and a light red, *Roter Bok*. The menu lists schnitzels, roasts, and soups, but the house specialty is shish kebabs. The salad bar is very fresh. Between April and December, most nights between 7 and 9pm, informal operettas are presented in a pavilion in the garden. Access to the show, a four-course meal, and a quarter-liter of wine costs 490AS ($32.85) per person. Open mid-March to mid-January, daily 1 to 11:30pm, mid-January to mid-March, open only Friday to Sunday 1 to 11:30pm.

Grinzinger Hauermandl. Cobenzlgasse 20, Grinzing. ☎ **01/320-3027.**

Many of the guests at this rustic Grinzing inn are lively Viennese escaping the Inner City for an evening. Enter through a garden where a Gypsy wagon perches on the roof. The robust farm-style cooking includes chicken noodle soup and two kinds of schnitzels—pork schnitzels priced at 95AS ($6.35) and veal schnitzels priced at 150AS ($10.05). A quarter-liter of wine (about two glasses) costs 30AS ($2). The tavern is open year-round, Monday to Saturday from 6:30pm to midnight.

Mayer. Am Pfarrplatz 2, Heiligenstadt. ☎ **01/370-3361,** or 01/370-1287 after 4pm.

This historic house was some 130 years old when Beethoven composed sections of his *Ninth Symphony* while living here in 1817. The same kind of fruity dry wine is still sold to guests in the shady courtyard of the rose garden. Original heurigen music completes the traditional atmosphere. The menu includes grilled chicken, savory pork, and a buffet of well-prepared country food. Reservations are suggested. It's open Monday to Saturday from 4pm to midnight and on Sunday and holidays from 11am to midnight. The innkeepers, the Mayer family, sell wine for 31AS ($2.10) a glass, with meals beginning at 165AS ($11.05). Closed December 21 to January 15.

✪ **Weingut Wolff.** Rathstrasse 50, Neustift. ☎ **01/440-3727.**

Only 20 minutes from the center of Vienna, this is one of the most enduring and beloved Heurigen. Although aficionados claim the best Heurigen are "deep in the countryside" of lower Austria, this one comes closest to offering an authentic experience near Vienna. In summer, you're welcomed into a flower-decked garden set against a backdrop of ancient vineyards. You can fill up your platter with some of the best wursts (sausages) and roast meats (especially the delectable pork), along with freshly made salads. Save room for one of the luscious and velvety-smooth Austrian cakes. Find a table under a cluster of grapes and sample the fruity young wines, especially the Chardonnay, Sylvaner, or Gruner Veltliner. The tavern is open daily 11am to 1am with main courses ranging from 85 to 240AS ($5.70 to $16.10).

Zum Figlmüller. Grinzinger Strasse 55, Grinzing. ☎ **01/320-4257.**

One of the city's most popular wine restaurants is this suburban branch of Vienna's Figlmüller's. Although there's a set of indoor dining rooms, most visitors prefer the flowering terrace with its romantic garden. The restaurant prides itself on serving only wines produced under its own supervision, beginning at 33AS ($2.20) per glass. Meals include a wide array of light salads as well as more substantial food, such as enormous Wiener schnitzels for 156AS ($10.45). Open from late April to mid-November, Monday to Saturday from 4:30pm to midnight.

5 More Entertainment

A CASINO

Casino Wien. Esterházy Palace, Kärntnerstrasse 41. ☎ **01/512-4836.** No cover.

You'll need to show your passport to get into this casino, opened in 1968. There are gaming tables for French and American roulette, blackjack, and chemin de fer, as well as the ever-present slot machines. The casino is open daily from 11am to 4am, with the tables opening at 3pm.

FILMS

Burg-Kino. Opernring 19. ☎ **01/587-8406.** U-Bahn: Karlsplatz.

This theater often shows films in English and every summer presents Carol Reed's classic *The Third Man,* starring Orson Welles and Joseph Cotten. The film was set in occupied Vienna and remains an enduring favorite. Tickets range from 75 to 100AS ($5.05 to $6.70) but are specially priced on Monday at 70AS ($4.70). Look for listings in the local newspapers.

Filmmuseum. In the Albertina, Augustinerstrasse 1. ☎ **01/533-7054.** U-Bahn: Karlsplatz.

This *cinemathèque* shows films in their original languages and presents retrospectives of such directors as Fritz Lang, Erich von Stroheim, Ernst Lubitsch, and many others. The museum presents avant-garde and experimental films, as well as classics. A monthly program is available free inside the Albertina, and a copy is posted outside. The film library inside the government-funded museum includes more than 11,000 book titles, and the still collection numbers more than 100,000. Two recent retrospectives were a comprehensive survey of Jean-Luc Godard, and an overview of Japanese art films from the 1970s. Admission costs 65AS ($4.35), but you must be a member. Membership for 24 hours costs 60AS ($4); membership for a full year costs 230AS ($15.40).

6 Only in Vienna

We've recommended a variety of nightspots, but none seem to capture the true Viennese spirit quite like the establishments below. Each has its own atmosphere and decor and each continues to remain uniquely Viennese.

Alt Wien. Bäckerstrasse 9 (1). ☎ **01/512-5222.** U-Bahn: Stephansplatz.

Set on one of the oldest, narrowest streets of medieval Vienna, a short walk north of the cathedral, this is the kind of smoky, mysterious, and shadowy cafe that—with a bit of imagination—evokes subversive plots, doomed romances, and revolutionary movements being hatched and plotted. During the day, it's a busy, workaday restaurant patronized by virtually everybody. But as the night progresses, you're likely to rub elbows with denizens of late-night Wien who get more sentimental and schmaltzy with each beer. Foaming mugfuls sell for 28AS ($1.90) each and can be accompanied by heaping platters of goulash and schnitzels. Main courses range from 95 to 175AS ($6.35 to $11.75). Open daily from 10am to 4am.

Kaffeehäuser Drechsler. Linke Weinzeile 22. ☎ **01/587-8580.** U-Bahn: Karlsplatz.

It's the best antidote for insomnia in Vienna, and a worthy early-morning diversion for the jet lagged. Established around 1900, this is the largest and busiest cafe in the Naschmarkt neighborhood, that vast open-air food market that sits on what used to be a branch of the Danube. The cafe's bizarre hours reflect those of the wholesale food industry itself: Monday to Friday from 3am to 8pm, Saturday from 3am to 6pm. Platters of hearty food (concocted from very fresh ingredients procured at the stalls outside) sell for 65AS to 80AS ($4.35 to $5.35). You won't be alone if you order a beer to accompany the sunrise. And if you need a dose of caffeine, coffee pours out of urns like a Danube flood.

Karl Kolarik's Schweizerhaus. In the Prater, Strasse des Ersten Mai, 116. ☎ **01/728-01-52.** U-Bahn: Praterstern.

References to this old-fashioned eating house are about as old as the Prater itself. Awash with beer and Central European kitsch, it sprawls across a *biergarten* landscape that might remind you of the Habsburg Empire at its most indulgent. Indulgence is indeed the word—the vastly proportioned main dishes could feed an entire 19th-century army. If you're looking for *neue kuchen,* this isn't the place. The menu stresses old-fashioned schnitzels and its house specialty, roasted pork hocks (*Hintere Schweinsstelze*) served with dollops of mustard and horseradish. Wash it all down with mugs of Czech *Budweiser.* A half-liter of beer costs 36AS ($2.40); main courses range from 90 to 180AS ($6.05 to $12.05). During clement weather, the action moves outside to a green area close to the entrance of Europe's most famous amusement park, the Prater. Open April to September only, daily from 10am to 11pm.

Möbel. Burggasse 10. ☎ **01/524-9497.** U-Bahn: Volkstheater.

Neighborhood residents perch along the long, stainless steel countertop for a glass of wine, a coffee, and light platters of food. But what makes it unusual is the hyper-modern furniture that's for sale in this cafe-cum-art gallery. Everything sold is functional, utilitarian, and contemporary looking. Depending on what's being featured that month, you're likely to find coffee tables, reclining chairs, book shelves, kitchen equipment, and even a ceramic-sided woodburning stove priced at 18,000AS ($1,206). Sandwiches cost 35 to 50AS ($2.35 to $3.35), glasses of wine from 18 to 28AS ($1.20 to $1.90). It's open Monday to Friday from noon to 1am, Saturday and Sunday from 10am to 1am.

Pavillion. Burgring 1. ☎ **01/532-0907.** U-Bahn: Volkstheater.

Even the Viennese stumble when trying to describe this civic monument from the Sputnik-era of the 1950s. By general consensus, it's usually considered a music cafe. During the day, it's a nice cafe, with a multigenerational clientele and a sweeping garden overlooking the Heldenplatz (forecourt to the Hofburg). Come here to peruse the newspapers, chat with locals, and drink coffee, wine, beer, or schnapps. The place grows much more animated after the music (funk, soul, blues, and jazz) begins around 8pm. Platters of Viennese food are priced at from 70 to 160AS ($4.70 to $10.70). Open daily from 11am to 2am.

Schnitzelwirt Schmidt. Neubaugasse 52 (7). ☎ **01/523-3771.** U-Bahn: Mariahilfer-strasse. Tram: 29.

The waitresses wear dirndls, the portions are huge, and the cuisine—only pork and some chicken—celebrates the culinary folklore of central Europe. The setting is rustic, a kind of tongue-in-cheek bucolic homage to the Old Vienna Woods, and schnitzels are almost guaranteed to hang over the sides of the plates. Regardless of what you order, it will be accompanied by French fries, salad, and copious quantities of beer and wine. The dive packs them in because of good value, an unmistakably Viennese ambience, and great people-watching. Main courses cost 65 to 125AS ($4.35 to $8.40). Open Monday to Saturday from 11am to 10pm. Closed Sunday.

Wiener Stamperl (The Viennese Dram). Sterngasse 1. ☎ **01/533-6230.** U-bahn: Schwedenplatz.

Named after a medieval unit of liquid measurement, this is about as beer-soaked and as rowdy a nighttime venue as we're willing to recommend. It occupies a battered, woodsy-looking room reeking of spilled beer, stale smoke, and the unmistakable scent of hundreds of boisterous drinkers. This is about as real and colorful as it gets. At the horseshoe-shaped bar, order foaming steins of Ottakinger beer or glasses of new wine from nearby vineyards served from an old-fashioned barrel. The menu consists entirely of an array of coarse bread slathered with spicy, high-cholesterol ingredients, such as various forms of wursts and cheeses, and for anyone devoted to authentic old-time cuisine, lard specked with bits of bacon. Sidewalk tables contain the overflow from the bar, but only during nice weather. Come here for local color and a friendly and rough-and-ready kind of alcohol-soaked charm. Open Monday to Friday from 11am to 2am, Saturday and Sunday from 6pm to 4am.

10 | Side Trips from Vienna

Exciting day trips on Vienna's doorstep include the Vienna Woods, the villages along the Danube, particularly the vineyards of the Wachau, and the small province of Burgenland, between Vienna and the Hungarian border.

Lower Austria (*Niederösterreich*), known as the "cradle of Austria's history," is the biggest of the nine federal states that make up the country today. Though this province should be *upper* Austria by its geographic location, it is named "Lower Austria" because the Danube flows into it from the east. The province is bordered on the north by the Czech Republic, on the east by Slovakia, on the south by the province of Styria, and on the west by Upper Austria.

This historic area was once heavily fortified, as some 550 fortresses and castles (often in ruins) testify. The medieval Kuenringer and Babenberger dynasties had their hereditary estates here. There are historic monasteries, churches, and abbeys, and the province is covered with vineyards. In summer it booms with music festivals and classical and contemporary theater.

Lower Austria is divided into five distinct districts. The best known is the **Wienerwald (Vienna Woods),** still completely surrounding Vienna (see "Tales of the Vienna Woods" box in chapter 6), although the woods have been thinned out on the eastern side.

The district of **Alpine Lower Austria** lies about an hour's drive south of Vienna, with mountains up to 7,000 feet (1,800 m) high.

The **foothills of the Alps** begin about 30 miles west of Vienna, and extend to the borders of Styria and Upper Austria. This area has some 50 open-air swimming pools and nine chairlifts that go up to the higher peaks, such as Ötscher and Hochkar (both around 6,000 feet (2,100 m).

One of the most celebrated districts is the **Waldviertel-Weinviertel** (a *viertel* is a traditional division of Lower Austria). The *wald* (woods) and *wein* (wine) areas contain thousands of miles of marked hiking paths and, of course, many mellow old wine cellars.

Another district, **Wachau-Nibelungengau,** has both historical and cultural significance. It's a land of castles and palaces, abbeys and monasteries, as well as vineyards. This area begins about 40 miles west of Vienna and lies on both banks of the Danube.

Some 60% of Austria's grape harvest is produced in Lower Austria, from the rolling hillsides of the Wienerwald to the terraces of the Wachau. Many visitors like to take a "wine route" through the province, stopping at cozy taverns to sample the vintages from Krems, Klosterneuburg, Dürnstein, Langenlois, Retz, Gumpoldskirchen, Poysdorf, and other towns.

Lower Austria is also home to more than a dozen spa resorts, such as Baden, the most popular. These resorts are family-friendly, and most hotels accommodate children up to 6 years old free; between ages 7 and 12 they stay for half price. Many towns and villages have attractions designed just for kids.

It's relatively inexpensive to travel in Lower Austria, where prices are about 30% lower than those in Vienna. Finding a hotel in these small towns isn't a problem; they're signposted at the various approaches to the resort or village. You may not always find a room with a private bathroom in some of the area's old inns (unless otherwise noted, however, all recommended accommodations have private bathrooms). Parking is also more accessible in the outlying towns, an appealing feature if you're driving, and, unless otherwise noted, you park for free. Note that some hotels have only a postal code for an address (if you're writing to them, this is their complete address).

Burgenland, the newest and easternmost province of Austria, is a stark contrast to Lower Austria. It's a little border region, formed in 1921 from German-speaking border areas of what was once Hungary. Burgenland voted to join Austria in the aftermath of World War I, although when the vote was taken in 1919, its capital, Ödenburg, now called *Sopron,* chose to remain with Hungary. The Hungarian city of Sopron actually lies to the west of Lake Neusiedl (*Neusiedler See*), a popular haven for the Viennese.

The province marks the beginning of a flat steppe (*puszta*) that reaches from Vienna almost to Budapest. It shares a western border with Styria and Lower Austria, and the long eastern boundary separates Burgenland from Hungary. Called "the vegetable garden of Vienna," Burgenland is mostly an agricultural province, producing more than one-third of all the wine made in Austria. Its Pannonian climate translates into hot summers with little rainfall and moderate winters. For the most part you can enjoy sunny days from early spring until late autumn.

The capital of Burgenland is **Eisenstadt,** a small provincial city. For many years it was the home of Joseph Haydn, and the composer is buried here. Each summer there's a festival at Mörbisch, using Lake Neusiedl as a theatrical backdrop. **Neusiedl** is the only steppe lake in Central Europe. If you're visiting in summer, you'll most certainly want to explore it by motorboat. Lots of Viennese flee to Burgenland on weekends for sailing, birding, and other outdoor activities.

Accommodations in this province are extremely limited, but they're among the least expensive in the country. The area is relatively unknown to North Americans, which means fewer tourists. Like Lower Austria, Burgenland contains many fortresses and castles, often in ruins, but you'll find a few castle hotels. The touring season in Burgenland lasts from April to October.

1 The Wienerwald (Vienna Woods)

The Vienna Woods—romanticized in operetta, literature, and known worldwide through the famous Strauss waltz—have already been introduced in chapter 6, "Exploring Vienna."

The woods stretch from Vienna's city limits to the foothills of the Alps to the south. You can hike through the woods along marked paths or drive through, stopping off at country towns to sample the wine and the local cuisine, which is usually hearty and reasonably priced. The Viennese and a horde of foreign visitors, principally German, usually descend on the wine taverns and cellars here on weekends—we advise you to make any summer visit on a weekday. The best time of year to go is in September and October, when the grapes are harvested from the terraced hills.

TIPS ON EXPLORING THE VIENNA WOODS

You can visit the expansive and pastoral Vienna Woods by car or by public transportation. We recommend renting a car so you can stop and explore some of the villages and vineyards along the way. Public transportation will also get you around, but it will take much more time. Either way, you can easily reach all of the destinations listed below within a day's trip from Vienna. If you have more time, spend the night in one or more of the quintessential Austrian towns along the way, where you can feast on traditional Austrian fare and sample the exquisite local wines.

Before you go, visit the tourist office for **Lower Austria,** Heidenschuss 2, A-1010 (☎ **01/536-100**) in Vienna. It is the best source of information and maps for the Vienna Woods. You can also contact **Niederösterreich Information,** Walfischgasse 6, A-1010 Vienna (☎ **01/5333-11428**). Both offices are open Monday to Friday from 8:30am to 5pm, Saturday from 10am to 4pm. Tourist offices for some of the smaller towns in the area appear in their individual listings.

If you don't want to go on your own, **Vienna Sightseeing Tours,** Stelzamer-gasse 4 Suite 11 (☎ **01/7124-6830;** fax 01/714-1141), operates a 4-hour tour called **"Vienna-Mayerling."** It goes through the Vienna Woods past the Castle of Liechtenstein and the old Roman city of Baden. There's also an excursion to Mayerling, where Crown Prince Rudolf and his mistress met violent deaths. Other highlights include a trip to the Cistercian abbey of Heiligenkreuz-Höldrichsmühle-Seegrotte and a boat ride on Seegrotte, the largest subterranean lake in Europe. The office is open for tours April to October, daily from 6:30am to 8pm; and November to March, daily from 6:30am to 5pm. The cost is 400AS ($26.80) for adults and 200AS ($13.40) for children, including admission fees and a guide.

KLOSTERNEUBURG

On the northwestern outskirts of Vienna, Klosterneuburg is an old market town in the major wine-producing center of Austria. The Babenbergs established the town on the eastern foothills of the Vienna Woods, making it an ideal spot to stay if you want to enjoy the countryside and Vienna, 7 miles (11.27 km) southeast.

ESSENTIALS

GETTING THERE   **Motorists** from Vienna can take Route 14 northwest, following the south bank of the Danube to Klosterneuburg. If you opt for public transportation, take the U-Bahn (U4, U6) to Heiligenstadt, and catch **bus** no. 239 or 341 to Klosterneuburg; or by **train,** catch the Schnellbahn (S-Train) from Franz-Josef Bahnhof to Klosterneuburg-Kierling.

VISITOR INFORMATION   Contact the Klosterneuburg **tourist information office** at Niedermarkt 4, A-3400, (☎ **02243/32038;** fax 02243/26773; www.klosterneuburg.com). Open Monday to Friday from 8am to 8pm.

Austrians gather in Klosterneuburg annually on November 15 to celebrate St. Leopold's Day with music, banquets, and a parade.

VISITING THE ABBEY

○ **Klosterneuburg Abbey (Stift Klosterneuburg).** Stiftsplatz 1. ☎ **02243/411-212.** Museum 60AS ($4); English-language tour of monastery 70AS ($4.70); combined ticket to monastery and museum, 85AS ($5.70) adults, 50AS ($3.35) children under 12. Monastery: year-round, tours daily 9am–noon and 1:30–4:30pm; English-language tour Sun 2pm. Museum: May to mid-Nov Tues–Sun 10am–5pm; closed mid-Nov to Apr.

East of the Upper Town, the Augustinian abbey of Klosterneuburg is the most significant abbey in Austria. The monastery was once the residence of Habsburg emperor

Lower Austria, Burgenland & the Danube Valley

CZECH REPUBLIC

Gmünd
Retz
Laa
Horn
303
Mistelbach

WALDVIERTEL

NIEDERÖSTERREICH
(LOWER AUSTRIA)

WEINVIERTEL

303

Stockerau
7
SLOVAKIA

Ottenschlag
Krems
3
Tulln
A22
Korneuburg

OBER-
ÖSTERREICH
(UPPER
AUSTRIA)

33
Dürnstein
Danube River
Klosterneuburg

1
Herzogenburg

Kapelln
VIENNA

Marbach
3
Melk
St. Pölten
A1

Amstetten
Perchtoldsdorf
Hinterbrühl
16
10

A1
Heiligenkreuz Abbey
Mayerling
A2
Parndorf

NIEDERÖSTERREICH
(LOWER AUSTRIA)

Baden bei Wien
Neusiedl am See
51

Waidhofen
20
Purbach am See
Neusiedler See
Podersdorf

50
Eisenstadt
Illmitz

Annaberg
Wiener Neustadt
Rust

25
Puchberg
17
Mattersburg

Waidhofen
Semmering
20

115

S6

Forchtenstein

Sopron

S31

BURGENLAND

Kapfenburg
A2

STEIERMARK
(STYRIA)
Oberwart
HUNGARY

A9
335

54

Köflach
Graz
A2

KÄRNTEN
(CARINTHIA)
A9

Deutschlandsburg

Maribor

SLOVENIA

Skiing

0   20 mi
0   20 km
N

AUSTRIA
Vienna

169

Charles VI. It was originally founded, however, in 1114 by the Babenberg margrave Leopold III (called "the Saint").

Today, much of the monastery is the domain of ordained scholars, many of them on sabbatical study leaves from religious and monastic organizations around the world. They devote part of each day to study, contemplation, and review of the thousands of valuable books in the monastery's library. (The library is usually closed to the public, but academics can obtain written permission in advance.) The tour includes the cathedral of the monastery, the former well house, the residential apartments of the Habsburg emperors, the Gothic Cloister, and St. Leopold's Chapel. The chapel is the site of the famous enameled altar of Nikolaus of Verdun, created in 1181, perhaps the finest example of medieval enamel work in the world. Note also the chapel's beautiful 14th-century stained-glass windows. Additional art treasures and exhibits concerning the abbey and the religious traditions of Lower Austria are displayed in the museum.

The museum can be visited without a guide, but the monastery is accessible only by guided tours that take place daily at hourly intervals. Except for the Sunday English-language tour, most tours are conducted in German (with occasional snippets of English if the guide is able). If you require an English-language tour outside of the above-mentioned hours, arrangements must be made in advance.

The abbey has an old restaurant, the **Stiftskeller,** Albrechtsbergergasse 1 (☎ **02243/411-603**), where you can enjoy classic Austrian specialties for 90 to 250AS ($6.05 to $16.75). The kitchen is especially known for its fish dishes, and the menu, which is translated into English, also features dishes low in calories and sodium. The restaurant (child-friendly and with a playground) also has one of the largest and most beautiful outdoor terraces in the area, with old chestnut trees and views over Klosterneuburg. It's open year-round, Monday to Saturday from 11am to 11:30pm, and on Sunday from 11am to 5pm.

Nearby, guests can relax in the cozy **Stiftskaffe** (coffee shop), which is open Tuesday to Sunday from 9am to 6pm. It serves coffee and pastries, among other items. There also several Heurigen in the district, with good wine, good country food, and good cheer.

WHERE TO STAY & DINE

Hotel Josef Buschenretter. Wienerstrasse 188, A-3400 Klosterneuburg. ☎ **02243/ 32385.** Fax 02243/3238-5160. 40 units. TEL. 760–870AS ($50.90–$58.30) double. Rates include breakfast. No credit cards. Closed Dec 15–Jan 15. Free parking.

Built in 1970 a mile south of the town center, this hotel is white walled with a mansard roof rising above the balcony on the fourth floor. A terrace on the roof, an indoor swimming pool, and a bar provide diversion for hotel guests. The medium-size bedrooms are comfortably furnished and well kept, and some of the more expensive doubles contain a minibar and TV; all accommodations have phones.

Hotel Schrannenhof. Niedermarkt 17-19, A-3400 Klosterneuburg. ☎ **02243/32072.** Fax 02243/320-7213. E-mail: pveit@ins.at. 13 units. TV TEL. 980–1,100AS ($65.65–$73.70) double; 1,250AS ($83.75) suite. Rates include breakfast. AE, DC, MC, V. Free parking.

Originally dating from the Middle Ages, this hotel was completely renovated and modernized in 1986. The owners rent guest rooms with large living and sleeping rooms and small kitchens, as well as quiet and comfortable double rooms with showers. International and Austrian specialties are served in Veit, the hotel's cafe-restaurant next door. The hotel also runs the Pension Alte Mühle (see below).

Pension Alte Mühle. Mühlengasse 36, A-3400 Klosterneuburg. ☎ **02243/37788.** Fax 02243/377-8822. www.klosterneuburg.com/altemuhle. 13 units. TV TEL. 820–970AS ($54.95–$65) double. Rates include breakfast. AE, DC, MC. Free parking.

Housed in a simple two-story building, this hotel is gracious and hospitable. The breakfast room offers a bountiful morning buffet; the comfortable restaurant-cafe, Veit, is only 2,300 feet (690 m) away. Bedrooms are furnished in a cozy, traditional style, with good beds and well-maintained, if small, private bathrooms. The Veit family owns the place, and in summer their pleasant garden lures guests.

PERCHTOLDSDORF

This old market town with colorful buildings is referred to locally as Petersdorf. It's one of the most popular spots in Lower Austria for Viennese on a wine tour. You'll find many Heurigen, where you can sample local wines and enjoy good, hearty cuisine. Perchtoldsdorf is not as well known as Grinzing, but many visitors find it less touristy. It has a Gothic church, and part of its defense tower dates from the early 16th century. A vintners' festival held annually in early November attracts many Viennese. Local growers make a "goat" from grapes for this festive occasion.

ESSENTIALS

GETTING THERE   **Motorists** can head for Liesing (23rd District) via Wienerstrasse to Perchtoldsdorf, 11 miles (17.71 km) southwest of the city center. By **train,** from the Westbahnhof, you can take a *Schnellbahn* (S-Bahn) heading for Liesing. From here, Perchtoldsdorf is just a short ride away by taxi (cabs are found at the train station). **Bus** 256 runs infrequently from Vienna.

VISITOR INFORMATION   Contact the **tourist information office** in Perchtoldsdorf (☎ **01/536100;** www.noe.co.at). Open Monday to Friday from 8:30am to 5pm.

WHERE TO DINE

Restaurant Jahreszeiten. Hochstrasse 17. ☎ **01/865-3129.** Reservations recommended. Main courses 300–330AS ($20.10–$22.10); fixed-price lunch 330–500AS ($22.10–$33.50); fixed-price dinner 520–690AS ($34.85–$46.25). AE, DC, MC, V. Tues–Fri and Sun 12:30am–2pm; Tues–Sat 6–10pm. Closed July 25–Aug 15. AUSTRIAN/FRENCH/INTERNATIONAL.

Set within what was a private villa in the 1800s, this restaurant—the best in town—provides a welcome and romantic haven for Viennese escaping to the country. In a pair of elegantly rustic candlelit dining rooms, you can enjoy such dishes as rare poached salmon with herbs and truffled noodles, Chinese-style prawns as prepared by the Japanese cooks in the kitchens, fillet of turbot with morels and asparagus-studded risotto, and braised fillet of roebuck with autumn vegetables. Try one of the soufflés for dessert. The staff is polite, hardworking, and discreet.

HINTERBRÜHL

In this hamlet, you'll find good accommodations and good food. This is no more than a cluster of country homes, much favored by Viennese escaping the city for a long weekend. Hinterbrühl holds memories of composer Franz Schubert, who wrote *Der Lindenbaum* here.

Part of the village was built directly above the stalactite-covered waters of Europe's largest underground lake, the Seegrotte, which is accessible from a clearly marked entrance a few hundred yards from the edge of the town. Below a steep flight of stairs are the extensively illuminated waters of a shallow, very still, and very cold underground lake. It's famous throughout the region as a natural marvel. During World War II, the world's first jet plane was constructed in adjoining caverns. You can take a 20-minute boat ride, with a running commentary in German and broken English explaining the lake's ecological and historical significance.

ESSENTIALS

GETTING THERE   This village is 16 miles (25.76 km) south of Vienna, just west of Mölding, the nearest large town. To reach Hinterbrühl from Vienna, **drive** southwest along the A21, exiting for the signs to Gisshubel. From here, follow the signs posted to Hinterbrühl (which you'll reach first) and Mölding (a few miles after Hinterbrühl). To reach Hinterbrühl by public transport, take the S-Bahn **train** from the Südbahnhof to Mölding (trip time: 15 minutes), then catch a connecting bus to Hinterbrühl, the last stop, 12 minutes away.

VISITOR INFORMATION   Contact the **tourist information office** in Mölding (☎ 02236/26727; www.moldingtourist.at). Open Monday to Friday from 9am to 6pm.

WHERE TO STAY AND DINE

Hotel Beethoven. Bahnplatz 1, A-2317 Hinterbrühl. ☎ **02236/26252.** Fax 02236/277017. www.members.aon.at/hotel-hbeethoven. 20 units. MINIBAR TV TEL. 1,200–1,350AS ($80.40–$90.45) double. Rates include breakfast. AE, DC, MC, V. Free parking.

This hotel in the heart of the hamlet boasts one of the village's oldest buildings, a private house originally constructed around 1785. In 1992, the hotel built a new wing and most of the interior was renovated. The average-size bedrooms are cozy, traditional, and well maintained, with good beds and adequate bathrooms. There's no formal restaurant on the premises, although management maintains an all-day cafe where coffee, drinks, pastries, ice cream, salads, and platters of regional food are served daily from 9am to 11pm.

Restaurant Hexensitz. Johannesstrasse 35. ☎ **02236/22937.** Reservations recommended. Main courses 190–280AS ($12.75–$18.75); fixed-price lunch 250AS ($16.75); fixed-price dinner 450AS ($30.15). AE, MC, V. Tues–Sun 11:30am–2pm; Tues–Sat 6–10pm. AUSTRIAN/INTERNATIONAL.

This restaurant celebrates the subtleties of Austrian country cooking in an upscale setting with impeccable service. Established in 1985 by Alfred and Ulriche Maschitz, it's in a century-old building with a trio of dining rooms outfitted with wood paneling and country antiques. In summer, the restaurant expands into a well-kept garden studded with flowering shrubs and ornamental trees. It offers daily changing dishes, such as asparagus-cream soup; Styrian venison with kohlrabi, wine sauce, and homemade noodles; medallions of pork with spinach and herbs; and sea bass with forest mushrooms. Desserts are luscious and highly caloric. The restaurant's name, incidentally, translates as "the Witch's Chair," a reference to a regional fairy tale.

MAYERLING

This beautiful spot, 18 miles (28.98 km) west of Vienna in the heart of the Wienerwald, is best known for the unresolved double suicide/homicide of Archduke Rudolf, son of Emperor Franz Joseph, and his mistress in 1889. This event, which took place in a hunting lodge (now a Carmelite convent), altered the line of Austro-Hungarian succession. The heir apparent became Franz Joseph's nephew, Archduke Ferdinand, whose murder in Sarajevo sparked World War I.

ESSENTIALS

GETTING THERE   **Driving,** head southwest on A-21 to Alland and take 210 to Mayerling. Or, take **buses** 1123, 1124, or 1127 marked *Alland,* from Vienna's Südtirolerplatz, (trip time: 90 minutes). From Baden, hop on bus 1140 or 1141.

Twilight of the Habsburgs

Mayerling was the setting on January 30, 1889, for a grim tragedy that altered the line of succession of the Austro-Hungarian Empire and shocked the world. On a snowy night, Archduke Rudolf, the only son of Emperor Franz Joseph and Empress Elisabeth, and his 18-year-old mistress, Maria Vetsera, were found dead in the hunting lodge at Mayerling. It was announced that they had shot themselves, although no weapon, if found, ever surfaced for examination. All doors and windows to the room had been locked when the bodies were discovered. All evidence that might have shed some light on the deaths was subsequently destroyed. Had it been a double suicide or an assassination?

Rudolf, a sensitive eccentric, was locked in an unhappy marriage, and neither his father nor Pope Leo XIII would allow an annulment. He had fallen in love with Maria at a German embassy ball when she was only 17. Maria's public snubbing of Archduchess Stephanie of Belgium, Rudolf's wife, at a reception given by the German ambassador to Vienna led to a heated argument between Rudolf and his father. Because of the young archduke's liberal leanings and sympathy for certain Hungarian partisans, he was not popular with his country's aristocracy, which of course gave rise to lurid speculation about a cleverly designed plot. Supporters of the assassination theory included Empress Zita von Habsburg, the last Habsburg heir, who in 1982 told the Vienna daily *Kronen Zeitung* that she believed their deaths were the culmination of a conspiracy against the family. Franz Joseph, grief-stricken at the loss of his only son, ordered the hunting lodge torn down and a Carmelite nunnery built in its place.

Maria Vetsera was buried in Heilgenkreuz at a village cemetery, the inscription over her tomb reading *Wie eine Blume sprosst der mensch auf und wird gebrochen* ("Human beings, like flowers, bloom and are crushed"). In a curious incident in 1988, her coffin was exhumed and stolen by a Linz executive, who was distraught by the death of his wife and obsessed with the Mayerling affair. It took police 4 years to recover the coffin.

As it turned out, if Rudolf, who died at age 30, had lived, he would have succeeded to the already-tottering Habsburg throne in 1916, in the middle of World War I, shortly before the collapse of the empire.

VISITOR INFORMATION Contact the local authorities at the **Rathaus,** in nearby Heiligenkruz (☎ **02258/8720;** www.heilingenkreuz.at). Open Monday to Friday from 8am to noon and 2 to 5pm.

SEEING THE SIGHTS

Jagdschloss. Mayerling. ☎ **02258/2275.** Admission 30AS ($2). Mon–Sat 9am–12:30pm and 1:30–5pm (til 6pm in summer).

A Carmelite abbey stands on the site of the infamous hunting lodge where Rudolf and his mistress supposedly committed suicide (see "Twilight of the Habsburgs," above). The hunting lodge, if it hadn't been torn down, would be a much more fascinating—if macabre—attraction. Although nothing remains of the lodge, history buffs enjoy visiting the abbey.

✪ **Abbey Heiligenkreuz (Abbey of the Holy Cross).** Heiligenkreuz. ☎ **02258/8703.** Admission 70AS ($4.70) adults, 30AS ($2) children. Tours: daily at 10 and 11am and 2, 3, and

4pm (3pm last tour Oct–Easter). Visiting hours: Daily 9–11:30am and 1:30–5pm (Nov–Feb closes 4pm). From Mayerling, take Heiliqenkreuzstrasse 3 miles (4.83 km) to Heiligenkreuz.

The abbey was founded by Margrave Leopold III. It was built in the 12th century, but there has been an overlay of Gothic and baroque additions in subsequent centuries, with some 13th- and 14th-century stained glass still in place. The Romanesque and Gothic cloisters date from 1240, with some 300 pillars of red marble. Some of the dukes of Babenberg were buried in the chapter house, including Duke Friedrich II, the last of his line. Heiligenkreuz has more relics of the Holy Cross than any other site in Europe except Rome.

Today, a vital community of 50 Cistercian monks lives in Heiligenkreuz. In summer at noon and 6pm daily, visitors can attend the solemn choir prayers.

WHERE TO STAY AND DINE

Mayerling's best-managed hotel and restaurant enclave is in one interconnected complex of buildings in a verdant forest about half a mile from the town center. Managed by members of the Hanner family, it was originally built in the 1930s and enlarged in 1962 and again in 1985. Within its well-scrubbed confines, you'll find a hotel and two restaurants, the most popular and best recommended in town.

Hotel Kronprinz Mayerling (also known as Landgasthof Marienhof). Mayerling 1, A-2534 Mayerling. ☎ **02258/237846.** Fax 02258/237841. 28 units. MINIBAR TV TEL. 1,200–1,400AS ($80.40–$93.80) double. Rates include breakfast. AE, DC, MC, V. Free parking.

Clean, comfortable, unpretentious, and well maintained, this hotel offers simple but cozy bedrooms and decent bathrooms. Guests appreciate the proximity of the hotel's two restaurants (see below) and the abundance of natural beauty outside.

✪ **Restaurant Kronprinz.** Mayerling 1. ☎ **02258/237846.** Reservations required. Main courses 260–420AS ($17.40–$28.15); fixed-price menu 450–700AS ($30.15–$46.90). AE, DC, MC, V. Wed–Sun noon–3pm and 6–9:30pm. AUSTRIAN/FRENCH.

Self-taught owner/chef Heinz Hanner runs the most elegant restaurant in the region. This small-scale hideaway is decorated in beige marble, with large windows providing sweeping views of verdant forest. The French and Austrian cuisines have been praised by gastronomes throughout Austria and include a series of delectable dishes that change with the seasons and the whim of the chef. There might be truffled pâté of goose liver with artichokes, cream of zucchini soup with black truffles and Parmesan, medallions of venison with wild mushrooms and fried onions, and braised breast of Bresse chicken with paprika noodles.

Restaurant Landhaus. Mayerling 1. ☎ **02258/237846.** Reservations not required. Main courses 160–300AS ($10.70–$20.10); 6-course, fixed-price meal 790AS ($52.95). AE, DC, MC, V. Daily noon–2:30pm and 6–10pm. AUSTRIAN.

Unlike its more glamorous cousin (see above), this restaurant makes no attempts at modern cuisine. Instead, the kitchen turns out filling plates of *tafelspitz*, Wiener schnitzel, fresh salads, schnitzels of pork, perfectly done roast lamb, and—throughout the day—steaming bowls of soup and strong cups of coffee. In a rustic, woodsy set of dining rooms the staff and at least some of the guests are likely to appear in traditional Austrian costumes (*dirndls* and *trachten*).

2 The Spa Town of Baden bei Wien

Tsar Peter the Great of Russia ushered in Baden's golden age by establishing a spa here at the beginning of the 18th century. Following in his footsteps, the Soviet army used the resort city as its headquarters from the end of World War II to the end of the Allied occupation of Austria in 1955. But there's not much that's Russian about Baden, which was once known as "the dowager empress of health spas in Europe."

The Romans, who didn't miss many natural attractions, began in A.D. 100 to visit what they called Aquae, which had 15 thermal springs whose temperatures reached 95°F. You can still see the Römerquelle (Roman spring) in the Kurpark, which is the center of Baden today.

This lively casino town and spa in the eastern sector of the Vienna Woods was at its most fashionable in the early 18th century, but it continued to lure royalty, sycophants, musicians, and intellectuals for much of the 19th century. For years the resort was the summer retreat of the Habsburg court. In 1803, when he was still Francis II, emperor of the Holy Roman Empire, the monarch began summer visits to Baden—a tradition he continued as Francis I of Austria, after the Holy Roman Empire ended in 1806.

During the Biedermeier era (mid- to late 19th century), Baden became known for its ochre Biedermeier buildings, which still contribute to the spa city's charm. The **Kurpark,** Baden's center, is handsomely laid out and beautifully maintained. Public concerts performed here keep the magic of the great Austrian composers alive.

Emperor Karl made this town the Austrian army headquarters in World War I, but a certain lightheartedness persisted. The presence of the Russians during the post–World War II years brought the lowest ebb to the resort's fortunes.

The **bathing complex** was constructed over more than a dozen sulfur springs. In the complex are some half a dozen bath establishments, plus four outdoor thermal springs. These thermal springs reach temperatures ranging from 75° to 95°F. The thermal complex also has a "sandy beach" and a restaurant. It lies west of the town center in the Doblhoffpark, a natural park with a lake where you can rent boats for sailing. There's also a garden restaurant in the park.

The resort is officially named Baden *bei Wien* to differentiate it from other Badens *not* near Vienna.

ESSENTIALS

GETTING THERE   From Vienna, Baden is 15 miles (24.15 km) southwest. If **driving,** head south on Autobahn A-2, cutting west at the junction of Route 210, which leads to Baden.

If you go by **train,** Baden is a local (rather than an express) stop. From 4:40am until 11:15pm trains depart Vienna's Südbahnhof every 8 to 20 minutes. The trip takes 20 minutes, with two stops en route. For schedules, call ☎ **05/1717** or 02252/8936-2385. Also, the *Badner Bahn* train leaves every 15 minutes from the State Opera (trip time: 1 hour). **Buses** to Baden leave out of Vienna's Westbahnhof.

VISITOR INFORMATION   Visitors should head to the Baden **tourist information office** at Brusattiplatz 3 (☎ **02252/22-600-600;** www.tiscover.com/baden). Open Monday to Saturday from 9am to 6pm, Sunday from 9am to noon.

SEEING THE SIGHTS

In the **Hauptplatz** (main square), the **Trinity Column,** built in 1714, commemorates the lifting of a plague that swept over Vienna and the Wienerwald in the Middle Ages. Also here is the **Rathaus** (town hall) (☎ 02252/86800).

At **Beethovenhaus,** Rathausgasse 10 (☎ **02252/86800**), a little museum has been set up. The composer lived here in the summer from 1821 to 1823. It's open year-round Tuesday to Sunday from 4 to 6pm. Admission is 30AS ($2) for adults and 15AS ($1) for children.

Among the other sights in Baden, there's the celebrated death mask collection at the **Städtisches Rolletmuseum,** Weikersdorfer-Platz 1 (☎ **02252/48255**). The museum possesses many items of interest to history and art lovers. Furniture and art of the Biedermeier period are especially represented. The museum is open Monday to Wednesday and Friday to Sunday from 4 to 6pm. Admission is 30AS ($2) for adults, 10AS (65¢) for children. To reach the museum from Hauptplatz in the center, cut south onto Josefs Platz, then continue south along Vöslauer Strasse, going right when you come to Elisabeth Strasse, which leads directly to the museum's square.

Northeast of Hauptplatz on the Franz-Kaiser Ring is the **Stadttheater** (Municipal Theater; ☎ **02252/48338**), built in 1909; and on Pfarrgasse, the nearby parish church, **St. Stephan's** (☎ **02252/48426**), which dates from the 15th century. Inside, there's a commemorative plaque to Mozart, who allegedly composed his "Ave Verum" here for the parish choirmaster.

The real reason, however, to come to Baden is the sprawling and beautiful ✪ **Kurpark,** north of town. Here, you can attend concerts, plays, and operas at an open-air theater or try your luck at the casino (see "Baden After Dark," below). The **Römerquelle** (Roman Springs) can be seen gurgling from an intricate rock basin that is surrounded by monuments of Beethoven, Mozart, and the great Austrian playwright Grillparzer. Visitors can stroll along numerous paths with views of Baden and the surrounding hills.

TAKING A BATH

The **Kurhaus,** Brussatiplatz 3 (☎ **02252/44531**), is open daily from 10am to 10pm for the Römertherme (hot mineral baths). Admission is 110AS ($7.35) for a 2-hour visit, 130AS ($8.70) for a 3-hour visit, and 150AS ($10.05) for a 4-hour visit. A full day costs 250AS ($16.75). No advance reservations are needed.

Once you're inside, access to the sauna costs an additional 45AS ($3), and any massage or health/beauty regimes cost extra, on a pay scale that is labyrinthine.

Relatively wealthy clients head for the **Wellness Center,** also within the Kurhaus, which has a wider array of facilities. It operates somewhat like a medical clinic and requires advance reservations for a clinician, massage therapist, or other services. It's open daily from 7am to 8pm.

WHERE TO STAY
EXPENSIVE

✪ **Grand Hotel Sauerhof zu Rauhenstein.** Weilburgstrasse 11-13, A-2500 Baden bei Wien. ☎ **02252/41251.** Fax 02252/48047. www.sauerhof.at. 95 units. MINIBAR TV TEL. 2,500–2,900AS ($167.50–$194.30) double; 3,900–4,500AS ($261.30–$301.50) suite. Rates include buffet breakfast. Half board 300AS ($20.10) per person extra. AE, DC, MC, V. Free parking.

Although the history of this estate dates back to 1583, it became famous in 1757 when a sulfur-enriched spring bubbled up after a cataclysmic earthquake in faraway Portugal. The present building was constructed in 1810 on the site of that spring, which continues to supply water to its spa facilities today. During the 19th century, visitors included Beethoven (who wrote his *Wellington Sieg* here and enjoyed a dinner with Karl Maria von Weber) and Mozart's archrival, Salieri. Since then, the property has served as an army rehabilitation center, a sanatorium during the two world wars, and as headquarters for the Russian army. In 1978, after extravagant renovations, the Sauerhof reopened as one of the region's most upscale spa hotels.

Today, the neoclassical building with a steep slate roof rambles across a wide lawn. Few of the original furnishings remain, although the management has collected a handful of vintage Biedermeier sofas and chairs to fill the elegant but somewhat underfurnished public rooms. A covered courtyard, styled on ancient Rome, has a vaulted ceiling supported by chiseled stone columns. The generous bedrooms with firm mattresses are outfitted in a contemporary decor.

Dining/Diversions: There's a collection of Russian icons and a series of medieval halberds in the richly decorated, farmer-style restaurant, which serves some of the best food in town.

Amenities: Two tennis courts, a jogging course, an indoor swimming pool, a terrace, a spa (offering such treatments as sulfur baths, mud wraps, and electro-acupuncture), and a nearby golf course. Room service and laundry service are available.

MODERATE

Hotel Gutenbrunn. Pelzgasse 22, A-2500 Baden bei Wien. ☎ **02252/48171.** Fax 02252/ 45758. www.tiscover.com/hotel.gutenbrunn. 80 units. MINIBAR TV TEL. 1,490–1,890AS ($99.85–$126.65) double; 1,760–2,270AS ($117.90–$152.10) suite. Rates include breakfast. AE, DC, MC, V. Free parking.

This hotel in the town center, a minute's walk from the main square, was named after the healthful waters (*Gutenbrunn*) that bubbled out of the earth nearby. In 1480, Holy Roman Emperor Friedrich III paid a visit to the hotel's predecessor. By around 1890, visitors from throughout the Austrian Empire were staying in the neo-baroque building. Today, the Old World pink-and-white facade sports a hexagonal tower and a slate roof with a baroque steeple; a wing was added in 1972. The interior has a skylit reception area with a double tier of neoclassical loggia. The moderate size bedrooms are well furnished, with good beds. In back of the hotel, guests can promenade in the privately owned park dotted with old trees. A passageway connects the hotel to the town's spa. The hotel has a restaurant, a sauna, and indoor and outdoor swimming pools. Babysitters and laundry service are available, as is room service from 7am to 10pm.

Krainerhütte. Helenental, A-2500 Baden bei Wien. ☎ **02252/44511.** Fax 02252/44514. www.krainerhutte.ort. E-mail: krainerhutte@aon.at. 113 units. MINIBAR TV TEL. 1,800AS ($120.60) double; 2,600AS ($174.20) suite. Rates include breakfast. Half board 250AS ($16.75) per person extra. AE, MC, V. Parking 150AS ($10.05).

Run by Josef Dietmann and his family, this hotel stands on tree-filled grounds 5 miles west of Baden at Helenental. It's a large A-frame chalet with rows of wooden balconies. The interior has more detailing than you might expect in such a modern hotel. There are separate children's rooms and play areas. The medium-size bedrooms and small bathrooms are well maintained. In the cozy restaurant or on the terrace, you can dine on international and Austrian cuisine; the fish and deer come from the hotel grounds. There's an indoor swimming pool, plus a tennis court, a sauna, and an exercise room. Hiking in the owner's forests and hunting and fishing are possible. "Postbus" service to Baden is available all day.

Parkhotel. Kaiser-Franz-Ring 5, A-2500 Baden bei Wien. ☎ **02252/44386.** Fax 02252/ 80578. www.tiscover.com/parkhotel.baden. E-mail: parkhotel-baden@netway.at. 92 units. MINIBAR TV TEL. 2,000AS ($134) double; 2,360AS ($158.10) suite. Rates include breakfast. AE, DC, MC, V. Free parking.

This contemporary hotel is in the middle of an inner-city park dotted with trees and statuary. The high-ceilinged lobby has a marble floor padded with thick Oriental carpets and ringed with richly grained paneling. Most of the good-size sunny bedrooms have their own loggia overlooking century-old trees; each contains a radio, duvet-covered firm mattresses, and good bathrooms with plenty of shelf space. The hotel has a heated indoor swimming pool, two Finnish saunas, a restaurant, a coffee shop, and a terrace overlooking the park.

Schloss Weikersdorf. Schlossgasse 9-11, A-2500 Baden bei Wien. ☎ **02252/48301.** Fax 02252/4830-1150. www.austriahotel.co.at/weikersdorf. 104 units. MINIBAR TV TEL. 1,900AS ($127.30) double. Rates include breakfast. AE, DC, MC, V. Free parking.

The oldest part of the hotel has massive beams, arched and vaulted ceilings, an Italianate loggia stretching toward the manicured gardens, and an inner courtyard with stone arcades. Accommodations, which include 69 bedrooms in the main house plus 35 in the annex, are handsomely furnished and most comfortable. The rooms in the newer section repeat the older section's arches and high ceilings, and sport ornate chandeliers and antique or reproduction furniture. The nearby sports center has an indoor swimming pool, bowling alleys, tennis courts, and a sauna. On the premises are a charming baroque bar and two restaurants.

WHERE TO DINE

Badner Stüberl. Gutenbrunnstrasse 19. ☎ **02252/41232.** Reservations recommended. Main courses 70–210AS ($4.70–$14.05); set menus 88–98AS ($5.90–$6.55). No credit cards. Wed–Mon 11:30am–2:30pm and 6–10pm (last order). AUSTRIAN.

Several generations of the Ackerl family have impeccably maintained this old-fashioned coffeehouse and restaurant. It's in a house built in the 1860s in Baden's oldest neighborhood. You can order such Austrian staples as *tafelspitz* (which is served every Sunday), *Zwiebelrostbraten* (onion-flavored roast beef), goulash soup, very fresh salads, grilled steak, pork and veal schnitzels, and in season, venison and pheasant. The cooking is old-fashioned; the ingredients are fresh.

BADEN AFTER DARK

Casino Baden. In the Kurpark. ☎ **02252/444960.** Free admission. 300AS ($20.10) worth of chips cost 260AS ($17.40). Daily 3pm to 3am.

The major attraction in town is the casino, where you can play roulette, blackjack, baccarat, poker (seven-card stud), the money-wheel, and slot machines. Many visitors from Vienna come down to Baden for a night of gambling, eating, and drinking; on the premises are two bars and a restaurant. Guests are often fashionably dressed, and you'll feel more comfortable if you are, too (men should wear jackets and ties). A less formal casino, the Casino Leger, is open daily from noon to midnight.

3　Wiener Neustadt

Wiener Neustadt was once the official residence of Habsburg Emperor Friedrich III, and this thriving city between the foothills of the Alps and the edge of the Pannonian lowland has a strong historical background.

The town was founded in 1192, when Duke Leopold V of the ruling house of Babenberg built its castle. He had it constructed as a citadel to ward off attacks by the Magyars from the east. From 1440 to 1493 Austrian emperors lived in this fortress in the southeastern corner of what is now the old town. Maximilian I, called "the last of the knights," was born here in 1459 and lies buried in the castle's Church of St. George. In 1752, on Maria Theresa's orders, the castle was turned into a military academy.

Unfortunately, Wiener Neustadt was a target for Allied bombs during World War II. It's where the routes from Vienna diverge, one going to the Semmering Pass and the other to Hungary via the Sopron Gate. The 200-year-old military academy that traditionally turned out officers for the Austrian army may have been an added attraction to bombers—German General Erwin Rommel ("the Desert Fox") was the academy's first commandant after the Nazi Anschluss. At any rate, the Allies bombed the city—more than any other in the country—leveling an estimated 60% of its buildings.

ESSENTIALS

GETTING THERE   Wiener Neustadt is 28 miles (45.08 km) south of Vienna. **Drive** south along Autobahn A-2, until you reach the junction with Route 21, where you head east to Wiener Neustadt. **Trains** leave for Wiener Neustadt daily from Vienna's Südbahnhof, from 5:30am until midnight (trip time: between 27 and 44 minutes, depending on the number of stops). For schedules, call ☎ **05/1717;** www. oebb.at. **Buses** depart daily from the Wiener Mitte bus station every 15 to 30 minutes (trip time: 65 minutes) In Weiner Neustadt, buses drop off passengers in the town center, at Ungargasse 2. Most visitors opt for the train.

VISITOR INFORMATION   The Wiener Neustadt **tourist information office** (☎ **02622/29551**) is at Hauptpaltz in Rathaus. Open Monday to Friday from 8am to 6pm.

SEEING THE SIGHTS

You can visit the **Church of St. George,** Burgplatz 1 (☎ **02622/3810**), daily from 8am to 6pm. The gable of the church is adorned with more than 100 heraldic shields of the Habsburgs. It's noted for its handsome interior, decorated in the late Gothic style.

Neukloster, Neuklostergasse 1 (☎ **02622/23102**), a Cistercian abbey, was founded in 1250 and reconstructed in the 18th century. The New Abbey Church (Neuklosterkirche), near the Hauptplatz, is Gothic with a beautiful choir. It contains the tomb of Empress Eleanor of Portugal, wife of Friedrich III and mother of Maximilian I. Mozart's Requiem was first presented here in 1793. Admission is free; open Monday to Friday from 9am to noon and from 2 to 5pm.

Liebfrauenkirche, on the Domplatz (☎ **02622/23202**), was once the headquarters of an Episcopal see. It's graced by a 13th-century Romanesque nave, but the choir is Gothic. The west towers have been rebuilt. Admission is free, and the church is open daily from 8am to noon and from 2 to 6pm.

In the town is a **Recturm,** Babenberger Ring (☎ **02622/279-24**), a Gothic tower said to have been built with the ransom money paid for King Richard the Lion-Hearted of England. It's open March to October, on Tuesday to Thursday from 10am to noon and from 2 to 4pm, and on Saturday and Sunday from 10am to noon only. Admission is free.

WHERE TO STAY

Hotel Corvinus. Bahngasse 29-33, A-2700 Wiener Neustadt. ☎ **02622/24134.** Fax 02622/24139. www.hotelcorvinus.at. 68 units. MINIBAR TV TEL. 1,500AS ($100.50) double. Rates include breakfast. Children under 12 stay free in parents' room. AE, DC, MC, V. Parking free.

The best hotel in town, built in the 1970s, this place has a color scheme of white and weathered bronze. It sits in a quiet neighborhood near the city park, a 2-minute walk south of the main rail station. The good-size bedrooms have modern comforts, such as firm beds and well-maintained bathrooms. Hotel guests can use the sauna, Turkish bath, and whirlpool. There's also an inviting bar area, a parasol-covered sun terrace, and a lightheartedly elegant restaurant serving Austrian and international dishes.

WHERE TO DINE

Gelbes Haus. Kaiserbrunnen 11. ☎ **02622/26400.** Reservations recommended. Main courses 190–300AS ($12.75–$20.10); fixed-price dinner 650AS ($43.55). DC, MC, V. Tues–Sat noon–2pm and 7–10pm. Closed Christmas, New Year's Day, and Easter. AUSTRIAN/ INTERNATIONAL.

Set in the historic heart of town, this old and well-respected restaurant takes its name from the vivid ochre color of its exterior (ca. 1911–13). Inside, you'll find a stylish and comfortable art nouveau dining room. The Austrian and international cuisine is prepared with fresh ingredients, imagination, and flair. Examples include a succulent version of *tafelspitz* (boiled beef); an assortment of carpaccios arranged with herbs, truffle oil, goose liver, and exotic mushrooms; a savory duck breast in orange sauce; fresh Canadian lobster; and fillets of pork in red wine sauce with cabbage and herbs.

4 The Wachau-Danube Valley

The Danube is one of the most legendary rivers in Europe, rich in scenic splendor and surrounded by history and architecture. The Wachau, a section of the Danube Valley northwest of Vienna, with rolling hills and fertile soil, is one of the most beautiful and historic areas of Austria. Traveling through the Wachau, you'll pass ruins of castles reminiscent of the Rhine Valley, some of the most celebrated vineyards in Austria, famous medieval monasteries, and ruins from the Stone Age peoples, the Celts, the Romans, and the Habsburgs. Unrelentingly prosperous, the district has won many awards for the authenticity of its historic renovations.

If you like the looks of this district, take a paddleboat steamer trip. Most of these operate only between April 1 and October 31. You can travel the countryside from armchair on the ship's deck.

If you're really "doing the Danube," you can begin your trip at Passau, Germany, and go all the way to the Black Sea and across to the Crimean Peninsula, stopping over at Yalta. However, the Vienna–Yalta portion of the trip alone takes nearly a week, and few travelers can devote that much time. Most visitors limit themselves to a more restricted look at the Danube by taking one of the many popular trips offered from Vienna. (See the "Cruising the Danube" box in chapter 6.)

TIPS ON EXPLORING THE DANUBE VALLEY

If you only have a day to see the Danube Valley, we highly recommend the tours listed below. If you have more time, however, rent a car and explore this district yourself, driving inland from the river now and then to visit the towns and sights listed below. You can also take public transportation to the towns we've highlighted (see individual listings).

The Danube and Wachau Valley contain some of the most impressive monuments in Austria, but because of their far-flung locations, many readers find an organized tour convenient. The best of these are conducted by **Vienna Sightseeing Tours,** Stelzhamergasse 4, Suite 11 (☎ **01/7124-6830;** fax 01/714-1141), which offers guided tours by motorcoach in winter and both motorcoach and boat in summer. Stops on this 8-hour trip include Krems, Durnstein, and Melk Abbey. Prices are 800AS ($53.60) for adults, 400AS ($26.80) for children under age 12, and does not include lunch. Advance reservations are required. (Also see the "Cruising the Danube" box in chapter 6.)

Before you venture into the Danube Valley, pick up maps and other helpful information at the **tourist office for Lower Austria,** Heidenschluss 2, A-1010, Vienna (☎ **01/536-100;** fax 0222/5138-02230; www.noe.co.at).

TULLN

This is one of the most ancient towns in Austria. Originally a naval base called Comagena and later a center for the Babenberg dynasty, Tulln, on the right bank of the Danube, is "the flower town" because of the masses of blossoms you'll see in spring and summer. It's the place, according to the Nibelungen saga, where Kriemhild, the Burgundian princess of Worms, met Etzel, king of the Huns. A famous "son of Tulln" was Kurt Waldheim, former secretary-general of the United Nations and one of Austria's most controversial former presidents due to his previous Nazi affiliations.

ESSENTIALS

GETTING THERE   From Vienna, by **car,** head 26 miles (41.86 km) north and west along Route 14 to reach Tulln. S-Bahn **trains** depart from both the Wien Nord Station (at Praterstern) and, more frequently, from the Franz-Josefs Bahnhof, daily from 4:30am to 8:30pm every 50 to 120 minutes (trip time: from 27 to 45 minutes). Although Tulln lies on the busy main rail lines linking Vienna with Prague, most local timetables will list Gmund, an Austrian city on the border of the Czech Republic, as the final destination. For more information, call ☎ 05/1717; www.oebb.at. A bus ride to Tulln from Vienna is not recommended, because it would require multiple transfers in at least two (and sometimes three or more) suburbs. Between mid-May and late September, river cruisers owned by the **DDSG Blue Danube Steamship Co.** (☎ **01/588800;** fax 01/58880-440) leave Vienna on Sunday at 8:30am, arriving in Tulln around 11:15am.

VISITOR INFORMATION   The **tourist information office** in Tulln (☎ **02272/ 65836;** www.tulln.at) is at Albrechtsgasse 32. Open Monday to Friday from 9am to 6pm.

SEEING THE SIGHTS

The twin-towered **Church of St. Stephan** on Wiener Strasse grew out of a 12th-century Romanesque basilica. Its west portal is from the 13th century. A Gothic overlay added in its early centuries succumbed to the baroque craze that swept the country in the 18th century. A 1786 altarpiece commemorates the martyrdom of St. Stephan. Ogival vaulting was used in the chancel and the nave.

Adjoining the church is the polygon **karner** (charnel or bone house). This funeral chapel is Tulln's major sight, and the finest of its kind in the entire country. Built in the mid–13th century, it's richly decorated with capitals and arches. The Romanesque dome is adorned with frescoes.

In a restored former prison, Tulln has opened the **Egon Schiele Museum,** Donaulände 28 (☎ **02272/645-70**), devoted to its second most famous son, born here in 1890. Schiele is one of the greatest Austrian artists of the early 1900s. The prison setting might be appropriate, as the Secessionist painter spent 24 days in jail in 1912 in the town of Neulengbach—he was sentenced to 3 days' imprisonment for possession of what back then was regarded as "pornography." While awaiting trial, he produced 13 watercolors, most of which are now in the Albertina Collection in Vienna. The works of this great artist, who died in Vienna in 1918, now sell for millions of dollars. The Tulln museum has more than 90 of his oil paintings, watercolors, and designs, along with much memorabilia. It's open daily 9am to 7pm. Admission is 50AS ($3.35) for adults and 25AS ($1.70) for children.

WHERE TO STAY & DINE

Hotel/Restaurant Römerhof Stoiber. Langenlebarnerstrasse 66, A-3430 Tulln an der Donau. ☎ **02272-62954.** www.tiscover.com/romerhof-tulln. 49 units. MINIBAR TV TEL. 860AS ($57.60) double. Rates include breakfast. MC, V. Closed Mon. Free parking.

Built in 1972, this hotel near the train station has a simple modern facade of white walls and unadorned windows. The interior is warmly outfitted with earth tones, a macramé wall hanging, and pendant lighting fixtures. The bedrooms are comfortable but utterly functional, with duvet-covered but somewhat thin mattresses. Bathrooms have hair dryers, but limited storage space. A restaurant serves well-prepared meals in an attractive, rustic setting; traditional and good-tasting specialties include Wiener schnitzel and roast beef in sour-cream sauce. Meals in the restaurant range from 120 to 175AS ($8.05 to $11.75) each. Only dinner is served, May to October, from 6 to 8:30pm. There's also a little beer garden.

Hotel zur Rossmühle. Hauptplatz 12, A-3430 Tulln an der Donau. ☎ **02272/24110.** Fax 02272/241133. 57 units. TV TEL. 880–1,380AS ($58.95–$92.45) double. Rates include breakfast. AE, MC, V. Free parking. Coming from Germany, exit the autobahn at St. Christopher; from Vienna it's a 30-minute drive west on Route 14.

Despite the building's relative newness (constructed in 1977), this hotel combines many old-fashioned architectural features. Located on the town's main square, the hotel has an arched entryway protected by a wrought-iron gate, a collection of antique furniture, and crystal chandeliers. About half the bedrooms are in an older annex nearby and are less expensive than the 56 rooms in the newer main building. Regardless, the bedrooms are outfitted in a modernized country-baroque style, with good beds and small bathrooms.

   The hotel contains one of the region's most glamorous restaurants, an all-Austrian ode to good food and *Gemütlichkeit*. Fixed-price specials of the day range from 68 to 78AS ($4.55 to $5.25), but if you feel like celebrating opt for the full-blown, five-course Egon Schiele menu, named after the hometown boy and world-famous artist, costing 440AS ($29.50). Meals are served daily from noon to 2pm and 7 to 10pm.

HERZOGENBURG

To get to the monastery in Herzogenburg, **drive** 7 miles (11.27 km) south of Trais-mauer, take Wiener Strasse (Route 1) out of St. Pölten. Head east for 8 miles (12.88 km) toward Kapelln, but turn left at the sign onto a minor road to Herzogenburg.

✪ **Augustinian Herzogenburg Monastery.** A-3130 Herzogenburg. ☎ **02782/83113.** Admission 70AS ($470) adults, 40AS ($2.70) students, 50AS ($3.35) seniors. Apr–Oct daily 9am–6pm. Tours daily on the hour, 9–11am and 1–5pm.

Founded in the early 12th century by a German bishop from Passau, the monastery has a long history. The present complex of buildings comprising the church and the abbey was reconstructed in the baroque style (1714–40). Jakob Prandtauer and Josef Munggenast designed the buildings, along with Fischer von Erlach. The magnificent baroque church has a sumptuous interior, with an altarpiece by Daniel Gran and a beautiful organ loft. The most outstanding art owned by the abbey is a series of 16th-century paintings on wood; they are displayed in a room devoted to Gothic art. The monastery is known for its library, which contains more than 80,000 works.

   You can wander around on your own or join a guided tour. There's a wine tavern in the complex where you can eat Austrian specialties and drink the product of local grapes.

KREMS

In the eastern part of the Wachau on the left bank of the Danube lies Krems, a city some 1,000 years old. Krems is a mellow town of courtyards, old churches, and ancient houses in the heart of vineyard country, with some partially preserved town walls. Just as the Viennese flock to Grinzing and other suburbs to sample new wine in the Heurigen, so the people of the Wachau come here to taste the vintners' products, which appear in Krems earlier in the year.

ESSENTIALS

GETTING THERE   Krems is 50 miles (80.5 km) west of Vienna and 18 miles north of St. Pölten. To reach Krems from Vienna, **drive** north along the A22 super-highway until it splits into three near the town of Stockerau. Here, drive due west along Route 3, following the signs to Krems.

Trains depart from both the Wien Nord and the Wien Franz-Josefs Bahnhof for Krems, daily from 5am to 8:30pm. Many are direct, although some will require a transfer in Absdorf-Hippersdorf or St. Pölten (trip time: 60 to 95 minutes). Call ☎ **05/1717** (www.oebb.at) for schedules. Traveling by bus to Krems is not recommended; however, Krems is well connected by local buses to surrounding villages. Between mid-May and late September, the **DDSG-Blue Danube Steamship Co.** (☎ and fax **01/588800**) has a boat departing Vienna on Sunday at 8:30am. It arrives in Krems around noon.

VISITOR INFORMATION   The Krems **tourist information office** (☎ **02732/ 82676;** www.krems.at) is at Undstrasse 6. Open Monday to Friday from 9am to 7pm, Saturday and Sunday from 10am to noon and 1 to 6pm.

SEEING THE SIGHTS

The most interesting part of Krems today is what was once the little village of **Stein.** Narrow streets are terraced above the river, and the single main street, **Steinlanderstrasse,** is flanked with houses, many from the 16th century. The **Grosser Passauerhof,** Steinlanderstrasse 76 (☎ **02732/82188**), is a Gothic structure decorated with an oriel. Another house, at Steinlanderstrasse 84, combines Byzantine and Venetian elements among other architectural influences; it was once the imperial toll house. In days of yore, the aristocrats of Krems barricaded the Danube and extracted heavy tolls from the river traffic. Sometimes the tolls were more than the hapless victims could pay, so the townspeople just confiscated the cargo. In the Altstadt, the **Steiner Tor,** a 1480 gate, is a landmark.

Pfarrikirche St. Viet (Parish Church of St. Viet; ☎ **02732/857100**) stands in the center of town at the Rathaus, reached along either Untere Landstrasse or Obere Landstrasse. It's heavily adorned, rich with gilt and statuary. Construction began on this, one of the oldest baroque churches in the province, in 1616. In the 18th century, Martin Johann Schmidt painted many of the frescoes inside the church.

You'll find the **Weinstadt Museum Krems** (Historical Museum of Krems), Körnermarkt 14 (☎ **02732/801567**), in a restored Dominican monastery. The abbey is in the Gothic style of the 13th and 14th centuries. It has a gallery displaying the paintings of Martin Johann Schmidt, a noted 18th-century artist better known as Kremser Schmidt (mentioned earlier). The complex also has an interesting **Weinbaumuseum** (Wine Museum), exhibiting artifacts, many quite old, gathered from the vineyards along the Danube. The cost of admission is 45AS ($3) for access to both areas of the museum. The museum is open only between March and November, Tuesday to Sunday from 1 to 6pm.

Nearby Attractions

Eighteen miles north of Krems at St. Pölten is the Museum of Lower Austria, formerly located in Vienna. Now called **Shedhalle St. Pölten,** it's at Franz-Schubert-Platz (☎ **2742/200-5011**). This museum exhibits the geology, flora, and fauna of the area surrounding Vienna. It also exhibits a collection of arts and crafts, including baroque and Biedermeier; temporary shows featuring 20th-century works are also presented. Admission is 100AS ($6.70) adults, 50AS ($3.35) children. Open daily from 10am to 6pm.

WHERE TO STAY

Donauhotel Krems. Edmund-Hofbauer-Strasse 19, A-3500 Krems. ☎ **02732/87565.** Fax 02732/875-6552. E-mail: donauhotel-krems@aon.at. 60 units. TV TEL. 980AS ($65.65) double. Rates include breakfast. Half board 180AS ($12.05) per person extra. AE, DC, MC, V. No parking.

This large glass-walled hotel built in the 1970s has a wooden canopy stretched over the front entrance. The bedrooms are comfortably furnished and well maintained. They are a little small for long stays but suitable for an overnight, as the beds are fluffy and the bathrooms are spotless. Austrian fare is available in the airy cafe, on the terrace, or in the more formal restaurant. The hotel's fitness center includes a sauna and solarium.

Hotel-Restaurant am Förthof. Donaulände 8, A-3500 Krems. ☎ **02732/83345.** Fax 02732/833-4540. E-mail: hotelforthof@netway.at. 20 units. TV TEL. 1,400–1,600AS ($93.80–$107.20) double. Rates include breakfast. Half board 300AS ($20.10) per person extra. AE, DC, MC, V. Free parking.

In the Stein sector of the city, this big-windowed hotel has white-stucco walls and flower-covered balconies. A rose garden surrounds the base of an al fresco cafe; inside are Oriental rugs and a scattering of antiques amid newer furniture. Each of the high-ceilinged bedrooms has a foyer and a shared balcony. Most bedrooms are fairly spacious, and mattresses are frequently renewed. Bathrooms, though small, are adequate for overnight stopovers. On the grounds is an outdoor swimming pool bordered in stone.

WHERE TO DINE

✪ **Restaurant Bacher.** Südtiroler Platz 208, A-3512 Mautern. ☎ **02732/82937.** Fax 02732/74337. Reservations required. Main courses 230–375AS ($15.40–$25.15); fixed-price lunch Wed–Fri 395AS ($26.45); fixed-price dinner 695–895AS ($46.55–$59.95). DC, MC, V. Wed–Sat 11:30am–2pm and 6:30–9:30pm; Sun 11:30am–9pm. Closed mid-Jan to mid-Feb. AUSTRIAN/INTERNATIONAL.

Lisl and Klaus Wagner-Bacher operate this excellent restaurant-hotel, with an elegant dining room and a well-kept garden. Lisl cooks à la Paul Bocuse, serving an imaginative array of fresh ingredients. Specialties include crabmeat salad with nut oil and zucchini stuffed with fish and two kinds of sauces. Dessert might be *beignets* with apricot sauce and vanilla ice cream. She has won awards for her cuisine, as her enthusiastic clientele will tell you. The wine list includes more than 600 selections.

Eight double and three single rooms are available. Rooms contain TVs, minibars, phones, and radios, and each is attractively furnished with good beds. The rates are 1,590 to 1,950AS ($106.55 to $130.65) in a double. Bacher is 2½ miles from Krems.

DÜRNSTEIN

Less than 5 miles west of Krems is, in our opinion, the loveliest town along the Danube, Dürnstein, despite the throngs of tour groups in summer. Terraced vineyards mark this as a Danube wine town, and the town's fortified walls are partially preserved.

ESSENTIALS

GETTING THERE   Dürnstein is 50 miles (80.5 km). west of Vienna. To reach it by **car,** take Route 3 west from the city. From Krems, continue driving west along Route 3 for 5 miles. **Train** travel to Dürnstein requires a transfer in Krems (see above). In Krems, trains leave every 2 hours on river-running routes to Dürnstein. Call ☎ **05/1717** in Vienna for schedules. There's also **bus service** (trip time: 20 minutes) between Krems and Dürnstein.

VISITOR INFORMATION   Dürnstein has a little **tourist office** (☎ **02711/200**), housed in a shed in the east parking lot, called Parkplatz Ost. It's open only from May to October. Hours are Monday, Thursday, and Friday from 1 to 7pm, Saturday and Sunday from 11am to 7pm.

SEEING THE SIGHTS

The ruins of a **castle fortress,** 520 feet above the town, link the town with the Crusades. Here Leopold V, the Babenberg duke, held **Richard the Lion-Hearted**, king of England, prisoner in 1193. It seems that Richard had insulted the powerful Austrian duke in Palestine during one of the Crusades to return the Holy Lands to Christian hands. The story goes that when Richard was trying to get back home, his boat went on the rocks in the Adriatic and he tried to sneak through Austria disguised as a peasant. Somebody probably turned stool pigeon, and the English monarch was arrested and imprisoned by Leopold.

For quite some time nobody knew exactly where Richard was incarcerated in Austria, but his loyal minstrel, Blondel, had a clever idea. He went from castle to castle, playing his lute and singing Richard's favorite songs. The tactic paid off, the legend says, for at Dürnstein Richard heard Blondel's singing and sang the lyrics in reply. This discovery forced Leopold to transfer the English king to a castle in the Rhineland Palatinate, but by then everybody knew where he was, so Leopold set a high ransom on the king's head, which was eventually met and Richard was set free.

The castle was virtually demolished by the Swedish army in 1645, but you can visit the ruins if you don't mind a vigorous climb (allow an hour). The castle isn't much, but the view of Dürnstein and the Wachau is more than worth the effort.

Back in the town, stroll along the principal artery, **Hauptstrasse,** which is flanked by richly embellished old residences. Many of these date from the 1500s and have been well maintained through the centuries. In summer the balconies are filled with flowers.

The 15th-century **pfarrkirche** (parish church) also merits a visit. The building was originally an Augustinian monastery and was reconstructed when the baroque style swept Austria. The church tower, identified by its reddish color, is the finest baroque example in the whole country and is a prominent landmark in the Danube Valley. There is also a splendid church portal. Kremser Schmidt, the noted baroque painter, did some of the altar paintings here.

WHERE TO STAY & DINE

Gartenhotel Pfeffel. A-3601 Dürnstein. ☎ **02711/206.** Fax 02711/12068. www.tiscover. com/gartenhotel-pfeffel. E-mail: gartenhotel-durnstein@netway.at. 40 units. TEL. 1,120–1,200AS ($75.05–$80.40) double; from 1,560AS ($104.50) suite. Rates include breakfast. MC, V. Closed Dec–Feb. Free parking.

This black-roofed, white-walled hotel is partially concealed by well-landscaped shrubbery. One of the best bargains in town, the hotel takes its name from its garden courtyard with flowering trees, where tasty (but not fancy) meals are served. The public rooms are furnished with traditional pieces. The bedrooms are handsomely furnished in a traditional Austrian motif, with comfortable armchairs, good beds, and medium-size bathrooms. Leopold Pfeffel, your host, serves wine from his own terraced vineyard. He's also added a swimming pool.

Gasthof-Pension Sänger Blondel. A-3601 Dürnstein. ☎ **02711/253.** Fax 02711/2537. E-mail: sangerblondel@aon.at. 16 units. TEL. 1,090–1,330AS ($73.05–$89.10) double. Rates include breakfast. MC, V. Closed Dec–Feb and the first week in July. Parking 85AS ($5.70).

Lemon-colored and charmingly old-fashioned, with green shutters and clusters of flowers at the windows, this hotel is named after the faithful minstrel who searched the countryside for Richard the Lion-Hearted. Bedrooms are furnished in an old-fashioned, rustic style and are quite comfortable, containing such amenities as hair dryers in the small bathrooms. All have good beds with relatively new mattresses and fresh linen. Each Thursday an evening of zither music is presented. If the weather is good, the music is played outside in the flowery chestnut garden near the baroque church tower. There's a good and reasonably priced restaurant serving regional cuisine.

✪ **Hotel Schloss Dürnstein.** A-3601 Dürnstein. ☎ **02711/212.** Fax 02711/212-30. www. schloss.at. E-mail: hotel@schloss.at. 39 units. MINIBAR TV TEL. 2,900–4,400AS ($194.30–$294.80) double; from 4,600AS ($308.20) suite. Rates include half board. AE, DC, MC, V. Closed Nov 10–Mar 25. Parking 100AS ($6.70). A pickup can be arranged at the Dürnstein rail station.

The baroque tower of this Renaissance castle rises above the scenic Danube. It's one of the best-decorated hotels in Austria, with white ceramic stoves, vaulted ceilings, parquet floors, Oriental rugs, gilt mirrors, and oil portraits of elaborately dressed courtiers. Below the ochre facade of one of the wings, an ivy-covered wall borders the swimming pool. A beautiful shady terrace is only a stone's throw from the river. Elegantly furnished bedrooms come in a wide variety of styles, ranging from those large and palatial enough for an emperor to rather small and modern. Modern bathrooms have been put in all the bedrooms, though sometimes in cramped conditions. The restaurant serves well-prepared dishes from the kitchen of an experienced chef. Fixed-price menus begin at 390AS ($26.15), including appetizer.

✪ **Romantik-Hotel Richard Löwenherz.** A-3601 Dürnstein. ☎ **02711/222.** Fax 02711/22218. www.richardlowenherz.at. E-mail: lowenherz@duernstein.at. 40 units. TV TEL. 1,500–1,750AS ($100.50–$117.25) double. Rates include breakfast. AE, DC, MC, V. Closed Nov–Mar. Free parking.

This establishment was founded as a hotel in the 1950s on the site of a 700-year-old nunnery, originally dedicated to the sisters of Santa Clara in 1289. Its richly historical interior is filled with antiques, Renaissance sculpture, elegant chandeliers, stone vaulting, and paneling that has been polished over the years to a mellow patina. An arbor-covered sun terrace with restaurant tables extends toward the Danube. Best of all, the hotel has a swimming pool; you'll see the apse of a medieval church reflected in the water. The spacious bedrooms, especially those in the balconied modern section, are filled with cheerful furniture. The duvet-covered beds are the finest in the area, with extra-thick mattresses.

The restaurant offers a fine selection of local wines as well as fish from the Danube among its many regional specialties. The dining room is open daily from 11:30am to 11:30pm. A fixed-price menu costs 380AS ($25.45).

MELK

The words of Empress Maria Theresa speak volumes about Melk: "If I had never come here, I would have regretted it." The main attraction here is the Melk Abbey, a sprawling baroque abbey overlooking the Danube basin. Melk marks the western terminus of the Wachau and lies upstream from Krems.

ESSENTIALS

GETTING THERE Melk is 55 miles (88.55 km) west of Vienna. **Motorists** can take Autobahn A1, exiting at the signs for Melk. If you prefer a more romantic and scenic road, try Route 3, which parallels the Danube but takes 30 to 45 minutes longer. **Trains** leave frequently from Vienna's Westbahnhof to Melk, with two brief stops en route (trip time: about 1 hour). Between mid-May and late September, river cruisers owned by the **DDSG Blue Danube Steamship Co.** (☎ **01/588800;** fax 01/58880-440) leave Vienna only on Sunday at 8:30am, arriving in Melk around 1:40pm.

VISITOR INFORMATION   The **Melk tourist office** (☎ **02752/523-0732** or 0733; www.tiscover.com/melk) is at Babenbergerstrasse 1 in the center of town. Open Monday to Saturday from 9am to 7pm, Sunday from 10am to 2pm.

SEEING THE SIGHTS

✪ **Melk Abbey.** Dietmayerstrasse 1, A-3390 Melk. ☎ **02752/52312** or 02752/5231-2232 for tour information. Guided tours 110AS ($7.35) adults, 70AS ($4.70) children; unguided tours 80AS ($5.35) adults, 40AS ($2.70) children. Tours daily 9am–5pm.

The abbey and the abbey church are the major attractions here. However, Melk has been important since the Romans established a fortress here on a promontory over a tiny "arm" of the Danube. Melk also figures in the *Nibelungenlied,* the German epic poem, in which it is called *Medelike.*

The rock-strewn bluff where the abbey now stands was the seat of the Babenberg dukes, who ruled Austria from 976 until the Habsburgs took over. In the 11th century, Leopold II ("the Saint") presented Melk to the Benedictine monks, who turned it into a fortified abbey. It became a center of learning and culture, and its influence spread all over Austria, a fact familiar to readers of *The Name of the Rose* by Umberto Eco. However, it did not fare well during the Reformation, and it also felt the force of the 1683 Turkish invasion, although it was spared a direct attack when the Ottomans were repelled outside Vienna. The construction of the new building began in 1702, just in time to be given the full baroque treatment.

The abbey is one of the finest baroque buildings in the world. Architect Jakob Prandtauer (1660–1727), who also contributed to the Herzogenburg Monastery, designed most of the building. Its marble hall, the Marmorsaal, contains pilasters coated in red marble. A rich allegorical painting on the ceiling is the work of Paul Troger. The library, rising two floors, again with a Troger ceiling, contains some 80,000 volumes. The Kaisergang, or emperors' gallery, 650 feet long, is decorated with portraits of Austrian rulers.

Despite all the adornment in the abbey, it is still surpassed in lavish glory by the **Stiftskirche,** the golden abbey church. Damaged by fire in 1947, the church has been fully restored even to the regilding with gold bouillon of statues and altars. The church has an astonishing number of windows, and it's richly embellished with marble and frescoes. Many of the paintings are by Johann Michael Rottmayr, but Troger also contributed. The Marble Hall banquet room next to the church was also damaged by the fire, but it has been restored to its former ornate elegance.

Melk is still a working abbey, and you may see black-robed Benedictine monks going about their business or schoolboys rushing out the gates. Visitors head for the terrace for a view of the river. Napoléon probably used it for a lookout when he made Melk his headquarters during his Austrian campaign.

Tours depart every 15 to 20 minutes, depending on business. The guides make efforts to translate into English a running commentary in German.

WHERE TO STAY

Hotel Stadt Melk. Hauptplatz 1, A-3390 Melk. ☎ **02752/52475.** Fax 02752/524-7519. www.hotelstadtmelk.com. E-mail: hotel.stadtmelk@netway.at. 15 units. MINIBAR TV TEL. 950–1,200AS ($63.65–$80.40) double; 2,100AS ($140.70) suite. Rates include breakfast. AE, DC, MC, V. Parking free.

Just below the town's palace, a 5-minute walk from the train station, this four-story hotel has a gabled roof and stucco walls. Originally built a century ago as a private home, it was eventually converted into this cozy, family-run hotel. The simply furnished bedrooms are clean and comfortable with sturdy beds, firm mattresses, and well-maintained bathrooms that, though small, are still adequate. Rooms in the rear open onto views of the abbey. The pleasant restaurant has leaded-glass windows in round bull's-eye patterns of greenish glass. Meals, beginning at 400AS ($32), are also served on a balcony, decorated with flowers, at the front of the hotel. The food is quite good. There's a sauna on the premises.

WHERE TO DINE

Stiftrestaurant Melk. Abt-Berthold-Dietmayrstrasse 3. ☎ **02752/52555.** Fixed-price menus 180–220AS ($12.05–$14.75). AE, MC, V. Daily 8am to 6pm. BURGENLANDER.

For the visitor to Melk, this is required eating. Don't allow the cafeteria-like appearance to sway you from the very fine cuisine. This place is well equipped to handle large groups: 3,000 visitors a day frequent the restaurant during peak season. The dining rooms are typically Austrian clean, and the price is reasonable. From their fixed-price menu you might opt for the asparagus and ham soup with crispy dumplings; hunter's roast with mushrooms, potato croquettes, and cranberry sauce; and a choice of desserts, possibly the famed, highly caloric Sachertorte.

5 Eisenstadt: Haydn's Home

When Burgenland joined Austria in the 1920s, it was a province without a capital. In 1924 its citizens agreed to give Eisenstadt the honor. This small town lies at the foot of the Leitha mountains, at the beginning of the Great Hungarian Plain. Surrounded by vineyards, forests, and fruit trees, it's a convenient stopover for exploring Lake Neusiedl, 6 miles (9.66 km) east.

Even before assuming its new administrative role, Eisenstadt was renowned as the place where the great composer Joseph Haydn lived and worked while under the patronage of the aristocratic Esterházy family. For a good part of his life (1732–1809), Haydn divided his time between Eisenstadt and the Esterházy Castle in Hungary. Prince Esterházy eventually gave him his own orchestra and a concert hall in which to perform.

ESSENTIALS

GETTING THERE   From Vienna, Eisenstadt is 31 miles (49.91 km) southeast. **Motorists** can take Route 10 east to Parndorf Ort, then head southwest along Route 304 to Eisenstadt. **Trains** for Eisenstadt leave from the Südbahnhof daily, heading toward Budapest. Change at the railway junction of Neusiedl am See, where connections are carefully timed to link up with the trains to Eisenstadt (trip time: around 90 minutes). Call ☎ **05/1717** for schedules. You can take a **bus** from the City Air Terminal at the Vienna Hilton. Buses marked EISENSTADT-DOMPLATZ depart daily every 20 minutes.

VISITOR INFORMATION   When you arrive, go directly to the **Eisenstadt tourist office,** Franz-Schubert-Platz 1 (☎ **02682/63384**), which distributes information about Eisenstadt and Burgenland and also books rooms. Open October to May Monday to Friday from 9am to 5pm; June to September daily from 9am to 6pm.

SEEING THE SIGHTS

Bergkirche (Church of the Calvary). Josef-Haydn-Platz 1. ☎ **02682/62638.** Free admission Church; Haydn's tomb, 30AS ($2) adults, 15AS ($1) students, 20AS ($1.35) seniors. Daily 9am–noon and 1–5pm. Closed Nov–Mar. From Esterházy Platz at the castle, head directly west along Esterházystrasse, a slightly uphill walk.

If you want to pay your final respects to Haydn, follow Hauptstrasse to Esterházy-strasse, which leads to this church containing Haydn's white marble tomb. Until 1954, only the composer's headless body was here. Haydn's head was stolen a few days after his death, and it took 145 years for head and body to reunite! His skull was in the Music Museum in Vienna, where curious spectators were actually allowed to touch it.

Franz-Liszt-Geburtshaus (Franz Liszt's Birthplace). Raiding. ☎ **02619/7220.** Admission 20AS ($1.35) adults; 10AS (65¢) children, students, and seniors; 40AS ($2.70) family ticket. Mon–Fri 9am–noon and 1–5pm. Closed Nov–Easter. Take Route S31 south of Eisenstadt, then cut east onto a minor, unmarked road at Lackenbach (follow the signs to Raiding from there).

In the small nearby village of Raiding (south of Eisenstadt), this museum contains many mementos of Liszt's life, including an old church organ he used to play. Liszt's father worked as a bailiff for the princes of Esterházy, and this was his home when little Franz was born in 1811.

Haydn Museum. Haydn-Gasse 19-21. ☎ **02682/62652.** Admission 60AS ($4) adults, 40AS ($2.70) children, seniors, and students. Daily 9am–noon and 1–5pm. Closed Nov–Easter. Pass Schloss Esterházy and turn left onto Haydn-Gasse.

Haydn's little home from 1766 to 1778 is now a museum honoring its former tenant. Although he appeared at the court nearly every night, Haydn actually lived very modestly when he was at home. The museum has collected mementos of his life and work.

✪ **Schloss Esterházy.** Esterházy Platz. ☎ **2682/7193000.** Admission 60AS ($4) adults, 40AS ($2.70) children, seniors, and students. Daily 9am–5pm. From the bus station at Domplatz, follow the sign to the castle (a 10-minute walk).

Haydn worked in this château built on the site of a medieval castle and owned by the Esterházy princes. The Esterházy clan was a great Hungarian family who ruled Eisenstadt and its surrounding area. They claimed descent from Attila the Hun. The Esterházys helped the Habsburgs gain control in Hungary. So great was their loyalty to Austria, in fact, that when Napoléon offered the crown of Hungary to Nic Esterházy in 1809, he refused.

The castle, built around an inner courtyard, was designed by the Italian architect Carlone and fortified because of its strategic position. Carlone started work on the castle in 1663, but many architects had a hand in remodeling it. In the late 17th and early 18th centuries it was given a baroque pastel facade. On the first floor, the great baronial hall was made into the Haydnsaal, where the composer conducted an orchestra Prince Esterházy had provided for him. He often performed his own works for the Esterházy court. The walls and ceilings of this concert hall are elaborately decorated, but the floor is bare wood, which, it is claimed, is the reason for the room's acoustic perfection.

A complete tour of Esterházy Palace takes 45 to 55 minutes and costs 60AS ($4) per person; a tour of only the Haydnsaal lasts about 20 minutes and costs 20AS ($1.35) per person. Both tours are conducted for a minimum of 10 people.

WHERE TO STAY & DINE

Hotel Burgenland. Schubertplatz 1, A-7000 Eisenstadt. ☎ **02682/696.** Fax 02682/65531. www.austriahotels.co.at/burgenland. 88 units. MINIBAR TV TEL. 1,675AS ($112.25) double; from 2,500AS ($167.50) suite. Rates include breakfast. AE, DC, MC, V. Parking 110AS ($7.35).

The Hotel Burgenland opened in 1982 and quickly established itself as the classiest in town. A mansard roof, white-stucco walls, and big windows form the exterior of this contemporary hotel in the center directly northeast of the bus station at Domplatz. The comfortable bedrooms have lots of light, wood-grained headboards, functional furniture, and radios. A swimming pool, a sauna, two restaurants, and a cafe are on the premises.

One of the best restaurants in Burgenland is the hotel's G'würzstockl, open Sunday and holidays from noon to 2:30pm and Monday to Friday from 6 to 10pm. It serves such traditional and old-fashioned dishes as cabbage soup, veal steak with fresh vegetables, and a host of other platters, some Hungarian. Fixed-price menus cost 200 to 700AS ($13.40 to $46.90), with à la carte meals running 135 to 320AS ($9.05 to $21.45). Reservations are suggested. A less formal option is the Bianankorb, a cafe-restaurant open daily from 7am with last orders taken at 9pm.

Wirtshaus zum Eder. Hauptstrasse 25, A-7000 Eisenstadt. ☎ **02682/62645.** Fax 02682/ 626455. www.wirtshaus.online.at. 13 units. 590AS ($39.55) double. Rates include breakfast. AE, DC, MC, V. Free parking.

Filled with modern furniture, deer antlers, and iron chandeliers, this family-style guesthouse also has a garden terrace surrounded by a thick wall of greenery. It's in the town center, north of the bus station at Domplatz. The simple bedrooms are clean and comfortable with good beds but small bathrooms. The hotel's restaurant serves Austrian and Hungarian specialties at reasonable prices. Meals cost from 150 to 300AS ($10.05 to $20.10) and are served daily from 11am to 11pm.

6 Lake Neusiedl

The Neusiedl Lake region is a famous getaway for the Viennese, and North Americans will find it just as desirable. The lake offers countless diversions, making it an ideal destination for families and active travelers. The steppe landscape is great for strolls and hikes, and the geological anomaly of Neusiedler See (see box below) will intrigue you.

It's better to have a car if you're exploring Lake Neusiedl, although there are bus connections, departing several times daily from the Domplatz bus station at Eisenstadt.

NEUSIEDL AM SEE

On the northern bank of Lake Neusiedl is this crowded summer weekend spot. Water sports prevail here; you can rent a sailboat and spend the day drifting across the lake. The Gothic parish church is noted for its "ship pulpit." A watchtower from the Middle Ages still stands guard over the town, although it's no longer occupied. Many vineyards cover the nearby countryside. If you plan to be here on a weekend in summer, make advance reservations.

ESSENTIALS

GETTING THERE   Neusiedl am See lies 28 miles (45.08 km) southeast of Vienna and 21 miles (33.81km) northeast of Eisenstadt. Neusiedl am See is a gateway to the lake, less than an hour by express **train** from Vienna's Südbahnhof station. **Motorists** can reach it by taking the A-4 or Route 10 east from Vienna. If you're in Eisenstadt, head northeast along Route 50, cutting east along Route 51 for a short distance. **Buses** depart several times daily from the Domplatz bus station in Eisenstadt.

VISITOR INFORMATION   The **Neusiedler See tourist office** is in the Rathaus (town hall) at Hauptplatz 1 (☎ **02167/2229**), and it distributes information about accommodations in the area and will also explain how to rent sailboats. Open Monday to Friday from 8am to 7pm, Saturday from 10am to 3pm, and Sunday from noon to 4pm.

WHERE TO STAY AND DINE

Gasthof zur Traube. Hauptplatz 9, A-7100 Neusiedl am See. ☎ **02167/2423.** Fax 02167/24236. E-mail: zur-traube@aon.at. 7 units. TV TEL. 650–720AS ($43.55–$48.25) double. Rates include breakfast. No credit cards. Free parking.

The Capricious Lake

The **Neusiedler See** (Lake Neusiedl) is a popular steppe lake in the northern part of Burgenland. But this strange lake should never be taken for granted—in fact, from 1868 to 1872 it completely dried up, as it has done periodically throughout its history. This creates intriguing real-estate disputes among bordering landowners. The lake was once part of a body of water that blanketed all of the Pannonian Plain. It's between 4¼ and 9¼ miles wide and about 22 miles (35.42 km)long. Today, it's only about 6 feet (1.8 m) deep at its lowest point, and the wind can shift the water dramatically, even causing parts of the lake to dry up. Because of the curvature of the earth, the middle of the lake is about 80 feet (24 m) deeper than its edges.

A broad belt of reeds encircles its huge expanse, about 115 square miles. This thicket is an ideal habitat for many species of water fowl. In all, some 250 different species of birds inhabit the lake, including the usual collection of storks, geese, ducks, and herons. The Neusiedler See possesses no natural outlets; it is fed by underground lakes. The water is slightly salty, so the plants and animals here are unique in Europe. Alpine, Baltic, and Pannonian flora and fauna meet in its waters.

The Viennese come to the lake throughout the year, in summer to fish and windsurf and in winter to skate. If you're a sunbather, nearly every village has a beach (although on any given day it might be swallowed up by the sea or end up miles from the shore, depending on which way the wind blows). The fertile soil and temperate climate surrounding the west bank is ideal for vineyards. Washed in sun, the orchards in Rust produce famous, award-winning vintages.

This small hotel stands on the bustling main street of town. The pleasant restaurant on the ground floor is filled with country trim and wrought-iron table dividers. You can stop in for a meal from 11am to 10pm or book one of the cozy upstairs bedrooms for an overnight stay (you have to register at the bar in back of the restaurant). In summer, guests can relax in the garden. Franz Rittsteuer and his family are the owners.

Hotel Wende. Seestrasse 40-50, A-7100 Neusiedl am See. ☎ **02167/8111.** Fax 02167/ 811-1649. E-mail: anfrage@hotelwende.at. 106 units. MINIBAR TV TEL. 1,596–1,796AS ($106.95–$120.35) double; 3,854AS ($258.20) suite. Rates include breakfast. AE, DC, MC, V. Closed last week in Jan and first 2 weeks in Feb. Parking garage 110AS ($7.35). Free pickup at the train station.

This place is actually a complex of three sprawling buildings, interconnected by rambling corridors. Set at the edge of town on the road leading to the water, the hotel is almost a village unto itself. The aura here is one of clean but slightly sterile propriety, although the indoor pool and sauna, along with the glass-enclosed clubhouse, offer diversion. The bedrooms are well furnished, with firm mattresses and well-maintained bathrooms with hair dryers.

The best food and best service, as well as the most formal setting, are found in the hotel's restaurant. Under a wood-beamed ceiling, the rich and bountiful table of Burgenland is set to perfection. In summer, tables are placed outside overlooking the grounds. Because Burgenland is a border state, the menu reflects the cuisines of Hungary and Austria. The menu includes a savory soup made with fresh carp from nearby lakes; pork cutlets with homemade noodles, bacon-flavored rösti, baby carrots, and fresh herbs; breast of chicken with polenta and fresh herbs; fillet of zander in a potato crust with a sherry-cream sauce and wild rice; Hungarian crêpes stuffed with minced veal with paprika-cream sauce; and for dessert, iced honey parfait with seasonal fresh fruits, or perhaps a strudel studded with fresh dates with marzipan-flavored whipped cream. Main courses cost 192 to 370AS ($12.85 to $2480); open daily from noon to 2pm and 6 to 9pm.

PURBACH AM SEE

If you take Route 50 south from the northern tip of Lake Neusiedl, your first stopover might be in this little resort village, which has some nice accommodations. Purbach boasts a well-preserved circuit of town walls, which were built to stop Turkish invasions during the 16th and 17th centuries. It's also a market town, where you can buy some of Burgenland's renowned wines from local vendors.

ESSENTIALS

GETTING THERE   Purbach is 31 miles southeast of Vienna and 11 miles northeast of Eisenstadt. From Eisenstadt, you can take a daily **bus** leaving from the station at Domplatz. **Motorists** in Eisenstadt head northeast along Route 50; motorists from Vienna can cut southeast along Route 10 or Autobahn A4.

VISITOR INFORMATION   Contact the **Neusiedler See tourist office** in Neusiedl am See, Hauptplatz 1 (☎ 02167/2229). Open Monday to Friday from 8am to 7pm, Saturday from 10am to 3pm, and Sunday from noon to 4pm.

WHERE TO STAY

Am Spitz. A-7083 Purbach am See. ☎ **02683/5519.** Fax 02683/551920. E-mail: amspitz@ aon.at. 16 units. TV TEL. 840–900AS ($56.30–$60.30) double; 1,200AS ($80.40) apt. Rates include breakfast. MC, V. Closed Christmas to Easter. Free parking. The hotel will pick up guests at the bus station.

The main building of this hotel has a gable trimmed with baroque embellishments. The Holzl-Schwarz family are your hosts here, where a hotel has stood for more than 600 years. The current incarnation includes accommodations with wonderful views of the lake. The hotel staff takes care and pride in the maintenance of its average-size rooms and small but quite serviceable bathrooms. The hotel is well directed, conservative, and deserving of its three-star rating. The adjoining restaurant, rustically decorated and cozy, is one of the best places in the region for Burgenland cuisine. Specialties include chicken soup, bacon salad, and lamb cutlets with potatoes and spinach, all with local wines. It is closed on Monday and Tuesday, and reservations are suggested.

WHERE TO DINE

Romantik-Restaurant Nikolauszeche. Bodenzeile 3. ☎ **02683/5514.** Reservations recommended. Main courses 80–290AS ($5.35–$19.45); fixed-price menu (including wine) 250–1,000AS ($16.75–$67). AE, DC, MC, V. Thurs–Mon 12:30–3pm; Wed–Mon 6–11pm. Closed Dec 12–Mar 15. AUSTRIAN.

This upscale restaurant is housed in what was once, 5 centuries ago, a cloister for monks. The authentically regional menu changes every 2 weeks. Diners can order the rich bouillon or cabbage soup, the *fogosch* (a white fish), and the chef's special ham crêpes. The wine list is well chosen. Accordion or organ music is played. If you want privacy and calm, you can find a quiet corner in the interior courtyard.

RUST

South of Purbach, Rust is a small resort village with limited accommodations. It's famous for its stork nests, which are perched on chimneys throughout the town. The antiquated, charming town center is well preserved and clean. Its walls were built in 1614 for protection against the Turks.

Rust, capital of the Burgenland lake district, is surrounded by lush vineyards that produce the Burgenlander grape. If it's available, try the *Blaufränkisch,* a red wine that seems to be entirely consumed by locals and visiting Viennese. Sometimes you can go right up to the door of a vintner's farmhouse, especially if a green bough is displayed, and sample the wine before buying it on the spot.

The taverns in the town play lively Gypsy music. Some local residents, when the wine is in their blood, even dress up in regional costume. You're left with the distinct impression that you're in Hungary.

Rust has a warm and friendly atmosphere, especially on weekends. Summers are often hot, and the lake water can get warm. You can rent sailboats and windsurfers on the banks of the shallow Neusiedler See.

ESSENTIALS

GETTING THERE   Rust is 11 miles (17.71 km) northeast of Eisenstadt and 44 miles (70.84 km) southeast of Vienna. From Eisenstadt, head east on Route 52. From Purbach, **motorists** can take Route 50 south toward Eisenstadt. At Seehof take a left fork to Oggau and Rust. There is no train to Rust, however, there are several **buses** a day leaving from Eisenstadt that connect with Rust. For information, call the bus station in Eisenstadt at ☎ **02682/2350.**

VISITOR INFORMATION   The **Rust tourist office** (☎ **02685/502**) is in the Rathaus (town hall) in the center of the village. It can arrange inexpensive stays with English-speaking families. Open Monday to Friday from 9am to noon and 2 to 6pm, Saturday from 9am to noon, and Sunday from 10am to noon.

WHERE TO STAY & DINE

Hotel-Restaurant Sifkovitz. Am Seekanal 8, A-7071 Rust. ☎ **02685/276.** Fax 02685/36012. www.sifkovitz.at. E-mail: hotel@sifkovitz.at. 35 units. 860–1,260AS ($57.60–$84.40) double with bath. Rates include breakfast. AE, DC, MC, V. Closed Dec–Mar. Free parking.

Attracting summer visitors from Vienna and Hungary, this hotel has an older building and a new wing, both fully renovated in the mid-1980s. The facade is concrete and stucco, and the older building has red-tile roofs and big windows. The sunny bedrooms are comfortably furnished with rather functional pieces. Bathrooms, although not large, are well maintained. Singles are very hard to get during the busy summer season. Facilities include a sauna, an exercise room, a cafe, and a sun terrace. There is access to tennis courts, but they're on the grounds of another hotel nearby (the staff will make arrangements). Austrian and Hungarian-inspired cuisine is served daily from 11am to 3pm and 5:30 to 9:30pm.

Seehotel Rust. A-7071 Rust. ☎ **02685/382.** Fax 02685/381419. www.trendhotels.at. E-mail: seehotel@trendhotels.at. 110 units. MINIBAR TV TEL. 1,820AS ($121.95) double. Rates include breakfast. AE, DC, MC, V. Free parking.

Seehotel Rust is one of the most attractive hotels in the lake district. Set on a grassy lawn at the edge of the lake, this well-designed hotel remains open year-round. It has an appealing series of connected balconies, rounded towers that look vaguely medieval, and a series of recessed loggias. The hotel offers pleasantly furnished bedrooms with frequently renewed mattresses and clean bathrooms. The rooms are a little too "peas-in-the-pod" for most tastes; however, an overnight stopover can be just fine. On the premises are an indoor swimming pool, a sauna, two tennis courts, and a bar area.

Offerings in the restaurant include *tafelspitz* (boiled beef) with chive sauce, calves' brains with a honey vinegar, watercress soup, and sole meunière. Meals begin at 190AS ($12.75). A Gypsy band provides entertainment.

ILLMITZ

This old *puszta* (steppe) village on the east side of the lake has grown into a town with a moderate tourist business in summer. From Eisenstadt, **motorists** should take Route 50 northeast, through Purbach, cutting southeast on Route 51, via Pordersdorf, to Illmitz. The 38-mile (61.18-kilometer) trip from Eisenstadt to Illmitz seems long because traffic must swing around the northern perimeter of the lake before heading south to Illmitz.

NEARBY ATTRACTIONS

Leaving Illmitz, head east on the main route, then cut north at the junction with Route 51. From Route 51, both the little villages of St. Andrä bei Frauenkirchen and Andau are signposted. Near the Hungarian border, the hamlet of **St. Andrä bei Frauenkirchen** is filled with thatch houses. Known for its basket weaving, the town makes for a nice shopping expedition.

A short drive farther on is **Andau,** which became the focus of world attention in 1956 during the Hungarian uprising. Through this town, hundreds of Hungarians dashed to freedom in the West, fleeing the Soviet invasion of Budapest.

Starting in the late 1940s, the border with Hungary was closely guarded, and people who tried to escape into Austria were often shot. But now all that has changed. In 1989, the fortifications were rendered obsolete as hundreds of East Germans fled across the border to the West and freedom. Before the year was out, the Iron Curtain had fallen.

The surrounding marshy area of this remote sector of Austria, called **Seewinkel,** is a haven for birds and rare flora, plus many small *puszta* animals. This large natural wildlife sanctuary is dotted with windmills and huge reed thickets, used for roofs.

This area is relatively unknown to North Americans or even to most Europeans. The landscape is perfect for an offbeat adventure.

WHERE TO STAY & DINE

Weingut-Weingasthof Rosenhof. Florianigasse 1, A-7142 Illmitz. ☎ **02175/2232.** Fax 02175/22324. www.rosenhof.cc. E-mail: illmitz@rosenhof.cc. 15 units. 1,540–1,880AS ($103.20–$125.95) double. Rates include breakfast. No credit cards. Closed Nov–Easter. Free parking.

A block from the main highway running through the center of town, this charming baroque hotel has an arched gateway in its gold-and-white facade and a rose-laden courtyard filled with arbors. A tile-roofed building, capped with platforms for storks' nests, contains cozy bedrooms, which are maintained in mint condition. Rooms are a bit small, but the beds are good, and the bathrooms have hair dryers, but not a lot of extra room.

In an older section you'll find a wine restaurant whose star attraction is the recent vintage produced by the Haider family's wine presses. Many of your fellow diners live in the neighborhood. Hungarian and Burgenland specialties might include dishes as exotic, for example, as marinated wild boar with walnuts. Local fish, such as carp, are available, including the meaty zander from the Danube. In the autumn, the inn serves *Traubensaft* from freshly harvested grapes—delectable grape juice consumed before it ferments. In the evening, musicians fill the air with Gypsy music. Meals are served daily from 11am to 3pm and 5pm to midnight, costing 100 to 190AS ($6.70 to $12.75).

PODERSDORF

Podersdorf am See is one of the best places for swimming in the mysterious lake, as its shoreline is relatively free of reeds. As a result, the little town has become a modest summer resort. The parish church in the village is from the late 18th century. You'll see many storks nesting atop chimneys, and some of the cottages have thatched roofs. The Viennese like to drive out here on a summer Sunday to go for a swim and to purchase wine from the local vintners.

ESSENTIALS

GETTING THERE   Podersdorf lies 9 miles (14.49) south of the major center along the lake, Neusiedl am See (see box above). It's most often visited by car, although **buses** run throughout the day from Eisenstadt, going via Neusiedl am See. **Motorists** leaving Eisenstadt can head northeast along Route 50, via Purbach, cutting southeast at the junction with Route 51, driving through Neusiedl am See before cutting south along the lake to Podersdorf.

VISITOR INFORMATION   A small **tourist office** operates during summers only in Pordersdorf at Hauptstrasse 2 (☎ **02177/2227**). Open Monday to Friday from 8am to noon and 1 to 4pm.

WHERE TO STAY

Gasthof Seewirt. Strandplatz 1, A-7141 Podersdorf. ☎ **02177/2415.** Fax 02177/246530. 16 units. TV TEL. 980–1,240AS ($65.65–$83.10) double. Rates include breakfast. No credit cards. Closed Dec 1–Feb 15. Free parking.

Built in 1924, then gutted and renovated in 1979, this hotel sits at the edge of the lake, a short walk from the expanses of marshland. It charges the same prices and shares the same owners as the roughly equivalent but newer Haus Attila (see below). Bedrooms are clean, comfortable, and utilitarian, with duvet-covered comfortable beds. Bathrooms are a bit cramped but spotless. Public rooms include one of the best restaurants at the resort (see "Where to Dine" below). There's a sauna on the premises and touches of personalized charm from the hardworking, English-speaking owners.

Haus Attila. Strandplatz 8, A-7141 Podersdorf. ☎ **02177/2415.** Fax 02177/246530. 36 units. 980–1,240AS ($65.65–$83.10) double. Rates include breakfast. No credit cards. Free parking.

Newer and more recently renovated than its sibling, the Seewirt, this hotel was built in 1975, and renovated and enlarged in 1992. The light-grained balconies are partially shielded from public scrutiny by a row of trees, and many overlook the lake. Each of the bedrooms is clean, comfortable, and filled with durable, utilitarian furniture. The bathrooms are tidily maintained but rather tiny.

Seehotel Herlinde. Strandplatz 7, A-7141 Podersdorf. ☎ **02177/2273.** Fax 02177/2420. 40 units. MINIBAR TV TEL. 1,130–1,330AS ($75.70–$89.10) double. Rates include breakfast and lunch. No credit cards. Free parking.

An excellent two-star choice, this holiday hotel is on the beach of Lake Neusiedl away from the main highway. All the functionally furnished bedrooms have their own balconies; the best ones have views of the lake. Bathrooms are small and lack counter space, but are well maintained by daily maid service. Food and wine are plentiful, the latter often enjoyed on a 200-seat terrace.

WHERE TO DINE

Gasthof Seewirt Café Restaurant. Strandplatz 1. ☎ **02177/2415.** Main courses 130–185AS ($8.70–$12.40). MC, V. Daily 9am–9pm. Closed Dec 1–Feb 15. Closed Mon–Tues Feb 16–Apr 30 and from Sept 15–Nov 30. BURGENLANDER/INTERNATIONAL.

This likable and unpretentious restaurant offers bountiful meals served by formally dressed waiters who are knowledgeable about the local cuisine. The Karner family, well-known vintners whose excellent Rieslings, red and white *pinots*, and *weisserburgundens* are available for consumption, are proud of their long-established traditions and a local cuisine that in some ways resembles that of neighboring Hungary. A specialty of the house is *palatschinken marmaladen,* tender roast beef glazed with apricot jam; and a dessert called *Somloer Nockerl,* vanilla pudding, whipped cream, raisins, and nuts encased in a biscuit shell. The goulash soup is very similar to that served across the Hungarian border. Other dishes include baked Danube zander, veal cordon-bleu, a succulent version of Wiener schnitzel, and eel.

7 Forchtenstein

You could easily pass through this town without taking much notice. It resembles so many others along the way. However, Forchtenstein is home to one of the most famous of the Esterházy castles, reason enough to stop over.

ESSENTIALS

GETTING THERE   Forchtenstein is 44 miles (70.84 km) south of Vienna. From Eisenstadt, **motorists** take Route S31 southwest to Mattersburg, then follow the signs along a very minor road southwest to Forchtenstein. Three **buses** per day run from Vienna's bus station to Forchtenstein.

VISITOR INFORMATION   In lieu of a tourist office, information about the area is provided by the **town council** in the mayor's office at Hauptstrasse 54 (☎ **02626/ 63467**).

SEEING THE SIGHTS

Visitors come here chiefly to visit **Burg Forchtenstein** (Forchtenstein Castle), Burgplatz 1 (☎ **02626/81212**), 9 miles southeast of Wiener Neustadt in Lower Austria. The castle was constructed on a rocky base by order of the counts of Mattersdorf in the 13th century. The Esterházy family had it greatly expanded around 1636.

The castle saw action in the Turkish sieges of Austria, both in 1529 and in 1683. A museum since 1815, the castle holds the Prince Esterházy collections, which consist of family memorabilia, a portrait gallery, large battle paintings, historical banners, and Turkish war booty and hunting arms. It's the largest private collection of historical arms in Austria. Legend has it that Turkish prisoners carved out the castle cistern more than 450 feet deep. From a belvedere here you can see as far as the Great Plain of Hungary.

Admission is 70AS ($4.70) for adults and 40AS ($2.70) for children, and the castle is open April to October, daily from 9am to 5pm. From November to March, they offer tours only when requested in advance. A guide shows you through.

WHERE TO STAY

Gasthof Sauerzapf. Rosalienstrasse 39, A-7212 Forchtenstein. ☎ and fax **02626/81217**. 11 units. 650–690AS ($43.55–$46.25) double. Rates include breakfast. No credit cards. Closed Wed. Free parking.

A long, grangelike building, this hotel has two stories of weathered stucco, renovated windows, and a roofline that's red on one side and black on the other. The updated, immaculate interior is cozy and appealing, if simple. Anna Daskalakis-Sauerzapf, the owner, rents modestly furnished rooms that are reasonably nice for the price— comfortable beds, just adequate bathrooms, but an inviting place, nonetheless. The restaurant serves good regional food and a variety of local wines.

Gasthof Wutzlhofer. Rosalia 12, A-7212 Forchtenstein. ☎ **02626/81253**. 9 units. 800–1,100AS ($53.60–$73.70) double. Rates include breakfast. No credit cards. Closed Mar. Free parking.

Built in the 1640s as a private house, but greatly enlarged and improved over the years, this place became a hotel in 1955. The view from the rooms of this family-run guesthouse encompasses the whole valley and many square miles of forested hills. Don't expect luxury or frills here, but you do get good comfort, with duvet-covered beds, firm mattresses, and well-kept but small private bathrooms. Herbert Wutzlhofer, the owner, offers one of the bargains of the area—good food and comfort.

The hotel's restaurant, which attracts a lot of locals, has a deserved reputation for hearty cuisine. Unfortunately, it closes with the hotel in winter. Main courses cost 110 to 150AS ($7.35 to $10.05).

WHERE TO DINE

Reisner. Haupstrasse 141. ☎ **02626/63139.** Reservations recommended. Main courses 150–260AS ($10.05–$17.40); 5-course fixed-price menu 520AS ($34.85), 4-course fixed-price menu 430AS ($28.80), 3-course fixed-price menu 240AS ($16.10). No credit cards. Fri–Tues 11:30am–2:30pm and 6–10pm. Closed 3 weeks in Feb. AUSTRIAN.

This restaurant, the best in the area, has expanded over the years from its original century-old core. Well managed, it features the wines and cuisine of Burgenland. The main dining room is perfectly acceptable, but our favorite area is the cozy, rustic Stüberl, which the locals prefer as well. Besides the especially good steaks, you might enjoy trout fillet served with a savory ragoût of tomatoes, zucchini, potatoes, and basil. The five-course fixed-price menu is a gargantuan meal.

Appendix A:
Vienna in Depth

As Vienna moves into a new millennium, it is sometimes good to look back at its rich history—classical, culinary, and historical—to appreciate its present more deeply. The royal seat of the Habsburgs for 600 years, Vienna has always stood out as a center of art and music, as well as architecture.

1 Vienna Today

Now into the 21st century, Vienna is no longer the sleepy "backwater capital" that it was under Allied occupation in the 1940s. Once more, the city is at the "crossroads of Europe." Vienna is a major European power broker, a position it hasn't enjoyed since the collapse of the Austro-Hungarian Empire.

But all is not rosy, at least politically. Austria's flirtation with right-wingers has led to some of the most notorious international headlines for the country since the war. In February 2000, the newly formed governing coalition included the rightist Freedom Party of Jörg Haider.

European Union governments reacted by freezing relations with Austria, and the United States withdrew its ambassador, as did Israel. The EU announced a series of punishing sanctions against Austria.

Austria is dependent on the $14 billion it earns from world tourism. Even though Haider resigned as head of the Freedom Party, a pall remains, and tourism declined in 2000. Famous guests, including Catherine Deneuve and the president of Portugal, refused to attend the Vienna Opera Ball in 2000.

"There is disruption," one official in Vienna admitted, "but not to the extent we at first feared."

Travel officials in Vienna have quickly responded with goodwill tours, plus letters to the world's major travel agencies, assuring them that Vienna remains a hospitable city to visit. On its Web site, Austria goes so far as to admit that it is "quite aware that our country carries the burden of a deplorable past" and understands international concern over the makeup of the new government.

Politics aside, one reason for the slight downward drift in tourism is Vienna's daunting prices. As a cafe owner told us, "We must change our attitudes from complacency and haughtiness to service with a smile. We're going to have to not only improve service but drop prices to bring the world back to our door."

Environmental awareness is also on the rise, especially among the younger generation, who feel that they live in one of the most beautiful countries on earth and need to preserve it. Recycling is more evident in Vienna than in any other European capital; in fact, recycling bins are commonplace on the city's streets, and the Viennese are often seen sorting their paper, plastic, and tin cans.

In 1998, continuing the effort to lay the past to rest, Austrian officials agreed to return to their rightful owners art confiscated by the Nazis. At the turn of the millennium, this effort has continued. The Austrian minister of culture, Elisabeth Gehrer, said she wanted to correct what she termed "immoral decisions" made at the end of World War II. This bold move has sent reverberations throughout the museum world of Europe and the United States.

Visitors today will find a newer and brighter Vienna, a city with more *joie de vivre* than it's had since before World War II. It's still the city where the "music never stops." Much of the empire's glory and grandeur remain—its treasures now stock the museums, its palaces are open to visitors—in spite of two world wars. Vienna has been called an "architectural waltz"—baroque buildings, marble statues, lovely old squares, grand palaces, famous concert halls are all still here, as if the empire were still flourishing.

Wolfgang Seipel, who waits tables in a local cafe, told us, "We have our guilt, the famous Viennese schizophrenia. We've condoned atrocities, and there have been some embarrassing Nazi revelations. If Freud were still with us, I'm sure he'd wear out a couch every month. But in spite of it all, Vienna still knows how to show you a hell of a good time."

2 History 101

Vienna's history has been heavily influenced by its position astride the Danube, midway between the trade routes linking the prosperous ports of northern Germany with Italy. Its location at the crossroads of three great European cultures (Slavic, Teutonic, and Roman/Italian) transformed the settlement into a melting pot and, more often than not, a battlefield, even in prehistoric times.

EARLY TIMES The 1906 discovery of the Venus of Willendorf, a Stone Age fertility figurine, in the Danube Valley showed that the region around Vienna was inhabited long before recorded history. It's known that around 1000 B.C., the mysterious Indo-European Illyrians established a high-level barbarian civilization around Vienna. After them came the Celts, who migrated eastward from Gaul around 400 B.C. They arrived in time to greet and resist the Romans, who began carving inroads into what is now known as Austria.

Around A.D. 10, the Romans chose the site of modern-day Vienna for a fortified military camp, Vindobona. This strategic outpost is well documented—its location is bordered today by Vienna's Rotenturmstrasse, St. Rupert's Church,

Dateline

- **23,000 B.C.** Venus of Willendorf, a representative of a Danubian fertility goddess, crafted near Vienna.
- **1000 B.C.** Illyrian tribes establish a society near Vienna.
- **400 B.C.** Vendi tribes migrate from Gaul eastward to regions around Vienna.
- **100 B.C.** Romans make military inroads into southern Austria.
- **A.D. 10** Vindobona (Vienna) established as a frontier outpost of the Roman Empire. Within 300 years, it's a thriving trading post.
- **400** Vindobona burnt and rebuilt, but the event marks the gradual withdrawal of the Romans from Austria.
- **500** Vienna overrun by Lombards.
- **630** Vienna taken by the Avars.

continues

- **803** Charlemagne conquers the Danube Valley and site of Vienna, labeling what's now Austria as "Ostmark."
- **814** Death of Charlemagne signals dissolution of his empire.
- **881** First documented reference to Vienna ("Wenia").
- **955** Charlemagne's heir, Otto I, reconquers Ostmark.
- **962** Otto I anointed as the first official Holy Roman Emperor by the Pope.
- **976** Leopold von Babenburg, first of his dynasty, rises to power in the Danube Valley.
- **996** Austria is referred to for the first time with a derivation (Ostarrichi) of its modern name.
- **1030** Vienna, after Cologne, is the largest town north of the Alps.
- **1147** A Romanesque predecessor of St. Stephan's Cathedral is consecrated as the religious centerpiece of Vienna.
- **1192** English king Richard the Lion-Hearted is arrested and held hostage by the Viennese. His ransom pays for construction of the city's walls, completed in 1200.
- **1221** City charter granted to Vienna, with trading privileges.
- **1246** Last of the Baben- burgs, Friedrich the Warlike, dies in battle. He's succeeded by the brief reign of Bohemian king Ottokar II.
- **1278** Ottokar II is killed at Battle of Marchfeld. Rudolf II of Habsburg begins one of the longest dynastic rules in European history.
- **1335 and 1363** Habsburgs add Carinthia and the Tyrol to Austrian territory.
- **1433** Central spire of St. Stephan's completed.
- **1453** Friedrich II elected as Holy Roman Emperor and rules from Vienna.

continues

the Graben, and Tiefer Graben. Vindobona marked the northeastern border of the Roman Empire, and it functioned as a buffer zone between warring Roman, Germanic, and Slavic camps.

BABENBURGS & BOHEMIANS   In 803, the Frankish emperor Charlemagne swept through the Danube Valley establishing a new territory called *Ostmark* (The Eastern March). When Charlemagne died in 814 and his once-mighty empire disintegrated, Vindobona struggled to survive. The earliest known reference to the site by the name we know today (*Wenia*) appeared in a proclamation of the archbishop of Salzburg in 881.

In 976, Leopold von Babenburg established control over Austria, the beginning of a rule that lasted for 3 centuries. Commerce thrived under the Babenburgs, and Vienna grew into one of the largest towns north of the Alps. By the end of the 10th century, Ostmark had become *Ostarrichi*, which later changed into *Österreich* (Austria).

Toward the end of the 12th century, Vienna underwent an expansion that would shape its development for centuries to come. In 1200, Vienna's ring of city walls was completed, financed by the ransom paid by the English to retrieve their king, Richard *Coeur de Lion*, who had been seized on Austrian soil in 1192. A city charter was granted to Vienna in 1221, complete with trading privileges that encouraged the town's further economic development.

In 1246, when the last of the Babenburgs, Friedrich II, died without an heir, the door was left wide open for a struggle between the Bohemian, Hungarian, and German princes as to who would control Austria. The Bohemian king Ottokar II stepped into the vacuum. However, Ottokar, who controlled an empire that extended from the Adriatic Sea to Slovakia, refused to swear an oath of fealty to the newly elected emperor, Rudolf I of Habsburg, and the opposing armies joined in one of Vienna's most pivotal battles, the Battle of Marchfeld, in 1278. Though Ottokar's administration was short-lived, he is credited with the construction of the earliest version of Vienna's Hofburg.

THE HABSBURG DYNASTY   Under Rudolph of Habsburg a powerful European dynasty was launched, one of the longest lived in history. The Habsburg grip on much of central Europe would last until the end of World War I in 1918. During the next two centuries a series of annexations and consolidations of power brought both Carinthia (1335) and the Tyrol (1363) under Habsburg control.

Many of these Habsburg rulers are long-forgotten figures in history, including a string of Rudolfs, although Rudolf IV (1339-65), known as "The Founder," laid the cornerstone of what was later consecrated as St. Stephan's Cathedral. He also founded the University of Vienna as a competitive response to the university in neighboring Prague. In 1433 the spire of St. Stephan's in Vienna was completed into the form visitors see today.

A turning point in the dynasty came in 1453 when Friedrich II was elected Holy Roman Emperor and ruled from a power base in Vienna. By 1469 Vienna had been elevated to a bishopric, so the city had both wide ranging secular and religious authority.

Friedrich's power was not always steady, as he lost control of both Bohemia and Hungary, each of which elected national kings. After many years of precarious rule, he was driven from Vienna in 1485 by the Hungarian king, Matthias Corvinus, who ruled for a 5-year period from Vienna's Hofburg.

In 1490, Corvinus died and civil war broke out in Hungary. Maximilian I (1459-1519) Friedrich's son, took advantage of the civil raging in Hungary to intervene and regain control of much of the territory his father had lost.

The Habsburgs did not always conquer territory. Sometimes they succeeded through politically expedient marriages, a series of which brought Spain, Burgundy, and the Netherlands into their empire. In 1496, 4 years after Spanish colonization of the New World, a Habsburg, Phillip the Fair, married the Spanish infanta (heiress), a union that produced Charles I (Carlos I), who became ruler of Spain and its New World holdings in 1516. Three years later he was crowned Holy Roman Emperor as Charles V. Charles ceded control of Austria to his Vienna-based younger brother, Ferdinand, in 1521. Ferdinand later married Anna Jagiello, heiress to Hungary and Bohemia, adding those countries into the growing empire.

In 1526, discontent in Vienna broke into civil war. Ferdinand responded with brutal repression and a new city charter that placed the city directly under Habsburg control.

PLAGUES & TURKISH INVASIONS

Unfortunately, Vienna's "sea of troubles" had

- **1469** Vienna elevated to a bishopric.
- **1485–90** Hungarian king Matthias Corvinus occupies Vienna's Hofburg for a 5-year domination.
- **1490** Maximilian I recaptures Hungary and lost dominions.
- **1496** A Habsburg son marries the Infanta of Spain, an act that eventually places a Habsburg in control of vast territories in the New World.
- **1519** Charles I, Habsburg ruler of Spain, is elected Holy Roman Emperor as Charles V.
- **1521** Charles V cedes Vienna and the central European portion of his holdings to his brother for more effective rule.
- **1526** Rebellion in Vienna leads to brutal repression by the Habsburgs.
- **1529** The first Turkish siege. Half of Vienna is destroyed in a fire.
- **1533** Vienna declared the official Habsburg capital.
- **1556** Charles V cedes his position as Holy Roman Emperor to his brother Ferdinand, the Austrian king.
- **1560** Strengthening of Vienna's city walls.
- **1571** Ferdinand grants religious freedom to all Austrians. Before long, 80% of Austrians have converted to Protestantism.
- **1572** Establishment of the Spanish Riding School.
- **1576** A reconversion to Catholicism of all Austrians begins. Beginning of the Counter-Reformation.
- **1600–1650** Hundreds of Catholic monks, priests, and nuns establish bases in Vienna as a means of encouraging the reconversion and strengthening the Habsburg role in the Counter-Reformation.

continues

- **1618–48** Thirty Years' War almost paralyzes Vienna.
- **1679** In the worst year of the plague, 75,000 to 150,000 Viennese die.
- **1683** Turks besiege Vienna but are routed by the armies of Lorraine and Poland.
- **1699** Turks evacuate strongholds in Hungary, ending threat to Europe.
- **1700** Death of the last of the Spanish Habsburgs, followed a year later by the War of the Spanish Succession.
- **1740** Maria Theresa ascends the Austrian throne after initial tremors from the War of the Austrian Succession (1740–48).
- **1769** Schönbrunn Palace completed.
- **1770** Relations are cemented between Austria and France with the marriage of a Habsburg princess (Marie Antoinette) to Louis XVI of France.
- **1780** Death of Maria Theresa, and accession to power of her liberal son, Joseph II.
- **1789** Revolution in France leads to the beheading of Marie Antoinette.
- **1805 and 1809** Vienna is occupied twice by armies of Napoléon.
- **1810** Marriage of Napoléon to Habsburg archduchess Marie-Louise.
- **1811** Viennese treasury is bankrupted by military spending.
- **1814–15** Congress of Vienna rearranges the map of Europe following the defeat of Napoléon.
- **1832** First steamship company organized to ply the Danube.
- **1837** Austria's first railway line.
- **1815–48** Vienna's Biedermeier period, supervised by

continues

really just begun. In 1529, half of the city was destroyed by fire. Also during that year, Turkish armies laid siege to the city for 18 anxious days. When the Turks withdrew, they left Vienna's outer suburbs in smoldering ruins but never breached the inner walls. Partly as a gesture of solidarity, Ferdinand I declared Vienna the site of his official capital in 1533.

In the 16th century, the whole of Europe was shaken by the Protestant Reformation. In the second half of the century, under the tolerant Maximilian II, Vienna was almost 80% Protestant and even had a Lutheran mayor. However, Ferdinand II was rigorous in his suppression of Protestantism, and returned Vienna to Catholicism. By the first half of the 17th century, Vienna was a bastion of the Counter-Reformation.

Incursions into the Balkans by Ottoman Turks continued to upset the balance of power in Central Europe. During the same period, there were outbreaks of the Black Death, which reached their peak in 1679, when between 75,000 and 150,000 Viennese died. Leopold I commemorated the city's deliverance from the plague with the famous Pestaule column. It stands today on one of Vienna's main avenues, the Graben.

The final defeat of the Turks and the end of the Turkish menace came in September 1683. Along with a decline in plague-related deaths, this victory revitalized the city.

MARIA THERESA & POLITICAL REFORM Freed from military threat, the city developed under Charles VI (1711–40) and his daughter, Maria Theresa, into a "mecca of the arts." Architects like Johann Bernhard Fischer von Erlach and Johann Lukas von Hildebrandt designed lavish buildings, and composers and musicians flooded into the city.

In 1700, Charles II, last of the Spanish Habsburgs, died without an heir, signaling the final gasp of Habsburg control in Spain. Fearful of a similar fate, Austrian emperor Charles VI penned the Pragmatic Sanction, which ensured that his daughter, Maria Theresa, would follow him. Accordingly, Maria Theresa ascended to power in 1740 at the age of 23, and retained her post for 40 years. The only glitch was the War of the Austrian Succession (1740–48), which contested her coronation.

Austria entered into a golden age of the baroque. During Maria Theresa's reign, the population of Vienna almost doubled, from 88,000 to 175,000. Her most visible architectural legacies include sections of Vienna's Hofburg and her preferred residence, Schönbrunn Palace, completed in 1769. Modern reforms were implemented in the National Army, the economy, the civil service, and in education.

Maria Theresa was succeeded by her son, Joseph II, an enlightened and liberal monarch who eschewed elaborate ritual, introduced many reforms—especially in the church—made himself available to the people, and issued an "Edict of Tolerance."

NAPOLÉON & THE CONGRESS OF VIENNA
The 19th century had a turbulent start. Napoléon's empire building wreaked havoc on Vienna's political landscape. His incursions onto Habsburg territories began in 1803 and culminated in the French occupation of Vienna in 1805 and 1809. Napoléon dissolved the Holy Roman Empire and ordered the new Austrian emperor, Franz I, to abdicate his position as Holy Roman Emperor. The Viennese treasury fell bankrupt in 1811, causing a collapse of Austria's monetary system.

In one of the 19th century's more bizarre marriages, Napoléon married the Habsburg archduchess Marie-Louise in 1810. His days of success were numbered, however, and he was finally defeated in 1814.

METTERNICH
Organized to pick up the pieces and to redefine national borders after Napoléon's defeat, the pivotal Congress of Vienna (1814–15) was attended by representatives of all Europe's major powers. The Congress was a showcase for the brilliant diplomacy and intrigue of Austria's foreign minister, Klemens von Metternich, who restored Austria's pride and influence within a redefined confederation of German-speaking states.

Metternich's dominance of Austria between 1815 and 1848 ushered in another golden age. The Biedermeier period was distinguished by the increased prosperity of the middle class. Virtually kept out of politics, the bourgeoisie concentrated on culture. They built villas and the first big apartment houses and encouraged painting, music, and literature.

Advancing technology changed the skyline of Vienna as the 19th century progressed. The first of many steamship companies to navigate the Danube was established in 1832, and Austria's first railway line (linking the provinces to Vienna) opened in 1837.

- Metternich, marks the triumph of the bourgeoisie.
- **1848** Violent revolution in Vienna ousts Metternich, threatens the collapse of Austrian society, and ushers 18-year-old Franz Joseph I into power.
- **1850** Vienna's population reaches 431,000.
- **1859** Austria loses control of its Italian provinces, including Venice and Milan.
- **1862** Flooding on the Danube leads to a reconfiguration of its banks to a channel within Vienna's suburbs.
- **1867** Hungary and Austria are merged as the Austro-Hungarian Empire, headed by the emperor, Franz Joseph I.
- **1869** Completion of Vienna's State Opera House.
- **1873** Vienna World's Fair.
- **1889** Controversial death of Crown Prince Rudolf at Mayerling.
- **1890–1900** Vienna's outer suburbs are incorporated into the city as Districts 11 to 20.
- **1914** Assassination of the heir to the Habsburg Empire, Archduke Ferdinand, sparks World War I.
- **1916** Death of Franz Joseph, who is succeeded by Charles I, last of the Habsburg monarchs.
- **1918** End of World War I, defeat of Austria, abdication of Charles I, and the radical dismantling of the Austro-Hungarian Empire.
- **1919** Liberalization of Austrian voting laws enacts monumental changes in the social structure of Vienna. Beginning of "Red Vienna" period; the city swings radically to the left.
- **1927** Violent discord rocks Vienna.
- **1929** Worldwide economic depression.

continues

- **1933** Austria's authoritarian chancellor, Dollfuss, outlaws the Austrian Nazi party.
- **1934** Dollfuss assassinated by Nazis.
- **1938** German Nazi troops complete an amicable invasion of Austria that leads to the union of the two nations (Anschluss) through World War II.
- **1943–45** Massive bombings by Allied forces leave most public monuments in ruins.
- **1945** Defeat of Germany and Austria by Allied forces. Vienna is "liberated" by Soviet troops on April 11. On April 27, Austria redefined as a country separate from Germany, and divided, like Germany, into four zones of occupation. Vienna also subdivided into four separate zones.
- **1955** Evacuation of Austria by Allied forces; Vienna capital of a neutral Austria.
- **1961** Summit meeting in Vienna between President Kennedy and Soviet Chairman Khrushchev.
- **1979** Summit meeting in Vienna between Brezhnev and Carter.
- **1986** Investigations into the wartime activities of Austrian chancellor Kurt Waldheim profoundly embarrasses Austria.
- **1989** The last heiress to the Habsburg dynasty, Empress Zita of Bourbon-Parma, in exile since 1919, dies and is buried in one of the most elaborate funerals in Viennese history.
- **1995** Austria, along with Sweden and Finland, admitted into the European Union.
- **1997** After 10 years, longtime chancellor Franz Vranitzky steps down, turning over leadership of Social Democratic Party.

continues

In the meantime, despite his brilliance as an international diplomat, Metternich's domestic policies almost guaranteed civil unrest. They led to the eradication of civil rights, the postwar imposition of a police state, and the creation of an economic climate that favored industrialization at the expense of wages and worker's rights.

In March 1848, events exploded not only in Vienna and Hungary but across most of Europe. Metternich was ousted from power and fled the city (some of his not-so-lucky colleagues were lynched). In response to the threat of revolutionary chaos, the Austrian army imposed a new version of absolute autocracy.

Emperor Franz Joseph I, the last scion of the Habsburg dynasty, was the beneficiary of the restored order. At the age of 18, he began his autocratic 68-year reign in 1848.

THE METROPOLIS OF EUROPE Franz Joseph I's austere comportment created the perfect foil for an explosion of artistic development in the newly revitalized city. A major accomplishment was the vast Ringstrasse, the boulevard that encircles Vienna's 1st District. Franz Joseph ordered it built over the remnants of the old city walls, and the construction of the "Ringstrassenzone" became a work of homogeneous civic architecture unparalleled throughout Europe.

Meanwhile, advanced technology helped launch Vienna into the Industrial Age, transforming the city into a glittering showcase. The empire's vast resources were used to keep Vienna's theaters, coffeehouses, concert halls, palaces, and homes well lit, cleaned, and maintained. The water supply was improved, and the Danube regulated. A new town hall was built, and a new park, the Stadtpark, was opened.

The foundations of the Habsburg monarchy were shaken again in 1889 by the mysterious deaths of 30-year-old Crown Prince Rudolf, an outspoken and not particularly stable liberal, and his 18-year-old mistress, at the royal hunting lodge of Mayerling. The possibility that they were murdered, and the insistence of his family that every shred of evidence associated with the case be destroyed, led to lurid speculation. It became clear that all was not well within the Austro-Hungarian Empire.

In 1890, many of the city's outer suburbs (Districts 11 through 19) were incorporated into the City of Vienna, and in 1900 a final, 20th district, Brigittenau, was also added. In

1906 women received the right to vote. By 1910, Vienna, with a population of 2 million, was the fourth-largest city in Europe, after London, Paris, and Berlin.

- 1998 Austria decides to return art that Nazis plundered (much of it in museums).
- 1999–2000 Right-wing Freedom Party stirs worldwide protests against Austria.

WORLD WAR I & THE VERSAILLES TREATY   During the *belle époque,* Europe sat on a powder keg of frustrated socialist platforms, national alliances, and conflicting colonial ambitions. The Austro-Hungarian Empire was linked by the Triple Alliance to both Germany and Italy. Europe leapt headfirst into armed conflict when Franz Joseph's nephew and designated heir, the Archduke Ferdinand, was shot to death by a Serbian terrorist as Ferdinand and his wife, Sophie, rode through Sarajevo on June 28, 1914. Within 30 days, the Austro-Hungarian Empire declared war on Serbia, signaling the outbreak of World War I. An embittered Franz Joseph died in 1916, midway through the conflict, and he was succeeded by the last of the Habsburg monarchs, Charles I, who was forced to abdicate in 1918 as part of the peace treaty.

The punitive peace treaty concluded at Versailles broke up the vast Austro-Hungarian territories into the nations of Hungary, Poland, Yugoslavia, and Czechoslovakia. The new Austria would adhere to the boundaries of Charlemagne's *Ostmark.*

This overnight collapse of the empire caused profound dislocations of populations and trade patterns. Some of the new nations refused to deliver raw materials to Vienna's factories or, in some cases, food to Vienna's markets. Coupled with the punitive effects of the Versailles treaty and the massive loss of manpower and resources during the war, this quickly led Vienna to the brink of starvation. Despite staggering odds, the new government—assisted by a massive loan in 1922 from the League of Nations—managed to stabilize the currency while Austrian industrialists hammered out new sources of raw materials.

In 1919, voting laws in Vienna were liberalized, and Vienna immediately took an abrupt turn toward socialism, a period known as "Red Vienna."

THE ANSCHLUSS   In 1934, social tensions broke out into civil war, Europe's first confrontation between fascism and democracy. Austrian nationalism under the authoritarian chancellor, Engelbert Dollfuss, put an end to progressive policies. Vienna's liberal city council was dissolved, along with all social programs. Later that year, Austrian Nazis assassinated Dollfuss, and Nazis were included in the resultant coalition government. In 1938, Austria united with Nazi Germany (the Anschluss). Hitler returned triumphantly to Vienna, several decades after he lived there as an impoverished and embittered artist. In a national referendum, 99.75% of Austrians voted their support.

WORLD WAR II & ITS AFTERMATH   The rise of Austria's Nazis devastated Vienna's academic and artistic communities. Many of their members, including Sigmund Freud, fled to safety elsewhere. About 60,000 Austrian Jews were sent to concentration camps, and only an estimated 2,000 managed to survive; Austria's homosexual and gypsy populations were similarly decimated.

Beginning in 1943, Allied bombing raids demolished vast neighborhoods of the city, damaging virtually every public building of any stature. The city's most prominent landmark, St. Stephan's Cathedral, suffered a roof collapse and fires in both towers. The city's death rate was one of the highest in Europe. For the Viennese, at least, the war ended abruptly on April 11, 1945, when Russian troops moved into the city from bases in Hungary.

During a confused interim that lasted a decade, Austria was divided into four zones of occupation, each controlled by one of the four Allies (the United

Der Dritte Mann

The 1949 film *The Third Man,* starring Joseph Cotten, Orson Welles, and Alida Valli, remains one of the best records of a postwar Vienna in ruins. Graham Greene, who wrote the screenplay (published by Penguin Books), found a "city of undignified ruins which turned February into great glaciers of snow and ice." The Danube was a "gray, flat muddy river," and the Russian zone, where the Prater lay, "smashed and desolate and full of weeds."

In the closing weeks of World War II, the city suffered major aerial bombardment. In the waning summer of 1944, Vienna tried to save itself, closing all theaters and public areas. The work week was extended to 60 hours. A dreaded mass recruitment, the *Volksturm* rounded up all males between the ages of 16 and 60 for a final defense. Hitler was in his Berlin bunker when he learned that the city of his youth, Vienna, had fallen to the Allies.

The victors found a wasted city on the verge of starvation. By 1945, Vienna had recorded the highest death rate in Europe. Bombings had destroyed 20% of its buildings, and some 270,000 Viennese were left homeless. The entire roof of St. Stephan's Cathedral had collapsed, as its towers caught fire.

The city was divided into four zones of occupation by the Allies. *The Third Man* immortalized the "four men in a jeep"—that is, four military policemen from the quartet of occupying powers—patrolling the beleaguered city. The black market, on which the events in the film turn, became the way of life in Vienna.

Even today, the Viennese have bitter memories of the occupation, especially by the Soviet Union. A reminder of those dreaded years is found at Schwarzenbergplatz (reached from Karlsplatz by walking along Friedrichstrasse/Lothringerstrasse). Under the Nazis, this square was called Hitlerplatz. Today, a patch of landscaped greenery surrounds a fountain and a statue left by the Russians. The city has been none too happy with this "gift" from its former conquerors. Three times officials have tried to demolish the memorial, but so far Soviet engineering has proven indestructible. Viennese have nicknamed an anonymous Soviet soldier's grave "the Tomb of the Unknown Plunderer."

In May 1955, the Austria State Treaty, signed by the four Allied powers and Austria itself, reestablished full Austrian sovereignty. Why did it take so long? One reason is that the Soviets were seeking heavy reparations from Austria. But as dust settles over history, another possibility arises. Stalin may have planned to stick around in Vienna, as he did in Berlin. After all, a toehold in Vienna would have given the Soviets a deep penetration into the West at the peak of the Cold War. As it was, Vienna became a center of Cold War espionage and spying—real James Bond country.

States, the Soviet Union, Britain, and France). Vienna, deep within the Soviet zone, was also subdivided into four zones, each occupied by one of the victors. Control of the inner city alternated every month between each of the four powers. It was a dark and depressing time in Vienna; rubble was slowly cleared away from bomb sites, but the most glorious public monuments in Europe lay in ashes. Espionage, black market profiteering, and personal betrayals proliferated, poisoning the memories of many older Viennese even today.

POSTWAR TIMES On May 15, 1955, Austria regained its sovereignty as an independent, perpetually neutral nation. As a neutral capital, Vienna became the obvious choice for meetings between Kennedy and Khrushchev (in 1961) and Brezhnev and Carter (1979); many international organizations (including OPEC and the Atomic Energy Authority) established branches or headquarters there.

Once again part of a republic, the Viennese aggressively sought to restore their self-image as cultural barons. Restoring the State Opera house and other grand monuments became a top priority.

However, Vienna's self-image received a blow when scandal surrounded Austria's president, Kurt Waldheim, elected in 1986. Waldheim had been an officer in the Nazi army and had countenanced the deportation of Jews to extermination camps. The United States declared him *persona non grata*. Many Austrians defiantly stood by Waldheim; others were deeply embarrassed. Waldheim did not seek reelection, and in May 1992, Thomas Klestil, a career diplomat, was elected president, supported by the centrist Austrian People's Party.

In 1989, the last heiress to the Habsburg dynasty, Empress Zita of Bourbon-Parma, in exile since 1919, was buried in one of the most lavish and emotional funerals ever held in Vienna. At age 96, the last empress of Austria and queen of Hungary had always been held in some degree of reverence, a symbol of the glorious days of the Austrian empire.

In the spring of 1998, the Austrian government stunned the art world by agreeing to return artworks confiscated from Jews by the Nazis. Many Jewish families, including the Austrian branch of the Rothschilds, fled into exile in 1938. Although they tried to regain their possessions after the war, they were not successful. Austrian journalist Hubertus Czernin wrote, "The art was stolen by the Nazis and stolen a second time by the Austrian government." One museum director claimed Austria had "a specific moral debt," which it was now repaying.

The noble gesture was soon forgotten as uglier news grabbed headlines. In 1999 elections, the Freedom Party won notoriety and 27% of the vote, by denouncing the presence of foreigners in Austria. Echoing Nazi rhetoric, the party blames foreigners for drugs, crime, welfare abuse, and the spread of tuberculosis. The party remains racist and Nazi-admiring in spite of the resignation of its leader, Jörg Haider, its most controversial member.

The party still is a defining force in the current government of Austria. The United States, Israel, and fellow members of the European Union have taken steps to distance themselves from Austria.

3 Exploring Vienna's Architecture

Vienna is best known for the splendor of its baroque and rococo palaces and churches. It also contains a wealth of internationally renowned Gothic and modern architecture.

GOTHIC ARCHITECTURE

Although there are no remains in Vienna of early medieval buildings, a number of Gothic buildings rest on older foundations. During the 1300s, ecclesiastical architecture was based on the *Hallenkirche* (hall church), a model that originated in Germany. These buildings featured interiors that resembled enormous hallways, with nave and aisles of the same height. The earliest example of this style was the choir added in 1295 to an older Romanesque building, the abbey church of Heiligenkreuz, 15 miles west of Vienna.

The most famous building in the Hallenkirche style was the first incarnation of St. Stephan's Cathedral. Later modifications, however, greatly altered the details of its original construction, and today only the foundations, the main portal, and the modestly proportioned western towers remain. Much more dramatic is the cathedral's needle-shaped central spire, completed in 1433, which still soars high above Vienna's skyline. St. Stephan's triple naves, each the same height, are a distinctive feature of Austrian Gothic. Other examples of this construction can be seen in the Minorite Church and the Church of St. Augustine.

During the late 1400s, Gothic architecture retreated from the soaring proportions of the Hallenkirche style and focus turned to more modest buildings with richly decorated interiors. Stone masons added tracery (geometric patterns) and full-rounded or low-relief sculpture to ceilings and walls. Gothic churches continued to be built in Austria until the mid-1500s.

FROM GOTHIC TO BAROQUE

One of the unusual aspects of the Viennese skyline is its relative lack of Renaissance buildings. Vienna was periodically besieged by the Turks from 1529 until the 1680s, forcing city planners to use most of their resources to strengthen the city's fortifications.

Although Vienna itself has no Renaissance examples, Italian influences were present for more than a century before baroque gained a true foothold. Late in the 16th century, many Italian builders settled in the regions of Tyrol, Carinthia, and Styria. In these less threatened regions of Austria, Italian influence produced a number of country churches and civic buildings in the Renaissance style, with open porticoes, balconies, and loggias. The most famous building constructed during this period was the Landhaus (the old city hall) in Graz.

THE FLOWERING OF THE BAROQUE

The 47-year rule of Leopold I (1658–1705) witnessed the beginning of the golden age of Austrian baroque architecture. Italian-born Dominico Martinelli (1650–1718) designed the **Liechtenstein Palace,** built between 1694 and 1706 and inspired by the Renaissance-era Palazzo Farnese in Rome.

Austria soon began to produce its own native-born architects. The architecture of the high baroque fell into the hands of two great Austrian architects, Fischer von Erlach and Lukas von Hildebrandt.

Johann Bernhard Fischer von Erlach (1656–1723) trained with both Bernini and Borromini in Rome. His style was restrained but monumental, drawing richly from the great buildings of antiquity. Fischer von Erlach knew how to transform the Italianate baroque of the south into a style that suited the Viennese. His most notable work is the **Karlskirche,** built in 1713. He also created the original design for Maria Theresa's **Schönbrunn Palace.** He had planned a sort of super-Versailles, but the project turned out to be too costly. Work was started on a modified building, but Maria Theresa chose architect Nikolaus Pacassi to expand it into a summer residence. Only the entrance facade remains of Fischer von Erlach's design. The **Hofbibliothek** (National Library) on Josephsplatz and the **Hofstalungen** are other notable buildings he designed.

Von Erlach was succeeded by another great name in the history of architecture: **Johann Lukas von Hildebrandt** (1668–1745). Von Hildebrant's design for Prince Eugene's **Belvedere Palace**—a series of interlocking cubes with sloping mansard-style roofs—is the culmination of the architectural theories initiated by Fischer von Erlach. Other von Hildebrandt designs in Vienna include the **Schwarzenberg Palace** (converted after World War II into a hotel) and **St. Peter's Church.**

The **rococo style** developed as a more ornate, somewhat fussier progression of the baroque. Gilt stucco, brightly colored frescoes, and interiors that drip with embellishments are its hallmarks. Excellent examples include the **Abbey of Durnstein** (1731–35) and **Melk Abbey,** both in Lower Austria. One of the most powerful proponents of rococo was Maria Theresa, who used its motifs so extensively within Schönbrunn Palace during its 1744 renovation that the school of Austrian rococo is sometimes referred to as "late-baroque Theresian style."

In response to the excesses of rococo, architects eventually turned to classical Greece and Rome for inspiration. The result was a restrained neoclassicism that transformed the skyline of Vienna and lasted well into the 19th century. The dignified austerity of Vienna's **Technical University** is a good example.

ECLECTICISM & VIENNA'S RING

As Austria's wealthy bourgeoisie began to impose their tastes on public architecture, 19th-century building grew more solid and monumental. The neoclassical style remained the preferred choice for government buildings, as evidenced by Vienna's **Mint** and the **Palace of the Provincial Government.**

But the 19th century's most impressive Viennese architectural achievement was the construction of the **Vienna Ring** (1857–91). The medieval walls were demolished, and the Ring was lined with showcase buildings. This was Emperor Franz Joseph's personal project and his greatest achievement. Architects from all of Europe answered the emperor's call, eager to seize the unprecedented opportunity to design a whole city district. Between 1850 and the official opening ceremony in 1879, the Ring's architecture became increasingly eclectic: French neo-Gothic (the Votivkirche), Flemish neo-Gothic (the Rathaus), Greek Revival (Parliament), French Renaissance (Staatsoper), and Tuscan Renaissance (Museum of Applied Arts). Regrettably, some of the Ring's charm is diminished by the volume of traffic circling Old Vienna. Nevertheless, a circumnavigation of the Ring provides a panorama of eclectic yet harmonious building styles.

SECESSIONIST & POLITICAL ARCHITECTURE

By the late 19th century, younger architects were in rebellion against the pomp and formality of older architectural styles. In 1896, young **Otto Wagner** (1841–1918) published a tract called *Moderne Architektur,* which argued for a return to more natural and functional architectural forms. The result was the establishment of **art nouveau** (*Jugendstil,* or, as it applies specifically to Vienna, *Sezessionstil*). The Vienna Secession architects reaped the benefits of the technological advances and the new building materials that became available after the Industrial Revolution. Wagner, designer of Vienna's **Kirche am Steinhof** and the city's **Postsparkasse** (Post Office Savings Bank), became a founding member of the movement.

Joseph Hoffman (1870–1955) and **Adolf Loos** (1870–1933) promoted the use of glass and the newly developed steel alloys and aluminum. In the process they discarded nearly all ornamentation, a rejection that contemporary Vienna found profoundly distasteful and almost shocking. Loos was particularly critical, even hostile, toward the buildings adorning the Ringstrasse. His most controversial design is the **Michaeler Platz Building.** Sometimes referred to as "the Loos House," it was erected on Michaeler Platz in 1908. The streamlined structure was bitterly criticized for its total lack of ornamentation and its similarities to the "gridwork of a sewer." According to gossip, the emperor found it so offensive that he ordered his drivers to avoid the Hofburg entrance on Michaeler Platz altogether.

Architectural philosophies were also affected during the "Red Vienna" period by the socialist reformers' desire to alleviate public housing shortages, a grinding social problem of the years between world wars. The Social Democratic Party began erecting "palaces for the people." Based on cost-effective construction techniques and industrial materials, these buildings are reminiscent of some of the Depression-era WPA projects in the United States, but on a staggering scale. The most obvious example is the **Karl-Marx-Hof** (Heiligenstadterstrasse 82-92, A-1190), which includes 1,600 apartments and stretches out for more than half a mile.

TO THE PRESENT DAY

After World War II, much of Vienna's resources went toward restoring older historic buildings to their prewar grandeur. New buildings were streamlined and functional; much of Vienna today features the same kind of neutral modernism you're likely to find in postwar Berlin or Frankfurt.

Postmodern masters, however, have broken the mold of the 1950s and 1960s. They include the iconoclastic mogul Hans Hollein, designer of the silvery, curved-sided **Haas Haus** (1990) adjacent to St. Stephan's Cathedral. The self-consciously avant-garde **Friedenreich Hundertwasser** is a multicolored, ecologically inspired apartment building at the corner of Löwengasse and Kegelgasse that appears to be randomly stacked.

Lately, Hermann Czech has been stirring architectural excitement, not so much by building new structures as developing daring interiors for boutiques and bistros; examples are the **Kleines Café** (Franziskanerplatz 3) and **Restaurant Salzamt** (Ruprechtsplatz 1).

4 Art Through the Ages

Vienna's location at the crossroads of the Germanic, Mediterranean, and Eastern European worlds contributed to a rich and varied artistic heritage.

EARLY ECCLESIASTICAL ART

Most art in the early medieval period was church art. From the Carolingian period, the only survivals are a handful of **illuminated manuscripts,** now in Vienna's National Library. The most famous is the *Cutbercht Evangeliar* from around 800, a richly illuminated copy of the four gospels.

The Romanesque period reached its peak between A.D. 1000 and 1190. Notable from this time is the *Admont Great Bible,* crafted around 1140, one of the prized treasures of Vienna's National Library. In 1181, the famous goldsmith Nicolas de Verdun produced one of the finest **enamel works** in Europe for the pulpit at Klosterneuberg Abbey. Verdun's 51 small panels, crafted from enamel and gold, depict scenes from the religious tracts of the Augustinians. After a fire in the 1300s, the panels were repositioned onto an altarpiece known as the "Verdun Altar" at Klosterneuberg, where they can be seen today.

THE GOTHIC AGE

The Gothic Age in Austria is better remembered for its architecture than its painting and sculpture. Early Gothic sculpture was influenced by the *Zachbruchiger Stil* (zigzag style), identified by angular and vivid outlines of forms against contrasting backgrounds. The era's greatest surviving sculptures date from around 1320 and include *The Enthroned Madonna of Klosterneuburg* and *The Servant's Madonna,* showcased in Vienna's St. Stephan's Cathedral.

By the late 1300s, Austrian sculpture was strongly influenced by Bohemia. The human form became elongated, exaggerated, and idealized, often set in graceful but unnatural S curves. Wood became increasingly widespread as an artistic medium and was often painted in vivid colors. A superb example of **Gothic sculpture** is *The Servant's Madonna* in St. Stephan's Cathedral. Carved around 1320, it depicts Mary enthroned and holding a standing Christ child.

By the end of the Gothic Age, the artistic vision of Western and Central Europe had merged into a short-lived union known today as **International Gothic.** Especially evident in the illumination of manuscripts, the movement was encouraged by the Catholic Church and partially funded by a group of feudal aristocrats. The finest assemblage of Gothic paintings in Austria is in the Orangery of Belvedere Palace.

FROM THE RENAISSANCE TO THE 18TH CENTURY

During most of the Renaissance, Vienna was too preoccupied fending off invasions, sieges, and plagues to produce the kind of painting and sculpture that flowered in other parts of Europe. As a result, in the 17th and 18th centuries, Vienna struggled to keep up with cities like Salzburg, Munich, and Innsbruck.

Most painting and sculpture during the baroque period was for the enhancement of the grandiose churches and spectacular palaces that sprang up across Vienna. Artists were imported from Italy; an imported artist, **Andrea Pozzo** (1642–1709), produced the masterpiece *The Apotheosis of Hercules* that appears on the ceilings of Vienna's Liechtenstein Palace. Baroque painting emphasized symmetry and unity, and a trompe-l'oeil illusion was used to give extra dimension to a building's sculptural and architectural motifs.

The first noteworthy Austrian-born baroque painter was **Johann Rottmayr** (1654–1730), the preferred decorator of the two most influential architects of the age, von Hildebrandt and Fischer von Erlach. Rottmayr's works adorn some of the ceilings of Vienna's Schönbrunn Palace and Peterskirche. Countless other artists contributed to the Viennese baroque style. Notable are the frescoes of **Daniel Gran** (1694–1754), who decorated the Hofbibliothek. He also has an altarpiece in the Karlskirche.

Vienna, as it emerged from a base of muddy fields into a majestic fantasy of baroque architecture, was captured on the canvas in the landscapes of **Bernardo Bellotto** (1720–80), nephew and pupil of the famous Venetian painter Canaletto. Brought to Vienna at the request of Maria Theresa, Bellotto managed to bathe the city in a flat but clear light of arresting detail and pinpoint accuracy. His paintings today are valued as social and historical as well as artistic documents.

Dutch-born, Sweden-trained **Martin van Meytens** (1695–1770), court painter to Maria Theresa, captured the lavish balls and assemblies of Vienna's aristocracy. His canvases, though awkwardly composed and overburdened with detail, are the best visual record of the Austrian court's balls and receptions. In 1730, van Meytens was appointed director of Vienna's Fine Arts Academy.

Sculptors also made their contribution to the baroque style. **Georg Raphael Donner** (1693–1741) is best known for the remarkable life-size bronzes of the Fountain of Providence in the Neuer Markt. **Balthasar Permoser** (1651–1732) is responsible for the equestrian statues of Prince Eugene of Savoy in the courtyard of the Belvedere Palace. The famous double sarcophagus in the Kapuzinerkirche designed for Maria Theresa and her husband, Francis Stephen, is the masterpiece of **Balthasar Moll** (1717–85).

Equally influential was **Franz Xaver Messerschmidt** (1737–83), the German-trained resident of Vienna who became famous for his portrait busts.

His legacy to us is accurate and evocative representations of Maria Theresa, her son Joseph II, and other luminaries.

THE REVOLT FROM "OFFICIAL ART"

During the early part of the 19th century, Viennese painting was academic, grandiose, and sentimental. "Official art," however, contrasts with the hundreds of folk-art sculptures and paintings produced in and around Vienna during the same era.

In rebellion against "official art," a school of **Romantic Realist** painters emerged, drawing on biblical themes and Austrian folklore. Scenes from popular operas were painted lovingly on the walls of the Vienna State Opera. Landscape painting was influenced by the 17th-century Dutch masters.

Georg Waldmüller (1793–1865), a self-proclaimed enemy of "academic art" and an advocate of realism, created one of the best pictorial descriptions of Viennese Biedermeier society in his *Wiener Zimmer* (1837). More than 120 of his paintings are on display at the Upper Belvedere museum.

Another realist was **Carl Moll** (1861–1945), whose graceful and evocative portrayals of everyday scenes are prized today. **Joseph Engelhart** (1864–1941) was known for his voluptuous renderings of *belle époque* coquettes flirting with Viennese gentlemen.

THE SECESSIONIST MOVEMENT

The Secessionist Movement (*Sezessionstil*) was founded in 1897 by young painters, decorators, and architects from Vienna's Academy of Fine Arts. The name captures their retreat (secession) from the *Künstlerhaus* (Vienna Artists' Association), which they considered pompous, sanctimonious, artificial, mediocre, and mired in the historicism favored by Emperor Franz Joseph. Their artistic statement was similar to that of the art nouveau movement in Paris and the Jugendstil movement in Munich.

The Secessionist headquarters, on the Friedrichstrasse (at the corner of the Opernring) was inaugurated in 1898 as an iconoclastic exhibition space for avant-garde artists. Foremost among the group was **Gustav Klimt** (1862–1918) whose work developed rapidly into a highly personal and radically innovative form of decorative painting based on the sinuous curved line of art nouveau. His masterpieces include a mammoth frieze, 110 feet long, encrusted with gemstones, dedicated to the genius of Beethoven. Executed in 1902, it's one of the artistic focal points of the above-mentioned Secessionist Pavilion. Other pivotal works include *Portrait of Adèle Bloch-Bauer* (1907), an abstract depiction of a prominent Jewish Viennese socialite. Its gilded geometric form is reminiscent of ancient Byzantine art.

THE MODERN AGE

Klimt's talented disciple was **Egon Schiele** (1890–1918). Tormented, overly sensitive, and virtually unknown during his brief lifetime, he is now considered a modernist master whose work can be placed alongside that of van Gogh and Modigliani. His works seem to dissolve the boundaries between humankind and the natural world, granting a kind of anthropomorphic humanity to landscape painting. One of his most disturbing paintings is the tormented *The Family* (1917), originally conceived as decoration for a mausoleum.

Modern sculpture in Vienna is inseparable from the international art trends that have dominated the 20th century. **Fritz Wotruba** (1907–75) introduced a neo-cubist style of sculpture. Many of his sculptural theories were manifested in his "Wotruba Church" (Church of the Most Holy Trinity), erected toward the end of his life in Vienna's outlying 23rd District. Adorned with his sculptures and representative of his architectural theories in general, the building is an important sightseeing and spiritual attraction.

Oscar Kokoschka (1886–1980) was one of Vienna's most important contemporary painters. Kokoschka expressed the frenzied psychological confusion of the years before and after World War II. His portraits of such personalities as the artist Carl Moll are bathed in psychological realism and violent emotion.

5 Musical Vienna

Music is central to Viennese life. From the concertos of Mozart to Johann Strauss's waltzes, from opera to operetta to folk tunes, the Viennese are surrounded by music—and not only in the concert hall and opera house but at the heuriger (wine tavern) as well.

THE CLASSICAL PERIOD

The classical period was a golden age in Viennese musical life. Two of the greatest composers of all time, Mozart and Haydn, worked in Vienna. Maria Theresa herself trilled arias on the stage of the Schlosstheater at Schönbrunn, and she and her children and friends often performed operas and dances.

Classicism's first great manifestation was the development of *Singspiele,* a reform of opera by **Christoph Willibald Ritter von Gluck** (1714–87). Baroque opera had become overburdened with excessive ornamentation, and Gluck introduced a more natural and graceful musical form. In 1762, Maria Theresa presented Vienna with the first performance of Gluck's innovative opera *Orpheus and Eurydice.* It and *Alceste* (1767) are his best-known operas, regularly performed today.

Franz Joseph Haydn (1732–1809) is the creator of the classical sonata, which is the basis of classical chamber music. During his lifetime, Haydn's patrons were the rich and powerful Esterházy family, whom he served as musical director. His output was prodigious. He wrote chamber music, sonatas, operas, and symphonies. His strong faith is in evidence in his oratorios; among the greatest are *The Creation* (1798) and *The Seasons* (1801). He also is the composer of the Austrian national anthem (1797), which he later elaborated in his quartet Opus 76, no. 3.

The most famous composer of the period was **Wolfgang Amadeus Mozart** (1756–91). The prodigy from Salzburg charmed Maria Theresa and her court with his playing when he was only 6 years old. His father, Leopold, exploited his son's talent—"Wolferl" spend his childhood touring all over Europe. Later, he went with his father to Italy, where he absorbed that country's fertile musical traditions. Leaving Salzburg, he settled in Vienna, at first with great success. His influence effected fundamental and widespread changes in the musical life of the capital. But eccentric and extravagant, he was unable to keep patronage or land any lucrative post; he finally received an appointment as chamber composer to the emperor Joseph II at a minimal salary. Despite hard times, Mozart refused the posts offered him in other cities, possibly because in Vienna, he found the best of all musical worlds—the best instrumentalists, the finest opera, the best singers. He composed more than 600 works in practically every musical form known to the time; his greatest compositions are unmatched in beauty and profundity. He died in poverty, buried in a pauper's grave in Vienna, the whereabouts of which are uncertain.

Shall We Waltz?

Dictionaries define it as a form of "round dance," but anyone who has ever succumbed to its magic invariably defines it as pure enjoyment, akin to falling in love—a giddy, romantic spinning associated with long ball gowns, men in formal clothing, and elaborate ballrooms.

Many people think that the Strausses—father and son—actually invented the dance. However, the waltz has roots throughout Europe and began its life in theaters and inns. Fashionable hostesses considered it vulgar. At court, highly stylized dances like the minuet and the gavotte were the rule. The waltz, gaining propriety in the second half of the 18th century, brought a greater naturalism and zest to grand parties with its rhythmic lilt and uninhibited spinning.

A violinist and composer of dance music, Johann Strauss the Elder (1804–49) introduced his famous *Tauberlwalzer* in Vienna in 1826. As a dance musician for court balls, he became indelibly associated with the social glitter of the Austrian court. In the years to follow, his fame grew to such an extent that he began a series of tours (1833–40), which took him to England, where he conducted his music at Queen Victoria's coronation.

His famous son, Johann Strauss the Younger, was "the King of the Waltz." He formed his own dance band and met with instant success. He toured Europe and even went to America, playing his waltzes to enthusiastic audiences. By 1862, he relinquished the leadership of his orchestra to his two brothers and spent the rest of his life writing music. He brought the waltz to such a high degree of technical perfection that eventually he transformed it into a symphonic form in its own right.

The waltz lives on today in his most famous pieces, *The Blue Danube* (1867), *Tales from the Vienna Woods* (1868), *Weiner Blut,* and the *Emperor Waltz.* His genius ushered in the "golden age of operetta." Perhaps the best beloved of his operettas, *Die Fledermaus* (1874), is given a splendid performance every New Year's Eve at the Vienna State Opera. The heritage left by "the Waltz King" forms a vital part of Austria's cultural self-image.

THE ROMANTIC AGE

Franz Schubert (1797–1828), the only one of the great composers actually born in Vienna, was of the Biedermeier era and the most Viennese of musicians. He turned *lieder,* popular folk songs often used with dances, into an art form. He was a master of melodic line, and he created hundreds of songs, chamber music works, and symphonies. At the age of 18, he showed his genius by setting the words of German poet Goethe to music in *Margaret at the Spinning Wheel* and *The Elf King.* His Unfinished Symphony has remained his best-known work, but his great achievement lies in his chamber music and song cycles.

THE 19TH CENTURY

After 1850, Vienna became the world's capital of light music, exporting it to every corner of the globe. The **waltz,** originally developed as a rustic Austrian country dance, was enthusiastically adopted by Viennese society.

Johann Strauss (1804–49), composer of more than 150 waltzes, and his talented and entrepreneurial son, **Johann Strauss the Younger** (1825–99), who developed the art form further, helped spread the stately and graceful rhythms of the waltz across Europe. The younger Strauss also popularized the operetta, the genesis of the Broadway musical.

The tradition of Viennese light opera continued to thrive thanks to the efforts of **Franz von Suppé** (1819–95) and Hungarian-born **Franz Lehár** (1870–1948). Lehár's witty and mildly scandalous *The Merry Widow* (1905) is the most popular and amusing light opera ever written.

Vienna did not lack for important serious music in the late 19th century. **Anton Bruckner** (1824–96) composed nine symphonies and a handful of powerful masses. **Hugo Wolf** (1860–1903), following in Schubert's footsteps, reinvented key elements of the German lieder with his five great song cycles. Most innovative of all was **Gustav Mahler** (1860–1911). A pupil of Bruckner, he expanded the size of the orchestra, often added a chorus and/or vocal soloists, and composed evocative music, much of it set to poetry.

THE NEW VIENNA SCHOOL

Mahler's musical heirs forever altered the world's concepts of harmony and tonality, and introduced what were then shocking concepts of rhythm. **Arnold Schoenberg** (1874–1951) expanded Mahler's style in such atonal works as *Das Buch der Hangenden Garten* (1908) and later developed a 12-tone musical technique referred to as "dodecaphony" (*Suite for Piano*, 1924). By the end of his career, he pioneered what was referred to as "serial music," patterns or series of notes with no key center, shifting from one tonal group to another. **Anton von Webern** (1883–1945) and **Alban Berg** (1885–1935), composer of the brilliant but esoteric opera *Wozzeck,* were pupils of Schoenberg. They adapted his system to their own musical personalities.

Finally, this discussion of Viennese music would not be complete without mention of the vast repertoire of folk songs, Christmas carols, and country dances that have inspired both professional musicians and ordinary folk for generations. The most famous Christmas carol in the world, **"Stille Nacht, Heilige Nacht"** ("Silent Night, Holy Night"), was composed and performed for the first time in Salzburg in 1818 and heard in Vienna for the first time that same year.

6 A Taste of Vienna

It's pointless to argue whether a Viennese dish is of Hungarian, Czech, Austrian, Slovenian, or even Serbian origin. Personally, we've always been more interested in taste than in tracing the province in which a dish was born. Our palates respond well to *Wienerküche* (Viennese cooking), a centuries-old blend of foreign recipes and homespun concoctions. Viennese cooking, however, tends to be rich and heavy, with little regard for your cholesterol levels.

FROM WIENER SCHNITZEL TO SACHERTORTE

Of course everyone knows Wiener schnitzel, the breaded veal cutlet that has achieved popularity worldwide. The most authentic local recipes call for the schnitzel be fried in lard, but everyone agrees on one point: The schnitzel should have the golden-brown color of a Stradivarius violin.

Another renowned meat specialty is boiled beef, or *tafelspitz,* said to reflect "the soul of the empire." This was Emperor Franz Joseph's favorite dish. For the best, try it at Hotel Sacher; if you're on a budget, then order *tafelspitz* at a *beisel,* cousin of the French bistro.

Roast goose is served on festive occasions, such as Christmas, but at any time of the year you can order *eine gute fettgans,* a good fat goose. After such a rich dinner, you may want to relax over some strong coffee, followed by schnapps.

The Legendary Sachertorte

In a city fabled for its desserts, the Sachertorte has emerged as the most famous. At a party thrown for Prince Wenzel Clemens Metternich in 1832, Franz Sacher first concocted and served the confection. It was an instant success, and news of the torte spread throughout the Austro-Hungarian Empire. Back then, everyone wanted the recipe, but it was a closely guarded secret.

In 1876, Sacher's son, Eduard, launched the Hotel Sacher. Eduard's cigar-smoking wife, Frau Anna, transformed the place into a favorite haunt of Austrian aristocrats, who drank wine and devoured Sachertortes into the wee hours. Memory of this pastry faded during the tragedy of the two world wars, but in 1951 the Sachertorte returned to the hotel's kitchen and reclaimed the renown it enjoyed in the 19th century. Today almost every pastry shop in Vienna sells the Sachertorte, and some confectioneries will ship it around the world.

Like all celebrities, the Sachertorte has even been the subject of a lawsuit. A 25-year-old legal battle over the exclusive right to the name "Original Sachertorte" was waged between the Hotel Sacher and the patisserie Demel. An Austrian court in 1965 ruled in favor of the Hotel Sacher.

After endless samplings of the torte from both the Demel and the Hotel Sacher, only the most exacting connoisseur can tell the difference—if there is any. Here, with permission of the Hotel Sacher, is their recipe for Sachertorte:

Ingredients:
- ½ cup butter
- ½ cup confectioners' sugar
- 1 tsp vanilla
- 6 eggs (separated)
- 5 oz dark chocolate
- ½ cup granulated sugar
- 1 cup flour
- apricot jam (as desired)

Add the softened butter, the confectioners' sugar, and the vanilla and mix well. Add the egg yolks and beat. Mix in the chocolate. Whip the egg whites until stiff and add to the mixture, along with the granulated sugar. Knead with a wooden spoon. Add the flour; then place in a mold and bake at 340°F for 15 minutes with the oven door ajar, then for 1 hour more with the door shut. Turn out of the mold and allow it to cool for 20 minutes. Coat with warm apricot jam.

Ingredients for Icing:
- ⅘ cup confectioners' sugar
- ½ cup water
- 6 oz chocolate

Heat the sugar and water (5 to 6 minutes), add the melted chocolate, and stir with a wooden spoon until the mixture is moderately thick. Layer the cake with the icing (¼ inch) and allow to cool.

For a taste of Hungary, order a *goulash*. Goulashes (stews of beef or pork with paprika) can be prepared in many different ways. The local version, *Wiener gulasch,* is usually lighter on the paprika than most Hungarian versions. And don't forget *gulyassuppe* (a Hungarian goulash soup), which can be a meal in itself.

Viennese pastry is probably the best in the world, both rich and varied. The familiar *strudel* comes in many forms; *apfelstrudel* is the most popular, but you can also order cherry strudel or other flavors. Viennese cakes defy description— look for *gugelhupf, wuchteln,* and *mohnbeugerl.* Many of the *torten* are made with ground hazelnuts or almonds in the place of flour. You can put whipped cream on everything. Don't miss *rehruken,* a chocolate "saddle of venison" cake that's studded with almonds.

Even if you're not addicted to sweets, there's a gustatory experience you mustn't miss: the Viennese Sachertorte. Many gourmets claim to have the authentic, original recipe for this "king of tortes," a rich chocolate cake with a layer of apricot jam. Master pastry baker Franz Sacher created the Sachertorte for Prince von Metternich in 1832, and it is still available in the Hotel Sacher. Outstanding imitations, however, can be found throughout Vienna.

COFFEE

Although it may sound heretical, Turkey is credited with establishing the famous Viennese coffeehouse. Legend holds that Turks retreating from the siege of Vienna abandoned several sacks of coffee, which, when brewed by the victorious Viennese, established the Austrian passion for coffee for all time. The first *kaffeehaus* was established in Vienna in 1683.

In Vienna, *jause* is a 4pm coffee-and-pastry ritual that is practiced daily in the city's classic coffeehouses. You can order your coffee a number of different ways—everything from *verkehrt* (almost milk-pale), to *mocca* (ebony-black). Note that in Vienna, only strangers ask for "einen Kaffee" ("a coffee"). If you do, you'll be asked what kind you want. Your safest choice is a large or small *brauner*—coffee with milk. *Kaffee mit schlagobers* (with whipped cream) is perfect for those with a sweet tooth. You can even order *doppelschlag* (double whipped cream).

BEER, WINE & LIQUEURS

Vienna imposes few restrictions on the sale of alcohol, so except in alcohol-free places you should be able to order beer or wine with your meal—even if it's 9am. Many Viennese have their first strong drink in the morning, preferring beer to coffee to get them going.

In general, **Austrian wines** are served when new, and most are consumed where they're produced. We prefer the white wine to the red. More than 99% of all Austrian wine is produced in vineyards in eastern Austria, principally Vienna, Lower Austria, Styria, and Burgenland. The most famous Austrian wine, *Gumpoldskirchen,* which is sold all over Vienna, comes from Lower Austria, the country's largest wine producer. At the heart of the Baden wine district, the *Sudbahnstrecke,* is the village of Gumpoldskirchen, which gives the wine its name. This white wine is heady, rich, and slightly sweet.

Located in an outer district of Vienna, Klosterneuburg, an ancient abbey on the right bank of the Danube, produces what is—arguably—the finest white wine in Austria. Monks have been making *Klosterneuburger* at this Augustinian monastery for centuries. The Wachau district, to the west of Vienna, also produces some fine, delicate wines, including *Loibner Kaiserwein* and *Duernsteiner Katzensprung,* which are fragrant and fruity.

By far the best red wine, and on this there is little disagreement, is *Vöslauer* from Vöslau. It's strong but, even though red, not quite as powerful as Gumpoldskirchen and Klosterneuburger. From Styria comes Austria's best-known rosé, *Schilcher,* which is slightly dry, fruity, and sparkling.

Because many Viennese visiting the *Heurigen* (wine taverns) outside the city didn't want to get too drunk, they started diluting the new wine with club soda or mineral water. Thus, the spritzer was born. The mix is best with a very dry wine.

In all except the most deluxe restaurants, it's possible to order a carafe of wine, *offener Wein,* which will be much less expensive than a bottle.

Austrian beers are relatively inexpensive and quite good, and they're sold throughout Vienna. Vienna is home to what we believe is the finest beer in the city, *Schwechater. Gösser,* produced in Styria, is one of the most favored brews and comes in both light and dark. *Adambräu,* another native beer, is also sold in Vienna's bars and taverns, along with some lighter, Bavarian-type beers like *Weizengold* and *Kaiser.* For those who prefer the taste without the alcohol, *Null Komma Josef* is a local alcohol-free beer.

Two of the most famous and favored **liqueurs** among Austrians are *slivovitz* (a plum brandy that originated in Croatia) and *barack* (made from apricots). Imported whisky and bourbon are likely to be lethal in price. When you're in Vienna, it's a good rule of thumb to drink the "spirit of the land."

The most festive drink is **bowle** (pronounced *bole*), which the Viennese often serve at parties. It was first made for us by the great Austrian chanteuse Greta Keller, and we've been devotees of it ever since. She preferred the lethal method of soaking berries and sliced peaches overnight in brandy, then pouring three bottles of dry white wine over the fruit, and letting it stand for another 2 to 3 hours. Before serving, she'd pour a bottle of champagne over it. In her words, "You can drink it as a cocktail, during and after dinner, and on . . . and on . . . and on!"

THE HEURIGEN

In 1784, Joseph II decreed that each vintner in the suburbs of Vienna could sell his own wine right on his doorstep to paying guests. And thus a tradition was born that continues today. *Heurig* means "new wine" or, more literally, "of this year."

These wine taverns lie on the outskirts of Vienna, mainly in Grinzing but also in Nussdorf and Sievering. Heurigen are often designated by a branch above the doorway. In summer, in fair weather, much of the drinking takes place in vine-covered gardens. In some of the more old-fashioned places, on a nippy night you'll find a crackling fire in a flower-bordered ceramic stove. There's likely to be a Gypsy violinist, an accordionist, or perhaps a zither player entertaining with schmaltzy Viennese songs. Most Heurigen are rustic, with wooden benches and tables, and it's perfectly acceptable to bring your own snacks. But today there are many that are, in fact, quite elaborate restaurants, serving a buffet of meats, cheeses, breads, and vegetables.

Beware: The wine is surprisingly potent, in spite of its innocent taste.

Appendix B:
Glossary of Useful Terms

English is widely spoken throughout Austria, especially in cities such as Vienna, and children are taught English in school. However, when you encounter someone who doesn't speak it or if you're trying to read a menu or sign the following might be useful.

1 Glossary

Altstadt old part of a city or town
Anlage park area
Apotheke pharmacy
Bad spa
Bahn railroad, train
   Bahnhof railroad station
   Hauptbahnhof main railroad station
   Stadtbahn (S-Bahn) commuter railroad
   Strassenbahn streetcar, tram
   Untergrundbahn (U-Bahn) subway, underground transportation system in a city
Beisl Viennese bistro, usually inexpensive
Berg mountain
Brücke bridge
Brunnen spring or well
Burg fortified castle
Dom cathedral
Domplatz cathedral square
Drogerie shop selling cosmetics, sundries
"Evergreen" or Schrammel alpine traditional music
Gasse lane
Gasthof inn
Gemütlichkeit (adj. gemütlich) comfort, coziness, friendliness
Graben moat
Gutbürgerliche Küche (German) home cooking
Heurige traditional wine tavern
Hof court (of a prince), mansion
Insel island
Jugendstil art nouveau
Kai quay
Kanal canal
Kammer room (in public building)
Kapelle chapel

Kaufhaus department store
Kino cinema
Kirche church
Kloster monastery
Konditorei pastry shop
Kunst art
Marktplatz market square
Neustadt new part of city or town
Oper opera
Platz square
Rathaus town or city hall
Ratskeller restaurant in Rathaus cellar serving traditional German food
Reisebüro travel agency
Saal hall
Schauspielhaus theater for plays

Schloss palace, castle
See lake (*der* See) or sea (*die* See)
Sezessionstil Viennese art movement
Spielbank casino
Stadt town, city
Steg footbridge
Strand beach
Strasse street
Tankstelle service station
Tor gateway
Turm tower
Ufer shore, riverbank
Verkehrsamt tourist office
Weg road
Zimmer room

2 Menu Terms

SOUPS (SUPPEN)

Erbsensuppe pea soup
Gemüsesuppe vegetable soup
Gulaschsuppe goulash soup

Kartoffelsuppe potato soup
Linsensuppe lentil soup
Nudelsuppe noodle soup

MEATS (WURST, FLEISCH & GEFLÜGEL)

Aufschnitt cold cuts
Brathuhn roast chicken
Bratwurst grilled sausage
Ente duck
Gans goose
Gulasch Hungarian stew
Hammel mutton
Kalb veal
Kaltes Geflügel cold poultry
Kässler Rippchen pork chops

Lamm lamb
Leber liver
Nieren kidneys
Rinderbraten roast beef
Rindfleisch beef
Schinken ham
Schweinebraten roast pork
Truthahn turkey
Wiener Schnitzel veal cutlet
Wurst sausage

FISH (FISCH)

Forelle trout
Hecht pike
Karpfen carp
Krebs crawfish

Lachs salmon
Makrele mackerel
Schellfisch haddock
Seezunge sole

EGGS (EIER)

Eier in der Schale boiled eggs
Mit Speck with bacon
Rühreier scrambled eggs

Spiegeleier fried eggs
Verlorene Eier poached eggs

SANDWICHES (BELEGTE BROTE)

Käsebrot cheese sandwich
Schinkenbrot ham sandwich
Wurstbrot sausage sandwich

Schwarzbrot mit Butter
pumpernickel with butter

VEGETABLES (GEMÜSE)

Artischocken artichokes
Blumenkohl cauliflower
Bohnen beans
Bratkartoffeln fried potatoes
Erbsen peas
Grüne Bohnen string beans
Gurken cucumbers
Karotten carrots
Kartoffelbrei mashed potatoes
Kartoffelsalat potato salad
Knödel dumpling

Kohl cabbage
Reis rice
Rotkraut red cabbage
Salat lettuce
Salzkartoffeln boiled potatoes
Sauerkraut sauerkraut
Spargel asparagus
Spinat spinach
Tomaten tomatoes
Vorspeisen hors d'oeuvres
Weisse Rüben turnips

DESSERTS (NACHTISCH)

Blatterteiggebäck puff pastry
Bratapfel baked apple
Käse cheese
Kompott stewed fruit

Obstkuchen fruit tart
Obstsalat fruit salad
Pfannkuchen sugared pancakes
Torten pastries

FRUITS (OBST)

Ananas pineapple
Apfel apple
Apfelsine orange
Banane banana
Birne pear

Erdbeeren strawberries
Kirschen cherries
Pfirsich peach
Weintrauben grapes
Zitrone lemon

BEVERAGES (GETRÄNKE)

Bier beer
Kaffee coffee
Milch milk
Rotwein red wine

Schokolade hot chocolate
Tee tea
Wasser water

CONDIMENTS & TABLE ITEMS

Brot bread
Brötchen rolls
Butter butter
Eis ice
Essig vinegar
Gabel fork
Glas glass
Löffel spoon

Messer knife
Pfeffer pepper
Platte plate
Sahne cream
Salz salt
Senf mustard
Tasse cup
Zucker sugar

COOKING TERMS

Gebacken baked
Gebraten fried
Gefüllt stuffed
Gekocht boiled

Geröstet roasted
Gut durchgebraten well-done
Nicht durchgebraten rare
Paniert breaded

Glossary of Useful Terms

Index

See also Accommodations, Restaurant, and Cafe indexes, below.

General Index

RESTAURANTS

FROMMER'S® COMPLETE TRAVEL GUIDES

Alaska
Amsterdam
Arizona
Atlanta
Australia
Austria
Bahamas
Barcelona, Madrid & Seville
Beijing
Belgium, Holland & Luxembourg
Bermuda
Boston
British Columbia & the Canadian Rockies
Budapest & the Best of Hungary
California
Canada
Cancún, Cozumel & the Yucatán
Cape Cod, Nantucket & Martha's Vineyard
Caribbean
Caribbean Cruises & Ports of Call
Caribbean Ports of Call
Carolinas & Georgia
Chicago
China
Colorado
Costa Rica
Denmark
Denver, Boulder & Colorado Springs
England
Europe

European Cruises & Ports of Call
Florida
France
Germany
Greece
Greek Islands
Hawaii
Hong Kong
Honolulu, Waikiki & Oahu
Ireland
Israel
Italy
Jamaica
Japan
Las Vegas
London
Los Angeles
Maryland & Delaware
Maui
Mexico
Montana & Wyoming
Montréal & Québec City
Munich & the Bavarian Alps
Nashville & Memphis
Nepal
New England
New Mexico
New Orleans
New York City
New Zealand
Nova Scotia, New Brunswick & Prince Edward Island
Oregon
Paris
Philadelphia & the Amish Country

Portugal
Prague & the Best of the Czech Republic
Provence & the Riviera
Puerto Rico
Rome
San Antonio & Austin
San Diego
San Francisco
Santa Fe, Taos & Albuquerque
Scandinavia
Scotland
Seattle & Portland
Shanghai
Singapore & Malaysia
South Africa
Southeast Asia
South Florida
South Pacific
Spain
Sweden
Switzerland
Thailand
Tokyo
Toronto
Tuscany & Umbria
USA
Utah
Vancouver & Victoria
Vermont, New Hampshire & Maine
Vienna & the Danube Valley
Virgin Islands
Virginia
Walt Disney World & Orlando
Washington, D.C.
Washington State

FROMMER'S® DOLLAR-A-DAY GUIDES

Australia from $50 a Day
California from $60 a Day
Caribbean from $70 a Day
England from $70 a Day
Europe from $70 a Day

Florida from $70 a Day
Hawaii from $70 a Day
Ireland from $60 a Day
Italy from $70 a Day
London from $85 a Day

New York from $80 a Day
Paris from $80 a Day
San Francisco from $60 a Day
Washington, D.C., from $70 a Day

FROMMER'S® PORTABLE GUIDES

Acapulco, Ixtapa & Zihuatanejo
Alaska Cruises & Ports of Call
Bahamas
Baja & Los Cabos
Berlin
California Wine Country
Charleston & Savannah
Chicago
Dublin

Hawaii: The Big Island
Las Vegas
London
Los Angeles
Maine Coast
Maui
Miami
New Orleans
New York City
Paris

Puerto Vallarta, Manzanillo & Guadalajara
San Diego
San Francisco
Sydney
Tampa & St. Petersburg
Venice
Washington, D.C.

FROMMER'S® NATIONAL PARK GUIDES

Family Vacations in the
   National Parks
Grand Canyon

National Parks of the
   American West
Rocky Mountain

Yellowstone & Grand Teton
Yosemite & Sequoia/
   Kings Canyon
Zion & Bryce Canyon

FROMMER'S® MEMORABLE WALKS

Chicago
London

New York
Paris

San Francisco
Washington, D.C.

FROMMER'S® GREAT OUTDOOR GUIDES

New England
Northern California

Southern California & Baja
Southern New England

Washington & Oregon

FROMMER'S® BORN TO SHOP GUIDES

Born to Shop: France
Born to Shop: Italy

Born to Shop: London
Born to Shop: New York

Born to Shop: Paris

FROMMER'S® IRREVERENT GUIDES

Amsterdam
Boston
Chicago
Las Vegas

London
Los Angeles
Manhattan
New Orleans

Paris
San Francisco
Seattle & Portland
Vancouver

Walt Disney World
Washington, D.C.

FROMMER'S® BEST-LOVED DRIVING TOURS

America
Britain
California

Florida
France
Germany

Ireland
Italy
New England

Scotland
Spain
Western Europe

THE UNOFFICIAL GUIDES®

Bed & Breakfasts in
   California
Bed & Breakfasts in
   New England
Bed & Breakfasts in
   the Northwest
Bed & Breakfasts in
   Southeast
Beyond Disney
Branson, Missouri

California with Kids
Chicago
Cruises
Disneyland
Florida with Kids
Golf Vacations in the
   Eastern U.S.
The Great Smoky &
   Blue Ridge
   Mountains

Inside Disney
Hawaii
Las Vegas
London
Miami & the Keys
Mini Las Vegas
Mini-Mickey
New Orleans
New York City
Paris

San Francisco
Skiing in the West
Southeast with Kids
Walt Disney World
Walt Disney World
   for Grown-ups
Walt Disney World
   for Kids
Washington, D.C.

SPECIAL-INTEREST TITLES

Frommer's Britain's Best Bed & Breakfasts and
   Country Inns
Frommer's Britain's Best Bike Rides
The Civil War Trust's Official Guide
   to the Civil War Discovery Trail
Frommer's Caribbean Hideaways
Frommer's Adventure Guide to Central America
Frommer's Adventure Guide to South America
Frommer's Adventure Guide to Southeast Asia
Frommer's Food Lover's Companion to France
Frommer's Gay & Lesbian Europe
Frommer's Exploring America by RV
Hanging Out in Europe

Israel Past & Present
Mad Monks' Guide to California
Mad Monks' Guide to New York City
Frommer's The Moon
Frommer's New York City with Kids
The New York Times' Unforgettable
   Weekends
Places Rated Almanac
Retirement Places Rated
Frommer's Road Atlas Britain
Frommer's Road Atlas Europe
Frommer's Washington, D.C., with Kids
Frommer's What the Airlines Never Tell You